MW00882706

# LEGO®

# ALMANAC
# 1961-2020

## INVESTING IN LEGO® SETS - A DEEP DIVE
## THE UNOFFICIAL GUIDE TO INVEST IN LEGO® SETS

INCLUDING DETAILED INSIGHTS INTO MY PERSONAL LEGO PORTFOLIO WITH 533 LEGO® SETS AND A TOTAL VALUE OF OVER 60.000 EURO (AS OF 30.06.2022)

**FALCO ZIEHL / WWW.RENDITEBAUSTEIN.DE**

# LEGO®

# ALMANAC
# 1961-2020

## INVESTING IN LEGO® SETS - A DEEP DIVE
## THE UNOFFICIAL GUIDE TO INVEST IN LEGO® SETS

INCLUDING DETAILED INSIGHTS INTO MY PERSONAL LEGO PORTFOLIO WITH 533 LEGO® SETS AND A TOTAL VALUE OF OVER 60.000 EURO (AS OF 30.06.2022)

**FALCO ZIEHL / WWW.RENDITEBAUSTEIN.DE**

**Impressum**

© 2022      Falco Ziehl
Web:         https//www.renditebaustein.de
E-Mail:      info@renditebaustein.de
Instagram:   @LEGOalmanac

Production, Publisher and Imprint: Independently published

ISBN: 979-8-8761-5593-1

## Acknowledgement

Writing a reference book requires, above all, time. Therefore, I would like to thank my wife-to-be in particular. She supported me and gave me the freedom to complete this book project before our daughter will be born soon.

# Table of Contents

# 1.    Prologue

Anyone who has ever stepped barefoot on a LEGO brick will certainly not forget the colorful building bricks from Denmark so quickly. However, the little brick has long since outgrown children's rooms and is conquering diverse areas of our lives as a creative element. Engineering offices, scientific laboratories and artistic studios have all found interest and use in the studded toy. Nowadays there are also lots of books about LEGO. These deal with various products such as sets, individual bricks, parts, figures, building ideas and many more. By far the most successful product of The LEGO Group are LEGO sets. Such building sets consist of various individual bricks, parts, possibly (mini-) figures and other inserts. LEGO sets have been a major contributor to the success of the LEGO brand. The basic ingredient is LEGO bricks and in the past decades they have become a synonym for 3-dimensional Tetris.

Via detours, the children's toys developed into a new hobby for adults. The hobby quickly turned into a real passion of collecting. In the course of time, especially older and discontinued LEGO products reached high collector values.

In 2015, I bought the *LEGO set no. 21008-1 Burj Khalifa* of the *Architecture* theme series. The LEGO set remained in its original packaging and unopened in a box in the attic of my parents and eventually fell into oblivion. In 2018, I accidentally discovered that my LEGO set had nearly tripled in value. My personal interest in *LEGO investing* was born.

I began to look more closely at the subject of LEGO investment and in addition continued to buy new and sealed LEGO sets. With my growing interest in the further months, I found out that the topic of LEGO investment was not entirely unknown. At this (early) time there were few small groups in different internet boards, which discussed the topic. Eventually, during my research for this book, I became aware of a paper that specifically analyzes the changes in the value of LEGO sets. The authors and brothers *Ed Maciorowski* and *Jeff Maciorowski* analyze more than 2,000 LEGO sets in terms of value changes in their publication *The Ultimate Guide to Collectible LEGO Sets Identification and Price Guide*. The publication was a bang for the buck, but it was never considered a guide to LEGO as an alternative investment. Rather, the brothers label LEGO as a collectible and praise the toy specifically in terms of its value preservation.

In my perception, the research was too focused on the characteristics of individual LEGO sets. There is a lack of generally valid assessments whether LEGO products are generally worthwhile as an alternative investment. Nevertheless, I owe it to the book that my reawakened interest in LEGO toys met my passion for investing. I personally enjoy investing very much. For several years now, I have been diversifying my money on a large scale in order to escape inflation and the low interest rates on bank accounts. The LEGO market seems to have unimagined potential for this. Today, there is a huge secondary market for new and pre-owned LEGO sets. Every day, tens of thousands of LEGO sets are traded around the world. Returns on retired LEGO sets have reached breathtaking levels, giving the toy a lot of attention in the financial media.

This book investigates the historical returns of 14,068 LEGO sets to provide a comprehensive understanding of the attractiveness for LEGO as an alternative asset class for investors. Various factors that affect the value of a LEGO set are discussed. The result is a value-weighted LEGO price index for the period from 1961 to 2020, in which LEGO products have experienced very diverse performance. Historical returns and the most important influencing factors are analyzed. The performance and results are underpinned by numerous tables, figures and calculations. Analyzing individual LEGO sets to make future investment decisions is like reading a crystal ball. From the beginning, the statistical investigation was based on the large mass of LEGO products. All of a sudden, the topic of LEGO has a new dimension: *Data Science*.

If you are buying LEGO sets for your personal collection, this investigation will help you get a good sense of the fair market value of LEGO sets. In addition, I want to help LEGO investors to choose appropriate LEGO sets in order to increase values in the long term.

Before investing in LEGO products, you have to understand that, as with any form of investment, there are several key requirements to follow. LEGO investment is considered speculative and every investment bears risks, which must be assessed in advance. Also, LEGO products are still considered an exotic investment. And an exceptional investment requires exceptional measures in its handling. *LEGO investment* is a cash-intensive business. This business is on the border between online arbitrage1, resale and investment.

The present findings are the results of my very personal journey in LEGO investment. Like-minded people are most welcome here to accompany me on the further unexpected journey. Participation is always welcome. It is up to you whether you follow the same path or build your own individual strategy. And now I would like to wish you a lot of fun and an exciting journey in the young *LEGO Investment*.

---

[1] In economics, arbitrage is the exploitation of price differences at the same time in different places for the purpose of taking profits. For example, shares are bought at a low price in one market (e.g., New York) and sold again for a higher amount in another market (e.g., Frankfurt).

## 2.    An unexpected journey

The todays well know LEGO brick first appeared in the year 1949. The colorful plastic brick was instantly popular with children and adults. The unique and practical interlocking principle, which holds individual bricks and pieces together, was then patented in 1958. After more than 70 years, the modular system of plastic bricks is now produced in a wide variety of colors, shapes and sizes.

When hearing LEGO, many adults immediately think of their childhood and the countless hours spent building. It is not surprising that children take great pleasure in LEGO toys. In contrast to many other toys, there are no construction restrictions with LEGO bricks and parts. Each LEGO brick has tubes on the bottom and studs on the top that snap into the tubes for a precise fit. This is the basic principle of LEGO bricks and certainly one of the secrets of their success. Everything can be connected to each other, for example bricks from 1965 and 2020 can still be combined today. Therefore, it is up to everyone whether they build standard models or use their crea-tivity, imagination and fantasy.[1]

LEGO is a registered trademark of The LEGO Group (TLG) or LEGO A/S and has been providing joy and enthusiasm worldwide for decades. The colorful bricks were invented in Denmark, but there is probably no other toy that is more successful internationally. By far LEGO is one of the most pop-ular toys worldwide.

The bricks producer states that the main target group are children aged 5 to 12, as well as parents who are looking for LEGO products that their children can use to learn through play. Accordingly, the majority of adults consider LEGO products primarily as toys. However, the number of adult play children has been steadily increasing for many years. One of the foun-dations was laid by The LEGO Group itself. For example, the LEGO Technic theme was launched in Germany in 1975 with the slogan "*For men from the*

---

[1] For example, Google covered one of its first office computers with a case made of LEGO bricks.

*age of 9'*. For years, the percentage of adults in LEGO sales has been rising above the industry average. Around 8 percent of the sales volume of the entire games industry is attributable to this group, who buy toys for themselves and not for their children.[1] Surprisingly, the vast majority of adults do not play with LEGO products.[2] Instead, the colorful individual bricks and pieces inspire an enthusiastic passion for collecting among like-minded people. Adults have long since associated LEGO with more than just their childhood memories or their children's nubby toys. Thousands of adults around the world collect LEGO products (especially LEGO sets). LEGO bricks and pieces are used to build large-scale objects and real masterpieces of art. In addition, the assembled building sets are happily displayed within their home.

This generation of adults has often lived through a so-called *dark age*. The term describes the period between playing with LEGO products as a child and then regaining interest as an adult. However, adults are often ashamed of having such youthful interests. The end of the *dark age* occurs when the (adult) person makes a conscious decision to build or collect LEGO products again. The *dark age* creates a time gap in the history of many adult builders, where The LEGO Group continues to sell its products, but adult individuals do not purchase them. This is due the fact that LEGO products are outside of adult perception.

The brick manufacturer already realized this unusual trend some years ago. The LEGO Group has always tried to appeal to adults and buyers of advanced ages by addressing products in a specific way (e.g., through themes or licensing agreements) and ultimately winning adults as customers.

Driven by a fiercely competitive market over the last twenty years, The LEGO Group has been forced to increase its demographic reach. In this way, it has been able to manifest the popularity of the LEGO brand around the

---

[1] Consumer-Panel of the market research company npdgroup
[2] LEGO; Latin *lego*; I read, I collect

world. Certainly, this can be interpreted as a crucial turnaround, that nowadays even adults have the courage to openly express their interest in LEGO.

In the past, the adult group of buyers was indirectly addressed mainly through high pricing of individual LEGO products and an increased level of complexity in building the LEGO set. In the meantime, the Danish toy manufacturer has products in its range that are clearly visibly targeted at adults. With the indication *18+* on the packaging, The LEGO Group has developed a new marketing strategy that specifically addresses adults. An ongoing intensification of this strategy is very likely among experts. For example, between 2018 and 2019, one in ten Euro of the company's revenue was already spent on a product purchase by adults. Finally, the toy has attracted the interest of the grown-up group of buyers.

At this point, adult LEGO owners realized that there is a high demand for selling their used LEGO products. The reasons for selling can be manifold, but in general it is necessary to create room. By selling their LEGO products, LEGO owners are able to refinance their hobby in part or in whole and, more often to make a profit. In turn, the buyers rewarded themselves with LE-GO products, which are no longer available in retail. *LEGO Investment was born*.

Learnings about the value of the LEGO collection continued to evolve. The idea developed to the extent that LEGO products can now be used to build many unusual things, such as a diversified LEGO portfolio.[1] Solvent and mostly older interested consumers form a group of buyers who, beyond the passion for collecting, see LEGO exclusively as an alternative investment.[2] This phenomenon has long since become so prominent that LEGO Investment is associated with classic tangible assets such as property, real estate, stocks, classic cars, artwork, antiques, wine, precious metals as well

---

[1] The term diversification has its roots in the financial sector and describes the minimization of risk in capital investment by spreading the invested capital over various investment instruments such as stocks, real estate, commodities, but also cars or watches.

[2] Investment is a business or financial term that means spending money on something from which you expect a financial return (usually an increase in the value of the invested product).

as jewelry.[1] Whether comics or toys, many things from days long gone are nowadays increasingly precious and valuable, which is also reflected in the price of particularly rare and limited findings. All these objects have at least one thing in common: they are highly coveted by collectors or fans. The colorful LEGO brick with its studs does not have to hide at all in this comparison.

In this context, researchers have studied and compared the returns of LEGO products with alternative investments ranging from wine to classic cars. Surprisingly, LEGO products performed exceptionally well as an alternative investment.[2] For example, in 2013, the minifigure *LEGO No. col161 Mister Gold* was released in the tenth anniversary series of the theme *Collectable Minifigures*. This minifigure is strictly limited to 5,000 pieces and was hidden in so-called *blind bags*[3]. The casual buyers well invested the USD 1.99. During peak times, the rare minifigure traded around USD 3,000. In other words, this represents an incredible return of more than 150,000 percent.

LEGO set no. 10190-1 Market Street also became very famous. It is the first LEGO set of the popular theme Modular Buildings. The MSRP of this set was USD 89.99 in 2007. Today, those who still own the LEGO set in its original and unopened packaging can enjoy a hefty price increase up to USD 2,575 (depending on condition)[4]. This represents a return of over 2,700 percent.

The iconic plastic brick has long since made it into our auction houses, and someday we will certainly hear about a rare LEGO set being listed at *Sotheby's* in London or *Chriestie's* in New York. For a long time already,

---

[1] According to a survey conducted by Barclays in 2012, the average wealthy individual holds about 10 percent of their wealth in collectibles such as artwork, antiques, jewelry, wines, rare cars and other luxury goods or merchandise, to partially diversify their portfolios and hedge financial investments.
[2] https://www.theguardian.com/lifeandstyle/2021/dec/10/investing-in-lego-more-lucrative-than-gold-study-suggests
[3] A blind bag is a bag whose content is unknown.
[4] Bricklink, September 2020

actively managed investment funds[1] have been pooling clients' capital in order to invest it in wines, artworks, precious metals and gemstones.[2] This makes such assets accessible to private investors. We should not be surprised, if there is an investment fund for LEGO products in the future.[3] Those who still have old LEGO sets in their basement or attic should definitely check them for their completeness and rarity value. That way, high sums of money can be achieved in some cases.

---

[1] An investment fund is an investing company that collects money from investors and invests it, for example, in stocks, bonds, commodities or real estate.
[2] Sotheby's is a world leading company in the art and antiques market. Its most traditional auction houses include New York and London.
[3] Funds that deal with the collection of wines, artworks or precious metals improve the accessibility of such assets for private investors.

## 2.1  Future Retrospection

If you're looking more extensively into LEGO products as an alternative investment, you're likely to come across two publications sooner or later in your research. The book *The Ultimate Guide to Collectible LEGO Sets: Identification and Price Guide* was published by authors and brothers *Ed Maciorowski* and *Jeff Maciorowski* in 2015. The brothers studied the price or value trends of over 2,000 collectible LEGO sets across 25 themes between 1989 and 2014. The book illustrates the incredible value of LEGO bricks and pieces, not only from an entertainment and educational perspective, but also as collectibles.

The second research is *LEGO - The Toy of Smart Investors* by *Victoria Dobrynskaya* and *Julia Kishilova*, which was published in 2018. The paper compares the original prices (MSRP or Manufacturer's Suggested Retail Price) and the value development of more than 2,000 LEGO sets. The study concludes that the majority of LEGO sets increased in value between 1987 and 2015. According to the study, investors achieved a better return with LEGO products than with stocks, gold or interest on bank accounts during this period.

People say that the past performance of a stock is not an indicator of its future performance. A stock price is influenced by countless factors. A future forecast seems hopeless and is equivalent to reading from a crystal ball. The interplay of various influencing factors is extremely complex, so that logical links appear impossible.

This argument is certainly correct in principle, but there are numerous examples of correlations. Anyone who recognizes the interplay of action and reaction can identify patterns and is several steps ahead of many investors and can therefore make money on the stock market.

For example, the German stock index (DAX = Deutsche Aktien Index) recovered from a drop in value of more than 40 percent (today known as the *Corona crash low*) at the past highs of the dotcom bubble in 2000 and the global financial crisis in 2008. At these historic trading levels, the largest and best-known German stock index reversed and headed straight for new all-time highs. There are plenty of similar examples. The future performance of the stock market is thus not always entirely detached from the past, even if such findings are only confirmed in retrospect.

In order to understand LEGO products as an alternative financial investment and to conclude about the future performance, a retrospective as well as insights from the past are essential. The following fundamental questions have been on my mind in this regard:

- *Which LEGO products have performed exceptionally well or very poorly in the past?*
- *What are the reasons for this?*
- *Is a reference to future LEGO products possible?*

LEGO products are also considered to be highly complex. For example, LEGO sets consist of individual bricks, parts and minifigures in a wide variety of materials, colors, shapes, sizes and weights. Figure 1 shows a comparison of the different performances of LEGO products (in this case LEGO sets)[1], the most important international stock indices, an ordinary savings account and gold in the period from 1961 to 2020 inclusive.[2]

---

[1] The performance is calculated on the basis of the present study of the underlying 14,068 LEGO sets in the period from 1961 to 2020, whereby no data set is available for 1962 and is therefore not taken into account in the following. The return achieved for this comparison is based on the projection of a fictitious LEGO investor or LEGO index. It is highly unlikely that a person or institution bought exactly these LEGO products during the said period. The calculated returns do not take into account any fees such as transaction costs.

[2] Inflation, gold and savings account refer to the valuation in German currency at the period under review. The performance of the other assets refer to the currency of the representative country behind the corresponding stock index.

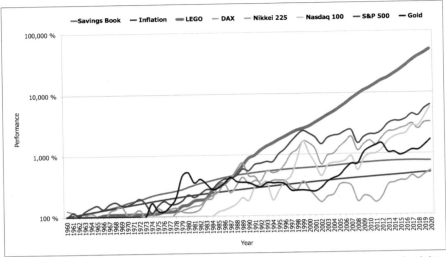

Figure 1 - Performances of LEGO products, selected stock indices, gold and savings book between 1961 and 2020 (without adjustment for inflation)

A stock index (singular) or also various stock indices (plural) refer to a predefined selection of stocks that are grouped together on the basis of certain decision criteria (e.g., level of market capitalization of the company listed on the stock exchange). Stock indices represent the development of financial activities on different submarkets. A submarket can represent either a country or an industry. Investment in corporate bonds in the form of equities is generally seen as risky and complex, although historically high yields can be achieved over the long term.

The *German stock index* or *DAX* represents the performance of the 40 largest and most liquid companies in Germany. It reflects around 80 percent of the market capitalization of listed stock corporations in Germany. It is the largest and most important German share index.

The *Standard & Poor's 500* or *S&P 500* lists the 500 largest U.S. companies and is thus one of the world's most important stock indices. It is considered an indicator for the development of the entire U.S. economy.

The *National Association of Securities Dealers for Automated Quotation 100* or *Nasdaq 100* lists 100 shares of non-financial companies (U.S.) with the highest market capitalizations.

The *Nikkei Heikin Kabuka 225* or *Nikkei 225* is the Japanese benchmark index and is based on prices of the 225 most important traded public companies. It is the most important stock index in Asia. The Nikkei 225 is therefore also considered an indicator for the development of the entire Japanese stock market.

*Gold* as a precious metal is the most important subclass of the asset class commodities. Gold is popularly regarded as a crisis currency and the best possible protection against financial and currency crises. The commodity is traditionally linked to the stock market by a negative correlation. If shares rise, the value of gold falls, vice versa.

In this comparison, the savings book or savings deposit is the simplest and most classic form of capital investments. This is usually a free savings account at a standard bank. The savings book is considered to be very safe and convenient. However, the historical interest rates and returns are significantly lower than for stocks, real estate and commodities.

All These asset classes are globally known and widely used. It is reasonable to compare LEGO products as alternative capital investments with these common capital investments. Overall, with regard to Figure 1, the returns of all asset products have developed positively as of December 31, 2020. The common basis is the acquisition of each individual asset class on January 1, 1960. If an asset class did not exist at that time, it was of course only taken into account on the later issue date.[1] For comparability of the value developments, a (fictitious) sale as of December 31, 2020 has been assumed. During this period, the values of the individual asset classes have developed very differently.

The average annual returns up to December 31, 2020 were calculated for all asset classes. The basis or starting point is 100 percent or USD 1. Interest

---

[1] For example, the NASDAQ 100 was first introduced in 1985.

is used to generate annual income. The interest or income earned is not paid out and is instead reinvested. In financial mathematics, this is referred to as reinvestment. This reinforces the so-called compound interest effect.

In a historical perspective, LEGO products show a very strong growth in value. Between the introduction of the LEGO brick as we know it today and December 31, 2020, LEGO products make it to the top of the comparison with a total growth of 50,273 percent. If you had invested the amount of 1 USD in LEGO products in 1961, it would have a value (without adjusting for inflation) of USD 502.73 as of December 31, 2020.

None of the remaining asset classes was able to keep up with the value growth of the toy manufacturer. In the end, they all had to accept defeat to the products of The LEGO Group. As of December 31, 2020, the S&P 500 is in on the second place with a gain of 6,272 percent. The Nasdaq 100 (5,747 %), DAX 30 (3,285 %), Gold (1,687 %), Savings (760 %) and Nikkei 225 (525 %) also lag behind. In some cases, the value growth of the competition is less than one tenth of the value growth of LEGO products. In contrast to LEGO products, stock indices and gold in particular are subject to strong fluctuations in value. Sometimes these fluctuations exceed by far 1,000 percent within only one decade. For example, between 1985 and 1996 (366 %) and 1985 and 2002 (439 %), the Nasdaq 100 increased in value to 1,653 percent in the peak year of 1999 or shortly before the turn of the millennium. Such volatile swings do not occur in the case of LEGO products.

Any fluctuations are in the lower double-digit percentage range. In addition, it is quite impressive that the weighted LEGO index has never recorded a negative return in a single year. This observation is again unique in the present comparison. Less surprisingly, the performances of the Nikkei 225 and the savings account are clearly the weakest. In fact, the Nikkei 225 is considered to be particularly sensitive to global political and economic events. As of December 31, 2020, the Nikkei 225 stands at just 525 percent (after adjusting for inflation) and is outperformed even by the savings account with an increase in value of 760 percent. In a historical context, the Nikkei 225 lags behind the European and U.S. stock markets. The savings account has long been considered an old-fashioned form of investment with low interest rates, especially in times of zero and negative interest rates. Nevertheless, the savings account is much less volatile. A factor that is important for many investors to be able to sleep peacefully at night.

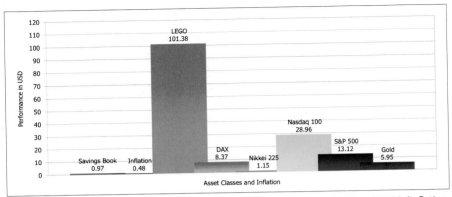

*Figure 2 - What became of 1 euro or USD by asset classes between 1985 and 2020 (inflation-adjusted)?*

The figure 2 illustrates how the seven asset classes and inflation have performed since the same starting date. For this purpose, the start date 1985 was chosen for all asset classes. The reason for this is that the Nasdaq 100 price index has only been calculated since 1985. From the comparison it can be concluded what is left of our money after an investment period of 36 years respectively between 1985 and 2020. If you had invested USD 1 in LEGO products back in 1985, it would be worth USD 101.38 in 2020, after adjustment for inflation. This corresponds to a considerable increase in value of 10,138 percent. The Nasdaq 100 has increased in value to 28.96 USD or 2,896 percent. Far behind are the S&P 500 (1,312 %), DAX (837 %), gold (595 %) and the Nikkei 225 (115 %). The savings account brings up the rear, being the only asset class to achieve a negative return of -3 percent over this period. If you had left your money in the form of cash without taking a return or interest rate into account during the period mentioned, only 48 pfennigs or DM 0.48 (approx. 0.25 Euro) would have been left over from DM 1 in 1985. This corresponds to a depreciation of 52 percent (starting from DM). In consequence, it generally makes sense to keep these comparisons in mind periodically in order to understand that leaving your money untouched is not an option at all.

I would draw special attention to the observation that only LEGO products have generated a positive return every single year between 1961 and 2020. On average, this is 11 percent per year. Of course, LEGO products were not perceived as an alternative investment at that time. Therefore, it can be assumed that a large part of the profit can also be attributed to this fact. LEGO products between 1984 and 1998 in particular contributed to this result with an above-average increase in value. In these years, the growth story picks up speed. LEGO products from this period first appeared under the logo we know today (red square with the word LEGO, in white, framed by black and yellow). And a predecessor of the minifigure we know today also makes its way into LEGO products. At that time, there was no thought that LEGO products could someday be an alternative investment.

Also, very little attention was given to the proper storage of LEGO products. Accordingly, nowadays well-preserved LEGO products from these bygone years are unique and rare. The value becomes even higher when the LEGO products are in new and unopened condition. Collectors rush to such treasures, if the price is justified.

It is also true for LEGO products that the return cannot be fixed for every year. It is to be assumed that a LEGO product for example from the year 1995 shows different values, if you look at them in the year 2000 or 2020. There are numerous reasons and factors for this. In the following figure 3 we see the comparison of the annual return (not adjusted for inflation) of all seven asset classes from 1961 to 2020.

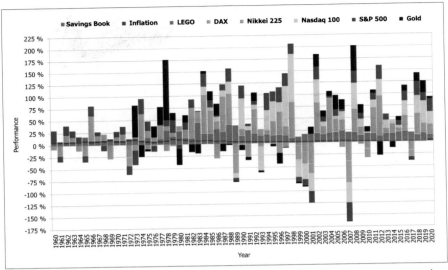

*Figure 3 - Annual average returns of LEGO sets, stock indices, gold and savings accounts between 1961 and 2020 (not adjusted for inflation).*

This method of presentation without taking inflation into account impressively illustrates how LEGO products have outperformed the field of asset classes in the past. A continuous positive return without major fluctuations led to success over the other asset classes in the long run. Since 1961 and the beginning of the recording of returns, LEGO sets have achieved an average of 11 percent per year.

In a direct comparison, LEGO products achieved the highest returns in only 12 of the total 60 years (1961 to 2020). The remaining 48 years are almost evenly divided between the DAX, Nasdaq 100 and S&P 500. Nevertheless, the returns of LEGO products in the period between 1961 and 2020 were impressive. The studded and colorful building bricks not only outperformed the competitors, but also outperformed annual inflation in 45 of the entire 60 years by an extremely wide margin. No other asset class outperformed inflation more often.

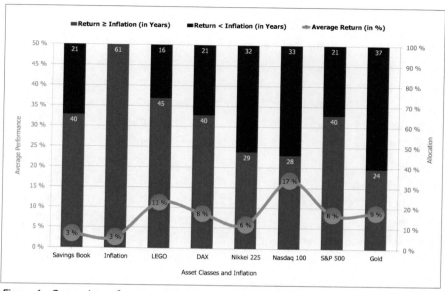

Figure 4 - Comparison of average annual returns of LEGO sets, stock indices, gold and savings accounts between 1961 and 2020 (not adjusted for inflation)

Since recording of returns in 1961 began, LEGO products have averaged 11 percent per year. The NASDAQ 100 has been calculated since 1985 and comes to an average return of 17 percent, ignoring inflation. The S&P 500 has an average return of 8 percent per year. Both stock indexes have beaten inflation in 28 and 40 of the entire 36 and 61 years, respectively. The DAX (8 %) and gold (9 %) rank below. Those who invested their money in Japan's Nikkei 225 could expect an average annual return of 6 percent. The Nikkei 225 has been recorded since 1973 and has beaten inflation in 29 out of 48 years. Unsurprisingly, savings accounts performed the worst in the comparison. The average annual return is just 3 percent.

There is no doubt that LEGO products have been an extremely profitable alternative investment in the past. The toy was more successful than either stock indices, precious metals or savings accounts. The underdog was able to impressively outperform the other asset classes.

19

## 2.2     Tangible Assets beat Monetary Asset

Basically, it can be said that when traditional forms of capital investment are considered unsafe, risky or unpromising, investors avoid monetary assets and flee with their savings into tangible assets. Simply explained, monetary assets describe the investment of money in money. These include savings books, savings bonds, instant-access savings accounts, fixed-term deposits and building loan contracts. All of these monetary assets are subject to a loss of value due to inflation and a lack of stability.

Inflation reduces the purchasing power of money. As a consequence, goods and services become more expensive. 100 Euro are still 100 Euro, but you can buy less for it. The main reason is that the manufacturer increases the prices of products. This happens primarily when the costs for companies change, for example, raw materials become more expensive or wages increase. In order to continue to generate profits, companies pass on the increased costs to consumers. The result is an increase in the price of goods and services.

Unlike monetary assets, tangible assets do not consist solely of paper or digital numbers. Tangible assets are primarily physical goods that can be touched. Tangible assets retain their value even if the value of money in a country declines due to inflation. In contrast to monetary assets, tangible assets are assumed to have a factual substance in terms of their real countervalue, whose value is independent of markets and politics. Tangible assets always require expertise. By common parlance, tangible assets are considered to be stable in value and are a favored capital investment, especially in times of crisis. They are considered less volatile and protect against inflation. Probably the best-known form of tangible asset is real estate or the precious metal gold. In legal terms, monetary assets and tangible assets differ in the sense that tangible assets are property or ownership interests, while monetary assets other than cash are merely written promises.

LEGO products are different. They are everyday products and their prices on the secondary market are determined by scarcity and collecting instinct once a LEGO product is no longer available in retail stores. According to a survey by Barclays in 2012, the average wealthy person holds about 10 percent of wealth in collectibles such as artwork, antiques, jewelry, fine wines, rare automobiles and other luxury items. These are often used to diversify the portfolio or hedge other financial investments. Tangible assets have many other different advantages and disadvantages, which are introduced in the following.[1]

## Advantages of tangible assets

■ **Object of value or utility value**
Unlike monetary assets, in the case of a drop in price, you still have a physical product to enjoy. Physical assets have a utility value in everyday life (e.g., you can play with LEGO products).

■ **Protection against inflation**
The majority of tangible assets make it possible not to suffer losses due to inflation.

■ **Crisis-proof**
Tangible assets outlive crises. Only their destruction can lead to a total loss. For example, LEGO products helped many people through the dark times of World War II (e.g., as wooden toys).

■ **Stable presence**
Tangible assets are difficult to multiply. Unlike money, the extraction and creation of tangible assets causes costs.

---

[1] https://www.svz.de/16552991

## Growing demand

The demand for many tangible assets is growing constantly. The main reason for this is the market in emerging countries. In principle, economic experts assume that tangible assets are determined by a long-term macro trend that is independent of the capital market and that price increases are therefore inevitable.

## Creditworthiness

Tangible assets can occasionally be used as security when applying for a loan.

## Disadvantages of tangible assets

## Fluctuaction in value

Although tangible assets by their classification are supposed to be stable, they are not protected from sometimes very strong fluctuations in value. Volatility can be very high. Success is determined by the market.

## Illiquidity

Tangible assets often have to be sold in a comparatively complex process. Above all, a resale at a certain time and a certain price (as high as possible) is not always possible.

## Over- and Undervaluation

Depending on the market period and the state of the industry, there might be significant fluctuations in value, which often do not reflect the actual value (e.g., insolvency of *Märklin*).

## Limited return on investment

Many tangible assets only give the opportunity to achieve a return through price increases. However, these are often relatively low.

- **Uncertain return on investment**

  Compared to bonds, fixed-term deposits and other monetary assets, tangible assets cannot be calculated precisely. The return is not fixed in certain time periods.

- **Exchange rate risk**

  Some tangible assets are exposed to exchange rate risk. For example, this is the case with foreign stocks or with commodities that are listed in USD.

- **Risk of concentration**

  Many tangible assets are quite cost-intensive to acquire. This makes appropriate diversification more difficult and price fluctuations have a greater impact on the investment.

- **Administration effort**

  Tangible assets often cause extensive administrative effort. Real estate in particular is at a clear disadvantage here.

- **Dispossession**

  Especially in a time of crisis, dispossession is possible. An example of this: Outside of political upheavals, the confiscation and subsequent prohibition of gold and silver in the U.S. from 1933 onwards.

- **Background knowledge**

  Many tangible assets require comprehensive background knowledge in order to recognize overvaluations or falsifications.

- **Speculations**

  Tangible assets can also become the target of speculators.

In present times of limited return opportunities, extraordinary investment ideas and strategies are becoming more and more popular. Speculation in later collector's items is really nothing special. However, the fact that the toys are made of plastic makes things much more exciting. The toy market has grown strongly in recent decades and classic toys sometimes achieve small fortunes in auctions. Toys offer extraordinary potential for value growth. Childhood favorites can evoke sentimental feelings that make them highly interesting collector's items.

*So why should this not also be the case with toys from today's world?* Overinvestment, overconfidence and the idea of easy money drive up the prices of almost everything, from 18th century vases and garlic to houses, groceries and property. But there are other examples that show the success of such creative ideas. People used to collect various figurines from Kinder Surprise on a grand scale, with individual specimens experiencing incredible price increases. Especially old and rare figurines of the earlier series from the 70s and 80s not rarely achieve three- and in exceptional cases four-digit sales proceeds. Teddy Bears from the world-famous Steiff factory are also popular collector's items. In the past, collectors were prepared to pay four to five figures for particularly rare examples of the bear with the button in its ear. There is hardly any upper price limit, and in individual cases, six-figure sums are sometimes paid. The prices for popular toy trains of Märklin have been experiencing a steady increase in value for years. The filing for insolvency on February 4, 2009 certainly played a decisive role in this. The demand is only served by a niche audience, whereby especially the male sex is enthusiastic about it. Some comic books of Batman, Spiderman, Mickey Mouse and Donald Duck are also experiencing sensational increases in value, although the rush has long since slowed.

Even the popular Smurf figurines are rarely valuable compared to LEGO products. Carrera racing tracks and their accessories do not seem to be a noteworthy value investment. Aircraft models from Herpa Wings are successful, but only reach a small number of collectors. Anyone who takes a closer look at the subject will quickly realize that LEGO products are more than a short-lived investment in difficult times. The colorful plastic bricks have long been bought and sold all year round, regardless of political and economic situations.

## 2.3 Morals, Ethics and Reputation in LEGO Investment

The availability of a LEGO product at retail is determined by its lifespan. In the LEGO universe, we talk about the so-called *EOL*. Originally, the abbreviation means *End of Line* or *End of Life*. In the overall context, the term *End of Lego* is probably the most appropriate. The term was invented by LEGO collectors and investors and describes the official end of the availability of a LEGO product in the online and retail market (so-called *primary market*). The LEGO product enters its well-deserved retirement. As a result, the LEGO product is no longer produced by The LEGO Group and in the following weeks and months, only remaining stocks are usually sold in the online and retail markets.

Excluding unusual events such as the Corona pandemic, The LEGO Group sells its products in over 150 stores in 15 countries. Thanks to its own online store, incoming orders are delivered to 42 of 193 countries. These countries range from North to South America, Europe, Middle East and Asia. The LEGO Group itself holds the largest selection of its own products compared to other retailers. The world's largest toy manufacturer is well aware of its dominance and tries to reach a large part of the world's population directly with its products.

Only The LEGO Group truly knows how long a LEGO product is available online and at retail. The following statistical analysis concludes that the average LEGO set is available for about 530 days or 1.5 years, before it is discontinued. After that, it can only be purchased on the secondary market[1]. The LEGO Group clearly sets the tone and does not simply lay its cards on the table. Since 2000, The LEGO Group has introduced more than 10,750 different LEGO sets to the online and retail markets. This corresponds to an average of more than 500 LEGO sets per year. The trend is clearly upward, with growth averaging about 4 percent per year since 2000. As a consequence, it seems almost impossible to own all LEGO sets since that time.

---

[1] The secondary market is a submarket on which market participants purchase or resell trading objects that are already in circulation.

On the one hand, unimaginable capacities are required for storage. In addition, the potential investor would have had to spend about USD 200,000 (without taking inflation into account) or USD 300,000 (adjusted for inflation) to acquire the toys. With so many new LEGO sets every year, it's certainly no surprise that old themes and products have to step aside for new ones.

On LEGO fan sites, forums and Facebook groups, it appears that the anger and resentment towards LEGO investors is growing. With increasing publicity of the phenomenon of LEGO investment, the tolerance level decreases. It is often assumed that LEGO investors purposefully buy up available LEGO sets in the primary market. The speculation on the future value of the LEGO products limits the availability for children, collectors, fans and building enthusiasts. LEGO investors are often blamed as the root cause when LEGO products simply disappear or become unavailable from online and retail stores. In this respect, the LEGO investor increasingly has a very bad reputation among LEGO fans.

A person who buys LEGO products purely for speculative reasons must accept the criticism that a truly interested and passionate LEGO fan is temporarily left empty-handed. The resulting contempt of many collectors and fans is often due to their own experiences with LEGO investors. LEGO products are no longer available online or in retail stores and the collector may have missed out on the LEGO product of desire. The accusation often comes from those who have missed out on the desired LEGO set. If this happens, the disappointed do not hesitate to voice accusations and harsh criticism. Especially on the Internet, people vent their anger and criticize the existence of LEGO investors in the strongest possible terms.

Investors cannot count on the mercy of others. An appropriate example is *LEGO set no. 10277-1 Crocodile Locomotive*, which went on sale exclusively at The LEGO Group in online and retail stores on July 01, 2020. The *Crocodile Locomotive* was essentially permanently sold out and unavailable anywhere during the first few months of its launch. Many times, it happened that a surprise availability in the LEGO online store was immediately announced on social media, so that the LEGO set was sold out again after only a few seconds. Often to the disappointment and frustration of many interested LEGO customers and fans. A homemade problem of The LEGO Group, whereby the manufacturer quite obviously failed to keep up with production. If the sought-after LEGO product was no longer available in stores, the offers on the secondary market, especially on the Internet, outnumbered each other. It was obvious that the resellers were mainly private sellers. Only a few hours after the start of the sale, hundreds of offers for the Crocodile Locomotive were posted on Ebay. The intention of the resellers is clear and is perceived accordingly by the public. LEGO investors, which also include resellers in the form of short-term speculators, therefore consistently enjoy a very bad reputation.

Resentment towards investors ranges from disapproval to savage abuse (e.g., greed, arrogance, ignorance, etc.). LEGO investors are accused of arbitrarily buying up the market with LEGO products and shamelessly exploiting supply or production bottlenecks. They are accused of hoarding LEGO products and offering them at inflated prices. LEGO investors are often not willing to negotiate the price of a LEGO product. They would rather not sell a LEGO product than not get the price they want. It is then said that LEGO investors are simply not interested in the LEGO hobby. Investors literally walk over dead bodies to increase their profit. The facts are interpreted negatively and are often completely twisted.

Surprisingly, some critics do not begrudge investors of the first hours and their success at that time. As a rule, critics and doomsayers refer in particular to the theme *Star Wars*, which has achieved exponential value growth in some cases in the past. The potential of other themes and products is completely ignored. Critics also predict in the same breath that the successes of the old days will not be repeated in the future. Critics have a variety of reasons for this. On the one hand, there are allegedly too many LEGO investors currently populating the market. On the other hand, the investment seems like a terrible idea in terms of time and effort. For example, unimaginable masses of LEGO products must be purchased in order to invest large amounts of capital. Also, the effort for research, purchase, storage, sale and shipping reduce the profit. Little or nothing remains of the former profit.

Admittedly, LEGO investors also provide useful services. Thanks to LEGO investors, the market gets more liquidity. Furthermore, they offer the possibility of getting LEGO products at a later date, when The LEGO Group is no longer producing them.

Before you start along the path of LEGO as an investment, it's important to keep in mind that you won't get a lot of likes with this type of investment. Of course, you should have fun and participate in social media discussions. Nevertheless, you should always keep in mind that you are tolerated, but actually not very welcome. Any form of investment aims to generate a return. Capitalists in the gambling segment are warmly unwelcome.

At the same time, every investment decision is embedded in a moral context. Each person must decide for himself whether it is ethically acceptable to buy the products of a toy manufacturer, knowing that other people, fans, interested parties, etc. may be left empty-handed. In this respect, a morally responsible investor is different from an investor who does not care about others. The responsible investor reflects the financial and ethical dimension of his investment decisions. Consequences and motivations of his investment are evaluated in such a way that they prioritize ethical demands over financial demands. Investors are therefore jointly responsible for the consequences of their investments.

Basically, the vast majority of current LEGO products are available to everyone. Exceptions are a few LEGO products that are only available regionally (e.g., SDCC or San Diego Comi-Con fair). Without a doubt, LEGO products are much more difficult to get in South-American or Africa. Here, a much smaller The LEGO Group product range is often available. The reasons for this are manifold, complex and can only be answered by The LEGO Group itself. For fans and buyers of the colorful bricks in such countries, this is a bitter message: they have simply missed the boat. That's life. Even LEGO investors can't change that. Of course, resellers and investors are not white knights who act completely selflessly. Rather, they have recognized and filled a niche that The LEGO Group leaves behind with the EOL of a product.

Of course, LEGO investors want to be rewarded for the risk taken and time invested. In addition, one should ask how prices of discontinued LEGO products would develop if there were no resellers and investors. The resulting significantly lower supply will most likely lead to significantly higher prices. This may be one of the reasons why The LEGO Group only lists its products for a limited period of time. Resellers and investors have long since taken over this task. In conclusion, if a LEGO product is too expensive for a prospective buyer, he has the free choice not to buy.

Of course, LEGO investors would like to be compensated for the risk they have taken and the time they have spent. In addition, we should ask ourselves how prices of discontinued LEGO products would develop if there were no resellers and investors. The noticeably lower supply associated with this would most likely lead to significantly higher prices. This is probably one of the reasons why The LEGO Group lists its products in the assortment only for a limited period of time. Resellers and investors have long since taken over this task. In conclusion, if a LEGO product is too expensive for a prospective buyer, he has the free choice not to buy.

## 2.4　Plastic-Juwels

There is a black market for everything, especially for valuable things. Criminals have long since recognized the value of the popular toy and go on an international LEGO heist. LEGO products are becoming increasingly popular among thieves. LEGO products are extremely popular around the world and already retail at high prices in some cases. Furthermore, it is almost impossible to track LEGO products. They do not have a unique identification or serial number. On top of that, LEGO products are very easy to sell. The LEGO secondary market for buyers and sellers is extremely liquid. Worldwide, thousands of LEGO products change hands every day. There are hundreds of examples that illustrate perfectly that LEGO products can increase in value and become very expensive.

In the recent past, toy stores have usually not been as well guarded as, for example, stores for electronic items. For example, a 53-year-old woman was charged with grand larceny after previously stealing 800 LEGO sets from a collector in Long Island, USA. She then attempted to sell the entire stolen collection on eBay for the equivalent of USD 59,000.

A few days later, the police succeeded in arresting a gang of four thieves in the American city of Phoenix who had stolen USD 40,000 worth of LEGO products from Toys'R'Us.

Even more unbelievable seems a robbery from England, where thieves had looted entire LEGO vans a few months earlier. The value of the stolen goods was approximately USD 150,000. One of the arrested perpetrators later had more LEGO stolen goods worth about 200,000 USD. The perpetrator hid the goods of 18 pallets in a special constructed warehouse. These horrifying stories can be continued endlessly.

The peak was reached in 2012, when SAP's CFO Thomas Langenbach was arrested while buying L*EGO set no. 9493-1 X-Wing Starfighter* at his local Target store (USA). Langenbach faked the product barcodes on the packaging. This novel scam allowed him to buy LEGO products at a significantly lower price afterwards. He did this by sticking the barcodes on LEGO products in stores, sometimes for less than a fifth of the actual price. By subsequently reselling the LEGO products on eBay, he earned more than USD 30,000. Langenbach was both a so-called flipper[1] and a fan of the LEGO bricks. The Santa Clara District Attorney's Office described his home as a mini-LEGOland. He had built and displayed many LEGO sets in his home. Otherwise, he had a large collection of individual LEGO bricks and pieces, separated by color, type and size. Langenbach served one month in prison for his crime, followed by five months of house arrest and three years of probation.

Among criminals, LEGO bricks are often associated with diamonds. Both are jokingly referred to as an untraceable commodity. Experts agree that the continued demand for LEGO products, which increase in value over time, as well as their difficulty to be tracked over the Internet, make the plastic toy attractive to thieves.

---

[1] The term *flipping* originally comes from the real estate industry and refers to the purchase of a profitable asset and the quick resale at a profit.

## 2.5    And if I just want to collect LEGO Products?

Basically, investors are to be distinguished from collectors. Collecting describes a systematic and passionate search, procurement and storage of things. Consequently, an investor is also a kind of collector. Both make a critical selection of the object or area to be collected. For this, particular expertise is required. The writer Sigismund von Radecki describes "collectors as people who gather rare things hoping that they will become even rarer."

Basically, everything can be collected. Collecting creates access to systematic thinking. It requires long-term planning, encourages patience, attention to detail, recognition of variety and in the case of exchanges the appreciation of values and special characteristics. The ambitious collector is driven by something else - something non-material. For him, collecting means acquiring objects for pleasure. It encompasses hobby, leisure activity and passion.

It is quite common for people who cannot control their passion(s) for collecting to tend to hoard. Hoarding is characterized by the accumulation of large quantities of material things that most people would consider worthless and useless. On the other hand, they have a particular emotional value for the hoarder.

*What drives collectors to accumulate various things in a selective or systematic way?* First and foremost, it's the enjoyment of the objects themselves. It is not just a purely hobby activity. Every purchase is perceived as personal enrichment. The acquisition of the collectible is not justified (exclusively) because of a possible increase in value. Rather, it is fun and pleasure that a collection can provide. The resulting purpose can be represented neither by purchase prices nor by key figures.

The collector's expertise grows with the scope of the collection. Among other things, this concerns the correct storage and care of the collectibles. Collectibles are often vulnerable to external influences, which is why they must be stored safely and if necessary, cared for.

Collecting opens the eyes, teaches seeing and understanding. Last but not least, collecting also creates social contacts with other collectors. This can create a sense of community. At the same time, the collector forms his individuality through his own expertise and the purchase or sale of rare objects. Within the community, his reputation grows with the representativity of his collection. Under these conditions, the increase in price and value often becomes irrelevant. Psychologically, it is even more interesting. Most people collect for fun and rarely sell their collection. The last happens in the rare case, if the collector wants to collect another object, for example. Isolated collectors nevertheless hope that the increasing age of the objects will drive the price up faster than the deterioration of the condition will lower it.

In principle, a passion for collecting must be considered apart from an investment approach. A collector willingly takes risks, accepts losses in value and constantly expands his collection. In principle, a collector buys a LEGO product to build or to complete his collection. According to the terminology, complementation is the result of his collecting. To understand the phenomenon of complementing, let's take a short excursion into psychology. Incomplete things as well as unfinished tasks lead to an unpleasant inner tension in humans, which motivate them to leave this state as quickly as possible (*Completion Behaviour Pattern*). An example of this is an incomplete puzzle.

When you buy a LEGO set to build, it is advisable to build the LEGO set as soon as possible. It will be much harder to build the LEGO set once it has reached a (significantly) higher value. If you store the LEGO set unopened for several years, it might be too late. The loss of value by opening the LEGO set can then become painfully expensive. One of the main problems with investing in LEGO products is that most investors are also fans. In principle, this is not a good match. LEGO sets are meant to be built. You have to be very disciplined to invest in LEGO sets and not open them for building.

In theory, we can differentiate between two types of collectors. The systematic collector wants to own a certain area (e.g., theme such as Star Wars) completely. In contrast, the non-systematic collector only collects

what he likes or reminds him of something (e.g., from childhood). Passionate hobby collectors often stick to their collecting activities for the rest of
their lives. Investors, on the other hand, are driven by returns. If a collecting
area loses lucrativeness, for example in the form of a drop in profits, investors are quickly tempted to leave the theme behind.

Collecting and investing need not be mutually exclusive, as a number of
similarities can also be identified. Collecting also means methodically select-
ing from various objects of comparison. A critical selection requires various
expertise (first and foremost specialist expertise).

There are LEGO collectors who sell some of their LEGO products and keep
the rest for their own collection. For example, on the Internet you can find
sales offers where LEGO sets are offered without minifigures. This is very
popular among minifigure collectors who do not need the actual main set
(usually consisting of individual bricks and pieces). This can also be a good
indication that minifigures of a particular LEGO set are already worth considerably more, so buying them individually is not really profitable for collectors. Experienced collectors estimate that they can recoup 50 to 75 percent of the cost of the entire LEGO set this way. Combined with discounts
on the purchase, even 100 percent is possible.

People who collect minifigures can do the opposite. They buy a LEGO set
because of the minifigures and sell the other individual bricks and parts. By
doing this, they reduce their initial costs or purchase price. LEGO enthusiasts
call this approach self-financing. Personally, I have also seen sales offers
where individual accessory of the LEGO set were sold. It is a popular way
to partially (re-)finance one's investment.

One final tip: Many investors are tempted to build a LEGO set from their
collection. From an investor's point of view, this is generally not a good idea.
The resulting loss in value afterwards is significant. Even if it seems to make
sense to satisfy one's building desire at certain intervals. The following tip
has become accepted among investors: Buy the LEGO set twice, which you
would like to build. This way you can always be sure that a LEGO set is
closed and sealed as an investment.

## 2.6 LEGO Investment Financial Bubble – Phenomenon and Myth

Financial bubbles are an allegorical phenomenon when investing and speculating in monetary and real assets. Usually, exaggerated expectations of future growth or other events lead to a sharp increase in rate, value or price. Consequently, high asset valuations occur within a particular industry or asset class. Also noted is a rapid increase in the trading volume of the assets as more buyers are attracted by the increased expectations. The overpriced purchase leads to an increase in value. Eventually, the time comes when new buyers are no longer willing to pay the inflated values or prices. At this point, supply exceeds demand. The prices or rates start to fall. The rapid rise is usually followed by an even faster decline of the value. If prices continue to fall, more investors sell their assets. This leads to a further acceleration of the price decline. The sharp fall in prices or values leads at times to panic selling on the part of many investors. Price or value declines of 30 to 50 percent within a few days are very common. This is the time when the bubble literally bursts. The bursting of the bubble is not over until prices or values have returned to a normal level.

Why a bubble finally bursts cannot be said exactly. Often, a connection is seen to the so-called *Greater Fool Theory*. In this investment strategy, a person buys an asset without looking deeper into valuation, use case, acceptance or underlying technology. The investor simply buys in the expectation that someone will undoubtedly buy later at an even higher price. According to the theory, this further buyer is an even bigger fool than oneself. It is therefore a strategy based purely on theoretical approaches. The purchase is always connected with the hope that someone will be found in the future who will be willing to pay an even higher price. The imminent losses have already brought many an investor into a serious financial predicament. A total loss cannot be ruled out either.

If you take a look on the Internet, it quickly becomes clear that the topic has already taken deep roots. One of the most famous crises is probably the speculation on phenomenal increases in the value of baseball player cards at the end of the 1980s. The euphoria surrounding baseball not only set ratings records on television. The excessive optimism became increasingly dangerous. All over the USA, a collecting fever spread with player cards. The collecting fever not only overcame school children, but also spread to adults like an addiction. Over time, a hobby developed into a billion-dollar business, driven by greed and herd behavior. Speculation on trading cards gained almost unstoppable popularity and value, only to crash rapidly a few years later and leave its collectors and investors with huge stocks of useless and worthless trading cards.

*Is history doomed to repeat itself again and a collapse of the LEGO market seems unstoppable?* Or are the fears, worries and divinations without any raison d'être? Basically, many things point to similarities between the two collecting passions:

a. Both the baseball card and LEGO product markets were originally designed for children. Both have experienced a large influx of adult investors who later became heavily involved in the life of the collectible.

b. Both markets are iconic and have existed for more than 50 years.

c. Both markets are experiencing a high level of fluctuation, with a large number of new variations being released each year.

d. Both markets have structured and highly disseminated price guides that show the overview of current prices and trends.

e. Both markets have deeply rooted and widely spread secondary markets with a large number of active users. For example, if you go to sales platforms like Ebay or Amazon, on any given day you will find that there are hundreds of thousands of sales listings in the United States, Germany or the United Kingdom. The number of offers in the United States exceeds those in Europe and the rest of the world on a daily basis.

f.   Both the market for LEGO products and baseball cards have long been among the largest collectibles markets in the world.

The following differences are worth noting:

a.   Unlike baseball cards, LEGO products are real toys that both children and adults can play with and give freedom to their creativity.

b.   Baseball trading cards and LEGO products are popular across all age groups.    Baseball trading cards and LEGO products are popular across all age groups. However, the first has gone through a change, with adults being its main customers nowadays. On the other hand, the majority of LEGO customers are mainly children or younger generations. Also, the main themed areas (e.g., Ninjago, Friends or City) are un-doubtedly aimed at minors. Investing is the last thing on children's minds. Rather, it is the fun of building that strengthens the brand now and in the future.

c.   Baseball cards are mainly an American phenomenon and dependent on the popularity of the sport itself.[1] LEGO products are bought, played with and sold all over the world. This helps the LEGO brand maintain a solid foundation around the world. In this regard, the more people who buy products from The LEGO Group, the better the secondary market for LEGO products will be after a product is retired.

d.   The LEGO Group releases a large swarm of new products each year to keep theme areas contrasting with fresh ideas. In comparison, the base-ball card market is literally flooded with thousands of cards every year.

e.   LEGO products are comparatively expensive to produce. Because of this, The LEGO Group does not want to risk warehouses with unsold inven-tory. On the other hand, the storage options for baseball cards are sig-nificantly easier compared to LEGO products.

---

[1] Notwithstanding a few Latin American countries and Japan.

f.   There is no replacement for a toy like LEGO. There are other, smaller competitors, but the original LEGO brick is far superior and loved more than ever. It's also undeniable that new technology is outpacing old hobbies, such as card collecting. Video games and smartphones are the new toys for many kids. But there is still a desire for people to use their imagination and build something (out of LEGO bricks). Today's playing kids are tomorrow's adult LEGO builders and collectors. It is this cycle that keeps The LEGO Group profitable, even in difficult economic times, and helps to keep the value of LEGO products high.

g.   In conclusion, baseball cards investment failed mainly because the underlying sport (baseball) lost popularity considerably. It is not the most popular sport in the world, nor do baseball cards have any sustainable intrinsic value.

In fact, there are some similarities between the two markets. Nevertheless, the contradictions outweigh the similarities. The key difference stems from the physical products themselves. Baseball cards are merely highly materially simplified trading cards, with no superior educational purpose. The majority of LEGO products are purchased by or for children. In contrast to the baseball card market, adult investors or buyers are the minority. They are responsible for only a fraction of The LEGO Group's total consolidated sales. Certainly, collectors and resellers have some influence on secondary market prices, but not to the extent that many may believe. The few tens of thousands of collectors and speculators are thus offset by millions of children and parents who do not view LEGO products as an investment.

The baseball card market was doomed by exactly this. The main buyers were no longer just children and fans. Rather, adults sought additional opportunities to profitably multiply money. What was initially intended for children was literally driven into worthlessness by speculation and overproduction. Baseball card manufacturers sensed their opportunity in the turnaround of the buying public and produced billions of cards. As a result, the market was flooded with worthless paper. Resellers and collectors stockpiled masses of cards, not realizing that manufacturers were already flooding the market with supply.

Investing in collectibles is always accompanied by ups and downs. Ultimately, they invest in perceived value, not intrinsic value. In this respect, LEGO products have a very low intrinsic value. The main material, plastic, is generally inexpensive. A circumstance that is difficult to imagine with LEGO products.

A long-term oversupply of LEGO products can be a good indicator of the formation of a bubble. However, in this aspect, The LEGO Group acts much more thoughtfully than the baseball card manufacturers and pursues a much more complex strategy. The quality of the products is at a very high level. LEGO products have a fixed life cycle, which makes the offer permanently varied. At the same time, The LEGO Group always keeps its eyes on the market and produces on demand. Theme areas sometimes disappear from the market after a short time, for example because customers are no longer enthusiastic about them. On the other hand, other topics can remain on the market for many years. A very intelligent and successful business practice. The company's action strategy runs counter to the typical formation of a bubble.

In summary, it is necessary to distinguish between the primary market[1] and the secondary market[2]. In the primary market, sales are made by The LEGO Group itself. The primary market is defined by The LEGO Group, whereby The LEGO Group sets the non-binding sales price. In the Secondary Market, LEGO products already in circulation are purchased and resold by various market participants. In the secondary market, prices are determined by the supply and demand of the participants. Admittedly, there is a possibility that the secondary market for certain themes or individual LEGO products may collapse (e.g., Star Wars).

---

[1] For instance, LEGO Onlineshop and Retail, WalMart, Costco and Amazon
[2] For instance, Ebay, Facebook Marketplace and Bricklink

In principle, a (financial) bubble bursts when the value of LEGO products reaches its peak. As a result, supply is disproportionately higher than demand. At present, this is not expected to be the case for all LEGO products. Rather, there will always be LEGO products that enjoy great popularity and therefore demand. A collapse of the entire LEGO market is therefore extremely unlikely. Nevertheless, it is certainly possible that some LEGO products may face sharp price corrections in the future. In contrast to this is the LEGO primary market. The LEGO Group keeps product prices very stable and inventories at a balanced level.

Without a doubt, the clearest indicators of an impending (financial) bubble are when the topic of LEGO investment is featured in major magazine and news coverage. Or when interest in LEGO products diminishes significantly and ultimately dies out completely. Although LEGO products are becoming more and more popular as an investment, the topic is not even close to being publicly present, like the topic of baseball trading cards was many years before the crash. The LEGO investment market has not yet collapsed under the pressure of supply. When the topic of LEGO as an investment reaches the public and pictures of rooms full of LEGO products are printed on the cover of relevant magazines, then it is time to exercise caution.

## 3.     A genuine Investment Option

*The crucial question that appears on the horizon is: Do LEGO products meet the basic requirements of a profitable investment?* We speak of an investment when capital is tied up in tangible or intangible assets over the certain term. A person who invests is called an investor. The investor expects a financial return from the investment. The return or yield is achieved through the increase in value of the tangible or intangible asset. Ideally, investors strive for a maximum multiplication of the invested capital. In this respect, investors are modern artists of finance, whereby their more artificial work are the returns, which are literally created out of nothing.

While looking for alternative ways to invest money, I started relatively late (around 2017) to explore the idea of whether LEGO products could be an investment. This is an unusual question, since I grew up with the company and its products. Unfortunately, anyone who knows the company, shares the company philosophy and appreciates the products cannot invest directly in the company at the given time, e.g., in the form of company shares (stocks).[1] The LEGO Group is a privately held, family-owned company. If The LEGO Group decides to take the company public, shares are issued to investors. The future shareholder is a co-owner of the company and thus has a say in what The LEGO Group can and cannot do with its products. It would also be conceivable for the company's profits to be shared with shareholders in the form of a dividend. However, it is highly unlikely that The LEGO Group will take this step. As long as The LEGO Group does not take the company public, it can continue to focus on its own vision without having to achieve specific financial goals or satisfy a large number of shareholders.

---

[1] The LEGO Group is by no means an exception. As with FC Bayern München AG, existing shares in The LEGO Group are not traded on international stock exchanges. Kiel Kirk Kristiansen, the grandson of the company's founder, currently holds 75 percent of the shares together with his three adult descendants. A further 25 percent is said to be held by the Oticon Foundation, which is dedicated to charitable activities.

Fortunately, there is a way to profit indirectly from the success of the building bricks. This can be done by purchasing physical LEGO products and speculating on their future price or value growth. This is currently the only way to invest in The LEGO Group. This observation brings us to the question at the beginning of the chapter: *Do LEGO products have the basic requirements to be a profitable investment?*

The foundation is set by the company itself: LEGO products are limited from the very beginning by its producer, The LEGO Group. On the other hand, there is huge demand in the form of the fan market, various collectors' markets, the secondary market for buying and selling, and numerous communities such as blogs, forums, and many more. The limitation of the supply is called artificial scarcity in market economy terms. The producer (The LEGO Group) keeps the supply below the demand by the consumer (customer or interested party). The result is a misbalance of supply and demand. This is pure market economy and works quite simply.

The fan-, collector- and secondary markets take place worldwide. The strongest markets are USA, Australia and Europe. But especially in the Asian region, a new generation of LEGO collectors and enthusiasts is currently growing up, who already have an increasing interest in older LEGO products (especially sets).

The rarity of a LEGO product determines its price or value. The reasons for this can be extremely manifold. Experience shows that the production capacity or supply is intentionally kept low. LEGO products such as sets, minifigures, but also individual bricks or parts are produced in fixed quantities and are only available for a certain period of time.[1] For example, collaborations in form of licensing agreements with Disney (e.g., Star Wars), Harry Potter or Marvel are expiring. New released products regularly replace the current product range. Discontinued LEGO products are no longer produced and disappear permanently from the (primary) online and retail markets. At this point, the LEGO product is only available on the secondary market.

---

[1] This limited period relates to the primary market.

There are opportunities and risks for LEGO investors to be evaluated. When a LEGO product is no longer available online or in retail stores, a collector's value usually begins to develop. LEGO investors can take advantage of this situation by buying relevant LEGO products and speculating on their increase in value.[1]

If LEGO products would be available at any time and in unlimited quantities in online or retail stores, there would be no increase in value or price on the secondary market. Supply would meet or even exceed demand. The result is saturation of consumer demand. The price and quantity of a LEGO product converge until both are at a level that allows anyone who wants to purchase a particular LEGO product for a price, he or she is willing to pay.

---

[1] We are already familiar with comparable procedures in the field of classic cars, sports cars, watches, handbags and sneakers, etc.

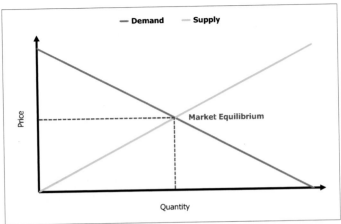

*Figure 5 - Price-Quantity Diagram, formation of a market price and a market quantity in market equilibrium*

Once the production of a LEGO product is discontinued, the maximum available quantity of the LEGO product on the market is regulated. Consequently, the price of a LEGO product that is available or offered on the market in a smaller quantity increases.[1] This is the basic idea behind buying a LEGO product as an investment that will soon cease to be sold.

*This brings us to the question why The LEGO Group keeps discontinuing LEGO products in the first place?* Well, The LEGO Group is also subject to the natural laws of the market and the social economy. As soon as the majority of potential buyers have purchased a LEGO set, the demand and therefore the total sales of the LEGO product can hardly be increased. The potential of the market is then largely exhausted. Nevertheless, saturation levels above 100 percent are possible in theory. On the demand side, this is made possible by several LEGO sets per household, e.g., as an extension of the existing set or in the case of replacement demand. Enthusiastic LEGO collectors are often prepared to pay many times the MSRP just to be able

---

[1] For example, an ideal scenario would be that you, as a LEGO investor, are the only person offering a LEGO product at a given point in time of demand.

44

to call LEGO sets, individual bricks, parts and minifigures their own. In the past, it was observed that various LEGO products achieved high returns. This can be explained by the fact that LEGO products were rarely if ever collected unopened in the past. Earlier sets are now rarer than ever. These are simple market economy laws. As a result, as of Dec. 31, 2020, about 90 percent of all LEGO sets have increased in value. Fundamentally, little has changed in the recent past except that discontinued LEGO products are experiencing much faster price increases. This unusual idea of alternative capital investment owes its origin not least to the development of the Internet. Online stores or comparison portals invite you to quickly search, compare and buy. The obstacles of the past have long since been forgotten. The right buyer can usually be found quickly, and he or she doesn't even have to be from the same country or speak the same language. Digital media have reduced this effort to a minimum and contribute to similar creative investment ideas. This puts LEGO products on a level with other tangible assets such as classic cars, watches or coins. Since the outbreak of the financial crisis and the low interest rate environment of recent years, tangible assets have become particularly popular investments, with returns in the two- to three-digit percentage range. But unlike LEGO products, many of these asset classes are characterized by a certain luxury, high craftsmanship or a wealthy clientele. Respectfully, it must be acknowledged that LEGO products have managed to create a sense of exclusivity. An exclusivity barrier that not everyone can jump over at will. But be vigilant. As soon as there are euphoric and exuberant reports about an investment, the best time to invest in this area is usually already over.

## 3.1    LEGO Investment is simple, but not easy.

Anyone who invests money wants to make money. Increasing money requires time, expertise and often start-up capital. Many private persons do not want to deal with the subject of investing capital. It costs them a lot of overcoming to put the thoughts into action. For beginners this is a big challenge at first. The majority of people often seem afraid of the complexity of the financial world. Yet everyone would have to deal with the subject on a regular basis. Many consumers turn to financial advisors who offer their help for a fee. If the consumer has no expertise or experience, he or she must be able to rely completely on the financial advisor. An uncomfortable notion. Advisors do not always act in the customer's best interest because they receive a commission for selling and brokering some financial products. The distrust of financial advisors is therefore correspondingly high today.

With self-confidence and initiative, it is not very difficult for beginners to take capital investment into their own hands. As a matter of principle, they should put aside any fears of contact. Personal involvement with capital investment inevitably leads to an improvement in understanding of business processes. Once the decision has been made to take wealth-creating measures on your own, the next hurdle comes. Nowadays, anyone who wants to invest his or her capital profitably is faced with an unmanageable choice of investment options. Beginners can quickly lose track of the amount of investment opportunities. Those who have made it to this book will certainly be familiar with alternative capital investments. Nowadays, countless media deal with the most diverse forms of capital investment.

The personal choice for the right type of investment depends on a variety of factors such as (prior) knowledge, experience, risk tolerance, capital assets and individual assumptions or restrictions that one imposes on oneself. It is also crucial to have a passion for investing and for the thing itself (LEGO products). Of course, it is possible to speculate soberly on high returns and profits. However, it has proven to be worthwhile to deny things with full conviction. It is no longer a secret that people are more successful when they do what they really feel like doing. Therefore, you should consider in advance whether you are on fire for the subject. On top of that, investing and the prospect of high and quick profits lead many an investor to a thrill similar to gambling.

Personally, I think it is not enough if the inner drive and one's own enthusiasm is only directed on high profit expectations. The following exemplary questions should be examined critically in advance:

### Can I identify myself with LEGO products?

Identification literally means equating and usually happens unconsciously. The more you identify with something, the more convincingly you represent it. The best motivation is identification. You have to believe in what you are doing. Successful people are never driven by money. The focus is on the cause itself, for example, improving a process, helping people, etc. Money is then often a (positive) by-product of success. If you invest a fair amount of your time in a particular thing, it can help you understand that product and enjoy it. Conversely, people are rarely interested in things in which we are not actively involved, or in this case, invested. It's like publicly traded companies. If you are not personally invested (e.g., in stocks), you are usually rather less interested in what is going on in the company, or even not interested at all. The Internet can be your constant source of information.

Online stores, online auctions, comparison portals and various information sites are just some of the many advantages. The information content is limitless and the community is growing at an almost unstoppable pace, so this medium is unavoidable. Continuous monitoring of the broad market is also crucial (e.g., podcasts, reviews in the LEGO online store, Amazon or Youtube, etc.). For example, visiting fairs, markets (this includes flea markets, weekly markets or supermarkets in the classic sense) or household liquidations can turn out to be beneficial. Many people - myself included - associate LEGO products with wonderful childhood memories. After many years of absence, my LEGO passion began unconsciously. I was working abroad at the time and during a visit to the observation deck of the Burj Khalifa, I bought the matching *LEGO set no. 21008-1 Burj Khalifa* from LEGO Architecture as a souvenir.

## Do I enjoy LEGO (-Investment)?

Enjoying the activity should be the first priority. Without motivation for the matter, the journey into the world of LEGO will not be long-lasting. Financial goals may be right and important from a certain point of view (e.g., in the area of controlling), but these goals rarely fill the individual with great enthusiasm. A passionate LEGO investor will gladly accept any detour on the weekend if it leads through the toy department of a retail store. Personally, I like to take such routes. However, I purchase the majority of my LEGO sets over the Internet. Along with this, I have not held the LEGO box or set in my hands before. Except for the few occasions in LEGO stores, I extremely rarely get to see LEGO sets in assembled condition, which I own as an investment myself. The assessment of a LEGO purchase is always based on facts. I try to keep emotions under control as far as possible (rule no. 1 on the stock market). That sounds easier than it really is. In any case, coming across LEGO sets at retail, which are on their way to me, is pure excitement every time. Passion can make you a better investor. But seriously, first decide why and how seriously you want to take investing LEGO products. Ask yourself: *Will you buy LEGO products solely for investment purposes? Do you collect LEGO products to part them out them and later resell individual LEGO bricks, parts and minifigures? Perhaps you combine fun or love for LEGO products?* Realize that every hour you spend sorting bricks and pieces, picking orders, or worrying about the safety of LEGO sets in the basement is an hour you can't spend doing something else.

## What do I expect from this investment?

Establishing goals is extremely important in any endeavor. It helps keep yourself accountable and to plan strategies. You need these to get what you want. Without a goal, the path doesn't matter. Usually, investors want to increase their invested capital because for instance they are saving for a specific purpose. In this case, the objective is clearly designed to maximize capital. On the other hand, their objectives may be of a temporal nature, in which they want to set aside money for retirement, for example. Decide in advance what your desired rate of return should be. If you decide to sell at double MSRP, then make that decision and stick to it. When it comes to investing, it can help to have an end goal in mind - even if it's just a number. Beyond that, safety and tax benefits play a big role. While not impossible, it seems extremely unlikely that they will get rich from LEGO investing. Rather, you should set yourself concrete goals, such as selling a certain number of LEGO products to be able to finance a vacation or build up some wealth. Don't underestimate the effect of being able to afford some of the profit from your investment.

## How long is your investment horizon?

Before investing in LEGO products, ask yourself the question of your planned investment horizon. *How many years do you want to keep your LEGO products before reselling them? Should LEGO products be bought with the aim of selling them quickly after purchase or keeping them for a long period of time?* The answers and decisions are entirely up to you. For example, studies show that holding stocks for the long term generates a higher return than trying to trade the swings (so-called ups and downs) of a stock price on a daily or even hourly basis. An investor who sets aside money for the proverbial bad times over the long term is more likely to achieve his or her financial goals than someone who merely looks to the market for quick profits. Patience is the key. *How long should you wait?* This is really a question of personal circumstances. There are many questions to ask yourself about this. *Do I have enough storage capacity to hold LEGO products for an indefinite period of time? How long can I do without the invested capital?* etc.

## How much money do you have available to invest?

The phrase "You need money to make money." is absolutely true here. It is especially important to consider how long you can invest money and live without it. There is definitely a correlation between the amount of capital you invest and the number of profits you can make with it. We all have obligations in life that quite often require the use of our capital. Whether the car needs to be serviced or the purchase of a new sofa is on the budget. Your capital investment should not tear a hole in the household budget. You should also have sufficient reserves available. Also, you should refrain from investing money that does not belong to you (e.g., borrowing money from family or incurring debt in the form of a bank loan). Consider whether you can do without the invested capital for an indefinite period of time. Get an overview of your personal finances to be able to quantify the amount of the LEGO investment. Putting all the money allocated to one asset class is risky. Diversification across multiple products is strongly recommended. Diversification sounds complicated, but it follows simple principles. Never put all your eggs in one basket. This advice describes the successful diversification principle. Successful investors spread their investment capital within and outside the asset class.

## How much risk are you willing to take?

Safety is a relative term. What one person sees as a safe haven may be another person's worst nightmare. Risk and return are inseparable. Confronting, assessing and defining your own risks are critical to success in investing. After all, you are investing your hard-earned money. Taking risks means that you dare to do a certain thing and don't know what will come out of it. In contrast, returns are compensation for risks investors take. As a rule, the more risks you take, the higher your chances of making a profit. At the same time, the probability of a (total) loss increases with the risk. Of course, a (total) loss must be avoided at all costs.[1] Especially in the beginning you should think about this. How can this be done in the case of LEGO investments? By defining a strategy, for example, that you buy only a certain quantity of a LEGO product. Buying the same LEGO product fifty times does not only increase your chances of making a profit. If the LEGO product is not very popular later on or flops completely, you will be especially upset about the loss of both money and time. But let me tell you, it is not impossible that your risk appetite will grow as you gain experience in a particular field. In the end, the choice of risks is usually yours. Stick to your strategy. It is essential to see the definition and refinement of a strategy as a never-ending process. Constant changes of your strategy do not demonstrate consistency. Therefore, it is difficult to learn from constant strategy changes (e.g., recognition of repetitive patterns).

■ **At what intervals do you buy LEGO sets?**
This question is in the context with the previous question "*How much money do you have available to invest?*" The question is intended as food for thought on how you plan to build your LEGO Investment or portfolio. The LEGO Group released over 12,500 LEGO sets between Feb. 1, 2000 and Dec. 31, 2020. This corresponds to approximately 600 LEGO sets per year. It is almost impossible that you have the possibilities to acquire all of these LEGO sets. In this respect, private investors are limited in terms of space, money, time, or all of the above. The majority of LEGO investors are restricted to invest a fixed amount each month. Alternatively, there are LEGO investors who really only buy when the available LEGO sets in online or retail stores meet their own expectations or fit into their strategy. These LEGO investors do

---

[1] For example, a total loss is the complete destruction (e.g., by fire) of the LEGO investment or portfolio.

not necessarily have to buy. From my own experience, I can confirm that due to the Corona Pandemic, LEGO offers have become weaker since March 2020. Due to the continuing high demand for LEGO products, retailers are cutting back on discounts. If you wait for the desired discount, you may run the risk of missing out the LEGO product. Therefore, combining different approaches certainly seems to be a good alternative.

## Can you handle financial losses?

With an investment you can not only make money, you can also lose money. A realized loss is always frustrating. You have invested time, money and energy in something that has ultimately developed against your expectations. It hits investors even harder when a total loss occurs, for example due to theft or complete destruction of LEGO products. The latter happens, for example, due to water or fire damage. In the case of a total loss, the investor loses his entire capital investment. What already sounds painful when trading shares on the stock market (e.g., insolvency of a company) is even crueler in LEGO investment: The total loss of a LEGO portfolio also destroys the physical value - the actual toy. Protective measures such as taking out insurance are strongly recommended. Investing evokes a roller coaster of emotions. Although thrill, hope, greed, lust, aggression, frustration, contentment, impatience, anger or joy are more likely to be emotions in the realm of stocks, they can also occur in LEGO investing. Those who do not have a robust mind or nerves can quickly become overwhelmed. Those who know their mental strengths and weaknesses, those who always keep a cool head, have an advantage.

## How would your partner react?

Many potential LEGO investors underestimate this matter or are not even aware of it. But some LEGO collectors can tell you that the topic can become very relevant. LEGO investment is above all one thing - multifaceted. Whether you want to invest a lot of money, spend hours researching future LEGO investments, LEGO sets are piling up in the basement, or you are angry because you missed out on a LEGO product. The topic is omnipresent once you get started. Be especially sensitive to your partner's understanding before both of you begin the unknown journey. The question should be a food for thought, but at the same time you should not let it scare you. The experiences that have been brought to my attention so far are as colorful as the popular bricks themselves. The hobby, which is often talked down, not infrequently takes on forms that exceed personal cost and time frames. Much to the displeasure of our beloved ones. Often the partner simply cannot understand the preference for the nubby toy. The Internet is also full of stories and testimonials about difficult disputes within relationships. Be aware of the following: There are an infinite number of situations in life in which your environment and the people around want to teach you. Think carefully about whether you really want to give up something you truly believe in because your environment disagrees with you. Passion for something is difficult to put into words, communicate or even scale. At the end of the day, you have to be comfortable with yourself and be able to sleep with a clean conscience. You will never be able to satisfy everyone. *What's the point if you really want to ride a motorcycle, but you are literally told not to do so?* In any case, you should inform your partner about your future plans. Some of us - myself included - enjoy the good fortune of having a partner who acknowledges, and not infrequently endorses the love to LEGO (Investment). Again, others may be much more authoritarian when it comes to the single USD in the household. I just want to raise the matter to avoid that they soon look into rolling eyes of their partner when he or she finds piles of LEGO products in the shared apartment.

## How much entrepreneurial spirit is in you?

For the majority of LEGO investors, this type of business is their first test as an entrepreneur. Anyone who wants to be an entrepreneur should have certain qualifications and character attributes. You need to think in a goal-oriented manner, weigh up risks and make solid decisions. Entrepreneurs have a sense for opportunities and dangers. *Are you prepared to work above average for a cause that is important to you? What about your business acumen? Can you handle money responsibly? Do you enjoy accounting?* The answers to these questions won't necessarily help them decide whether to sell LEGO sets, bricks, or parts, but they will be a factor in deciding how large and/or complex their business should be - or whether you want to turn your hobby into a business at all.

The previous questions are intended to introduce you to the topic of investing. Your personal answers are highly individual and rarely transferable. Likewise, there are neither right nor wrong answers. Be consciously critical of the questions, after all, the project will not only affect your financial future.

As with any type of investment, decisions must be made in LEGO investment. These decisions are unlikely to change your life. Nevertheless, these should be well considered, after all, it is your hard-earned money. In contrast, real estate, which can be theoretically as well as practically completely debt-financed. That means, they finance the purchase price of the real estate to a larger or whole part (inclusive additional expenses) by for example a bank credit. In the best case, you do not have to invest any of your own capital, which significantly improves your return. If you want to invest your money in LEGO products instead, you will always need initial funds or equity. Initial funds or equity capital is the amount of money that a LEGO investor must bring to the table at the beginning of their capital investment. It is important to realize that the LEGO investment significantly limits the flexibility and availability of your capital.

### 3.1.1 Principles of Investing

We all have different personalities, goals, interests and risk appetites. Investment markets are undeniably complex systems. They consist of many participants, numbers, formulas, risks, opportunities and news at breakneck speed. Anyone who wants to invest successfully should therefore know, understand and implement general principles of investing. The word principle is defined by its Latin origin *principium* translated as *beginning, start, origin* or *principle*. The specific meaning depends on the context. The most accurate is probably the combination of the scientific definition, where principle means several related scientific theories or general rules. Accordingly, principles are generally applicable rules and applicable to all forms of capital investment. Many of the simple principles described here have their origin in the stock market. Due to their psychological reference, they are also suitable for other capital investments. Therefore, these classical basic principles can also be applied to LEGO investment.

Without any doubt, the following basic principles are very easy to understand. In fact, you don't need above-average intelligence to act according to these basic principles. Investing is not a talent. It is a skill that people can acquire. A specific education in the field is certainly helpful, as almost everywhere, but not absolutely necessary. André Kostolany[1] describes it most aptly in his work *The Art of Thinking about Money*. A successful investor needs four competencies. They are instrumental in ensuring that a hard-nosed investor avoids the mistakes of the shaky investors and is one of the winners in the long run. In principle, the shaky investors pay for the profits of the hard-nosed investors.

---

[1] André Bartholomew Kostolany was born on Feb. 09, 1906 in Budapest, Austria-Hungary and was a journalist, writer and entertainer of Hungarian origin and U.S. citizenship who appeared as a stock exchange and financial expert as well as a speculator. He died on Sep. 14, 1999 in Paris.

## Money

Money is not necessarily a symbol of wealth, but rather depends on your financial circumstances, for example, whether you have debts or not. According to Kostolany, an investor has no money if, for example, he has 1 million Euro in shares, but maturities worth 2 million Euro. Trading and speculating with borrowed money ultimately lead to panic selling when prices correct and people fear they will not be able to repay their debts. As long as they continue to hold the income from their assets, their wealth grows at an increasing rate.

## Thoughts

Give enough consideration to the investment product you choose and learn to understand it. Being an investor is not a full-time profession. Just a few hours a month are enough. Knowledge and experience are the best protections against unwanted surprises. In general, you should only invest in what you understand. It will be easier for you to make decisions, define goals and minimize risks. Make sure that your goals are clear. Only if a measurable and realistic goal is defined, the way to reach it can be understood. Thoughts also represent, in a figurative sense, the strategy that you should always base your actions on. Wild speculation must be avoided as a matter of principle. Make sure that your strategic approach is as simple as possible, that you will still be able to follow it in 20 years as you did at the beginning. Make a clear determination regarding their long-term behavior. Think about it, develop a strategy, and stay true to it. It doesn't matter what friends, associates and the media say. Leave the herd instinct behind. Do not under any circumstances tend to give away returns or even to incur heavy losses by following the masses. In this context it is indispensable to minimize the risk by means of diversification. It has long been common knowledge that you should not put all your eggs in one basket, even in the stock market.

### Patience

Even major investors and entrepreneurs like Warren Buffett see patience as a long-lost virtue. The successful investor has a great degree of patience. He buys far below the fair value and sells far above the fair value. Falling prices and rates tempt investors to sell in panic. There is simply a lack of patience. *Why should a LEGO set bought for 40 percent below MSRP, for example, remain below that in 10 to 15 years?* Plan for the long term and avoid any attempts to get rich overnight. Do not be greedy. A rational approach is essential. Take your time. Life is stressful enough. Every day we have to make countless decisions, few of which can have a lasting impact like our wealth accumulation. Train yourself to be patient.

### Fortune

Every investor needs a portion of luck. Political and economic events, wars and natural disasters can affect capital markets and have a lasting impact on them. Due to their omnipresence and complexity, they can hardly be taken into account when planning a strategy. If you are lucky, everything goes as planned. If you are not lucky and your strategy vanishes into thin air, you have to take countermeasures as quickly as possible. Buying a LEGO product at a historically low price is also a form of luck.

It is critical to understand that these attributes are correlated with each other. The lack of money or the presence of debt is rarely consistent with patience. Strategy goes hand in hand with your thoughts. Thoughts are the basis of their strategy. Without knowing what you want, it becomes difficult to have patience for it. Such scenarios are known from the herd instinct. If everyone is buying, you will buy. And if everyone sells, you will probably do the same. If you lack luck, you will eventually lose faith in yourself and your thoughts or strategy.

### 3.1.2  Not all Investors are the same

In general, there are different types of investors in any capital invest-ment. LEGO Investment is no exception. The classic differentiation is first made between institutional investors (legal entities) and private investors (individuals). An institutional investor, unlike a private investor, has an es-tablished commercial business operation for the management of capital in-vestments. The volume for purchases and sales is much larger than for pri-vate investors. Mostly, institutional investors act on behalf of credit institu-tions, insurance companies, investment companies and corporations, pen-sion funds, social security institutions, health insurance companies, etc. It is not known whether institutional investors have invested in LEGO products to date. However, this is considered extremely unlikely. The majority of in-vestors are private. Private investors are more independent and not bound to third parties in their investment decisions. They use the investment mar-ket for personal purposes such as private asset management. Statistical sur-veys show that the majority of private investors are primarily concerned with security when investing their money. Private investors manage their own assets. Typically, the amounts of private investors are much smaller than those of institutional investors. Overall, private investors represent the larg-est group of LEGO investors.

Now that you know that you are a private investor, it is important to find out what type of private investor. Because understanding the different types helps to understand the approach, motivation, expectation or strategy, in-vestment amount, time horizon or risk management on an investment. The type of investor has an impact on the activities of the market or how people act here. Ultimately, they can also ensure a certain liquidity of the market. A high liquidity of the market is all the more likely to ensure a fair price determination.

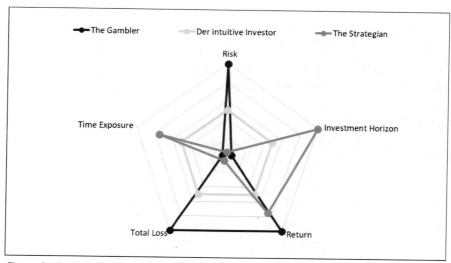

*Figure 6 - Profiles of investors you should know.*

In the following, it is necessary to determine which character attributes are helpful for the LEGO investment on the basis of the investor types presented. Strictly speaking, you can take a leaf out of every investor type's book and should not definitively commit to one profile. For most investors it is simply advisable to accept an average return. Based on this, each investor must decide for himself which type he wants to be. The different types of investors are shown in Figure 6 and will be presented below.

### 3.1.2.1 The Strategian

The strategist is conscious of the fact that he or she has to do something with the money he or she has saved. The subject of investment is a means to an end. The strategist wants to spend as little time as possible on it and feels little or no emotion about the matter itself. He or she relies primarily on fundamental analysis for decision-making. Strategists use the buy and hold strategy. As a result, they hold on to their investment decisions for a very long time, usually for years. The strategist does not follow an agreed time horizon and is experienced enough to recognize advantageous situations for buying or selling. Instead of making a quick buck, he or she is concerned with controlled wealth accumulation. Therefore, price fluctuations in the market do not shake that person, as they are usually short-term. The combination of these conditions allows a low-risk investment, in which investors can count on a steadily growing return. The strategian takes the time and observes the market quietly. He or she continues to act on the basis of his original strategy and keeps a cool head even in difficult times. This form of investment is in principle very sustainable and often pays off over the long term. The strategist is a conservative investor. For the conservative investor the security of the investment is in the foreground. They only want to take a small financial risk or none at all.

### 3.1.2.2 The intuitive Investor

As shown in Figure 6, the intuitive investor is ranked between the strategist and the gambler. His or her decisions take place subconsciously or are based on gut instinct. Intuition guides them halfway between emotions and reasons. He has a sense for recognizing patterns and shines through being diligent. Even in stormy times, they act with focus, concentration and keep an overview of the overall market. The person is not afraid to invest an above-average amount of time in capital investment. The intuitive investor keeps his or her goals in mind at all times, acquiring mixed LEGO products through the market in order to sell them in smaller batches. The profit goes into new products with full conviction. Their clearer dedication to the subject enables them (e.g., through more research work) on the one hand to acquire the chosen LEGO products cheaper through in-depth knowledge, and on the other hand to give the content (e.g., minifigures, theme series, unique bricks and parts, etc.) a much more efficient evaluation. This knowledge clearly comes to his benefit when it comes to later sales. Due to their clear multi-activity, they will improve their hunter instinct and collector instinct over time, which can have a noticeable effect on their risk behavior and return on investment. The Intuitive investor is a balanced investor. Investors of this profile care about a balance between security and return.

### 3.1.2.3  The Gambler

Unlike the strategist and the intuitive investor, the gambler is looking for a quick buck. The gambler is one of the offensive investors whose main goal is to achieve the highest possible return on investment. He has a solid capital base and is risk-averse towards losses. The gambler does not fear total loss. They believe they know what they are doing, but are rarely in control of the situation. Consequently, their short investment horizon resembles gambling to some extent. When asked specifically, this person will apparently have difficulties to explain in more detail what he or she is doing and for what reason. After all, a typical characteristic for a gambler is that he or she has no strategy. A gambler sees the activity more as a kind of hobby, which produces money on the side. In general, they hope that their LEGO products will all increase in value. Thus, his or her actions are defined in partially unconscious, hectic, capricious, and random interactions. Occasionally it happens that the gambler breaks the most important basic rule, when he or she takes on debts for the gambling and finally challenges his or her luck. The gambler takes on debts for his gambles and finally pushes his luck. The own psyche must be stable enough to keep a cool head even in hot phases. His continuous buying and selling are subject to the usual market fluctuations. In this respect, the gambler's trading is much more fast-paced, more intense, but also more hectic. Daily developments are taken up, processed and often want to be converted. This mainly includes people who hunt for bargains in the retail trade or sell *Gift-With-Purchase* (*GWP*) items immediately after purchase.

### 3.1.3   Typical Errors in Tangible Assets

As with all forms of investments, there are common investor mistakes to avoid in LEGO investing. Investment decisions are often considered complex and risky by private individuals. Especially as a new investor in the big wide LEGO universe, there are some points to consider in order to avoid at least the typical beginner's mistakes and not to step into every stumbling trap right from the start.

◻ **Do not put all your eggs in one basket.**
If you hold large quantities of the same LEGO product, it is like a lottery. Rather, you should buy LEGO products as independent of each other as possible. Independent in terms of theme series, individual bricks and parts, minifigures, etc.

◻ **Don't invest everything at once.**
Build up your portfolio gradually over the long term. A good example of this is an ETF savings plan.

◻ **Holding on to bad investments for too long.**
If you notice that a LEGO product is no longer increasing in value, you should consider selling it.

◻ **Instant consumption instead of long-term savings goals.**
Get in the habit of consistently following a savings plan every month.

◻ **The entry price is often overrated.**
If you are convinced of your choice, the purchase price is secondary.

◻ **Overreaction to present events.**
The rerelease or new release of a LEGO product does not automatically lead to the total loss of the previous model.

◻ **Repetition of mistakes already made in the past.**
All beginnings are difficult. Learn from your mistakes.

- **Beware of trends and excessive enthusiasm.**
  Avoid the herd instinct and make up your own mind about the LEGO products.

- **Trading without an investment strategy.**
  An old saying goes, "Back and forth makes pockets empty." Exercise to be patient.

- **Everything has to be perfect. Everything must be fast.**
  Even experienced investors rarely manage to buy at the lowest price and sell at the highest price.

- **You should not return to the market for fear of missing a price rally.**
  Do not act on greed and the herd instinct.

- **Inform yourself instead of blindly trusting.**
  Do not make the mistake of placing too much value on statements from friends and acquaintances and copying investment decisions.

### 3.1.4   Start lean and learn to master emotions

Emotions shape our character, our actions and consequently our life. Emotions are something very individual, beautiful and are an enrichment of our existence. In pretty much everything we do, we act emotionally and often instinctively. However, they have no place in capital investment. A common result are wrong decisions. Investment mistakes are unavoidable in our early days. These experiences are essential and important for our future investment behavior. Nevertheless, it is important to avoid repeating past mistakes. *What about our emotions when setbacks and losses occur or are not perceived?* In the following I would like to deal with an illustration, which is originally assigned to stock investors. However, this has frighteningly many parallels to other investment products. In principle, it deals with the typical behaviors of an investor.

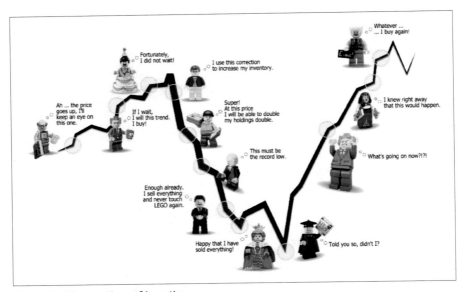

*Figure 7 - The emotions of investing*

The initial situation is well known. You buy a capital investment and wait that this decision is confirmed by a rising price or value. If this happens, you feel good and without any doubts. The investment idea proves to be correct. Apparently, nothing speaks against it, perhaps you even buy the product again. It gets interesting when the price or value starts to fall. Sentiment changes. Usually, a discussion begins with the inner self. The typical investor sells at an exaggeration downwards. Frequently, this leads to an underper-formance. More than ever, emotions ride a roller coaster of emotions. Losses feel like defeat. Especially at this time, investors tend to short-circuit reac-tions. But even with gains, our emotions are fickle. It is statistically proven that the majority of investors sell an investment that is in the profit zone too early. The main reason is that we become risk averse as the profit increases. On the other hand, it can turn out to be wrong to persist in an investment stubbornly and to follow the price or value from low to lower lows. In this case, the hope that the investment will rise again prevails. This is also a classic investment mistake. Basically, it is necessary to assess whether the current price or value is justified. Often, prices or values of investments experience exaggerations in both directions (up and down).

Discipline is the crucial imperative when it comes to investing. Here, above all, personal experience helps in dealing with such situations. With experience, some price swings seem almost logical and can be used to make a subsequent purchase or build up the investment size. Future investors are well advised to act less hastily. Set rules for yourself and your LEGO portfolio. Learn to play by the rules. Otherwise, you will be overrun by your own emotions. This is exactly one reason why many make bad decisions in investing. Because what evolution has set up so sensibly for human interaction tempts us to do exactly the wrong thing at important moments.

Emotions are often a poor guide when it comes to investing. There is a psychological challenge underlying this: We all assume that our investments are characterized by success and ignore the presence of mistakes. As investors, it is better to rely on solid rules rather than gut feelings. Warren Buffet's statement is particularly appropriate in this regard: "*The ability to say no is incredibly important and advantageous for an investor.*"

*Certainly, you wonder what all this has to do with LEGO Investment?* There will be moments when you find a variety of LEGO products on the Internet or in your local store. These LEGO products may even be on discount or advertised as discontinued. But let me tell you, just because a LEGO product is being sold at a discount of 40 percent or more does not guarantee an increase in value. Nevertheless, the chances are very good. It is still not guaranteed. Realize that a long-term investment period is possible when buying a LEGO product. But if the purchased LEGO product is then one, two, three or more years significantly in the loss, it demoralizes many investors. This is exactly where successful investors need to demonstrate their sovereignty. Only if you keep a LEGO product over the recommended holding period, you have chosen the right LEGO product. Remain steadfast and trust in the decisions you have made.

However, in the same way have to accept wrong decisions and sell such LEGO products. For example, it has often happened that a certain LEGO product initially rises in price or value for years. Until a time when, for example, a new release was introduced and the price or value of the predecessor initially falls. Not always is this short-term case of duration and consistency. Keep calm and evaluate the situation if necessary.

The simple display of LEGO products often leads to positive emotions and even enthusiasm. However, emotions are a difficult matter for everyone. Our emotions are with us from birth to our last day on this planet. Often, we do not even know why we feel in the way we do. It is important that you become clear when an unwanted emotion overtakes you. Notice it, acknowledge it, and confront it. You need to keep in mind that not every LEGO product is going to be a game changer. Of course, there is nothing wrong with occasionally going with your gut. But this should not become a habit. Concentrate on the essentials and act according to your list of criteria and requirements.

It is a myth that investors have to be exceptionally rich. There is a whole range of strategies that people can invest with less than USD 5,000 Euro up to USD 1 million or more. Do not panic if you have less to start with.

## 3.2     Wait, LEGO products are only toys!

LEGO products are truly not a low-cost toy. They never have been and probably never will be. The LEGO brand stands for the highest quality and has its price. When we are young, we have very little understanding of quality. Neither, we don't know the value of money, especially for toys we play with. By the age of three, parents spend an average of 1,131 Euro per child, the German Association of Toy Retailers (BVS) reported in 2013. Often, our parents work tirelessly to buy us the latest and most popular toys. We don't realize the effort that goes into making money. At some point we have our own job and earn our own money. Only then do we really appreciate the prices of toys that we had as children.

LEGO products have a reputation as children's toys. This reputation has been changing over the past few years. So-called AFOL's (Adult Fans Of LEGO) now represent a large part of the buying power in the LEGO market. There are thousands, maybe even millions of AFOL's in the world.[1] The passion of the adult fans is supported by their own websites as well as organized congresses all over the world. People meet in fan groups and clubs to philosophize about their common passion and to build the little bricks together. But it is not only about fun. The various groups and clubs are always trying to challenge each other with new and specially created LEGO constructions. In the recent past, there is also a great competition among the personal collections of each other.

In a time when nostalgia dominates entertainment, this trend may not be too surprising. After all, toys are the number one collecting category across all age groups, as Eric Bradley writes in his book *Pickers Pocket Guide - Toys: How to Pick Antiques Like a Pro* writes. Buying back a long lost or forgotten toy can bring back different feelings from childhood. While there are AFOL's who play with LEGO products like children, usually the approach for adults to LEGO products is different. AFOL's usually focus on collecting and displaying their own LEGO builds. Many adults make their own LEGO creations, known as *MOC's* (*My Own Creation*). The LEGO Group has made many efforts in recent years to reach out to the AFOL community.

In the 1990s, the company still believed that its products were intended exclusively for children. It was relatively late that The LEGO Group realized that adults were also extremely interested in LEGO products. From the beginning, LEGO sets in the Star Wars theme were particularly well suited to reach an older audience. This was largely because adults grew up with the movies. Through further licensing agreements such as Harry Potter, Lord of the Rings, Simpsons or Marvel, more and more adults found their way back to LEGO products.

---

[1] The number of AFOLs in the world is unknown. No records are available for this.

In addition to medium-sized licensed models, The LEGO Group also produces larger and significantly more complex LEGO sets. Currently, the most expensive LEGO set is listed with a suggested retail price of USD 799.99 and was released in the U.S. on Jan. 10, 2018.[1] We are talking about the *LEGO set no. 75192-1 Star Wars Millennium Falcon* with 7,541 individual bricks and parts. The age recommendation of 16 years and older refers to the size and complexity of the Millennium Falcon. For experienced LEGO builders, the construction time is a respectable 20 hours. It might be very difficult to motivate a child to build a LEGO set for such a long time. In addition, the Millennium Falcon is completely inappropriate for children to play with. After all, the weight of the structure is over 13 kilograms. The LEGO set is a new edition of the legendary *LEGO set no. 10179-1 Star Wars Millennium Falcon* from the *Ultimate Collector Series (UCS)*.

The LEGO Group is closely following the development of the new buyer segment and recently announced its intention to buy Bricklink, the largest online marketplace for buying and selling LEGO products. Clearly, this move signals the company's interest in being closely connected to the LEGO community. If you visit The LEGO Group's homepage, you are asked right from the start page whether the visitor is an adult or a child. Certainly not a common query from a toy manufacturer. Undoubtedly, the company has now understood that the products are also very popular with adults and that they contribute a significant portion of sales. The fact that The LEGO Group is increasingly targeting this group is shown by a look at the pricing of LEGO sets. Increasingly, The LEGO Group offers various sets in the high-priced range and cultivates cooperation with well-known companies for partnership licenses. There are a variety of LEGO products in limited editions to films of Star Wars or Batman, which later become collector's items. Limited editions or LEGO sets related to specific events are considered the most promising. Through the skillful use of popular licenses, The LEGO Group has experienced an unprecedented boom. The signs of this trend were evident early

---

[1] Personally, I don't know any child who has enough money to buy a LEGO set like the Millennium Falcon.

on, as statistics show that one-third of visitors to the first LEGOland in Billund were already adults without children.

It's not clear which the first LEGO set was specifically for adults. Officially, The LEGO Group released in the form of 18+ sets three iconic helmets from the Star Wars series in 2020:

- *LEGO set no. 75276-1 Stormtrooper Helmet*
- *LEGO set no. 75274-1 TIE Fighter Pilot Helmet*
- *LEGO set no. 75277-1 Boba Fett's Helmet*

Additional 18+ LEGO sets have been announced for 2020. LEGO products for adults often have sophisticated themes that reflect adult interests. LEGO sets in the 18+ category are often larger and more complex in design. Adult LEGO sets are also often more complicated, thanks to the use of many smaller individual bricks and pieces. The sets are the perfect way to turn a childhood pastime into a complex collectible and valuable display piece.

Toys from the 90s are now considered retro. The word originates from Latin and literally means as much as back or backwards. Strictly speaking, therefore, the idea of toys is to rediscover products from a person's youth. More and more people refer to the good taste of past times or are inspired by it. Thus, in recent days, more old toys have turned out to be unconscious capital investments. Collectors are increasingly willing to spend large amounts of money on rarities. Of course, the intactness and age play an important role. With the right condition, relics from childhood can be sold extraordinarily profitably. For example, unbelievable USD 12,400 and USD 60,000 have already been paid for various Disney VHS tapes at various auctions.[1] The English-language versions of the Black Diamond Classic, Platinum or Masterpiece editions have simply triggered a hype in the U.S. For example, the used Peter Pan Black Diamond edition is said to cost no less than USD 60,000. Gameboys and the accompanying games have also seen

---

[1] The VHS (Video Home System) cassette was popularly known as the video cassette. It is an analog recording and playback format for VCRs developed by JVC in Japan in 1976.

extraordinary price increases in some cases. However, if the Gameboy is not completely unused, it may be difficult to sell it for the aforementioned price. Furbies first hit the toy market in 1998 as garish, fluffy, electronic creatures. A Furby constantly babbles away with a vocabulary of several hundred words. After many years of apparent abstinence, collectors' love has recently been rekindled. Some collectors are willing to pay for an original Furby version 70-800, up to USD 250. Versions of other models are worth much less. The list can be continued seemingly limitless, be it Tamagotchis, McDonalds Happy Meal toys, old game consoles, Barbie dolls, Pokémon cards, etc.

### 3.2.1 Advantages - Why you should invest in LEGO!

The LEGO Group (Danish: Leg Godt; English: play well) was founded in 1932 in the small Danish town of Billund by Ole Kirk Kristiansen. Initially, it was a small family business that produced plain wooden toys. In 1942, the company lost its factory in a fire and rebuilt it in 1944. In 1946, the company acquired a new machine for the production of plastic toys. After several years of experimentation and some failures, the LEGO brick was finally born and patented in 1958 (2 x 4 studs on top, 3 tunnels on the bottom). About 8,000 employees produce a total of three trillion LEGO bricks and parts per year. A disposal problem for these enormous amounts of plastic has not seriously arisen yet. Children usually inherit old LEGO bricks and parts from their parents or older siblings. Since 1963, LEGO bricks and parts have been made of the harmless hard plastic acrylonitrile-butadiene-styrene copolymer. This durable raw material is the reason why children can still play with LEGO from their dad's childhood. The fact that LEGO bricks and pieces can be reused over and over again makes the play so outrageously appealing and varied.

As a private family business from Denmark, The LEGO Group sells its products all over the world. The LEGO Group's main competitors are Hasbro and Mattel. As of 2020, The LEGO Group is the largest toy manufacturer in the world. It is followed in second place by Mattel, which specializes in products such as Barbie, Hot Wheels, Matchbox cars and board games. Hasbro is an American company that owns several types of toy brands for puzzles, board games, dolls as well as electronic games. Hasbro is considered the third largest toy manufacturer in the world. According to Brand Finance Global 500, The LEGO Group was the strongest brand in the world in 2017.[1]

In addition, the company ranks as the largest manufacturer in the global toy market in terms of sales. The toy manufacturer thus stands impressively ahead of many well-known companies. Evaluated are the financial brand

---

[1] December 2017; http://brandfinance.com/images/upload/global_500_2017_locked_web-seiten.pdf

value, sustainability and strength of the brand, which is measured, among other things, by the popularity of its customers and employees. LEGO products are extremely popular with both children and adults. The company has expanded its brand presence with the help of successful investments and was therefore able to replace Ferrari, which for a long time was considered the strongest brand in the world. Extraordinarily impressive, considering that in 2004 The LEGO Group faced great difficulties from competitors Mattel and Hasbro and almost went bankrupt.

| No. | Corporation | Description |
|---|---|---|
| 01 | LEGO | The LEGO Group is a Danish company and the largest toy manufacturer in the world, which became famous for the classic toys (LEGO bricks). |
| 02 | Google | Google offers a variety of mostly ad-supported free services on the World Wide Web. These are mainly the search on various data sources. |
| 03 | NIKE | Nike Inc. is an internationally active, US-American sporting goods manufacturer founded in 1971. |
| 04 | Ferrari | Ferrari is an Italian automobile manufacturer of sports and Formula 1 cars with legal domicile in Amsterdam and administrative headquarters in Maranello, Italy. |
| 05 | VISA | Visa Inc. is a public company and, along with Mastercard, one of the two major international companies for credit cards, debit cards and credit cards and employed around 14,200 people in 2016. |
| 06 | Disney | The Walt Disney Company is an American media company. Disney became internationally known for the production of animated films and entertainment films for children and young people. |
| 07 | NBC | National Broadcasting Company is an American radio and television network. The broadcasting chain belongs to the NBC Universal media group and is headquartered in Rockefeller Center in New York City. |
| 08 | pwc | PricewaterhouseCoopers International is a global network of legally autonomous and independent companies in the fields of auditing, tax consulting and business and management consulting. |
| 09 | Johnson&Johnson | Johnson & Johnson is an American global pharmaceutical and consumer products company headquartered in New Brunswick, New Jersey, USA. |
| 10 | McKinsey&Company | McKinsey & Company is a management and strategy consulting firm represented in 65 countries and employed approximately 28,000 consultants worldwide in 2018. |

Table 1 - The ten most powerful brands in the world - as of 2017

## 3.2.1.1   The LEGO Group - The Market Leader

- The LEGO Group is known as an innovative company. The company is always striving to be as close as possible to the ravages of time. The *LEGO set no. 6979-1 Interstellar Starfighter* was already almost revolutionary when it was released in 2017. It is to date the first LEGO set with fiber optic cables that create an incredible alien glow.

- The LEGO Group is well known and loved. LEGO is one of the strongest brands in the world. In addition to the financial brand value, the strength of the brand is measured, among other things, by its popularity with customers and employees. The Danish toy manufacturer is extremely popular with children and parents alike.

- The manufacturer The LEGO Group has a first-class reputation, which is mainly due to its high-quality products.

- The company has managed to make its brand so strong that it has become a so-called generic term. This means that the LEGO brick is representative of an entire product category (interlocking bricks). We know similar phenomena from companies such as Vaseline, Jeep or Aspirin.

- The LEGO Group operates more than 600 retail stores in over 20 countries worldwide. For interested (private) investors, collectors or simply people who enjoy the products, LEGO products are therefore easily accessible both locally.

- If you believe the company, there is a high probability that The LEGO Group will produce all individual bricks and parts from sustainable materials in the future. The company's reputation and standing would presumably be considerably enhanced as a result.

- The LEGO Group puts great emphasis on having fun with its products. The company places an even greater emphasis on safety. The goal is therefore to design and manufacture LEGO products in a way that avoids product recalls. According to The LEGO Group, no products have had to be recalled since 2009.

- It is not likely that at some point people will lose interest in the LEGO brand, because it is (still) uncompetitive and too multifaceted. *How many brands do you know with their own toys, amusement parks, computer and console games, clothing collections or movies?* This is not expected to diminish in the future. On the contrary, they will try to expand the brand even more.

- In addition to The LEGO Group, there are other manufacturers of interlocking bricks that offer good quality bricks. LEGO products are especially convincing because of their unique minifigures. Counterfeits are known and will always exist. However, they are (still) relatively easy to detect. In addition, The LEGO Group (still) owns the trademark protection *three-dimensional Community trademark* of the LEGO minifigures known to us since the year 2000. Thus, counterfeiters may not copy the small figures identically. In this respect, The LEGO Group is taking extremely vigorous action against competitors (e.g., by suing for illegal copying).

- LEGO products are unique and some have iconic status. There are copies from the Far East, but these are not a real alternative in terms of price-performance ratio compared to LEGO bricks and parts.

- While LEGO products are strongly established in markets such as the U.S. and Western Europe, the importance of emerging markets such as China as a growth driver is increasing. For such markets, The LEGO Group developed special Chinese products in the past. A total of 80 new stores have been opened in China just in 2019. The future development of new markets promises new buyers for your LEGO investment.

- The LEGO Group is constantly investing in new collaborations and licenses of movies, games, books and sports. For example, The LEGO Group's licensing business with Star Wars began in 1990 and has continued for over 30 years. Through cooperation and licensing, the building ideas remain creative and up to date with current events. To be as close as possible to movie characters, Star Wars minifigures, were given their own hairstyles for the first time. Special minifigure heads were also designed.

- The constant renewal of partnerships and licenses is extremely attractive and also appeals to future buyers.
- If you decide to buy products from The LEGO Group, you will usually remain loyal to the company. Dealing with individual product areas or companies can prove to be a great advantage in toy investing (e.g., building up expert knowledge).
- The LEGO Group will continue to do well in bringing its own products directly to the customer. As long as the company does not interfere in the buying and selling market (e.g., Ebay), prices for LEGO products will continue to rise. Therefore, a much-cited LEGO bubble is considered extremely unlikely.
- It is often feared that The LEGO Group could change its philosophy, whereby all LEGO products would be permanently and indefinitely available for sale by the manufacturer itself. As a consequence, this would lead to a permanent saturation of the market, with the buying and selling market (and secondary market) likely to correct sharply. This scenario is extremely unlikely from a business point of view. The market and the LEGO brand thrive on new products. At present, there is absolutely no reason to believe that The LEGO Group will change its strategy. One decisive reason is that LEGO products are relatively expensive to manufacture. The constant availability would result in high storage costs of unsold inventory. The business consequences would be extraordinary. It is highly unlikely that demand for a LEGO product will continue indefinitely or even increase.

## 3.2.1.2 LEGO is more than just a toy

- In comparison with other classic tangible assets, LEGO products do not represent a luxury good and are relatively inexpensive. Even the MSRP is affordable for many buyers. From an economic point of view, this is an interesting market, whereby the target group has the necessary pocket money.
- A huge fan base from young to old enjoys LEGO products. LEGO enthusiasts live all over the world. There are exhibitions, countless clubs and meetings, social media groups, blogs and forums where like-minded people share their passion for the studded individual bricks and pieces. It is above all the fascination of being able to build almost realistic models from various building blocks that excites many people.
- The popularity of LEGO bricks is no coincidence. Psychologists have found out that it is a natural desire to exert power and control over our environment. If the big world does not bend to our will, at least this small cosmos must obey our powers of disposal.
- Nowadays, LEGO bricks and parts are still made of plastic. Years of use of the material is reflected in the very high quality of LEGO products. The colorful bricks are form-stable, limited elastic, UV-resistant, non-flammable and to a certain extent resistant to aging. LEGO bricks and parts are extremely durable. Extraordinary efforts are necessary to plastically deform or destroy a LEGO brick.
- The incredible attention to detail and many other factors that set LEGO products apart from the competition have been instrumental in ensuring that LEGO products continue to be favored by parents and children.
- Due to the precision of the production machines, there are very few bad LEGO elements. Only 18 out of one million or 0.0018 percent of the elements produced do not meet the company's high standards.
- The steady fluctuation of the LEGO assortment causes a manufacturer-induced scarcity of discontinued sets. In business terms, this automatically leads to an increase in the value of LEGO products.

- The LEGO Group takes great efforts to ensure that all bricks and parts function in the same way. This is achieved by a constant arrangement of interlocking points, which ensure a much better cohesion than other products on the market.
- Certain LEGO themes allow alternative build-up models (e.g., LEGO Creator 3 in 1 or partly LEGO Technic B-model) from the same individual bricks and parts of a LEGO set. This will address different buyers in the future.
- Every year, the LEGO Group launches more LEGO sets than the year before. Therefore, it is extremely unlikely that interested parties (e.g., collectors) will be able to buy all the LEGO sets they really want. It is increasingly common to have to limit purchases. This in turn leads to LEGO sets being bought more selectively. It is increasingly common for interest and desire for a particular LEGO set to persist into subsequent years when it is no longer available in stores. However, if a seller can be found on the secondary market who has the LEGO set in stock in new and unopened condition, it can be well worth it financially.
- Good toys can be versatile and used for a wide variety of games. The more varied the play possibilities, the longer the interest of the player can be maintained. LEGO bricks and pieces can be used to build castles, roads, houses and much more. There are unlimited possibilities.
- LEGO products not only bring back childhood memories. The diverse product range also offers exciting and relaxing activities, such as building together with your partner or your own children. There are no limits to your own creativity when it comes to building. Adults aim to make the built models look beautiful. The creation or building process is the creative phase. Children will rather try to play with the constructions they have built themselves.
- LEGO products are toys for eternity. So, LEGO bricks do not go in the trash, but are usually inherited.

- The assortment is regularly renewed. The LEGO Group cooperates with numerous companies in various industries. Partnerships and licenses expire at some point. This also helps to increase the value of a LEGO product.
- LEGO bricks and parts are changed regularly. Bricks from the 80s and 90s are partly no longer produced. Rare forms and colors can be traded at very high prices. Collectors are specifically looking for individual bricks and parts that are no longer produced in form and color, e.g., to create their own models or expand.

### 3.2.1.3　LEGO as a Financial Investment Tool

- LEGO products are an interesting investment to diversify your personal investment portfolio again exotically.
- The basic requirements for getting started with LEGO Investment are relatively simple. No special (fundamental) knowledge is required. There are also no bureaucratic requirements and no special securities account is needed.
- Unlike stocks, real estate, currencies or commodities, LEGO items are independent of world events. Political and economic influences have no or very little impact on the price or value of LEGO products.
- Unlike many other collectibles, there is no liquidity problem with LEGO products, as there is always a large demand. The demand for LEGO products is very high and it can be assumed that this will not change in the future. It is extremely unlikely that you will not be able to sell a LEGO product on the open market. The LEGO market is never saturated.
- There are no fees for e.g., custody account management or administration (as with stocks or funds). The purchase of funds, the conclusion of a building society savings contract or the saving of a certificate are often associated with costs that have a significant negative impact on the long-term return of the portfolio.
- LEGO products are a tangible asset that significantly minimizes the risk of loss of value due to inflation. With LEGO products you can even profit from inflation and rising prices, as tangible assets can also rise in these economic phases. There are many worthwhile examples from the past.
- Each investor is free to choose whether to invest USD 100 or USD 10,000.
- Compared to other capital investments, the process of selling LEGO products is much simpler. If, on the other hand, a person wants to turn

a property into cash, considerable bureaucratic requirements and re-sistance must be expected in some cases.

- LEGO Investment is based on flexible terms. In contrast, other financial products (e.g., bonds, house purchase, etc.) often require you to com-mit to a predefined time period.

- The fluctuation margin (volatility) of a LEGO value is considered to be very low. According to a study by researchers Nikita Shimkus, Satish Sharma, Savva Shanaev and Binam Ghimire, it averages less than one percent per year.

- Sales of LEGO products rose steadily between 1990 and 2010, despite the global financial crisis. During the same period, other toy manufac-turers have run into difficulties. As a result, we can expect a certain safe haven property of LEGO investment.

- If the LEGO investment is no longer profitable, it is not like the stock market that within a few weeks the prices or values fall massively. Nevertheless, profits of the LEGO investment of the past months or years can shrink. Experience has shown that those who simply sit on their LEGO products for a long time are well advised to do so.

- Not every LEGO investor remains permanently loyal to the LEGO in-vestment. It can be observed that again and again investors withdraw from the LEGO investment for various reasons, e.g., because there is no space for storage or people are in urgent need of the money. Others leave the LEGO investment because they want to invest higher sums. From higher sums, you need a lot of storage space and time. There-fore, large investors in the LEGO Investment are very unlikely.

- LEGO products can not be expropriated (by the state).

- The LEGO market is not regulated. There are no rules of the game. This is another reason why strong profits were possible in the past.

- LEGO products can be considered an investment in two ways: The sale of sealed and unopened LEGO products or of individual bricks, parts and minifigures. We are talking about the so-called Parting-Out

(Value). Parting-Out means listing and selling every single LEGO element of a set.

- It is inconceivable that collectors will be able to purchase missed LEGO products at a later date without the help of numerous resellers or investors. They are simply no longer manufactured by The LEGO Group and are therefore no longer available.
- As soon as LEGO sets are taken out of production, experience shows that the price or value of used sets increases.
- As with all speculative objects, the price trends of LEGO products cannot be estimated. We can only guess what collectors will be willing to pay for LEGO products in the future. In principle, the value of a LEGO product can fall to zero at most, while theoretically there is no limit to the increase in value.
- Now and then it happens that collectors do not own a theme completely, e.g., because they started collecting too late. To complete a theme, collectors are often willing to pay many times the MSRP in order to be able to call the missing LEGO set or the precious individual bricks, parts or minifigures their own.
- LEGO products are intentionally advertised by online and retail stores with discounts. Therefore, it is possible to buy LEGO products in convenient times. With the help of a savings plan you buy in economically favorable as well as in economically unfavorable times. An average purchase price results from the savings plan. According to research, regular saving with the help of the savings plan is more advantageous, because the saver automatically behaves anti-cyclically. In contrast, the so-called one-time investment, which is extraordinarily risky.
- The driving force in LEGO investment is children. This target group is the main reason why LEGO products can continue to be an interesting and worthwhile investment in the future. Today's children are tomorrow's collectors, who can spend money as they see fit. For example, LEGO set no. 10188-1 Star Wars Death Star (MSRP of USD 399.99) is certainly something few ten-year-olds can afford.

## 3.2.1.4 ... not to forget.

- In the unlikely event of a decline in value, there is always the physical LEGO product. After years of self-control, you can still build the LEGO product yourself.
- In addition, playing with LEGO products evokes a constructive aspect of children and adults.
- You control your investment. Through a targeted sale, the LEGO investor can pull out his money at any time and invest it in other forms of investment.
- LEGO products are decorative, especially sets around the theme Architecture.
- LEGO investment is possible for all ages.
- Even after many decades, the same LEGO individual bricks and parts can still be used and combined with today's bricks.
- LEGO products usually connect wonderful memories with our own childhood.
- Despite the Internet, there are still many unknowing people on the LEGO market who sell LEGO products significantly below value.
- Real LEGO collectors are purists who do not want to buy copies.
- LEGO products are likely to become even more attractive in the future as you can expect more complex, detailed and larger sets.
- LEGO products are much more expensive abroad than in Germany. This means that an increase in value due to currency differences is already inevitable. This is mainly due to the fact that Germany is the largest sales market for The LEGO Group. In addition, the majority of LEGO products are produced in Denmark. The short transport route has a significantly more favorable effect on the MSRP.
- Speculating is always worthwhile, even if only very few LEGO sets become valuable: You usually always get more than the purchase price.

- You don't have to be a ruthless investor when it comes to LEGO products as an investment. Many collectors or fans simply finance their LEGO hobby in this way. If profits from the sale of LEGO sets are realized, they can be used specifically for the acquisition of new LEGO products.
- Status can also play a major role for LEGO collectors and investors. The stories of spectacular sales and dream returns then tend to provide the supposedly rational legitimation.
- There can never be enough toys. LEGO bricks are colorful and there can never be enough of colorful things.
- It is scientifically accepted that collecting acts as a relaxing activity and counteracts hectic and stress. In addition, this passion can be interpreted into a certain kind of leisure activity.
- It is in the nature of LEGO that the possibility of the plug-in principle and the extensions animates to further purchase.
- It is simply fun.

## 3.2.2 Disadvantages – No Value without Buyers

### 3.2.2.1 Everything can and nothing will, because nothing must.

- In general, buying, holding and selling LEGO products results in a high time commitment.
- LEGO products are expensive in direct comparison. However, you have to keep in mind when it comes to pricing: The LEGO Group is based in Denmark and employs the majority of its people there. Denmark is not a low-wage country. Two large factories are located in the Czech Republic and Hungary, which largely supply the German market. In addition, The LEGO Group produces in Mexico and China. Both are considered low-wage countries.
- You have to restrain yourself and not open the original packaging or build LEGO sets.
- It is essential to ensure that LEGO products are complete and in immaculate condition. Even a single missing brick can cause collectors to lose interest. You can avoid this by not opening the LEGO products in the first place.
- LEGO products are mass-produced goods. Nevertheless, The LEGO Group does not publish any sales figures. The impact of *LEGO sets such as no. 10220-1 Volkswagen T1 Camping Bus*, which was available at retail for a good 10 years, is not yet foreseeable. It is questionable whether LEGO sets with such long runtimes will later achieve high prices or values. It is more likely that the market for such LEGO products is saturated.
- Be careful, some dramatization follows: There is a possibility that LEGO products are a cyclical product. When the economy is strong and people are earning decent money, they are more willing to buy even expensive LEGO products. In weak market phases (e.g., recession) demand may decrease.

- LEGO products are often capital- and space-intensive. If you want to actively approach the topic of LEGO investment, you should think about sufficient storage space. Especially voluminous LEGO products need to be stored well. In an ordinary rented apartment, this project seems ambitious and will quickly reach its limits.

- The fact that the storage of LEGO products requires considerable space as the stock or portfolio increases also limits investors in terms of the capital they can invest. You can't simply invest 500,000 Euro in LEGO products because the space requirements are immense. There is also the fact that there are probably not enough copies of the LEGO product or it is almost impossible to buy so many LEGO products at the same time. Depending on the retailer, purchases are often limited to a certain maximum number of the same LEGO product. The LEGO Group also limits the number of copies of a LEGO product for private buyers.

- The most obvious risk, however, is that the LEGO fan base may shrink or people may lose interest in LEGO products.

- The greatest risk of loss of value comes from The LEGO Group itself. If the company agrees to reintroduce a LEGO product that has already been discontinued (e.g., by reproducing it), this could reduce the value of the first edition.

- One factor that should not remain unmentioned. LEGO is made from plastic and thus petroleum. It is therefore not (yet) a green investment.

- Since the patent for the LEGO interlocking principle expired, there are many competitors today who copy LEGO products as well as individual bricks and parts. These copies are called interlocking bricks.

- It can be assumed that more investors are currently coming in than existing investors are leaving. This increases the risk of a higher supply. This in turn has a direct impact on demand and the price or value of a LEGO product.

- For four decades, The LEGO Group had a monopoly on the German market for all products with studs. However, LEGO bricks and parts are not protected by patents. These have long since expired. Patents protecting technical inventions are granted in Germany for a maximum of 20 years. After that, any competitor may use the once patented technology. It could therefore be that cheap copies will cause the price of LEGO products to fall in the future. At present, it is uncritical that copies have a big impact on the price of LEGO products. After all, real LEGO collectors are purists who do not buy and collect plagiarisms.
- Investment intentions when buying LEGO products are often met with criticism, loathing, accusations of profiteering, and personal insults from collectors or fans. Investors are not appreciated and have to put up with the accusation that the products are being bought straight away from genuine fans and interested parties.
- In principle, higher quantities of LEGO products over time lead to a much better saturation of the market. So far, The LEGO Group does not seem to have much interest in trying to control the buying and selling of LEGO products by investors.
- The past reveals a negative trend. The collecting passions of today's owners often find no interest in subsequent generations. With the passing of older collectors, future younger buyers are needed. Often the younger generations lack the connection to the hobbies of their parents and grandparents. With a lack of appreciation, the former hobby is forgotten and sometimes ends up in the trash. Examples of extinct collectibles are stamps, postcards, phone cards, surprise eggs, dolls, teddy bears, Mecki, Mainzelmännchen, Lurchi, Märklin Metall, Barbie, Tonka, Matchbox and many more.

## 3.2.2.2　An Asset Class with Risks

- LEGO investment could be a bubble, as it is uncertain how the (collector) market will develop.

- The value of exchange-listed companies is determined on the basis of corporate profits. As with many investments, the future price of a LEGO product is unknown. You can only guess what collectors are willing to pay in the future.

- A serious disadvantage is that the LEGO investment does not yield an ongoing return. In contrast, stocks (e.g., dividends) or real estate (e.g., rental income) pay interest on an ongoing basis.

- Investments in LEGO products significantly limit the flexibility or availability of personal capital. The invested capital is not available at any time, because the sale is comparatively time-consuming. You should be aware that you will not have short-term access to the money during the holding period.

- This form of investment is relatively complex if investors want to invest in large quantities of LEGO products. It is significantly easier to invest the same amount of capital in commodities, stocks, real estate or currencies.

- Sometimes it takes a while to sell a LEGO product. The liquidity of other investments, such as stocks, is much higher and therefore easier to sell.

- The colorful individual bricks and parts will tempt you to become addicted. You are likely to discover an exceptional bargain in every offer and discount.

- The growing influx of LEGO investors may lead to a dilution of the market. Consequently, supply would increase. Increasing supply leads to a decrease in demand and lower prices or values.

- You are completely dependent on The LEGO Group for the development of the price/value.

### 3.2.2.3 For information on risks and side-effects please read the pack insert.

- Depending on the sales platform, transaction fees may occur. In this case, it is worth waiting for so-called promotion days. In the example of Ebay, these are days on which you can sell at low or free conditions. Also, when selling internationally, sometimes high shipping costs, customs expenses or even damage during shipping must be taken into account.

- Strictly speaking, such speculative profits must be properly taxed. The background to this is that above a certain sales volume, you are no longer Classifieds as a private seller. Furthermore, it may be necessary to register a business.

- External influences such as water or fire can cause damage or the complete destruction of your LEGO products. In any case, investors should take out special additional insurance for their LEGO products.

- LEGO sets consist of individual bricks and pieces. These have no intrinsic value, such as the silver content of a silver coin or the gold content of a piece of jewelry. The material of LEGO bricks and pieces is strictly speaking worthless.

- There is no denying that it takes a certain amount of skill to choose the right LEGO products. It is necessary to correctly estimate the popularity and future demand for a product.

- The MSRP of a LEGO product is well known and relatively easy to find out. This may make it all the more difficult for future investors to want to pay the surcharge.

- Although there are tons of information available (e.g., internet), each one can claim and state something different. Only seldom are opinions the same and everyone thinks he or she knows better.

- The investor market for LEGO products is relatively new. A success that still has to prove itself.

## 3.3    Sciolism, Source: Internet

The entrepreneur and writer Rolf Dobelli Schweizer once said: "*If millions of people claim a stupidity, it does not become the truth because of it.*"

André Kostolany wrote in his book The Great Kostolany: "*The half-true information is more dangerous than the hundred% incorrect information, because a half-truth is a whole lie. The most dangerous is the wrong interpretation of a correct information, because it is the result of a wrong consideration and possibly also a lack of knowledge of the matter. Wrong interpretation of a wrong information, on the other hand, can lead to a good result, because negative times negative results in positive.*"

Half-knowledge is dangerous, especially when it comes to capital investments. There is a great danger of encountering dangerous half-knowledge on the Internet. Self-appointed experts insist on sharing tips, experiences, opinions and personal strategies with others. Generally, you should always step critically and with a healthy portion skepticism opposite insider tips or recommendations. If there is talk of great wealth, then there is actually no point in reading, watching or listening any further.

However, there are enough people who warn about LEGO products as an investment. These are doubters who see only risks and dangers. Chances are ignored partout. The group of crash prophets is quite extreme in this respect, predicting upcoming catastrophes in LEGO investment. Occasionally they are quite amusing, but in the long run they make investors constantly doubt their investment decisions and fear a crash. Crash prophets feed on investors' fear and always cause stress on the front of the capital markets.

There is nothing wrong with obtaining information from the Internet and exchanging views with like-minded people on forums and other social media channels about LEGO products, offers, and so on. At all times, you should critically question other points of view and not be naïve about them. Forums etc. offer a pleasant way of exchanging opinions and experiences. In addition, they offer the opportunity to assess the moods of market participants (e.g., with regard to subject themes, LEGO sets, new releases, etc.).

In everyday life between job and family, we have little time to review more in-depth information about LEGO products: *Which individual bricks and parts of a LEGO set are particularly desired?* or *Which minifigures are exclusive to a LEGO set?* There are numerous LEGO groups online and offline. These groups are made up of like-minded LEGO enthusiasts who are willing to help. In such groups, there is often give and take. You should not expect anyone to do the price research for you. However, if you are having trouble identifying individual bricks, parts, or minifigures, you can ask them for assistance. Online and retail stores can also help with questions. Comments under posts on blogs, for example, are also a great way to elicit additional thematic information.

Basically, investors have to think very economically. Furthermore, investors should always form their own opinion on the subject and not leave the thinking to others. Take your finances into your own hands and always judge all statements about money and finances in the daily media skeptically. Listen only conditionally to the qualified advice of outsiders, opinion makers as well as special advisors, which are primarily salesmen. It is clearly more reasonable to take yourself into the responsibility for possible wrong decisions. The same applies to success in investment.

Nowadays, people spend a lot of time thinking about and discussing EOL data of LEGO products. Again, it is important to check isolated information for its sources. *Is the website or member reputable and known for it or able to demonstrate a track record?* LEGO fans discuss the various pieces of information and often come to a loose consensus about when a LEGO product might be discontinued. Take this information and apply your own logic to it. Develop your own gut feeling. It's up to you whether you want to contribute your guesses to these discussions.

Just a few reflections on this: The time you spend on this is not wasted. You are actively engaged with your investment and giving input to other participants. This is not a waste of time. Perhaps you have already acquired expertise in some subjects, which can be helpful for the other investors. Nevertheless, you should bring in as little emotion as possible. This may sound easier than it is. Everyone has certainly already made the experience and has come across people on the Internet who are particularly hot tempered and emotional in their discussions. The reasons for this can be trivial and manifold. Avoid completely accepting other people's opinions in such a way that you literally adopt them and defend them yourself. Do not get angry and argue with and about other participants. Experience has shown that this is by far the most difficult hurdle. Always remember that feelings cannot replace arguments.

## 3.4    When LEGO Products retire

All good things come to an end and LEGO products are no exception. The past shows that every LEGO product is discontinued at a certain point. The LEGO product enters its well-deserved retirement. The product developers of the Danish toy producer are constantly designing new building concepts. They spend days and weeks developing new models, which are better, more innovative, more fun and more creative than before. The goal is to constantly delight customers in new ways. At the same time, this means that the company must stop continuing to produce older products. Because the production capacities of the factories and storage capacities of the company's own stores also have their limits.

This predetermined retirement (End Of Lego or End Of Line or End Of Life or EOL) defines the end of life of a LEGO product. Retailers are then often no longer able to restock these products, or only in very limited quantities. This is also known as discontinuing LEGO products. *But what role does this play in LEGO investment?* A very crucial one. When a LEGO product is sold off, the most attractive phase for the LEGO investor begins. To make it easier to understand, here is an example. Let's turn back the time. It's July 2016 when *LEGO set no. 42056-1 Porsche 911 GT3 RS* officially hits retail stores. For the example, let's assume that you, as a LEGO investor, purchased the LEGO set directly on the day of release at the MSRP of USD 299.99. In the US, the *Porsche 911 GT3 RS* was officially available at retail until April 2019. That much is already said, no one can predict this discontinuation date. The life span of the *Technic Porsche 911 GT3 RS* at the time was about 2.75 years. During this period, the price or value of the LEGO set is extremely stable and varies little. During the official availability of a LEGO product, there are regular price discounts due to reductions and offer prices in online or retail stores.

An increase in price and value is extremely unlikely in this period and should not be expected from you. Why should you, since the LEGO product is still available in retail stores and oftentimes even with discounts. It is extremely unlikely to find a fan, collector or investor who will pay a purchase price above MSRP at this time. Since the price is relatively stable during its lifetime, a sale should only be considered if it can't be avoided (e.g., need for money or space). If you make any profit at all on a sale during this time, it would certainly be modest.

Both your invested capital and the space required to store the *Technic Porsche 911 GT3 RS* are blocked during this period. Ideally, you want to keep both (capital and space requirements) to a minimum in order to get the maximum return as quickly as possible. *So, wouldn't it make more sense to simply buy the Technic Porsche 911 GT3 RS just before it is no longer available in retail?* The chance of gaining value increases significantly as the End-Of-Life begins. Unfortunately, it's not quite that simple. The problem is that no one can predict when a LEGO product will be discontinued. This is a key reason to look more closely at this important stage in the life of any LEGO product below.

Basically, the following strategy of The LEGO Group company has emerged. A new LEGO product is created from idea, to design, to production. The LEGO Group stores a certain quantity of each LEGO product. The number is of course not published, otherwise sophisticated investors could already recognize a possible investment interest from this. As soon as the inventory is empty and the product is sold out, the LEGO product disappears from online and retail stores and is no longer advertised in the company's own catalog. Only very occasionally are very few products reissued. This occurs, for example, when demand has been incorrectly estimated[1]. This has happened a time or two in the past. However, I would like to emphasize that these are rare exceptions. However, The LEGO Group has also had to admit that this measure was a negative business.

*You may wonder why The LEGO Group stops production and sales of older LEGO products, even though there is still demand for them?* With an experienced and powerful corporation like The LEGO Group, it is natural to

---

[1] Of course, limited products are excluded from this in advance.

assume that all sales are documented and available on an hourly, daily, weekly, monthly and annual basis at the click of a button. In addition, it can be assumed that at least a handful of the more than 20,000 employees[1] deal exclusively with the LEGO secondary market. If there is a noticeable and high demand in this market, a progressive company like The LEGO Group would have to take various measures. Quite obviously, it is missing this initiative and is taking a different path. *Why is that?* Here are a few thoughts.

On the one hand, The LEGO Group is affected by industry trends in the same way as, for example, technology companies or textile retailers. Industry trends are patterns or trends that occur within a particular industry and influence the buying behavior of customers. If a certain topic is in vogue, for example because there is a current movie or computer game about it, the topic receives increased attention and demand from customers. Companies like The LEGO Group try to identify trends early on and implement them profitably. Or even better, to set decisive trends themselves. Nowadays, there is nothing more distant for companies to compulsively hold on to products (e.g., by continuing production) when at the same time other trends are determining the industry. Recognizing relevant trends and incorporating them into the company's strategy is essential to survive in today's world. Due to the very high dynamics in the world, many trends are short-lived. German fashion designer Karl Lagerfeld was also aware of the short-lived nature of trends. In his opinion, trends that exist for only half a year are quickly forgotten. In turn, it is also a big mistake to ignore trends. For example, because the competition deliberately picks up on the theme or trend and thereby wins market share from the competition accordingly. This phenomenon is omnipresent in the interlocking bricks universe. For example, well-known competitors of The LEGO Group (e.g., Cobi or XingBao) specifically focus on the topics of military and war. The LEGO Group does not directly implement these thematic areas. Nevertheless, such topics are

---

[1] as of May 22, 2022

indirectly addressed through thematic areas such as Indiana Jones or Star Wars.

Another critical factor is that product storage costs companies like The LEGO Group a lot of money. Too much inventory leads to avoidably high storage costs and thus to higher selling prices. Excessive inventory is also referred to as overstocking. This happens, for instance, when older models cannot be sold off. The reason for this can be that the wrong quantities were originally calculated for a product. This affects not only the large warehouses, but also the (storage) areas in the retail or the official LEGO stores.

The display or storage areas in the LEGO stores are for the direct sale of LEGO products and are more limited in their total number. In the case of a LEGO product that is not well accepted by the clientele, the company would certainly do better to replace such disappointments with bestsellers at an early stage. In contrast to the storage possibilities, the creativity for designing new LEGO products is unlimited.

*Why can't The LEGO Group just keep producing a product despite the fact that it's being retired, but demand is still high?* Even The LEGO Group can't guess which products will be sought after by collectors and fans. Estimating the number of production units in advance seems difficult. It is usually not possible to change a production planned long in advance at short notice. So many factors are involved. Not all single bricks and parts are produced in the same factory. For example, not all molds are always available everywhere. External suppliers (e.g., printers) need a certain lead time. Capacities may also already be occupied with other products. In addition, there are other difficulties, such as the current Corona pandemic.

*Should The LEGO Group continue production even if the demand for a LEGO product has decreased?* Production capacity is limited to a certain number of components. As time goes on, it makes sense to focus on newer, more profitable lines and products. For example, the molds to produce LEGO bricks and pieces are extremely expensive. Each mold can only produce a certain number of LEGO bricks and parts before it needs to be replaced.

Furthermore, the key is production capacity. The LEGO Group can only produce a limited number of different bricks and parts for sets at any given time. In turn, if older LEGO products are to continue to be produced, fewer new LEGO products can be produced. The same applies, of course, to individual bricks, parts or minifigures.

New individual bricks and parts are often more functional or versatile than older individual bricks and parts. In addition, the overall quality is improved by using new and modern materials and processing methods. The number of parts in production is limited. In order to make room for newer individual bricks and parts, older ones must be phased out. Conversely, there is practically no chance to get older individual bricks and parts such as railroad tracks, motors or Samsonite gears. For example, older railroad tracks are much more fragile and not fully compatible with newer tracks. Despite some demand for the older tracks, it would not make sense for The LEGO Group to continue producing the older train tracks. In the end, there are plenty of reasons why The LEGO Group discontinues its products after a certain period of time and forgoes re-production.

In principle, The LEGO Group can discontinue its products from official retail at any point in time. It can be assumed that the company has a predetermined schedule for each product. Over the past few years, many people have studied this issue and have found all sorts of signs that indicate the retirement of a LEGO product. Until now, concrete information has never been released by The LEGO Group. Therefore, numerous websites and so-called insiders have made it their business to constantly determine LEGO products regarding their future retirement date. In the meantime, there are forums and groups (e.g., on Facebook) that deal exclusively with EOL dates of LEGO products. The goal is to make a LEGO investment as close as possible to the EOL date.

I would like to explain in the following what these indications may look like. As an investor, you must understand that these are exclusively speculations and likelihoods. None of these indications are set in stone. Only The

LEGO Group knows the exact discontinuation date of its products. Nevertheless, through years of experience of closely observing the buying public and fan community, a trend has now emerged.

## Retiring Soon - Marking

One of the most obvious signs in the life span of a LEGO product is when The LEGO Group itself marks a product with the '*retiring soon*' notice on its website. The LEGO Group now has a dedicated section on its website called '*Last Chance to Buy*', which identifies products that will soon be discontinued. Depending on the product, these can sometimes stay in this section for weeks to months. However, most products that are being retired never receive this label. For example, take *LEGO set no. 75827-1 Ghostbusters Fire Department Headquarters*, which was never marked with '*retiring soon*' in the near future. Rather, the LEGO set surprisingly disappeared straight into retirement from one day to the next. This type of transition is extremely common. In exceptions it happens that the LEGO product is again re-produced in new quantities. There is no guarantee for this. Likewise, it may be that The LEGO Group only wants to part with unpopular products. Still other sources claim that The LEGO Group only wants to boost its sales of the marked products with this approach. It is unclear whether The LEGO Group is really still producing in case of this, or whether simply the too large stocks cause the products to remain longer on the market. You can't blame The LEGO Group in this case, because there are never public statements about when exactly a product will be discontinued. In my experience and observation, the likelihood that there will be a follow-up production is extremely low. Examples from the past of post-productions are, for instance, *LEGO set no. 21318-1 Tree House* or *LEGO set no. 92176-1 NASA Apollo Saturn V.* The latter LEGO Set gained inglorious reputation because it is an identical re-release of *LEGO set no. 21309-1 NASA Apollo Saturn V.* This was a surprise to many LEGO investors in particular, who had very high expectations that the LEGO set would increase in value by the time it retires. The effects will only be seen in a few years. Depending on the LEGO set, you will have to react quickly when the '*retiring soon*' marking appears, because eager collectors and LEGO investors will buy the LEGO sets out of stock in no time. I have often made the experience that only a few minutes after marking I was left with an empty online shopping cart. The marking '*retiring soon*' does not indicate when exactly the LEGO set will be discontinued. This is certainly due to the unknown amount of stock. In the past, LEGO sets disappeared after a few weeks, some other LEGO set remained marked even after more than a year. In the end, the marking is to be considered rather sober and can only be seen as an indication. You can reach LEGO products with the marking '*retiring soon*' at *https://www.lego.com/en-us/categories/retiring-soon*.

## Unusually high discount in the LEGO Store

The LEGO Group is not extraordinarily known for offering heavy discounts. In the past, collectors and investors noted that this may be another indication. Unlike the 'retiring soon' marker, it is considered a sure indicator that in the short term a LEGO product will be retired if it experiences a heavy discount in the LEGO online and/or offline store. There is no limit to the level of discount. The EOL probability increases with the size of the discount. From experience, a discount of more than 30 percent is considered atypical, especially for LEGO sets, if it comes directly from The LEGO Group. You can expect the LEGO set to be retired within the next few days or weeks once the stock is sold off. You can reach the LEGO products in the sale section at https://www.lego.com/en-us/categories/sales-and-deals.

## Purchase limit (Number of Products)

The majority of shoppers who have already purchased from The LEGO Group online or in retail stores will probably be aware that for some time now, the number of identical products has been limited when pur-chasing. At first glance, this does not seem particularly unusual. You might think that The LEGO Group simply wants to guarantee that the largest possible number of different buyers can purchase the product. Often, a maximum value of five pieces per household applies. How-ever, this is more of a calculated strategy. The LEGO Group also notices all sorts of tricks from customers who, for example, register a second LEGO account on the wife of the same residential address. Such addi-tional orders are cancelled with extraordinarily high probability and the indication of the intended restriction or limit per household. In this re-gard, it is observed that the intended limitation changes extremely rarely until the EOL. Shortly before the retirement of a LEGO product, the limitation is often restricted even more. This is continuously re-duced until it eventually reaches one piece per household. So far, there is no clear evidence that this approach correlates with the evolving EOL. Unfortunately, this indicator does not always apply to all LEGO products either. Accordingly, the prescribed limitation can only be seen as an additional indicator and should by no means be considered in isolation from the other signs.

## Life cycle of comparable LEGO products

We already know that every LEGO product has a predetermined life cycle. The exact duration is not known to us and can just be estimated at best. This is where it gets tricky, because assumptions have to be made in order to estimate the duration. On the basis of these, the life cycle of a LEGO product can be estimated. Fortunately, the Internet nowadays allows us to monitor the life span of a LEGO product, some-times down to the day. Large data records exist for this purpose, es-pecially for the past twenty years. These data records offer much more information for further analysis. For example, patterns can be identified if all LEGO products are viewed in relation to a theme. Likewise, it is possible to look at all LEGO sets that have between 100 and 200 individual bricks and pieces. The available data sets allow to forecast the lifetime of a LEGO product more precisely. Of course, this forecast must be done taking into account current events (e.g., Corona pandemic, Ukraine war, supply shortages, etc.). At this point I would like to point out the website of Brickeconomy. The website shows very clearly the expected EOL date of a LEGO set. Unfortunately, it is not described on the website of Brickeconomy how the algorithm works and how the EOL dates are determined. It can be assumed that related or comparable LEGO products (e.g., from the same theme), which are already no longer available, serve as a basis for calculation. This would be obvious in the form that the release and discontinuation dates of past LEGO products are sometimes very well documented. An impressive example of this are the sets in the Seasonal or Chinese Traditional Festivals theme. For these LEGO sets, the future availability can now be determined very precisely on the basis of past LEGO sets. In Germany, Great Britain or the USA, this is almost exactly one year and varies only by a few days.

Another method allows you to find out if the LEGO product has already been discontinued in other countries. This can be seen, for example, via Brickset or the official LEGO website. If the product has been retired in other countries, it is likely that it will also be retired in your country soon. The LEGO Group has been known to change product retirement dates at the last minute. No one will be able to tell you when a LEGO product will be discontinued. It is not uncommon for employees of The LEGO Group only to know about a product shortly before it is due to be discontinued. The LEGO Group takes this issue very seriously, as they are aware of the new (hobby) investors. Specific inquiries about the expiration dates of LEGO products are not answered by The LEGO Group: "*We can tell you that we normally offer a LEGO set between 1 and 3 years. Unfortunately, we cannot provide expiration dates for LEGO sets.*"

Perhaps in the future The LEGO Group will publish the total number of products manufactured per part number with the end of production. This would be interesting and helpful because even unpopular LEGO products would probably be bought up quickly if they were only produced in very small numbers.

Finally, we note that determining the discontinuation date of a LEGO product is a difficult task. The availability in the official LEGO Store depends mainly on the individual product. It is advisable to watch the market carefully and pay close attention to the information provided. Nevertheless, it is often not even necessary to predict the discontinuation date of a LEGO product. As an investor, they are usually subject to budget and inventory constraints. Therefore, it is possible to wait until it seems very certain that the LEGO product will be discontinued. Only then should you focus on the rest at retail. Experience has shown that it is not particularly difficult to find the desired product in small quantities.

However, I must admit that in the past I have also purchased LEGO products well before retirement. Of course, you always realize this only in retrospect. Usually, the reason was that the product was offered at a particularly attractive price. It also happened that I bought a LEGO product well before the EOL, because I did not want to miss the product in any case. In fact, it has already happened to me several times that I wanted to wait for the perfect time to buy and therefore missed out on a LEGO product. *How does this have to be imagined?* Well, it's not every day that you look to see if a certain LEGO product is still available at sufficient retailers. There are simply too many LEGO products and retailers nowadays. Mostly you notice only after a few days, weeks or even months that the LEGO product is no longer available. This way I simply missed several very good LEGO products (e.g., *LEGO set no. 75827-1 Ghostbusters Fire Headquarters* or *LEGO set no. 70657-1 Ninjago City Harbor*). Meanwhile, both LEGO sets are attracting very high prices in the secondary market. This again reinforces my opinion that these LEGO sets would have been a very good investment. Nevertheless, you should not let this demotivate you. Over the past five years, The

LEGO Group has released an average of 657 LEGO sets per year. For the majority of LEGO investors, money and storage resources are limited, making it impossible to own all LEGO sets. Let me tell you: It is not possible to own all LEGO sets, which can be interesting for investment.

There is no reliable way to determine if or when a LEGO product will be retired. If you really don't want to miss a LEGO product, just buy it. Just don't take the risk of predicting the retirement date yourself. You run the risk of having to buy the LEGO product at higher prices in the secondary market. For many LEGO investors, the EOL comes far too quickly. For others, it comes much too late. And often the EOL comes quite unexpectedly or surprisingly. One day a LEGO product seems to be sufficiently available and the next day it is sold out.

Unless you are fortunate enough to work for The LEGO Group and have an up-to-date knowledge of product cycles, all is speculation and conjecture. For LEGO products, although specific discontinuation dates exist, occasionally products are no longer available before that date. Because as soon as the EOL status is known, many fans, collectors and investors still buy the LEGO product, with which one was uncertain so far. And since LEGO products are no longer produced, the available products are often gone faster than expected.

In my opinion, a good indicator is whether a LEGO set is still doing well after it is discontinued or retired. So, if a LEGO set is discontinued and you can't get one of those LEGO sets anywhere after it's discontinued, then that could be an indication that there was high demand. If a LEGO set is still available in stores six months after production ends, then there seems to be less demand for that LEGO set.

The best thing you can do is to take a clear and objective view of all these characters. There is certainly nothing wrong with using the existing EOL lists (e.g., StoneWars, Promobricks, Brickset or Brickmerge) as a guide. As a large investor it is much more difficult, because you have to stagger your LEGO purchases. There are also enough investors who do not even consider the EOL date and simply try to get the LEGO product at the lowest price, similar to stocks. If you are interested in this topic and want to lose yourself in the depths and vastness of the Internet, I suggest the following sites: *https://retiringsets.com* and *https://community.brickpicker.com/forums*

## 3.5 Buy and Hold or Flipping

When you invest in tangible assets, you have to ask yourself whether you want to hold them for several years or sell them immediately. The associated time horizon has a significant influence on risk and return. Nowadays, the majority of people are looking for a quick buck. In return, they are happy to take higher risks. With the time frame, we define not only the risk, but also the expectations for the investment. From this, different strategies can be defined. For example, you sell your LEGO investment if it doubles in price or value within a year. Another strategy might be to sell your LEGO investment only if fewer than five products of the same type of LEGO set are offered for sale on Ebay, within a certain period of time (e.g., one month). So, the investment horizon correlates with our strategy. To date, the following three investment horizons have been established in LEGO Investment.

- **Short Term (Weeks)**
  The so-called *flipping* refers to the purchase of a revenue-generating asset and its direct quick resale. The term originated in the USA and can be applied to any asset. The term applies most frequently to real estate and initial public offerings (IPOs[1]).

- **Mid Term (Months)**
  An investor who ties up his capital for the medium term usually follows a period of up to two years. As you can already see from the name, this is the period between short-term and long-term investment.

- **Langfristig (Years)**
  The so-called buy and hold, whereby the investor hopes for a price or value increase over several years to decades.

---

[1] An IPO (Initial Public Offering) is an event in which a company goes public or is listed on a stock exchange. This refers to the listing of a company's shares on an organized capital market. In other words, it takes place when a company decides to sell its shares to the public.

*Flipping* is recommended for advanced and experienced LEGO investors. It requires good knowledge and extensive (years of) experience in the LEGO market. In the LEGO universe, flipping is synonymous with the short-term investment horizon. It differs significantly from the medium and long-term horizon: Flipping is a kind of rapid sale of LEGO products. Investors flip LEGO products at any conceivable time in the life span of a LEGO product. It is very common that the LEGO product is not yet retired. This circumstance also makes flipping so tricky. Above all, LEGO investors try to take advantage of supply shortages or lack of supply and seasonal market conditions to quickly buy for a profit and eventually sell. In doing so, investors increasingly have their eyes on LEGO products, which are extraordinarily popular and often eagerly anticipated.

In the past, The LEGO Group has shockingly often failed to have enough stock available for potential buyers on the release date of a highly demanded LEGO product. Admittedly, this is not easy. Even The LEGO Group doesn't have a crystal ball to anticipate the demand. In such cases, companies always prefer rather to have fewer products in stock. The idea is to avoid sitting on a large inventory because the demand was wrongly estimated in advance. Flippers purposefully exploit this dilemma. There are numerous current examples of this, which I would like to list in the following:

**Example 1: LEGO no. 5006744-1 Ulysses Space Probe, 2021**
Launched in March 2021, the Ulysses Space Probe was revealed as a VIP-Reward. The set is a LEGO exclusive in collaboration with NASA[1]. Previously, The LEGO Group unveiled *LEGO set no. 10283-1 Space Shuttle Discovery* in an official press release. At the same time, The LEGO Group announced two VIP-Rewards that were to be released in the VIP Rewards Center with the launch of the Space Shuttle Discovery. After The LEGO Group sent out various announcements to VIP customers, Ulysses Space Probe was available in the German LEGO

---

[1] NASA (National Aeronautics and Space Administration) is the U.S. civilian federal space and flight science agency established in 1958.

Online Store just in time for 9 A.M. on April 14, 2021. The VIP Reward was available to purchase for 1,800 VIP points or the equivalent of 12 Euro. From that point on, the gamble turned into a tragedy. Barely any buyers had access to the VIP Reward Center. Rather, it collapsed due to various error messages (including high access numbers). According to unconfirmed sources, a total of 2,700 copies were sold. This small stock only withstood the rush for only a few minutes. It was by absolutely no surprise that a particularly large number of people wanted the VIP Reward. Prior to this, the VIP Reward was advertised with a high level of attention in all popular social media such as Instagram, Facebook, blogs, etc. After customers had managed to master the technical difficulties of the LEGO website, various sales offer gradually appeared on Ebay Germany. Prices for the LEGO Ulyssee Space Probe ranged from 200 to 700 Euro. As time passed, the offers on Ebay Germany increased. Quickly (about 2 to 3 days after the sale) the offer prices adjusted to 100 to 200 Euro. Unfortunately, there are no records how often and at which price the space probes changed their owners. As of May 2, 2021, there were more than 100 sold Ulyssee Space Probes on Ebay Germany, with prices ranging from 45 to 261 Euro. To May 2022 the average selling price is between 70 and 80 Euro. For comparable sales portals such as Facebook Marketplace, no sales figures can be verified. The LEGO Ulyssee Space Probe is considered the latest paragon of flipping. Nevertheless, it is always advisable to have a few VIP points in the LEGO account for such promotions.

## Example 2: LEGO no. 10277-1 Crocodile Locomotive, 2020

Another very applicable example is the *LEGO set no. 10277-1 Crocodile Locomotive*. The original MSRP of 97.47 Euro is considered moderate and the LEGO set was distributed exclusively by The LEGO Group at launch[1]. The LEGO set includes 1,271 individual bricks and parts, 2

---

[1] The MSRP is 99.99 Euro. The lower price of 97.47 Euro resulted from the Corona Pandemic related VAT reduction in Germany in 2020.

minifigures, optional upgrade of an engine and has been extremely in-demand since it was officially announced. This is hardly surprising, as it is widely known that trains have a huge fan base. In addition, this LEGO set is considered to be a re-release of the legendary and iconic *LEGO set no. 4551-1 Crocodile Locomotive* from 1991. *LEGO set no. 10277-1 Locomotive Crocodile* officially went on sale in the LEGO Online Store on July 1, 2020. Until the first calendar weeks of 2021, the LEGO set was unavailable for a long time. In order to allow as many customers as possible to purchase a Crocodile Locomotive, The LEGO Group had taken the precaution of placing a limit in the system that allowed buyers to purchase only one set per customer. During the pe-riod when the Crocodile Locomotive was limited, flipper had an easy time. The popular and desired LEGO set achieved selling prices on Ebay sometimes between 200 and 300 Euro. Even without a discount on the purchase, this corresponds to an excellent return for this short period. As of today (May 2, 2021), the set is available in the LEGO online store and is limited to five pieces per customer.

If these two examples were previously unknown to you as a reader, you might ask yourself how such lapses and failures can happen to a company like The LEGO Group in the 21st century. Well, unfortunately, we cannot attribute the sole cause to the Corona Pandemic-ridden year of 2020. At this point, we do not want to look for someone to blame, because we can only speculate about the reasons. There have been an extraordinary number of such examples in recent years. Especially eagerly awaited LEGO products in the pre-Christmas period are excellent for such speculation or flipping. The feast of love and the need of people to buy Christmas gifts quickly, has already let many LEGO products briefly explode in price. Often against a background that the supply chain stagnates. Short-term investors or flippers exploit these weaknesses in the logistics of the companies. Flippers do not hesitate to buy the LEGO products at MSRP. Despite the fact that an old merchant's rule says that the profit lies in purchasing. In conclusion, we can say that flipping new LEGO products can be very profitable, especially when the demand for a LEGO product is exceptionally high. The vast majority of buyers do not want to wait until The LEGO Group produces larger quantities and can meet the demand. This inevitably leads to sellers being able to charge significantly higher selling prices temporarily.

Since the beginning of the Corona Pandemic in 2020, this form of LEGO speculation has become extremely popular. It is becoming increasingly common for supposedly coveted LEGO products to be offered at very high prices on the relevant sales platforms before their official release. At this point, however, the product cannot yet be officially purchased.[1] Rather, the sales advertisement states that the LEGO product will be shipped shortly after it is released. This is obviously the riskiest form of flipping. The risk here is that the seller will not be able to buy the LEGO product on the day it appears. Meanwhile, sellers benefit from the fact that there are always buyers who do not fully read the sale ad before buying the LEGO product. For both buyers and sellers, this form is a win-win situation. The seller gets a percentage markup for the time and risk invested, while having to order the product on the release day or time. The seller's return is highly dependent on the demand for the LEGO product and how quickly it is sold out on the release day. The buyer benefits in the form that he or she can be sure to obtain the desired LEGO product on the day of its release. Of course, by detouring through the seller, the buyer will have to wait longer for the LEGO product. The LEGO Group will first ship the LEGO product to the seller, who in turn will ship it to the buyer upon receipt. The downside of this form of resale is clearly the reputation within the community. Especially among LEGO fans who end up without a product, the displeasure is extraordinarily high. From this you should come to your own conclusions and take appropriate action (e.g., do not post publicly on forums).

---

[1] For highly demanded products, The LEGO Group exclusively allows VIP members to purchase the LEGO product in retail stores for a certain period of time before the official sale.

Basically, the medium and long-term time horizon differs in the length of the holding period. In contrast to flipping, a LEGO product is most likely already retired and hopefully already experiencing its value appreciation. With this larger time window, the investor hopes for a higher return. The nostalgia factor kicks in from 10 to 30 years after EOL. However, the most significant difference is in the strategy itself: *Buy, Hold and Wait.* If the LEGO product benefits from a long-term price development, it will be sold

A profitable holding period of your LEGO investment cannot generally be determined in advance. For one thing, no one can say when the LEGO product will reach its highest price or value in the secondary market. Nor does anyone know how long a LEGO product will be available in stores before The LEGO Group retires it. And even then, a LEGO product can still be purchased indefinitely at retail as well as online. It is only when the majority of LEGO products have completely disappeared from retail stores that the crucial period begins to count for the investor. From now on, the LEGO product is retired.

Ideally, there will be a database in the future that records all bid and ask prices for LEGO products. This would give investors the opportunity to determine the best time at which the purchase price was the lowest and the sales price the highest. The conclusions about individual LEGO products, themes, etc. can be used as a basis for future LEGO investments.

## 3.6    Completeness, Quality and Storage

LEGO investment works as long as there are buyers. Future buyers, such as collectors, are your customers and have high expectations of LEGO products and the associated purchase. With any tangible asset investment, a safe storage of the valuable object is essential. Same applies to the LEGO Investment. Although LEGO bricks are virtually indestructible under normal conditions, LEGO products in their original packaging require special care. Top preservation plays an incredibly important role in LEGO products and is strongly influenced by the condition of the original packaging.

A complete LEGO set consists of the original individual bricks and parts, packaging, instructions, spare parts bag, labels and sticker sheets, minifigures and (if applicable) parts separators. If any of this is missing, buyers may quickly lose interest. If necessary, you can only regain interest by a (strong) downward correction of the price. The high-quality standard not only applies to the product, the packaging must also be convincing.

As investors and sellers, we have no control over the contents of a LEGO product. It is not possible to check the contents upon arrival, because LEGO products usually come in sealed packaging. Whether, for example, individual bricks are missing or the instruction manual is bent, the investor or owner of the sealed LEGO set can not judge and also not influence. However, there are generally few reports on the Internet that building instructions or sticker sheets arrive in the packaging already bent. This is of course only apparent when opening. The supposed cause is the back and forth slipping in the packaging v. a. by the transports. This is certainly a pity, as it does not meet the high-quality standards of The LEGO Group. In principle, however, it can be assumed that the content of LEGO products is always identical. Pricing a LEGO product in this way is done only by examining the original packaging, knowing full well that the contents are complete, however, if the packaging is sealed. A buyer literally buys a pig in a poke. Of course, buyers rely on The LEGO Group's high-quality standards, but such problems are the exception rather than the rule. If, for example, individual LEGO bricks are missing,

LEGO customer service is happy to help and will send the missing pieces free of charge. The extent to which the company will also resend missing individual bricks and parts if the LEGO product has been dormant for years (e.g., found in an attic) cannot be conclusively determined.

Most investors cannot imagine that the packaging of a LEGO product plays a very important role for future buyers. Outer packaging or sales packaging has many meanings and functions such as ease of handling for transportation, general protection (e.g., damage, contamination and loss of quantity, theft, environmental influences such as weather, etc.), marketing or easier storage. First and foremost, outer packaging reflects how gently and carefully the product has been handled in the past. As a general rule, outer packaging with significant signs of use (e.g., dents, dings, cracks, creases, extensive scratches, etc.) or completely missing packaging significantly reduces the value of a LEGO product.[1] The value of a LEGO product is also reduced if the packaging is open even though the bags of individual bricks are still closed. As a result, the buyer would have to check completeness with, for example, Bricklink to ensure that no LEGO individual bricks and pieces are missing. Many investors are afraid of the risk and the effort involved, which is why original sealed LEGO products are preferred.

Every investor will eventually buy a LEGO product where the packaging is not entirely free of defects. *The question is how to deal with a defective packaging?* Since you as a LEGO investor want to resell the LEGO product, it is necessary to distinguish between ordinary buyers and collectors. Ordinary buyers purchase LEGO products, for example, to build or play with them themselves (e.g., for their children) or to give them as gifts. This group of buyers sees the packaging more as a means to an end and minor damages are usually acceptable.

In contrast, a collector has much higher requirements for the packaging of the LEGO product. Basically, collectors are simply enthusiasts who love

---

[1] Special care and attention must be paid to very sensitive product packaging such as the Architecture theme series or many 18+ LEGO sets. The matte black packaging is particularly susceptible to scratches, which then appear unattractive white.

and desire a complete product. And that includes the packaging. The original packaging must remain in perfect condition for optimal value retention. Any form of damage such as dents, dings, cracks, creases, scratches, etc. must be avoided as far as possible. The seals must be completely intact. An opened or broken seal means a loss of value for the LEGO product. Many LEGO items have packaging that cannot be opened without breaking the seals. However, there are different types of seals. Conversely, seals are the unambiguous assurance that there is completeness and integrity of the contents. If only one seal is broken and the others are neatly intact, then it is still a new and sealed LEGO product with (some) signs of wear of the packaging.

The subject of seals has a high value in the LEGO investment and should not be taken too lightly. Personally, I have returned LEGO products to the shipper when I had concerns about a seal. When the LEGO product arrives, you should always check the seals. If you are selling a LEGO product, it is best to simply list all applicable images of the individual seals as well.

Otherwise, there may be various additional information on the packaging that does not have anything to do directly with the LEGO product. These include security or adhesive labels for securing goods, price tags or various adhesive labels, such as barcodes assigned to the retail trade. Opinions differ on existing and visible price tags. Many see a price tag as an advantage, as it shows the original RRP at that time. Still other buyers prefer packaging in its pure as-delivered state – e.g., without stickers and labels.

In general, adhesive residues from price tags and labels (depending on the size) lead to deductions in the sales price. Considering that you should avoid major damages on the packaging, it is better to refrain from removing an existing adhesive label. However, if you decide to remove the decorative label, there are various spray cans available in retail stores that make the removal easier. Alternatively, you can try heating the adhesive with a hair dryer. This should then be easy to remove. Personally, I have made with the second so far very good experience.

If the LEGO products are significantly older, collectors are more likely to accept damaged packaging. There is no time classification when a LEGO product is considered old. Experience shows that LEGO products that have been retired for at least 15 to 20 years are considered old. Here, the common rules from the collecting universe apply: *Expensive is what is rare and well preserved or has a unique history.* Extremely rare LEGO products are another exception. These can be a very good investment even in poor condition. If a LEGO product is only listed once on a sales platform such as Ebay or Amazon, buyers are more willing to accept defects in the packaging. On the other hand, if there are several or even hundreds of offers for a LEGO product, a buyer will be much more critical when assessing the condition.

In fact, there is no way to measure the condition of a LEGO package. Overall, the assessment of it is condition is subjective. The final price then results from the interaction of supply and demand. Especially with regard to storage periods of several years, investors have to consider many different influencing factors. This is to avoid unwanted damage during storage. However, up to now there is very little knowledge about storage periods of more than 10 years. Only an exceptionally small number of investors have stored unopened LEGO products in large quantities for 10 years or more. Current knowledge in this regard must be Classifieds as still very recent. Furthermore, the topic of storage is hotly debated in many forums and blogs. Self-proclaimed experts with a few years of experience in LEGO investment share their (best) knowledge in this regard. Basically, you must always question this advice. The prevailing conditions and storage capacities can sometimes differ significantly from investor to investor. When we talk about the storage of our LEGO products, we first have to clarify the following question:

*How and where should LEGO products be stored according to the latest knowledge and experience?* As a general rule, LEGO products should not be damaged during storage. The condition of the LEGO product between both phases of storage (start and end) should be unchanged. Otherwise, storage should take up as little space as possible. Stowage and storage space is always limited. This is often associated with costs and nerves. Nerves in the form that many collectors and investors choose to store LEGO products in their home. If you do not live alone, it is inevitable that this type of storage will have an impact on your relationship.

The type of storage also correlates directly with your investment strategy. If, for example, LEGO products have to be available for quick and short-term sales (*flipping*), a complex storage is not advisable. What is understood by a complex storage, I would like to list below:

- Always stow LEGO products in a solid outer packaging with little room for movement. Ideally, you use the shipping cartons in which the LEGO products were delivered to you. These can also be used for shipping after the sale. Personally, I store most of my LEGO sets in sturdy moving boxes.
- Unless you are storing LEGO products in additional outer packaging, it is strongly recommended that you use an overhead dust cover such as an old bed sheet.
- Furthermore, unless you store LEGO products in additional outer packaging, direct sunlight, LED light, excess heat from incandescent lamps and UV light should be avoided at all costs.
- You should always store heavy LEGO products downwards and upright (narrow side down). This way you can stack lighter LEGO products on top of them. Horizontal storage leads to unsightly deformation of the long side over time. Most of the time, this can be seen by the formation of a belly or a bell in the largest area. The contents of the LEGO product put such a strain on the packaging that a dent forms (due to the pressure from above and the lack of resistance at the bottom). This must be avoided at all costs.
- Storage directly on floors should be avoided. The LEGO product is exposed to various hazards in this way, such as water damage from neighbors' burst water pipes.

- If you store LEGO products on a shelf, make sure that you use intermediate shelves. This makes it easier to stack several LEGO sets on top of each other.
- LEGO products stored in damp rooms take on the moisture. Cartons show typical behavior here and bulge, swell, become wavy and get stains, etc. The formation of mold can also not be ruled out.
- You should store LEGO products only in rooms where conditions are not critical. The LEGO Group recommends that the room temperature should not exceed 40 degrees Celsius. If you decide to store your LEGO products in the attic or basement, you should consider possible temperature fluctuations. In addition, the rooms should be odorless. A musty cellar, fuel oil smell or cigarette smoke are not advantageous. Prevent possible external influences such as a burst water pipe or vermin or rodents. The storage facility should be dry and preferably without a heat source. With regard to the existing temperatures, the guideline or maximum temperature in a non-insulated attic in summer is 40 to 50 degrees Celsius for several days. The effect of such temperatures on instruction manuals, stickers, etc. is not yet known. For a basement room, temperature ranges between 14 and 20 degrees Celsius are considered ideal, with humidity not exceeding 55 percent.
- It may be necessary to use additional dehumidifiers and temperature regulators in the storage room. You can monitor whether the correct storage conditions are present by using a room climate meter (temperature and humidity). If you are not sure whether your storage facility is dry enough, a hygrometer can help you determine the humidity level. If the air conditions are too humid, you can use so-called *dry packs* to counteract this. You can also place mini dry packs in the outer packaging to ensure a perfectly dry atmosphere inside the stowage carton and prevent mold or similar.
- If the basement air is dry, perhaps even heating pipes run along the ceiling, this is usually not a problem. As a general rule, a dry indoor climate is preferable to a humid indoor climate.

- This does not change if you wrap the LEGO sets in foil or plastic bags. Sealing, additional bubble wrap or cling film leads to hermetic sealing of the LEGO product and should be avoided at all costs. This is even rather counterproductive, as (remaining) moisture can build up in the sealed films and accelerate the process. Instead, you should include so-called silica gel packs for moisture control in the outer packaging. If you are unsure, you can do a test with empty cartons.
- Depending on the size of the LEGO investment, additional insurance should be taken to cover, for example, theft, fire or water. In this context, you should constantly update your documentation regarding the market value. This is required as proof for the insurance company in the event of an insurance claim.
- Check the conditions for random LEGO products at frequent intervals. Constant conditions are advantageous. Strong fluctuations are in any case worse than a constant slight deviation of the temperature from the ideal range. The intermediate controls are also suitable, for example, to remove spin-nets, etc.

All these conditions represent an ideal situation for storage. These should make clear to you how complex and intensive the subject of storage can be. The preservation of the original packaging is of crucial importance. It is advisable to pack the original cartons in large, stable outer cartons. Basically, it is a matter of protecting the LEGO product or the packaging from external influences (e.g., sun or during shipping). Fading of the original packaging must be avoided at all costs. In the event of a future sale, this will give the impression that the LEGO investor or seller does not take care of his LEGO products.

This is where a significant advantage becomes apparent when buying LEGO products online. For example, online retailers always ship their goods in one or more outer packages. These are ideal for further storage.[1] Later,

---

[1] At this point, I would already like to point out that the use of outer packaging when buying online is not a matter of course. For example, I have already made the experience on Ebay or

the LEGO products can be sold or shipped in the same outer packaging. Online retailers usually use bubble wrap, foam wrap, packaging chips, bubble cushions, cardboard shredders or paper as filling material. All of these materials are included free of charge with your order and should be reused. If you decide to purchase LEGO products from a retailer, these materials would be an additional cost to you.

A serious disadvantage arises as soon as you own several hundreds of LEGO products. Dividing them up into many individual outer packages is tedious and time-consuming. In addition, you can quickly lose track of everything. A detailed documentation from the beginning is inevitable. Before you start stocking up, you need to know how big you want to make the LEGO investment. Their approach has a direct influence on the storage. Personally, I now only use very large moving boxes (length x width x height = 75cm x 41cm x 42cm). The advantages are obvious for me. Above all, this means that I have significantly fewer individual storage boxes in the total number. According to my experience fit in such an average 12 to 13 LEGO sets fit into such a moving box. Using a standardized moving box makes storage much easier than using different types of outer packaging. They can be used as building blocks, which makes stacking much easier. Moving boxes are extremely stable due to the use of stronger material. Also, against the background, if you have to move to a larger warehouse in the future, the use of moving boxes is recommended.

In order to maintain an overview, each moving box is numbered consecutively. This sequential number, the dimensions of the moving box and the LEGO products it contains are recorded in an Excel. Especially with large quantities of LEGO products, you save a lot of time. You don't have to open every moving box to see which LEGO sets are inside. For me personally, this system and method of storage has proven successful. I gladly accept the

---

Facebook Marketplace that the original LEGO box itself was used as a shipping box. The shipping label was glued directly to the box of the LEGO set. After the LEGO set arrived, these looked accordingly damaged. Consequently, these were completely inappropriate for a resale. Therefore, it is always advisable to point out to the seller to use an additional outer packaging.

additional costs for the moving boxes, also because these costs of 5.95 Euro per box are manageable. Nevertheless, additional costs due to additional purchases in the LEGO investment must be well considered: shelves, re-packaging, dehumidifiers or temperature controllers, etc. reduce your return on investment.

LEGO products from about 200 Euro are an exception. These are usually too large to be stored or temporarily stored in special boxes or moving boxes. For these, it is advisable to store them in the shipping box provided, if you bought the LEGO product from an online retailer. If, on the other hand, you bought the LEGO product in a retail store, you can use a classic plastic or garbage bag. This at least protects against dust and possible sun-light. Regardless of this, the already mentioned conditions for upright stor-age apply. Whether another product can be stacked on top of the LEGO product should be checked on a case-by-case basis.

Adequate storage is the main problem in LEGO investment and limits the ability of many investors to make large profits. In this respect, the issue of storage and spaces should be well planned before buying. Ideally, as an investor, you store all LEGO products in your home, but this simply reaches its limits at some point. This type of storage is only recommended for small LEGO investments or as temporary storage for flippers. Living space is an expensive resource. As a preventive measure, you should always discuss this project with your partner.

Alternatively, many LEGO investors switch to the basement or the attic. It is very rare to find LEGO investors who rent a warehouse. Especially the additional costs for renting frighten many investors. Such a high-cost factor does not leave a trace on their return or profit. On the other hand, there is the clear advantage that hundreds to thousands of LEGO products can be stored without any problems. Should the space become too small, it is usu-ally possible to switch to larger rooms for the corresponding additional amount.

The possibility of renting storage space (e.g., so-called self-storage) is now common almost everywhere. The price varies depending on the location. The advantage is that the providers usually have insurance coverage, which is based on the value of the stored items or goods. In addition, the climatic conditions in modern warehouses are much better than in a damp basement or attic without thermal insulation.

## 3.7    What quantities to buy?

Between the years 2000 and 2020, The LEGO Group released an average of 467 new LEGO sets annually. The total value based on inflation-adjusted MSRP is USD 257,558 for this period, or USD 12,265 per year. These figures are intended to show that it is nearly impossible to buy all LEGO sets. Nor is it even necessary for a successful LEGO investment. To anticipate the later evaluation, LEGO sets generate very different returns. It is therefore important to buy the right LEGO sets. Once a LEGO investor has identified a potential new LEGO set as an investment, the question quickly arises as to how often the identical set should be purchased. What are the pros and cons of buying the same product more than once as a LEGO investor? Collectors have found a simple strategy for this in the past. If one is interested in a certain LEGO set, it is recommended to buy two LEGO sets. One LEGO set to build and play with, and another LEGO set to store unopened immediately after purchase. To date, this strategy has proven successful. On the other hand, LEGO investors do not know how many identical LEGO sets should be purchased. Many investors are familiar with a very similar question when buying stocks. Again, the question arises as to how many stocks should you buy? After all, investors don't just buy one share. With both investments (shares as well as LEGO) there is the problem that you can never be 100 percent sure which LEGO set or stock company is the right one and will increase the most in price or value. If you decide to buy, for example, a LEGO set fifty times, you take several risks at the same time. On the one hand, you tie up your capital (to a large extent) in a single LEGO set. If it turns out later that the LEGO set is a flop, this can have a negative impact on the overall return. On the other hand, larger quantities take up a lot of space. Also, the sale should be carefully planned, because such quantities of LEGO sets at the same time to offer, can literally flood the secondary market. Large quantities of a LEGO set on the market affect the demand and consequently the price. By doing this, they are damaging the prices themselves. Another hurdle can be that it is extremely difficult to buy large quantities of the same LEGO set - especially for private individuals. LEGO investors are mostly private individuals and thus only able to get the LEGO sets they want multiple times through many individual purchases from different retailers. This in turn makes it difficult to buy LEGO sets for the same conditions (e.g., discount). Of course, this can also be an opportunity for them to buy LEGO sets at later times with better discounts. Consequently, your average purchase price for the LEGO set will decrease. Buying from one supplier also has the advantage of lower total shipping costs. You also have to take into account that LEGO sets are sold at lower discounts just before they are retired, based on experience. And it happens very often that you can no longer get the LEGO set in the desired quantity. Also, due to the many resellers, many online and retail stores have imposed limited quantities on buyers when purchasing LEGO sets. Basically, there is no need to buy the same LEGO sets in large quantities. Of course, as a LEGO investor, you want to get the most out of your investment. If you have a blockbuster in the portfolio, with value increases of, for example, over 300 percent, you naturally wish that you had higher quantities of the LEGO set. This is completely human and succeeds only exceptionally few LEGO investors. It is much more difficult to achieve the same return on investment for, say, 25 different LEGO sets. It seems to make the most sense to adjust the number of pieces of a LEGO set to your risk profile. There is no universally valid formula for this. Each LEGO investor must personally assess how risk-conscious they want to be in their LEGO investment. For example, if you have the opportunity to invest a large amount of money in LEGO sets, then fifty LEGO sets of the same type may be relatively modest.

# 4.     Statistical investigation of 16,891 LEGO products

It is common knowledge that we especially notice what exceeds our expectations. At regular intervals, we read headlines or hear stories about
LEGO sets that achieve record-breaking sales prices. Often three-, four- or
even five-digit so-called yield rockets are glorified in all kinds of media. In
the conclusion of these contributions LEGO products are praised as new star
at the investment sky. Once you have read through the various reports and
websites, you quickly realize that the very same LEGO sets are advertised
and hyped up over and over again. However, this is out of all proportion,
because LEGO sets have existed since 1949 and thus for over 70 years. As
far as is known and documented, 16,891 LEGO products have been released
during this period.[1]

The hype and speculation of a possible LEGO investment has caused the
*LEGO set no. 10179-1 Star Wars Millennium Falcon Ultimate Collectors Edi-
tion*. This model is a special edition limited to about 15,000 pieces. The most
expensive Ultimate Collectors Edition Millennium Falcon ever sold changed
hands for USD 15,000 at an auction in Las Vegas in 2014, an increase in
value of over 2,900 percent when measured against the MSRP of USD
499.99.[2] There is no question that this LEGO set literally went through the
roof and its price or value really exploded. The Ultimate Collectors Edition
Millennium Falcon is an impressive example of LEGO's success as an alternative investment. The LEGO set was unique at the time in its specifications
(number and type of bricks and parts, overall weight and size, etc.) and
construction methods.

In contrast, a comprehensive and critical examination of the development
of the value of LEGO sets can sometimes allow well-founded conclusions to
be drawn about the future development of prices and values. For quite some
time, I have already been occupied with various questions on this topic:

---

[1] Including books (475 items), sets (14,068 items), and other items (2,348 items) such as
key chains, magnets, clocks, etc., as of Dec. 31, 2018, Brickset.
[2] For simplicity's purposes, inflation was not taken into account here.

- *Are LEGO sets in general suitable as an investment?*
- *Which LEGO sets are particularly worth investing in and which ones are better left alone??*
- *What are the reasons for a good and bad LEGO invest-ment?*

For meaningful answers, a representative number of a wide variety of historical data from LEGO sets must be evaluated. The appropriate tool is a statistical survey, evaluation and interpretation.

Many types of investment, including LEGO investment, quickly tempt people to act emotionally. Whether market fluctuations or the preference for a particular LEGO set (e.g., because you associate it to your childhood) can influence the decision process of LEGO investors. Moreover, it is troublesome that emotional investors tend to follow the overall market, as their own decisions are too often influenced by the actions of others. If there is high sentiment about a LEGO set, they will buy. The purpose of evaluating and interpreting this statistical survey is to enable LEGO investors to make future investment decisions free of emotion. There is no room for feelings and emotions.

Statistics as a subfield of mathematics gives conclusions about the frequency of a certain search characteristic and is an optimal method to establish a systematic connection between experience and theory. The goal of mathematical statistics is to prove generally valid statements using the methods of pure mathematics (analysis and linear algebra). Statistics must be representative in order to be valid. Representativity describes the property of being able to draw conclusions about a much larger quantity from a small sample. The size of the sample to be drawn depends on the desired degree of accuracy of the statistical conclusions.

The size of the sample alone does not guarantee reliable results. Nevertheless, the statistics must be large enough and the stored data must be complete. However, '*large enough*' is relative. The general motto '*the more, the better* does not help either. Fortunately, nowadays the size of the sample can be determined by so-called sample calculators on the Internet[1]. Without going into too much detail, the sample size is 376 for 16,891 LEGO products. For example, if we want to investigate whether a license agreement has an influence on the price or value of a LEGO product, we must have the data of at least 376 LEGO products for this investigation to be representative.

The entire database for 16,891 LEGO products comes from three sources, some of which cooperate with each other, access the same data, or complement each other. Bricklink[2], Brickset[3] and Brickeconomy[4] are independent LEGO databases. The three platforms are well known among LEGO enthusiasts. The data collections are available free of charge, at any time and to anyone. To access the data collection no registration is necessary. Brickset and Brickeconomy are largely financed through affiliate marketing. This is a partnership between a seller (usually an online retailer of LEGO products) and the website operator on the Internet. The website operator promotes the seller's products through advertising opportunities on his website (e.g., via banners or links). In return, the website operator receives a commission. In turn, Bricklink sees itself as a sales market for LEGO products, sets, individual bricks, parts and minifigures. Meanwhile Bricklink has the reputation as Ebay for LEGO products. The main business of Bricklink is to provide the platform for buyers (demand) and sellers (supply) to find each other. Occasionally, Bricklink releases its own LEGO sets (through contests such as the AFOL Designer Program).

Throughout the year, The LEGO Group releases a variety of new products, which are continuously, immediately and without much delay added to these databases. In the process, various information is recorded, such as the number of individual bricks and parts, MSRP, and much more. It is certainly no

---

[1] https://www.surveymonkey.de/mp/sample-size-calculator
[2] https://www.bricklink.com
[3] https://www.brickset.com
[4] https://www.brickeconomy.com

surprise that the first LEGO sets from 1961 are significantly older than all three data platforms. Accordingly, the information of older LEGO sets is fragmentarily documented. Especially the MSRP information is often missing.

Furthermore, a survey, evaluation and interpretation of 16,891 LEGO products is only representative if the data records per LEGO product are complete and comparable with each other. Incomplete data sets can influence the statistical evaluation either positively or negatively. This should be avoided at best by always referring to the sample sizes mentioned.

In the first step, the data was transferred and merged. Due to the complexity and in order to be flexible in the evaluation later, the data records were merged in Microsoft Excel. For this purpose, all data sets were elaborately processed in the next step. Some of the data sets were incomplete, not available or differed on the three data platforms (Brickset, Bricklink and Brickeconomy). For example, for a large portion of LEGO products, the MSRP in Canadian Dollars and Euro was not recorded. Other LEGO products do not have any information about dimensions or weights.

By restricting the necessary and available data elements for each LEGO product to a minimum (theme, MSRP, availability in the LEGO Store from and until, number of individual bricks and parts, current sales offers on Bricklink in USD, sales in the last 6 months on Bricklink in USD, part-out value on Bricklink in USD), only 21 percent or 3,576 of the total 16,891 LEGO products remain. Fortunately, this is significantly more LEGO products than the calculated minimum sample size of 376 LEGO products suggests. However, this does not mean that the data of the remaining 13,315 LEGO products are irrelevant and without further use. These can be used for other questions.

Microsoft Excel was also used exclusively for the subsequent statistical analysis. Following the statistical analysis, Microsoft Excel enables the interpretation in the form of schematic illustrations by means of various charts, diagrams and tables. The interpretation is preferably limited to two points. First, we want to find out the roots behind value developments of LEGO products from the past by establishing a correlation to the characteristics of each LEGO product. Subsequently, we want to generalize these discoveries and derive them to high and low yielding LEGO products in the future.

## 4.1 Value-Investment through LEGO Part-Out-Value

The term *Value Investing* originally refers to an investment strategy based on the buying and selling decisions of bonds or stocks. The economist and investor Benjamin Graham is known as the founder of the *Value Investing* approach. A well-known adherent is Warren Buffett. The American large-scale investor puts it most aptly in his own words: *,Price is what you pay. Value is what you get.`* This core statement is transferable to LEGO investing

Pretty much everyone knows that price and value are not the same. In everyday life, there is often no clear distinction between the two terms. Price is the unit of money paid, resulting from supply and demand for goods or services. Value, on the other hand, is the utility that a buyer or seller attaches to a good or service. The value that a buyer attaches to a good or service represents his maximum willingness to pay. Goods or services are inexpensive or not worth their value. Therefore, the price and value of a good or service may differ. This also applies to LEGO products, because the price of a LEGO product can be lower than its value.

When you buy a LEGO product and you don't know its value, driven by the hope that the price will go up, you're not investing, you're speculating. There is a fine line between speculating and investing. No wonder they say: *To invest is to speculate with success.*

Only when the value of the LEGO product can be determined more precisely a well-founded and informed investment decision can be made. If this results in a purchase remains open to question. You compare the value with the price and only buy if the price is (significantly) below the value. Wealth accumulation is achieved through the difference between the purchase price and the true value. This is made on the assumption that the price will fluctuate around the value in the long term and thus will eventually rise in its direction. The further the purchase price of a LEGO product is below its fair value, the larger the margin of safety and the lower the risk of suffering losses in the long run. The *Value Investment* strategy is by definition the search for undervalued LEGO products.

*Value Investing* is particularly beneficial for private investors and small investors, as it allows them to focus specifically on LEGO products that are within their area of expertise. A clear disadvantage of the value strategy is that investors need to pay much attention to LEGO purchases. Otherwise, the investor cannot make a professional opinion and commit to a specific purchase decision.

With the help of the fundamental analysis of a LEGO product, a value investor can decide whether a LEGO product is of high quality and what an appropriate purchase price is. Of central importance is the so-called *Part-Out-Value* for LEGO sets. The *Part-Out-Value* describes the *intrinsic value* of a LEGO set. The *intrinsic value* is always determined for a point in time in an unknown and distant future. The *intrinsic value* or *Part-Out-Value* is the sum of the current average prices of the components belonging to the LEGO set, such as individual bricks, parts, minifigures, instructions and packaging. The total sum of all these individual prices or costs is a very good indicator of whether a LEGO set will tend to increase in price after the EOL.

This price can fluctuate day-to-day and ultimately depends on the supply and demand of the individual lots. Attractive buying opportunities for LEGO sets always occur when a LEGO set is significantly undervalued. This in turn means that the traded price is significantly below the *intrinsic value* or *Part-Out-Value*. The prices of LEGO sets follow the law of supply and demand. The price is always low when the supply is greater than the demand. Then there are more sales offers in the market than purchase interests.

Supply and demand are affected largely by the components contained in the LEGO set. When a new LEGO set is released, its individual bricks, parts and minifigures are initially available in very limited quantities. As time passes, more and more retailers will offer the individual bricks, parts and minifigures of the LEGO set for sale (e.g., Bricklink). This is called parting out. As the supply of individual bricks, parts and minifigures of the LEGO set increases, the *Part-Out-Value* of the same LEGO set will stabilize. If you include the *Part-Out-Value* in your strategy, it is advisable to consider it only after the LEGO set has been available on the market long enough to be able to trust the *Part-Out-Value* even better. Nevertheless, the *Part-Out-Value* is not ultimate at any point in time. It happens again and again that The LEGO Group uses identical individual bricks, parts or minifigures occasionally in new LEGO sets. In this way, more and more identical bricks, parts and minifigures find their way through dealers into the LEGO parts market. The rising supply of identical individual bricks, parts or minifigures has the consequence that, conversely, the respective prices fall. As the *Part-Out-Value* of a LEGO set is constantly determined by supply and demand, it is not possible to derive a general tendency when the *Part-Out-Value* of a LEGO set is at its highest or lowest. For this, you would probably have to track the retailer prices on Bricklink on a weekly basis.

In this research, I was able to prove that for 64 percent, or 3,716 out of 5,784 LEGO sets, the *Part-Out-Value* is higher than the current asking or selling price in USD on Bricklink. In fact, you achieve a higher selling price with the *Part-Out-Value*. Many retailers on Bricklink know this and have focused on parting out, well aware that this form of sale is much more costly than selling unopened LEGO sets. In addition, it can be observed that more and more new dealers are entering this (parts) market.

However, it has become common sense that the additional effort for parting out is compensated by a higher margin. In my study, I was able to prove that the *Part-Out-Value* is on average 106 percent higher than the current offer or sales price in USD on Bricklink. In simple words: If you currently offer your LEGO portfolio for sale on Bricklink at a total value of 20,000 Euro (new and unopened LEGO sets), the *Part-Out-Value* of the same portfolio is about 41,200 Euro.

Experience has shown that minifigures in particular are the price drivers. Nowadays, there are countless minifigure collectors who really rush for new minifigures in new LEGO sets. The high demand is usually offset by little supply, because there is comparatively more supply for an unopened or new LEGO set than the individual minifigures it contains. Of course, minifigure collectors like to avoid the unnecessary cost of the individual bricks and parts included with the LEGO set. In general, the focus is only on the mini-figures.

The additional revenue (in the above example, the difference of 21,200 Euro) from parting out compared to the sale of unopened or new LEGO sets must cover all associated costs. This includes, among other things, the time spent creating the offers (e.g., on Bricklink), all storage costs and all associated shipping costs. The time required for the separation is by far the largest expense item and includes the opening of the LEGO sets as well as the identification of individual bricks, parts and minifigures. Subsequently, the sales advertisements are placed on the various trading platforms.

At the same time, it is uncertain how many single orders you have to process and ship for a merchandise value of 20,000 or 41,200 Euro. Many small orders mean more shipping effort for you (e.g., preparing and packing the goods, traveling to the shipping service provider, etc.). It can make a significant difference whether you drive to the post office three times a day or once a week. These costs also reduce your profit. Likewise, returning goods and restocking them takes a lot of time and effort.

Only a few Bricklink dealers are able to execute this as a profitable business model on a continuous basis. The majority of dealers fail after some time. As a private investor with a comparatively small LEGO parts inventory, it is very difficult to compete against larger dealers on Bricklink. Many dealers on Bricklink deal with much larger quantities of individual LEGO bricks, parts and minifigures. You have to expect that once you own a particular LEGO set, Bricklink dealers will have well up to 100 units of it. As a result, the retailer on Bricklink will also have significantly more variety of supply. Of course, this also means that larger dealers on Bricklink can make better prices on individual bricks, parts, and minifigures. Shoppers on Bricklink know this. If you are a buyer looking for certain items, there is a much better chance that you will get it in the quantity you want from one of the larger dealers on Bricklink. In addition, the dealer may also have that one special LEGO set that you have been looking for for a long time. So, the buyer sometimes saves significantly on shipment costs by buying from the larger retailer than from you.

In general, the demand for individual bricks, parts and minifigures is higher than for unopened and new LEGO sets. This leads to the assumption that the *Part-Out-Value* reflects the actual value of a LEGO set. The consideration of the *Part-Out-Value* for the personal investment strategy is undoubtedly recommended. For example, you can buy LEGO sets where the *Part-Out-Value* is three to four times higher than the MSRP.

Finally, it should also be noted that the statistical survey of my personal LEGO portfolio showed that even 76 to 92 percent of my LEGO sets had a Part-Out-Value higher than the current asking or selling price on Bricklink and Ebay Kleinanzeigen[1], respectively. The 76 to 92 percent margin is due to the fact that different marketplaces (92 percent Ebay Kleinanzeigen and 76 percent on Bricklink) have different selling prices.

---

[1] Ebay Kleinanzeigen is the largest online Classifieds portal in Germany and is very much comparable to Facebook's Marketplace.

## 4.2　An Excursus on Inflation

Inflation is not a new age phenomenon. It already occurred in the 12th century in the Chinese Empire. Inflation is closely linked to the national economy of a country. It is a natural part of the financial system and should always be taken into account when investing in money and tangible assets. If the price level increases, we are talking about inflation. In the opposite case or when the price level falls, we speak of deflation. The price level is a key figure that indicates the average level of all prices for goods and services in an economy. An increase in the price level means that money loses value. When money loses value, the price level falls. In turn, we speak of so-called monetary stability when the same amount of money can buy the same quantity of goods or commodities as at an earlier point in time.

Usually, inflation refers to the period of one year. The reasoning is obvious, because inflation can also fluctuate significantly within a year. We have already learned that tangible assets are generally praised as inflation-proof. Strictly speaking, inflation also has an influence on LEGO products. *So why am I talking about an influence now?* It is probably because of the awkward terminology that has become popular. Rather, inflation protection means that the actual increase in value of the asset is higher than the inflation for the same period.

By contrast, the value of a coin or banknote is merely a promise made by the state and the banks. Coins and banknotes have no material value and are therefore strictly speaking worthless. As you can already imagine, the word inflation comes from Latin. It means as much as inflate. If inflation occurs in an economy, the proverbial inflation of various prices for goods and services occurs. As a result, prices rise for a very long time before falling again. Thus, inflation stands for a gradual loss of value of money and varies from state to state. Nevertheless, inflation also has positive effects. For example, it is a key driver for salaries for working people to rise over the long term. Ideally, salaries rise at least enough to cover inflation. If this is the case, price increases for goods and services are less problematic for our wallets. In this ideal case, the working person can at least continue his standard of living. Of course, it is the state's intention (at least in Germany) that the prosperity of the population should lead to an improvement in the individual's standard of living.

Surely you have noticed that in certain periods you have to spend more on goods and services than before. Our available money is worth less. If the price level continues to rise, the purchasing power of money decreases. Purchasing power indicates the amount of goods and services that can be purchased with one monetary unit. This becomes particularly clear if you look at the value of money over the past decades.

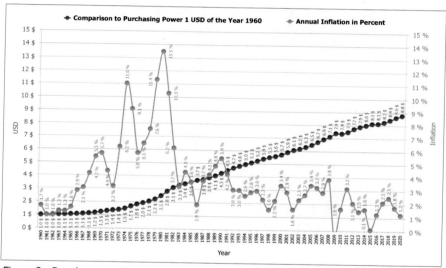

*Figure 8 - Development of inflation in the USA between 1960 and 2020*

Since 1960, the trend of inflation has known only one direction: Upward. Over the past 60 years, inflation has fluctuated between -0.36 and 13.5 percent. The average inflation rate was 3.68 percent. The years 1969 and 1970 as well as 1973 to 1982 are particularly remarkable, with even double-digit inflation rates being achieved at times. For example, between 1979 and 1981, average inflation was 11.72 percent. In this respect, inflation has

135

stabilized at a healthy level over the past two decades. In the overall context, USD 1 of 1960 is equivalent to the purchasing power of USD 8.78 in 2020. This results in an increase of USD 7.78 or 778 percent in the past 60 years. As a result, prices for goods and services in 2020 are on average 7.78 times higher than they were in 1960. In other words, USD 1 in 2020 could buy only 11.4 percent of the goods and services that the same money bought in 1960. In order to invest your money profitably in tangible or monetary assets over the same 60-year period, you had to beat at least the average annual inflation of 3.68 percent. The difference between the return on personal investments and inflation is called the *actual yield*.

In 2000, for example, *LEGO set no. 5987-1 Dino Research Compound* from the Adventurers theme series was available in the U.S. at an MSRP of USD 79.99. According to today's purchasing power or taking into account the current value of money, USD 79.99 from the year 2000 corresponds to USD 122.74 in 2020, which is an increase of 53 percent in 21 years or an average of 2.5 percent per year. In this respect, *LEGO set no. 5987-1* must maintain a value of at least 53 percent over this period in order to actually not make a loss with the LEGO set. In this respect, owners of the LEGO set no. 5987-1 could consider themselves truly lucky so far. Currently, there are only a handful of this LEGO set in new and unopened condition left for sale. The price of an original *LEGO set no. 5987-1 Dino Research Compound* is about USD 250[1]. Based on USD 122.74, the value appreciation of the LEGO set is USD 127.26 or 104 percent. This corresponds to an average annual return of 5.2 percent.

Alternatively, if you had chosen to keep the USD 79.99 in your savings account, it would be worth about USD 101.5 in 2020. Based on USD 122.74, that corresponds to a total loss in value of 21 percent, or an average loss in value of 1 percent per year, which is less than inflation at 2.5 percent annually. Due to lower interest rates and higher inflation, you would have less money today.

---

[1] current sale offers in USD on Bricklink, as of March 10, 2021

Unfortunately, the platform Brickset does not list prices for LEGO sets in the former currency Deutsche Mark (DM). With the introduction of the Euro on January 1, 2002, as many as 5,560 LEGO products, or 33 percent of the total 16,891 LEGO products, belong to the period of the Deutsche Mark. The majority of the MSRP in Euro were also not recorded until 2010. Thus, a comparison of the value development of LEGO products in Germany for the entire period is not possible, due to the lack of data records before January 1, 2002. Moreover, the MSRP's of LEGO sets in USD, by even taking into account the exchange rate at the time, cannot be validly converted into Deutsche Mark prices. This is because, according to The LEGO Group, there are several criteria for determining or calculating the MSRP of a LEGO set. These are not reproducible for outsiders, even with great effort.

To illustrate how complex LEGO set pricing is, we will look at two random LEGO sets in USD and GPB (Great Britain Pound) for each decade between 1970 and 2020 in the following. Again, I would have liked to use an average MSRP of all LEGO products for each decade. Unfortunately, there are comparably few MSRP's in GPB for LEGO products available on the Brickset platform. For example, not a single UVP is recorded in GPB for the period between 1961 and 1969. Therefore, it is not possible to draw a representative conclusion from one year to an entire decade. The following table compares the official exchange rate of the US Federal Reserve with that of The LEGO Group, which is obtained from the MSRP of a LEGO set in USD and GBP.

| Year | LEGO set no. | MSRP in GBP | MSRP in USD | Exchange Rate The LEGO Group (GBP / USD) | Official Exchange Rate (GBP / USD) | Exchange Rate Difference in Percent |
|---|---|---|---|---|---|---|
| 1974 | 200-1 | 1.25 | 4.99 | 4.00 | 2.34 | 71 % |
| 1974 | 360-1 | 4.55 | 13.99 | 3.08 | 2.34 | 31 % |
| 1986 | 6074-1 | 24.99 | 34.99 | 1.40 | 1.47 | -5 % |
| 1986 | 6312-1 | 3.75 | 5.75 | 1.53 | 1.47 | 4 % |
| 1991 | 4515-1 | 11.99 | 12.99 | 1.08 | 1.87 | -42 % |
| 1995 | 6125-1 | 3.25 | 3.99 | 1.23 | 1.58 | -22 % |
| 2001 | 6775-1 | 24.99 | 34.99 | 1.40 | 1.44 | -3 % |
| 2001 | 8548-1 | 22.99 | 34.99 | 1.52 | 1.44 | 6 % |
| 2010 | 7946-1 | 81.99 | 99.99 | 1.22 | 1.55 | -21 % |
| 2010 | 7147-1 | 9.99 | 12.99 | 1.30 | 1.55 | -16 % |
| 2020 | 21054-1 | 89.99 | 99.99 | 1.11 | 1.28 | -13 % |
| 2020 | 31103-1 | 19.99 | 24.99 | 1.25 | 1.28 | -2 % |

*Table 2 - Determination of the currency rate for GBP and USD by The LEGO Group using the example of various LEGO sets and time periods*

In principle, it can be assumed that The LEGO Group bases the pricing of its sets on the official exchange rate of the U.S. Federal Reserve. Nevertheless, it can be seen from Table 2 that the exchange rates or ratios between the two currencies are subject to ongoing fluctuations. The exchange rate chosen by The LEGO Group sometimes deviates significantly from the official exchange rate of the U.S. Federal Reserve. The variation range tends to be between -42 to +71 percent. Particularly eye-catching are the two *LEGO sets no. 200-1 and 360-1*, in which the currency difference is +31 and +71 percent above the official currency rate of the U.S. Federal Reserve. As a result, there is an extremely lucrative higher margin for The LEGO Group.

The calculated exchange rate is significantly higher for two of the twelve LEGO sets (+31 and +71 percent). Consequently, at this time, buyers in England purchased these two identical LEGO sets at a lower price than buyers in the United States. For five of the twelve LEGO sets, the exchange rate I determined for The LEGO Group can be considered fair. The deviation from the exchange rate of the U.S. Federal Reserve is only between -5 to +6 percent. It is also noticeable that most recently the trend is moving in a different direction, favoring American LEGO customers. Overall, the average deviation between the two exchange rates is -1 percent in the periods shown. Conversely, LEGO sets were 1 percent cheaper for buyers in the USA compared to buyers in the UK. LEGO sets in the U.S. were therefore relatively cheaper compared to the U.K.

The average fluctuation range between -42 and +71 percent can have various causes. In principle, strong currency fluctuations within a given period can be excluded. Such variations only occur in countries where the supply and demand of the currency fluctuate strongly (e.g., due to war). Nevertheless, it is possible that The LEGO Group, in setting the price or exchange rate, may have found itself in a period in which the official exchange rate of the US Federal Reserve was particularly good or bad. Accordingly, the exchange rate for The LEGO Group's pricing is comparatively poor. Only extremely rarely does The LEGO Group change the set MSRP's for online or retail sales.[1]

For the period between 1960 and 2020, the cumulative rate of inflation was 492 percent in the USA. Over the same period, inflation in Germany was only 350.55 percent.[2] This in turn means that prices for goods and services in Germany rose at a much slower rate over the same period. Conversely, the purchasing power of money was stronger in Germany. Due to lower inflation, LEGO sets were able to generate a higher return in Germany.

Inflation is measured with the help of a price index. The price index looks at the price increases of a representative shopping basket of around 750 different goods, services over a certain period of time. The goods include cars, food, package tours, electrical appliances and much more. Usually, one compares over a period of one year. Certainly, now they understand why inflation can vary from country to country. In fact, inflation varies from person to person. This is also referred to as *personal inflation*. The reason for this is that people have different spending habits. There is no question that not all of us consume the entire 750 goods per year. Not everyone buys a

---

[1] In contrast, it can be observed that Apple, as a U.S. hardware and software developer, always adjusts the prices of its products in different countries. The basis for this is the exchange rate to the USD.
[2] https://www.finanzen-rechner.net/inflationsrechner.php, March 14, 2021

car or a washing machine every year. Therefore, such goods are weighted lower in the price index.

It is often argued that the inflationary price development of all goods and services can also be applied to LEGO products. Strictly speaking, The LEGO Group would have to re-release a LEGO set at a later date, with the same number and type of bricks, parts, minifigures, etc. The LEGO Group would also have to re-release a LEGO set at a later date. Based on the new MSRP of the identical LEGO product, we could track a price trend for just that product. The pricing of a LEGO product takes into account all the costs that go into making the product. If the price of electricity on the manufacturing factory rises, that markup is guaranteed to be reflected in the MSRP. Otherwise, The LEGO Group as a company would earn less than before. This really doesn't seem like an option, since the majority of companies are generally growth- and profit-driven.

However, a comparison of different LEGO sets from two different years is not representative. Rather, product-specific criteria must be defined for a comparison. It is difficult to draw reliable conclusions from a random comparison of two LEGO sets without a common denominator. For example, the relationship between the MSRP and the number of individual LEGO bricks and pieces is suitable for this purpose. The number of individual bricks and parts is an important characteristic of LEGO sets. Using the ratio equation, an average brick can be assigned an average price. Admittedly, the criterion has weaknesses. For example, it ignores the fact that individual parts and elements have different shapes, colors and sizes. These characteristics do have an influence on the price, but will not be taken into account in the following.

For example, *LEGO set no. 717-1 Junior Constructor* from 1961 has 512 individual LEGO bricks and parts, according to Bricklink. The former MSRP is given by Brickset with USD 16.95. If you calculate the ratio of the MSRP to the individual brick or part, you will get 0.0331 USD/brick. Conversely, each brick or part of the LEGO set costs an average of US-cents 3.31 or USD 0.033. If you look for a comparable LEGO set from 2020, you can determine the price increase of the average LEGO brick. *LEGO set no. 31107-1 Space Rover Explorer* from 2020 has 510 individual bricks and pieces. The MSRP at that time was USD 39.99. Consequently, the average single brick or part price is US-cents 7.84. Compared to *LEGO set no. 717-1 Junior Constructor* from 1961, this represents a price increase of 137 percent. Over the same 59-year period, inflation was 492 percent, well above the 137 percent price increase.

If The LEGO Group would have adjusted the *LEGO set no. 717-1 Junior Constructor's* original MSRP of USD 16.95 for inflation, that would equate to a new MSRP of USD 83.39 in 2020. Compared to that the MSRP of the *LEGO set no. 31107-1 Space Rover* is only USD 39.99. Or in other words, *LEGO Set No. 31107-1 Space Rover Explorer* is half the price. This means that the average price increase has been set well below inflation.

*So, how is this possible? Is The LEGO Group sacrificing sales and profits for the benefit of the customer? How does The LEGO Group compensate the increase in inflation or the rising price level?*

First of all, the comparison carried out is not quite as representative as it first appears. What could be the reason for this? Ideally, the comparison should be carried out on a larger quantity of LEGO sets. This is to compensate for outliers. It is also possible that a lower MSRP was intentionally chosen for *LEGO set no. 31107-1 Space Rover Explorer*, for example to boost sales.

Surprisingly, the reason is quite different. For this we have to include other criteria in the comparison. Therefore, we look at the weights of the *LEGO set no. 717-1 Junior Constructor* as well as the *LEGO set no. 31107-1 Space Rover Explorer*. The *LEGO set no. 717-1* weighs 3,675 grams including packaging (1,955 grams). There are no building instructions for the LEGO set. Accordingly, the net weight excluding packaging is 1,720 grams. The *LEGO set no. 31107-1* has a total weight of 868 grams. If we subtract the packaging (175 grams) and the building instructions (317 grams) from that, the net weight is 376 grams. As a result, LEGO bricks and parts in *LEGO set no. 717-1* are more than five times heavier than in *LEGO set no.*

*31107-1.* An average individual brick or part in *LEGO set no. 717-1* weighs 3.36 grams. In contrast, the average weight in *LEGO set no. 31107-1* is only 0.74 grams per brick or piece. In this criterion both LEGO sets differ remarkably. Without looking at the detailed list of individual bricks and parts on Bricklink and due to the fact that there is a higher average weight, the individual bricks and parts in *LEGO set no. 717-1* must be larger.

Based on these observations, we have to consider the weight of two LEGO sets in addition to the number of individual bricks and parts in order to compare their price increases. Basically, the more criteria that are taken into account, the more representative or accurate the results obtained from a comparison will be. After further research, I came across two LEGO products with *LEGO set no. 102-2 Imagination Set 2* from 1971 and *LEGO set no. 8995-1 Thornatus V9* from 2009. Moreover, I paid attention to the fact that both LEGO sets do not have minifigures. Not quite ideal, there are only 39 years between the two LEGO sets. However, for an illustration of the price increase due to inflation, the example is useful. For a simpler overview, I have summarized the comparison in the following table.

| Year | LEGO Set No. | Number of Minifigures | Number of Items | Net Weight in Gram | Weight Per Brick | MSRP in USD |
|------|------|------|------|------|------|------|
| 1971 | 102-2 | 0 | 426 | 1,346 | 3.16 | 6.95 |
| 2009 | 8995-1 | 0 | 438 | 1,340 | 3.06 | 59.99 |

*Table 3 - Price increase due to inflation based on LEGO set no. 102-2 and 8995-1*

Table no. 3 illustrates that the two LEGO sets are approximately the same apart from the year of release and the MSRP. Again, we will check whether inflation has left any traces in the price increase from USD 6.95 to USD 59.99. Total inflation for the 39-year period, or between 1971 and 2009, is officially 455 percent, according to the Federal Reserve. This means that prices for goods and services in 2009 are about 4.55 times higher than in 1971. Accordingly, in 2009, USD 1 could buy only 22 percent of the identical goods and services that were last purchased in 1971. If we now put both

MSRP's of the two LEGO sets in relation to each other, we get the price increase that The LEGO Group has charged in 39 years. The result is an unbelievable 763 percent. As a reminder, inflation was only 455 percent.

For this particular example, we conclude that the 763 percent price increase seems disproportionate. Again, we have to admit that there can be many other reasons why the price increase is so significant. In 39 years, costs for raw materials and automation, among other things, fluctuate. Development work is also expensive. Based on the existing data, unraveling price increases over the past decades seems extraordinarily challenging. Profit is not a bad word; it is what drives companies to produce. If you want to know why prices are rising faster than inflation can explain, it may be that The LEGO Group charges a premium and has a high profit margin by industry standards.

## 4.3   Calculation of the Return of Investment

The key indicator for measuring the economic success of an investment is its return. The term *return* originally comes from the Italian word *rendita*. *Rendita* means *yield* or *return* in colloquial terms. In this respect, the total return describes the income generated by an invested capital or an investment over a certain period of time.

Private investors tend to put total return on a par with gross total return. Initially, there is nothing wrong with this, but a fundamental distinction must be made between gross and net total return. The gross total return always puts the invested capital in relation to the achieved profit. The gross total return is measured on the basis of the return on an investment and is usually expressed in percent.[1] Albert Einstein already believed that the strongest force in the universe is compound interest. The reason for that, we will see in the following statistical analysis.

There is a simple basic formula for the mathematical calculation of the gross total return. For the sake of simplicity, inflation and interest are first not taken into account.

$$Total\ Return_{Gross} = \left(\frac{Sale\ Price - Purchase\ Price}{Purchase\ Price}\right) \times 100$$

In order to understand the calculation of the gross total return better, a fictitious example can help. For this, I refer to my private LEGO portfolio. On November 16, 2018, I purchased *LEGO set no. 42064-1 Ocean Explorer* from the Technic themed series for 55.29 Euro (including shipping). The LEGO Group's suggested retail price is 89.99 Euro. Consequently, my purchase price represents a discount of about 38 percent. At the time of review on December 31, 2020, the LEGO set was in my inventory for 777 calendar days, or a little more than 2 years. As of December 31, 2020, the LEGO set

---

[1] Percentages are a ratio or auxiliary unit of measurement in which the size ratio is set in relation to a uniform basic value (hundred).

was traded at the following prices: 1) Ebay-Kleinanzeigen 130 Euro and 2) Current sales offers on Bricklink 169.27 Euro.

For the example, we proceed from the worse or lower price on Ebay Classifieds. We assume that we have successfully sold *LEGO set no. 42064-1 Ocean Explorer* on Ebay-Kleinanzeigen on December 31, 2020 for 130 Euro. Accordingly, we put the data into the formula to calculate the gross total return.

$$Total\ Return_{Gross} = \left(\frac{Sale\ Price - Purchase\ Price}{Purchace\ Price}\right) \times 100$$

$$Total\ Return_{Gross} = \left(\frac{130\ € - 55,29\ €}{55,29\ €}\right) \times 100$$

$$Total\ Return_{Gross} = 125{,}12\ \%$$

The increase in value or gross total return of *LEGO set no. 42064-1* amounts to 135.12 percent. The change in value is positive because it is greater than zero.

I would like to give another example from my private LEGO portfolio, which has generated a negative gross total return at the same observation date (December 31, 2020). I purchased the *LEGO set no. 71040-1 Disney Castle* from the Advanced Models theme series through an online retailer on June 18, 2019 for 325 Euro including shipping. The LEGO Group's suggested retail price is 349.99 Euro. Thus, my purchase price is just under 7 percent below the MSRP.[1] As of December 31, 2020, *Disney Castle* was trading at the following prices: 1) Ebay-Kleinanzeigen 290 Euro and 2) Current sale offers on Bricklink 459.70 Euro.

Again, for this example, we assume the worse or lower selling price on Ebay-Kleinanzeigen. Accordingly, we assume that *LEGO set no. 71040-1* was

---

[1] In this example, for the sake of simplicity, no further discount such as payback points, cashback, etc. has been taken into account.

sold on Ebay-Kleinanzeigen for 290 Euro on December 31, 2020. The period between purchase and sale corresponds to 563 calendar days or 1.5 years.

$$Total\ Return_{Gross} = \left(\frac{Sale\ Price - Purchase\ Price}{Purchace\ Price}\right) \times 100$$

$$Total\ Return_{Gross} = \left(\frac{290\ € - 325\ €}{325\ €}\right) \times 100$$

$$Total\ Return_{Gross} = -10{,}77\ \%$$

The loss in value or gross total return of LEGO set no. 71040-1 is -10.77 percent. The change in value is negative because it is less than zero. This is called depreciation, where the LEGO set has suffered a loss in value. In this example, we have assumed that the sale really took place, so we speak of a realized loss. On the other hand, we speak of a book loss if the LEGO set has a negative return at a certain period under consideration, but is not sold. The loss is therefore only documented in the books and not realized. This occurs, for example, if you continuously update your personal LEGO inventory list with regard to increases or decreases in value. Especially for long-term investments, inflation has a decisive influence on the performance of individual LEGO products and the return of your LEGO portfolio. Therefore, inflation has to be taken into account when determining the return of your LEGO products. Basically, it is recommended to take inflation into account if more than 365 calendar days or 1 year have passed since the purchase of a LEGO set. It is not necessary to take inflation into account if there are less than 12 months between purchase and sale. Ultimately, it is your decision. Even the Federal Reserve publishes a report on official inflation for the U.S. every month.

So far, we have only talked about the gross total return. However, this does not take into account all the costs related to the LEGO investment. These additional costs are caused by the purchase and sale of the LEGO products. Ongoing costs also have an impact on the total return of your

LEGO investment. Therefore, the real total return or net total return for investors is the key figure to measure the profit of the investment. In simple words: The net total return is what you actually get paid into your account.

There are various factors that influence the net total return. We have to differ between the factors that have a positive or negative influence on the net total return. Negative influencing factors reduce the total return and positive influencing factors increase the total return. From a practical point of view, it is up to you, which costs you take into account for the calculation of the financial return on your investment. The following negative factors are the most common.

### ◼ Costs due to the Acquisition

Method of Payment
The most common payment options in online and retail include Cash Payment, Bank Transfer (e.g., Payment in Advance), Cash on Delivery (e.g., Cash), PayPal, Credit Card, SOFORT (Instant Bank Transfer), Amazon-Payments, Purchase on Account, Klarna, Debit Note or Cryptocurrencies. The different service providers charge different fees. It is best to find out from the respective provider how high the estimated fees are.

Shipping Costs
Free shipping is not something that can be taken for granted. There are still a lot of companies that charge shipping fees when you buy from their online store. Usually these costs are displayed in the ordering process.

Custom Duties
It may happen that you buy a LEGO product from an international retailer (e.g., Amazon France, El Corte Inglés, etc.). The reasons for this are manifold, e.g., because the overseas retailer still has a popular LEGO set

in stock or advertises an unbeatable price. Depending on where the desired product comes from, customs duties may apply. Customs duties depend on the value of the goods, which is ideally shown on an invoice. Customs duties also affect your return on investment and should be factored in. The number of customs duties can be looked up on the official site of the customs (e.g., in Germany at www.Zoll.de).

Travelling Costs    Basically, costs must also be considered that arise from trips, e.g., to the retailer or picking up the package at the mail order center. These can be fuel costs, local transport ticket, costs for the use of car sharing and many more. It is also worth considering whether the costs for insurance, leasing and maintenance of the private vehicle should be included here on a pro rata basis. Often the vehicle is already available, the costs are incurred anyway, which is why many do not consider these costs further.

## Running Costs

Storage Costs    LEGO investment is extremely space-consuming. You have to deal with the question of how much you include storage costs in your financial return. The more honest you are about these costs, the more accurate your net return on investment will be. For example, if the LEGO investment seized a room in the basement of your house, you could, in principle, include the costs related to this from space or rent, electricity, heating, etc., on a pro rata basis. Practically speaking, these are often so-called "business as usual" costs. Associated costs arise to them independently of the LEGO investment. Of course, these types of costs must be taken into account if, for example, you rent extra storage space. All costs associated with this must be calculated into the return of your investment.

Insurance Costs    If you are planning to invest in LEGO, you may reach a point where your investment can reach a high value. To protect yourself against various types of damage (e.g., fire damage, water damage, etc.) or theft, it is recommended that you take out insurance. The insurance sum is determined by the value of your LEGO investment. It is recommended to contact your private household insurance company in this regard. In any case, they should constantly update the total amount.

## Costs due to Sale

Sale Costs    Nowadays, there is a wide range of online and offline sales platforms (e.g., Bricklink, Ebay, Amazon, Ebay-Classiefieds, flea markets, Facebook Marketplace, etc.). Nevertheless, most of them involve fees. These are not so much usage fees. Rather, they are fees that have to be paid to the provider when selling. It is common to charge percentage and/or fixed fees for posting, selling, or other costs associated with the sale, such as advertising or highlighting the sale ad. Which exact fees are charged, you can ask the respective provider or read up.

Shipping Costs    If the buyer of your LEGO product decides not to pick up the product himself, the most common delivery method is shipping by a service provider such as DHL, UPS, Hermes, GLS, etc. The seller is responsible for the shipping costs. Usually, for strategic reasons, it is best for the seller to pay the shipping costs. On top of that, they have to estimate material costs for e.g., cardboard box or shipping bags, tape, filling material etc. These additional costs need to be taken into account only to the extent that they bear them themselves.

Taxes The subject of taxes is extremely complex, and it is not easy to take a comprehensive look at it. You should consult a tax advisor for your personal case. You may be obliged to pay tax on profits from LEGO sales.

Furthermore, there are cost factors such as Internet and cell phone tariffs that you can also take into account. It is up to you how much you want to go into detail here and which total costs you include in the net total return. Basically, there are no rules. On the other hand, there are also various ways to positively influence or increase the net total return. These include z. So-called bonus systems such as cashback programs or the LEGO VIP model.

## Bonification

Cashback The term cashback literally means cash or money back. This is a bonus program in which cash is credited for every purchase in online or retail stores. As a rule, it is necessary to register with the cashback provider. Well-known German cashback providers are, for example, Shoop or iGraal.

LEGO VIP In contrast to Cashback, the LEGO VIP program is a re-ward point system directly from The LEGO Group. VIP members can collect points and have the opportunity to exchange points for non-cash assets (so-called rewards such as posters, keychains but also LEGO sets and much more). In addition, there is the possibility to buy LEGO products directly by means of collected points. Here, 1 LEGO VIP point is equivalent to 0.67 Euro. For every 1 Euro spent in the LEGO Shop, 7.5 points are credited, e.g., 5 Euro-Cents. This corresponds to a discount of 5 percent in the LEGO online store and the it's retail stores.[1] You can also use the VIP points you earn to purchase LEGO vouchers.

Payback

Another very common option in Germany is the so-called Payback points. One Payback point corresponds to one Euro-Cent. If you have accumulated several points, you can either have the points you have saved transferred to your account or redeem them as credit at one of the retailers.

Credit Cards with Bonus Program

Credit cards with bonus programs are becoming more and more common. Some providers include extra insurance or allow customers to collect points for rewards. Other providers grant discounts on certain products or services. Such bonus programs can be attractive if you use them wisely.

---

[1] December 20, 2021

This brings us in the following to the formal determination of the net total return.

$$Total\ Return_{Net} = \left(\frac{Sale\ Price + Bonification - Total\ Costs - Purchase\ Price}{Purchase\ Price}\right) \times 100$$

The calculated net total return is equal to the profit or loss of your investment. The profit is the excess and the loss is the deficit, which is generated in a certain period. If the result is zero, we speak of a neutral result, in which neither loss nor profit is achieved.

As you probably have already noticed, the influence of inflation has been ignored in the previous examples. It is absolutely necessary to take inflation into account. There are two approaches to the calculation with advantages and disadvantages.

For example, you can use the formula from financial mathematics for initial and final capital. This formula is as follows:

$$C_{End} = C_{Begin} \times \left(1 + \frac{p}{100}\right)^n$$

What may sound complicated to some laymen should already be known to investors. The variables of the formula explain themselves as follows:

$C_{End}$ = closing capital after financial return (here: sale price)
$C_{Begin}$ = opening capital before financial return (here: purchase price)
$n$ = number of years
$p$ = interest rate

The crucial disadvantage of this formula is the parameter $p$, which stands for the average inflation. If you look at the development of LEGO sets over a long period of time, the interest rate or inflation $p$ sometimes fluctuates considerably. Less often, inflation is the same in two or more consecutive years. We cannot account for this phenomenon with the above formula.

According to this formula, inflation $p$ is an invariant constant. Of course, one could arithmetically average the different inflation values over the corresponding period.[1] Nevertheless, this method is less accurate than the following second calculation approach.

This requires some up-front work, in which we list all official inflations between 1960 and 2020. For calculation purposes, we use the MSRP of the year of release and apply interest to this by means of all ongoing inflation up to the time of comparison (December 31, 2020). The result is the MSRP_New. In mathematics, this is referred to as *discounting*. Accordingly, the MSRP_New represents the identical LEGO set, whereby this would be published by The LEGO Group at a later point in time (December 31, 2020). Thus, it is possible to determine the value development of the LEGO set on the basis of the MSRP_New and the current value or sales price (December 31, 2020).

For an example, I choose LEGO set no. 42083-1 Bugatti Chiron from the Technic theme series. The set was released in 2018 at an MSRP of 329.99 Euro. To calculate the MSRP_New, we ignore the year of release, 2018, and focus on the performance of the subsequent two years, 2019 and 2020. In 2019, inflation was 2.49 percent, and in 2020, inflation was 4.29 percent.

$$1\ USD_{2020} = 1\ USD_{2018} \times \left(1 + \frac{p_{2019}}{100}\right) \times \left(1 + \frac{p_{2020}}{100}\right)$$

$$1\ USD_{2020} = 1\ USD_{2018} \times \left(1 + \frac{2{,}49\ \%}{100}\right) \times \left(1 + \frac{4{,}29\ \%}{100}\right)$$

$$1\ USD_{2020} = 1{,}0689\ USD_{2018}$$

$$Purchasing\ Power = \frac{1\ USD_{2020}}{1{,}0689\ USD_{2018}}$$

$$Purchasing\ Power = 0{,}936\ USD$$

---

[1] The arithmetic average calculates the median value by dividing the sum of the considered numbers by their number.

As a result, USD 1 from 2018 corresponds to the purchasing power of USD 1.0689 in 2020. This is associated with an increase of USD 0.0689 or 6.89 percent in 2 years. Conversely, the average annual inflation rate is 3.39 percent. Thus, from USD 1 in 2018, only USD 0.936 remained in 2020. Consequently, one could only buy 93.6 percent of the goods and services that one got for the same money in 2018.

The MSRP$_{New}$ is obtained by multiplying the original MSRP by the determined price increase.

$$MSRP_{New} = 329{,}99\ USD \times (1 + 6{,}89\ \%)$$

$$MSRP_{New} = 352{,}73\ USD$$

For comparison, I check the calculation using the (less accurate) initial and final capital formula. It can be assumed that the deviation will be insignificant, since the period of two years is extraordinarily short. The size of the deviations will increase with a longer period of time.

$$C_{End} = C_{Begin} \times \left(1 + \frac{p}{100}\right)^{n}$$

$$C_{End} = 329{,}99\ USD \times \left(1 + \frac{3{,}39}{100}\right)^{2}$$

$$C_{End} = 352{,}74\ USD$$

As already suspected, the deviation is very small and amounts to only 1 Cent. Nevertheless, I will use the more exact formula for the determination of the yields.

Now that we have all the basics, let's determine the change in value of *LEGO set no. 42083-1 Bugatti Chiron* as of December 31, 2020. As of December 31, 2020, the average sale price for the LEGO set on Bricklink is USD 471.63 (current sales listings). Consequently, we have yet to put the average sale price of USD 471.63 and our calculated MSRP$_{New}$ of USD 352.73 into proportion. The markup results from the difference of the two MSRP's and amounts to USD 118.90. This corresponds to an increase in value of 33.71 percent. It does not take into account possible acquisition costs, running costs, costs due to sale or possible bonification or cashback programs.

Comparing the total return of different LEGO products quickly reveals which LEGO investment performs more successfully in the long term. Unfortunately, this is less conclusive because LEGO products are available for different periods of time. If you compare a LEGO set from 2018 and 2019 to the 2020 observation period, the respective total return has to be evaluated on different time periods (namely 1 year and 2 years). Therefore, it is recommended to calculate the return per calendar year. In financial mathematics, this is referred to as *annualized return* or *return per annum* (in short: return p. a.). The average net return per year, based on the starting value of 100 percent (the capital invested or MSRP) is calculated as follows.

$$Annual\ Return_{Net} = \left( \frac{Total\ Return_{Net}}{100} + 1 \right)^{\frac{1}{n}} - 1$$

$$Annual\ Return_{Net} = \left( \frac{33{,}71\ \%}{100} + 1 \right)^{\frac{1}{2}} - 1$$

$$Annual\ Return_{Net} = 15{,}63\ \%$$

If we apply the net total return of 33.71 percent for a period of 2 years, this results in an annual net return of 15.63 percent per year. You have already calculated the annual return and made it comparable as a standardized measure of the success of your investment.

## 4.4    Hard and Soft Factors

The terms hard and soft factors are frequently used in the context of assessing a real estate location. These evaluate the attractiveness of the location, for example where a company would like to open additional branches or offices. Essentially, hard factors serve to measure success and have a sustained influence on the choice of location. This is also referred to as economic objectification through key figures. Hard factors describe objectively measurable and quantifiable facts. Hard factors result in key figures or ratios. They can be used to determine economic success or failure (positive or negative change in value or return). Hard factors do not change or change only rarely and very slowly. In their basic meanings, soft and hard factors can be applied to LEGO investment. The following hard factors exist in LEGO Investment.

| No. | Hard Factors | Source (December 31,2020) |
|-----|-------------|---------------------------|
| 01 | Official number of a LEGO set | Brickset |
| 02 | Official name of a LEGO set | Brickset |
| 03 | Related theme series to a LEGO set | Brickset |
| 04 | Related sub theme series to a theme series[1] | Brickset |
| 05 | Year of release of a LEGO set | Brickset |
| 06 | Availability of a LEGO set at *www.LEGO.com* for Germany, Great Britain and USA | Brickset |
| 07 | Total number of different and unique bricks and pieces (Regular Items, Extra Items, Counterparts Items and Alternate Items) in a LEGO set. | Bricklink |
| 08 | Total number of different and unique minifigures in a LEGO set | Bricklink |
| 09 | Manufacturer's suggested retail price of a LEGO set in Great Britain Pound (GBP), United States Dollar (USD), Canadian Dollar (CAD) and European Union (Euro). | Brickset |

| No. | Hard Factors | Source (December 31,2020) |
|-----|-------------|---------------------------|
| 10 | Dimensions and volume (width x height x depth) of LEGO Set packaging (cm or cm$^3$) | Brickset |
| 11 | Total weight of all individual bricks, parts, instructions, packaging, etc. per LEGO set | Brickset |
| 12 | Age range of the LEGO set recommended by The LEGO Group | Brickset |
| 13 | Existing license agreement of a LEGO set (yes/no) | Brickset |
| 14 | Registered Brickset users who own a LEGO set (number) | Brickset |
| 15 | Registered Brickset users who have a LEGO set on their wish list (number) | Brickset |
| 16 | Average rating of a LEGO set on Brickset | Brickset |
| 17 | Number of reviews of a LEGO set on Brickset | Brickset |
| 18 | Sales price of the LEGO set within the last 6 months (between 01.07.2020 and 31.12.2020) | Bricklink |
| 19 | Selling prices of current offers of a LEGO set (reporting date 31.12.2020) | Bricklink |
| 20 | Part-Out-Value of a LEGO set (as per December 31, 2020) | Bricklink |

Table 4 - Determination of the hard factors for the investigation

It is less simple with soft factors, because these are not measurable. The significance of soft factors is therefore less objective. They are considered to be qualitative indicators, and are based primarily on subjective assessments. Nevertheless, they are appropriate as metrics if the estimation methods are transparent. Soft factors are constantly changing and can therefore only be determined in the short term. Soft factors in LEGO investment include:

| No. | Hard Factors | Source (December 31,2020) |
|---|---|---|
| 01 | Designer of a LEGO set | Brickset |
| 02 | Exclusivity, rarity and limitation of a LEGO set | - |
| 03 | Stickers and printed individual bricks and pieces in a LEGO set | - |
| 04 | LEGO set as display model or play set | - |
| 05 | Scale of a LEGO set | - |
| 06 | Possible combinations of different themes series | - |
| 07 | Sold out LEGO set due to constant demand | - |
| 08 | Controversial LEGO sets | - |

*Table 5 - Determination of the soft factors for the investigation*

The mix of various hard and soft factors is the reason why LEGO sets differ from each other. This investigation aims to clarify which hard and soft factors ultimately cause a LEGO set to increase or decrease in value. The assessment of the hard and soft factors offers enormous potential for a statistical survey regarding the change in value of LEGO products. The necessary information of the hard and (partly) soft factors comes from the databases of Brickset and Bricklink. Both databases allow any person to retrieve detailed information on almost any LEGO product free of charge. In addition, the Brickset platform has been provided with the function to retrieve LEGO products of a certain year as an Excel spreadsheet. This applies to all listed years between 1949 and 2020.

The hard factors and (partial) soft factors in Tables 4 and 5 were sourced as of December 31, 2020. Both the Brickset and Bricklink information was incomplete at this time.

Both platforms do not only record information about LEGO sets. There are also LEGO books and other articles. In this respect, it is necessary to distinguish existing information for LEGO sets, LEGO books and LEGO other items.

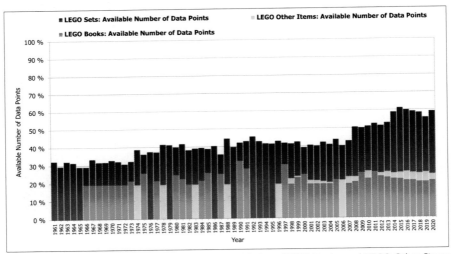

*Figure 9 - Available number of data points for LEGO Sets, LEGO Books and LEGO Other Items between 1961 and 2020*

All LEGO products in this statistical survey are assumed to be in new or unopened or sealed and original packaging condition. The condition of a LEGO product has a significant impact on its demand and therefore also on its price or value. The available number of data points on Brickset and Brick-link has the following influence on the statistical evaluation according to Figure 9:

| | |
|---|---|
| 1961 to 1973 | This 13-year period is difficult to reproduce in representative terms because the necessary information is very fragmentary. Statistical evaluations can only be carried out selectively. The available number of data points for LEGO sets averages 33 percent. Again, even fewer data points are available for LEGO Books and LEGO Other items. |
| 1974 to 2006 | After merging Brickset and Bricklink, the available number of data points for LEGO sets averages 43 percent. |

For LEGO Books and LEGO Other items, only 14 percent of data points are recorded. Consequently, the statistical survey of LEGO sets improves in quality, as relatively more LEGO sets can be examined and evaluated.

2007 to 2020    This 14-year period is the most extensively recorded. Particularly from 2007 onward, there is a significant jump in the available data points. As of 2007, an average of 64 percent of the data is available for LEGO sets.

In summary, the completeness of data points for LEGO products on Brickset and Bricklink can be rated as moderate. Nevertheless, there is no other database that provides so much information about LEGO products to the public. Of course, it must be assumed that The LEGO Group has significantly extensive data sets on its products. These data records are not publicly accessible and the website of the toy manufacturer does not offer any added value for the present statistical survey.

Nevertheless, the data records on Brickset and Bricklink are improving significantly over the past years. Last but not least, both databases are continuously busy recording additional hard and soft factors. For example, Brickset has recently been extended to document for current LEGO products whether they are subject to a license agreement or not. But Bricklink must also be highlighted at this point. The platform documents thousands of LEGO products (especially LEGO sets), including the respective individual bricks, parts, minifigures in type, shape and color. This type of platform is unique in the LEGO universe, also because you can trade on Bricklink.

## 4.4.1  Official Name / Official Number of LEGO Products

As of December 31, 2020, there are over 11,000 LEGO sets listed on Brickset. All LEGO sets have an official name and an official number. Both are assigned by The LEGO Group. Typically, the name associates what the LEGO model built represents. Therefore, it should come as no surprise that a model of a fire station is appropriately named *Fire Station* or *Fire Head-quarters*. In general, the name is short, concise and memorable. Nevertheless, this can lead to different LEGO sets having very similar or even the same names. The official name of a LEGO set is never unique.

For example, a search request for the keyword *fire station* returns twenty-three search matches (LEGO sets) on Brickset. LEGO set names can therefore appear both individually and repeatedly in the LEGO universe. This is true for the entire period from 1949 to 2020, since LEGO sets have existed. If you look at LEGO sets with very similar or even the same names, you will notice that they differ among themselves in various hard and soft factors. For example, this can concern the functions, number, shape, color of the individual bricks and parts, size of the packaging, MSRP and much more. Due to identically occurring names, a LEGO product cannot be clearly identified. The simplicity of the LEGO product names does not provide enough information to uniquely identify them among each other.

The LEGO Group is solving this problem by assigning very simple and individual identification numbers to each LEGO product. For a LEGO set this is the so-called *LEGO set number*. Currently, LEGO set numbers range from five to seven digits and are clearly visible on the packaging and building instructions for the LEGO set. In the past, LEGO Set Numbers ranged from one to four digits. The LEGO set number makes it much easier for you as an investor to e.g., find the right LEGO set on the internet. But also, for LEGO bricks and parts there are so called *LEGO part numbers* or *element numbers*. For new LEGO sets you can find them in the building instructions or on the corresponding brick or part. In addition to the element number, many parts have a four- or five-digit design number engraved on the inside

162

of the single brick and part. The design number along with the color is an excellent way to identify individual bricks and parts. In addition, the LEGO element number enables you to buy the individual brick or part in question, for example, in the LEGO online shop.

Sometimes LEGO set numbers appear twice (e.g., *LEGO set no. 7418-1 Scorpion Palace* and *LEGO set no. 7418-2 Scorpion Palace and Foam Scimitar*). You may have noticed that both LEGO Set numbers are additionally separated by a hyphen and another number (e.g., -1, -2, -3 etc.). There are several reasons why The LEGO Group has decided to occasionally duplicate set numbers.

- A LEGO set number is assigned to so-called sub-sets or groupings. An example of this are the *Collectable Minifigure Series*. The *Collectable Minifigure Series No. 10* has the *set no. 71001*, to which the number *71001-1* is assigned (1 random and complete minifigure in blister packaging) and *71001-2* (complete series with 16 complete minifigures in a box). Also included are all LEGO advent calendars. For example, *LEGO set No. 41353-1 Advent Calendar Friends* from 2018, this advent calendar contains 24 windows, with each individual window being a sub-set between *41353-2* to *41353-25*.
- Very occasionally, The LEGO Group may re-release or re-issue certain LEGO sets that have existed in the past and have been retired. For example, *LEGO set no. 4962-1 Duplo Baby Zoo* was released in 2006 and was retired from sale a year later. In 2015, the LEGO set was resold in a very similar fashion. Both LEGO sets consist of 17 individual bricks and pieces and one figure. In the new edition, some of the animals have been slightly revised.
- The LEGO Group may also change the design of the packaging, but the content (number of bricks, parts and minifigures) will remain unchanged. Examples of this are *LEGO set no. 7223-1 Yellow Truck*, which was released in a so-called polybag, and *LEGO set no. 7223-2 Yellow Truck*, which was released in a rigid cardboard box.

- Another reason for using duplicate LEGO set numbers may be when the reissue of an old LEGO set includes additional products. For example, *LEGO set no. 7075-1 Captain Redbeards Pirate Ship* and *LEGO set no. 7075-2 Captain Redbeards Pirate Ship Limited Edition with Motor*. Both are identical in construction and differ only in that the reissue (*LEGO set no. 7075-2*) contains an additional engine as an accessory in the polybag.
- In the latter case, The LEGO Group has in the past used the same LEGO set number for completely different LEGO sets. For example, *LEGO set no. 6648-1 Mag Racer* and *LEGO set no. 6648-2 Dump truck*.

Basically, the complete LEGO set number (e.g., 42081-1) is necessary to uniquely identify the LEGO set. Through my research, I could not locate an official designation for this additional number. Also, there is no official explanation why The LEGO Group does not print the complete set number on the packaging of LEGO products.

For quite some time, it can be observed that The LEGO Group increasingly assigns set numbers for a single LEGO set individually. This has happened with *LEGO set no. 21309-1 NASA Apollo Saturn V* from 2017 and *LEGO set no. 92176-1 NASA Apollo Saturn V* from 2020. Both LEGO sets are identical in construction with the same amount of individual bricks and parts. So, it can be called a reissue and despite this, The LEGO Group has decided to give the current NASA Apollo Saturn V a new LEGO set number.

Finally, I would like to mention two other LEGO products that share the same set number, but have different additional numbers. These are *LEGO set no. 7237-1 Police Station with Light Minifigure* and *LEGO set no. 7237-2 Police Station without Light Minifigure*. Only if you investigate further, you will learn that *LEGO set no. 7237-2* was released a year later, contains four more individual bricks and two more minifigures. However, the most significant difference is in the version of one particular minifigure. The police man from *LEGO set no. 7237-1* has an inconspicuous flashlight in his right hand, unlike the police man from *LEGO set no. 7237-2*. The flashlight is equipped with an additional function, whereby by pressing down the head, the flash-light begins to glow.

*Figure 10 - City Police Man (COP045) with blue tie, badge and white hat and flashlight with light function[1]*

This function was unique to date and has an extraordinary influence on the market price of the minifigure. As of March 26, 2021, the Police Man with flashlight (and function) is offered for an average of USD 44.99 (Current sale offers in USD on Bricklink). By the same date, the offered market price of the Police Man without flashlight (and function) from LEGO set no. 7237-2 averages just USD 3.58 (Current sale offers in USD on Bricklink).[2] A remarkable difference in value of USD 41.41 or 1,157 percent.

---

[1] https://www.Bricklink.com/v2/catalog/catalogitem.page?M=cop045#T=P, March 26, 2021
[2] Bricklink, March 26, 2021

## 4.4.2 Themes

They could not be more different: The themed areas of LEGO sets. A LEGO theme is a product line, where the associated LEGO sets are based on a central theme. Theme areas of LEGO sets are diverse, varied and embody a personal character by representing different worlds and motifs. As of December 31, 2020, 147 different LEGO themes are listed on Brickset for the period between 1949 and 2020. These include Architecture, BrickHeadz, Disney, Speed Champions, City, Star Wars and many more. LEGO themes simultaneously represent the development of The LEGO Group over the past decades. Whether it's the quality of the individual bricks and parts, minifigures, building ideas or the target group concerned: LEGO themes have undergone serious developments.

For years, there has been a persistent belief that the theme of a LEGO set has a significant influence on its value. Since LEGO sets have been achieving impressive increases in value, there has been a lot of discussion about the possible causes. Very often, the success of a LEGO theme is measured by whether there is a licensing cooperation for it. However, there are many other factors that must be taken into account when evaluating a LEGO theme:

- Content or Topic
- Popularity of a Theme
- Associated License or Cooperation
- Target- and Age Group
- Composition of Colors, Shapes as well as Number of Individual Bricks and Pieces
- Composition Colors, Shapes as well as Number of Minifigures
- Stickers and/or printed Bricks
- Number of LEGO Sets per Theme
- Duration or Time of Availability
- Composition of the MSRP

- Design of the Packaging
- Structure and Design of the Instructions
- Electronic Parts included (e.g., motors, remote control, etc.)
- Difficulty Level during Assembly
- Retail Availability (e.g., LEGO Exclusive)
- Themes with Augmented Reality (e.g., through digital AR app)[1]

At a later stage, many of these factors should be included in the evaluation of a LEGO theme.

---

[1] The LEGO Group combines toys with augmented reality. Augmented reality is an app function that allows the real LEGO world (e.g. the built-up LEGO set) to be scanned using the camera of a smartphone, tablet or gaming device. Digital elements are then added to the real LEGO world in the form of special effects.

### 4.4.3 Sub-Themes

Sub-themes represent a subordinate level of the thematic areas. Sub-themes are categories within the summarized superordinate theme. The easiest way to describe sub-themes is to look at famous movie series such as Harry Potter, Star Wars, or Jurassic Park. For example, the Harry Potter theme area, which has now existed for over 20 years. There are eight Harry Potter films in total, and The LEGO Group has produced various LEGO sets for a total of seven of the eight films. These seven sub-theme areas are thematically based on the corresponding films.[1]

Specifically with Harry Potter, you should know that the last two movies (Harry Potter and the Deathly Hallows Part 1 and Part 2) were combined by The LEGO Group as one sub-theme series. Usually, LEGO sets are released at the same time as the related movies or series. It is rather rare that The LEGO Group publishes related LEGO sets in the wake of movies or series. As of December 31, 2020, there are over 600 different sub-theme areas. Due to the volume, a more detailed analysis cannot be dealt with in this study.

---

[1] Part 1 - Harry Potter and the Philosopher's Stone, Part 2 - Harry Potter and the Chamber of Secrets, Part 3 - Harry Potter and the Prisoner of Azkaban, Part 4 - Harry Potter and the Goblet of Fire, Part 5 - Harry Potter and the Order of the Phoenix, Part 6 - Harry Potter and the Half-Blood Prince, Part 7 - Harry Potter and the Deathly Hallows Part 1 and Part 8 - Harry Potter and the Deathly Hallows Part 2.

### 4.4.4 Manufacturer's Suggested Retail Price (MSRP)

The Manufacturer's Suggested Retail Price (MSRP) is the suggested retail price of The LEGO Group to its resellers (e.g., toy stores such as Target, Walmart, Costco or online stores such as Amazon, and many others). With the MSRP, retailers receive a recommended resale price to their customers. Since the name already indicates that this is exclusively a recommendation by the manufacturer, it is not subject to any obligation. In turn, this leads again and again to price reductions of LEGO products. The term MSRP is not exclusive to LEGO products. Rather, the MSRP occurs wherever retailers sell products from manufacturers (e.g., in bookstores). The aim of the MSRP is to standardize prices for the same products between different locations.

In Germany, there is no vertical price fixing, which is generally prohibited by the antitrust law. In the case of vertical price fixing, a manufacturer (The LEGO Group) obligates its customer (online and retailer) to sell the goods at a fixed price. Excepted from the vertical price fixing are published products such as books and magazines.

Thus, online and retailers are allowed to independently determine what price they demand for a LEGO product. For years, it has been common practice for competing online and in-store to compete with each other by offering higher discounts on LEGO products. The chosen discount depends on many factors such as time of year, supply and demand, popularity, theme area, remaining shelf life, and many more. These factors are subject to seasonal and regional fluctuations. These swings make it impossible to include discounts in the analysis.

The recommended retail price was introduced in Germany on January 1, 1974. A similar suggested retail price was introduced in the USA, although there is no record of the exact date. The list price there is called manufacturer's suggested retail price (MSRP). The equivalence of the list price is often not directly comparable internationally. Goods and services sometimes have to meet different legal requirements. For example, the prices communicated to consumers must include taxes and duties in the EU. This, on the other hand, does not apply to the USA. In the USA, there is no national sales tax or value added tax. Instead, so-called sales taxes are decided at the state, county and local level. This varies from state to state and there can also be differences between counties. As of December 31, 2020, sales taxes vary from 2.9 to 7.25 percent among U.S. states. In addition, municipalities in 35 U.S. states impose an additional sales or use tax ranging from 1 to 5 percent. As a result, the list price reported by The LEGO Group's list price or suggested retail price in the U.S. does not include sales tax.

The MSRP of current LEGO sets can be found on The LEGO Group homepage and in retail catalogs. As soon as a LEGO product retires, the MSRP disappears from the homepage and the LEGO product will be removed from the catalog. After a few more weeks or months, the corresponding LEGO product page will also disappear permanently from the homepage.

Easier and without time limitation, the MSRP's of LEGO sets can be found in Brickset's database. On the Internet, Brickset has the largest record of MSRP's of past and current LEGO sets. These are always the most current MSRP. As described earlier, The LEGO Group may adjust the MSRP of a LEGO set as time passes. For example, *LEGO set no. 31109-1 Pirate Ship* of the Creator 3 in 1 theme was released with an MSRP of 99.99 Euro in 2020. Due to price adjustments in 2022, the former MSRP was raised from 99.99 Euro to 119.99 Euro. Currently, only the new MSRP of 119.99 Euro is listed at Brickset.

As of December 31, 2020, the Brickset database records the MSRP in four major currencies: Great Britain Pound (GBP), United States Dollar (USD), Canadian Dollar (CAD), and European Union currency (Euro). It is known that the MSRP of a LEGO product depends on the country. The main reason is the currency exchange rate difference. Of course, MSRP's also fluctuate due to supply and demand. According to The LEGO Group, popularity of certain (license) themes, purchasing power of target groups, prices of competing products from other manufacturers also play a role in setting the MSRP's. For the majority of LEGO sets on Brickset, the list price is available in USD. For much less LEGO sets the MSRP is also listed in CAD, GBP or Euro.

The MSRP forms the calculatory basis of this statistical survey. In the statistical survey, MSRP are used to calculate historical returns and to create variously dependent LEGO price indices. The MSRP of a LEGO product (especially LEGO sets) cannot be projected exclusively to the individual LEGO bricks and parts it contains. Of course, the MSRP includes not only all costs to produce the LEGO product, but also development costs, marketing costs, etc. These costs can vary significantly from LEGO product to product. For simplicity, we assume in this study that the MSRP of a LEGO product represents only the individual bricks and parts and minifigures contained in the LEGO product. Accordingly, costs for packaging, instructions and sticker sheets are not taken into consideration.

## 4.4.5  Date of Release

The release date is the day, month and year of the official release of a LEGO product. The production date is to be distinguished from the release date. Unlike the release date, the production date is marked on the product packaging in various ways. The production date is numbered in a code and can be printed or punched, depending on the localization. For example, it can be found on the adhesive strips or seals, in a separate white box on the side, or punched directly into the box.[1] For example, LEGO set no. 10252-1 VW Beetle of the Creator Expert theme was released in 2016 and is currently (as of October 2020) still in production. So production and release date can be different

Also, the production date of the same LEGO product may differ. One buyer may have the VW Beetle from 2017, while another buyer may have the VW Beetle from 2019. It has already been established that different production dates have an impact on a LEGO set (e.g., quality or color deviations in individual bricks and parts). In the past, it could already be determined that various defects from the first production series were corrected in later years. It would be particularly interesting to buy the same LEGO product several times with different production years and then compare them. Certainly, a comparison worth mentioning and interesting, especially with regard to LEGO sets that experience particularly long production periods, such as *LEGO set no. 10220-1 Volkswagen T1 Camper Van.*

This LEGO set was launched in 2011 and is currently still available in 2020. Continuously guaranteeing the same comprehensive quality over such a long period of time is possible but difficult. It is therefore conceivable that fluctuations in production quality will occur. Nevertheless, there is also the elimination of quality defects in production.

The exact release date is composed of day, month and year, and often varies from country to country. Also, the records on Brickset are incomplete,

---

[1] https://www.promobricks.de/schon-gewusst-das-verraet-der-code-auf-den-LEGO Set-verpackungen/48320/

whereby day and month were rarely documented, especially in the past. For the majority of the statistical survey, the year of release is already sufficient. An official release or appearance, or the start of sales of a LEGO product, can occur through The LEGO Group as well as specialty retailers such as toy stores, supermarkets, department stores, or online stores. Of course, The LEGO Group reserves the right to be the first to sell a LEGO Set.

The release date or year bundles all characteristics of a LEGO set in the published period between January 1 and December 31 of each year. Each year has brought completely different LEGO themes and sets. It can be assumed that the release date or year plays a central role in the development of value.

## 4.4.6   Expiration Date or End-Of-Life

In addition to the release date, it can be noted that in the past every LEGO product was discontinued sooner or later. In general, we speak of the discontinuation of the LEGO set on a retirement date. This predetermined retirement (so called End Of Lego / End Of Line / End Of Life; short: EOL) defines the official end of life of each LEGO product. It means that The LEGO Group will no longer produce a LEGO product and that it will disappear from retailers' shelves when it is sold out. Of course, it is also possible that the LEGO product has already been completely sold out. The End of Life of a LEGO product is crucial for its further performance in the LEGO investment.

It is important to note that The LEGO Group does not publish an exact date when a LEGO product will be retired. Rather, it is the case that the Brickset platform, for example, records a discontinuation date in the aftermath. This is in no way commented on or even confirmed by The LEGO Group. Therefore, it is not uncommon that there are inaccuracies in the discontinuation dates. These inaccuracies are not reported, but I have noticed them during the statistical survey. For example, it happens that LEGO sets are already retired after Brickset, but some of them were still available for a short time in The LEGO Group online store or retail. This proportion of inaccurate discontinuation dates is, however, assessed as low, which is why the focus is particularly on the mass of data and individual deviations appear irrelevant.

### 4.4.7 Age Group

For many years, The LEGO Group has been printing various age groups on the packaging of LEGO sets. For example, there are LEGO sets by ages *13+* or *4 to 99*. So far, there is no official explanation from The LEGO Group as to what these ages groups mean. The lack of an official meaning naturally leaves plenty of room for various speculations, which are hotly debated among building enthusiasts, collectors and investors.

If you believe one of these hypotheses, then the age indication is exclusively a recommendation, according to the respective developmental stage. For example, this should serve as an orientation for buyers, for which age group the LEGO set is suitable. Imagine the lovely grandmother standing in front of the lavishly filled LEGO set shelves to buy her grandson a birthday present, and this explanation seems quite logical.

Again, it cannot be denied that children evolve differently in terms of skills, dexterity, patience, spatial awareness, and so on. Therefore, such age recommendations are to be understood mainly for the general public.

So, the question is again to what degree this age recommendation is respected and accepted by customers. As already mentioned, some children aged 12 are certainly capable of building a LEGO set with the age recommendation *16+* on their own. Therefore, it must be basically questioned to what extent the age recommendations of The LEGO Group correspond to reality. This does not apply to LEGO products with an age rating of up to 3 years. Usually, these are Duplo bricks, which are significantly larger in their size. With smaller pieces, there is a risk that small children could swallow such pieces. Likewise, LEGO products are not known to use stickers up to the age of 3. From the age of 3 years LEGO parts and pieces become smaller and more detailed.

Likewise, the age level could be a classification of the level of difficulty. Strictly speaking, this is also an age restriction. Accordingly, The LEGO Group would have to specifically assign its products and especially sets to certain difficulty levels. At the same time, this would be equivalent to a marketing coup to directly address buyers in terms of maturity, skills and experience level. In general, adults are free to ignore this at their own peril. By statistically examining the age level, possible effects on the value changes of LEGO sets should be examined.

### 4.4.8  4.4.8 Packaging Dimensions and Volume

Due to the design of a few to several thousand individual bricks and parts, there are LEGO sets in various sizes, dimensions and therefore scales. The size of a LEGO set is defined in common language by the number of individual bricks and parts. The size of the assembled LEGO set and the size (dimension) of the packaging must be distinguished from this. The latter is documented on Brickset and is part of this chapter.

Unfortunately, there is no record of the dimensions of LEGO sets in the assembled state. This is certainly not surprising, because for this it would need, for example, a person who has built and measured all LEGO sets. Alternatively, this information could be requested by the community at Brickset. Anyone who has a particular LEGO set could contribute and report the dimensions voluntarily.

Nevertheless, Brickset records the dimensions of the packaging for a wide range of LEGO sets. For sets, the dimensions are given in length, width and height of the original packaging. The height dimension corresponds to the depth. All of these dimensions are in centimeters. Usually, The LEGO Group uses a fixed number of different packaging sizes. The number of individual bricks and parts may vary in these. It is also possible that The LEGO Group uses different sizes of packaging for LEGO sets with the same number of bricks and pieces.

It seems plausible to include other reference variables that are directly related. For example, the size of a LEGO set depends on the composition of the various individual bricks and parts. The number of individual bricks and parts also influences the total weight of a LEGO set. All three factors (number of bricks and pieces, total weight and dimensions) describe the physical composition of each LEGO set.

The dimensions of the packaging sizes are usually determined by the marketing department. In this context, the marketing department has determined that large representations of LEGO sets on the front of the packaging attract the attention of consumers and lead to higher sales figures.

The format of the front is even more important for the representation of the built-up LEGO set. It is interesting to note the ratio between the width and height of a package, which ranges from 1:1 to approximately 16:9. The majority of LEGO sets have packaging with an aspect ratio of 4:3. Conversely, a width of 4 cm is assigned a height of 3 cm.

| Set No. 42112-1 | Set No. 70651-1 | Set No. 4893-1 |
| Ratio (w/h) ≈ 16:9 | Ratio (w/h) ≈ 4:3 | Ratio (w/h) ≈ 1:1 |

*Figure 11 - Comparison of the three most common LEGO packages (Ratio 1:1 / 4:3 / 16:9)*

Figure 11 shows the three most common formats of LEGO set packaging. All three are standardized and are used in many areas. The origin of modern aspect ratios (e.g., 16:9 or 16:10) can be attributed to the golden ratio. The format of some computer screens, for example, is almost the same as the Golden Ratio (16:10), with a ratio of approx. 1:1.6. Today's screen standard 16:9 also approximates this format. The aspect ratio 1:1 and 4:3 are considered outdated and discarded classics. Nowadays, there are websites that specialize exclusively in the sale of LEGO packaging. It is obvious that there is a demand for them as well. This raises several questions, which will be answered in the statistical survey:

- *What value can be assigned to LEGO packaging (The packaging is the first thing customers or buyers see.)?*
- *Does the value of a LEGO set increase or decrease with its size?*

### 4.4.9 Weight

All LEGO sets are different from each other and the main difference between LEGO sets is their weight. Nowadays, the weight of LEGO sets is only
used when reselling used bricks and parts. Usually, the weight is given in
grams for smaller quantities or in kilograms for larger quantities. The weight
can be used in addition to the number of bricks and parts and the theme
etc. The weight can give information about the price or value development
of the LEGO set. For example, this can be when selling used LEGO bricks
and parts by comparing the part prices of different thematic areas.

However, the additional factor of weight is also important for new or unopened LEGO sets. For example, it is suspected that weight can also be used
as a value parameter for new LEGO sets. The weight is also the most important indicator for designers to find out whether a LEGO set is within the
estimated budget.

For a variety of LEGO sets, Bricklink and Brickset document the weight.
Gross weight includes packaging, assembly manuals, minifigures, individual
bricks, parts, and other accessories (e.g., stickers, occasional promotional
brochures, etc.). In addition, for many LEGO sets, the weights of the packaging and building instructions are available on Bricklink. Thanks to the indication of gross weights, the net weight (only individual bricks and parts)
can be calculated for LEGO sets. By referring and relating weight to MSRP,
weight to number of individual bricks and parts, year of release, etc., correlations will be revealed.

### 4.4.10 Type of LEGO Products

Unlike the previous factors, the categorization by *type* is not an official statement of The LEGO Group in its origin. Rather, in the course of statistical research, it was noticed that some LEGO set *types* are repeated at certain intervals. In this context, type is a categorization characterized by certain distinctive features. The content of a LEGO set is not always related to its name. By means of the categorization type the content or the essence is to be summarized keyword-like. Examples include helicopters, houses, trains, camper, transporters, ships, police and fire stations, and so on. This in turn leads to the fact that there are different variations of the above-mentioned LEGO products (especially sets). Categorization is intended to determine which types have increased or decreased in value.

### 4.4.11 License Agreements and Cooperations

Licensed products generate at least one third of The LEGO Group's total sales. In the US market, the share is significantly higher. Licenses therefore play an extraordinarily important role for the company. Through licenses and collaborations, The LEGO Group benefits from the brand recognition of other companies. It is simply a kind of free advertising for the licensee and licensor. Every dollar a manufacturer puts into a concession[1] saves it a portion of the marketing costs in return. A rule of thumb indicates that licensed products are generally suitable as a successful LEGO investment. How much truth or fantasy there is needs to be examined.

---

[1] A concession is the granting or transfer of the right to use a certain thing, e.g., the use of a license.

### 4.4.12 LEGO Set Owner (on Brickset)

Many LEGO websites offer the great possibility that their users can document their private LEGO collection on the relevant pages. This way you can keep track of your own collection even after years of collecting, building and investing. For the following reason I include this information in my evaluation.

The LEGO Group does not publicly release the number of LEGO sets produced. Occasionally we know that an edition is limited or even numbered. Of course, there is no question that not every LEGO set owner automatically documents his collection in such online portals. The Brickset platform currently has over 225,000 users. The goal is to determine whether a correlation between the number of registered users for a LEGO set and the change in value can be derived.

### 4.4.13 Wish List of Buyers of a LEGO Set (on Brickset)

Of course, it happens that for various reasons LEGO fans do not decide to buy a LEGO set or have to postpone the purchase. The reasons for this can be numerous: no capital, lack of space, indecision (e.g., which LEGO set), etc. At the same time, with the high number of new LEGO sets every year, you can lose track of them. To keep track, you can, for example, create a wish list on Brickset. Possibly the so-called wanted list gives us an insight about the popularity and furthermore about the potential future buying behavior of LEGO buyers.

### 4.4.14 Recension of LEGO Sets by members on Brickset

Brickset members can critique LEGO sets and give them up to five stars (1 = bad to 5 = very good). All rated stars are accumulated into an overall rating via their statistical mean to summarize the LEGO set into an overall score or rating. It is to be examined whether there is a connection between the evaluation and increase or decrease in value.

### 4.4.15 4.4.15 Number of Recension of LEGO Sets on Brickset

These are the number of recension on which the calculation of the overall rating is based.

### 4.4.16 Reviews of LEGO Sets on Brickset

In contrast to the recension, extensive text evaluations are written for so-called reviews. Users or members of Brickset have the opportunity to critically examine a LEGO set. Reviews refer among other things to the construction, individual bricks and parts, minifigures and much more. Advantages and disadvantages are mentioned. Each review should conclude with a personal opinion of the creator. In addition, the reviewer must rate five specified criteria (overall impression, building experience, parts, playability, and value for money) from 1 = poor to 5 = good

### 4.4.17 Bricks, Parts and Minifigures

Individual bricks, parts and minifigures are the basic ingredients of each LEGO set. To date, there are several thousand of each of these. To keep track of this, Bricklink, as the largest provider in this area, records a large number of individual bricks, parts and minifigures, as well as the composition of 14,068 LEGO sets.[1]

Bricklink has created different categories for the various individual bricks, parts and minifigures. These categories are called *Regular Items*, *Extra Items*, *Counterparts* and *Alternative Items*.[2] A typical summary at the end of each brick, part, and minifigure listing looks like this:

**Summary:**

| Type | Unique Lots | Total Qty |
|------|-------------|-----------|
| **Regular Items:** | | |
| **Parts** | 181 | 476 |
| **Minifigures** | 6 | 6 |
| **Extra Items:** | | |
| **Parts** | 33 | 34 |
| **Counterparts:** | | |
| **Parts** | 15 | 21 |
| **Alternative Items:** | | |
| **Parts** | 1 | 1 |

*Table 6 - Sample summary of individual bricks, parts and minifigures for LEGO sets on Bricklink.*

---

[1] Bricklink, December 31, 2020
[2] Bricklink does not guarantee that the inventory is correct. Therefore, the listing should always serve as a guide only.

Each of these categories has a specific meaning. Bricklink distinguishes here between type (Type), number of unique types (Unique Lots) and total number of types (Total Qty = Quantity). Basically, the total number and the number of unique pieces and parts can differ. On the other hand, the total number of unique bricks and parts is at least equal to or greater than the number of unique bricks and parts. This is logical because you cannot have a total of five bricks in a LEGO set, of which ten bricks are different. With the composition of LEGO sets, it is possible to calculate how often a single brick, part or minifigure appears in a LEGO set (e.g., average number). In addition, the ratio of the different categories to each other can be determined.

The example in Table 6 identifies 181 unique or different individual bricks and parts. In total there are 476 pieces. Conversely, a unique brick or part is present on average 2.6 times in the LEGO set.[1] This speaks for a great variety of individual bricks or parts. On the other hand, a LEGO set is considered to have little variety if the ratio between the total number and the number of unique bricks and pieces is particularly high in a LEGO set. In the same example, there are 6 different minifigures, but each minifigure exists only once in the LEGO set. Accordingly, the ratio between the total number and the number of unique pieces or parts is 1.0.

The statistical investigation of the compositions of LEGO sets reveals the effects of individual bricks, parts and minifigures on the value development of LEGO sets in many different ways. The meaning of the individual categories *Regular Items*, *Extra Items*, *Counterparts* and *Alternative Items* is explained in the following chapters.

---

[1] Total Qty / Unique Lots = 476 / 181 = 2.63

### 4.4.17.1 Regular Items

For LEGO sets applies especially: The more individual bricks and parts, the more possibilities. Possibilities as that the LEGO models can be made larger and more detailed. Nevertheless, it is not uncommon that identical regular individual bricks and parts occur several times in a LEGO set. For years, LEGO sets have been getting larger and larger. Many decades ago, LEGO sets were often composed of well under a hundred bricks and parts. As of December 31, 2020 the current largest *LEGO set no. 10276-1 Colosseum* has exactly 9,036 individual bricks and parts.

**Summary:**

| Type | Unique Lots | Total Qty |
|------|-------------|-----------|
| Regular Items: | | |
| Parts | 181 | 476 |
| Minifigures | 6 | 6 |
| Extra Items: | | |
| Parts | 33 | 34 |
| Counterparts: | | |
| Parts | 15 | 21 |
| Alternative Items: | | |
| Parts | 1 | 1 |

*Table 7 - Regular Items for LEGO Sets on Bricklink*

The category of *Regular Items* represents individual bricks and parts that are needed to build a LEGO set or an additional model (e.g., Creator 3 in 1 or Technic 2 in 1). Among buyers, LEGO set construction is often defined by its number, size, and color of associated individual bricks and parts. In addition, the composition of individual bricks and pieces gives the LEGO set both character and appearance.

Regular Items include the standard shapes such as the 2 x 4 brick, 1 x 1 brick, and many more. On the other hand, regular items include plates, wheels, doors, Technic elements, electronics, hoses, sticker sheets, and so on. Factory-assembled parts are also included. However, instructions and packaging are not part of this category. Thanks to Bricklink, it is possible to see in detail the individual regular items of a LEGO product.

### 4.4.17.2 Extra Items

Anyone who has already built a LEGO set will know the following phenomenon: Depending on the LEGO set size, there are always different numbers of LEGO bricks and parts left over. A special feature is that it is often very small individual bricks or parts (e.g., 1 x 1 plate). These so-called extra items are included in many LEGO sets by the factory. Until today, there is no official statement from The LEGO Group. This is enough reason for many fans to speculate about the existence of the Extra Items. There can be all kinds of explanations for the fact that these Extra Items are included in many LEGO sets.

**Summary:**

| Type | Unique Lots | Total Qty |
|---|---|---|
| **Regular Items:** | | |
| Parts | 181 | 476 |
| Minifigures | 6 | 6 |
| **Extra Items:** | | |
| Parts | 33 | 34 |
| **Counterparts:** | | |
| Parts | 15 | 21 |
| **Alternative Items:** | | |
| Parts | 1 | 1 |

*Table 8 - Extra Items for LEGO Sets on Bricklink*

For example, it must be assumed that The LEGO Group is well aware of the economic impact of those extra bricks and parts. Extra Items always cost money. Consequently, there must be a significant cause. The most likely reasons are the following:

The LEGO Group boxes all individual bricks and parts of a LEGO set in different bags. This is done by machine and automatically by weight instead

188

of by an exact count. Machines do not notice if any bricks or parts are missing. But every brick and piece is important when customers build the LEGO set strictly according to instructions. The customer experience is particularly affected by this.

The LEGO Group understands the importance to have all required bricks and parts to build a LEGO set. So, it seems much easier to include additional bricks and parts with the LEGO set. This is mainly to avoid that customers are forced to request missing bricks and parts from The LEGO Group later on. Certainly, many customers, being frustrated by the experience, would possibly turn their backs on LEGO sets. So, from The LEGO Group's point of view, it is more customer-oriented to add a few extra bricks and parts to the LEGO sets instead of not having the missing bricks or parts at all. The LEGO Group is well aware that occasionally bricks and pieces may be missing from a new LEGO set and has the following comments on this issue

---

### Missing Bricks and Parts in new LEGO Sets

*We are truly sorry that something is missing from your new LEGO set. We do our best to make every set perfect and take it very much to heart when a nonconforming set leaves our house. But don't worry: we'll send you the pieces you need!*

*Please click on "Missing Pieces" on our customer service page to order the part that is missing from your set.*

*If you don't find what you're looking for, please send us a full description of the part (the part number listed on the back of the assembly instructions would be very useful) and the number of the set. Once your piece is on its way, we will send you a shipping confirmation via email.*

*If some pieces get lost in the course of time, please use our replacement piece service*

---

*Figure 12 - Statement of The LEGO Group about missing bricks in new LEGO sets[1]*

It can be assumed that The LEGO Group keeps statistics on which bricks and parts may be missing due to production. At the end of the day, it costs The LEGO Group very little to produce these types of bricks and parts. It

---

[1] June 10, 2022, https://www.lego.com/de-de/service/help/new-sets-with-missing-parts-kA009000001dbloCAA

would cost the company more to increase call center staff to handle customer calls complaining about missing bricks and parts. Let's not forget that The LEGO Group wants to maintain its reputation.

In addition, we want to talk about the fact that the components are often very small. For example, in the case of LEGO City vehicles, these are individual bricks or parts for headlights, turn signals or brake lights. In the case of Advent calendars from the Harry Potter theme, three magic wands are included with the minifigures. It is remarkable that these are especially single bricks and parts that are easily lost or difficult to find again.

## 4.4.17.3 Counterparts

So-called *counterparts* are usually parts that are either assembled from regular individual bricks or parts or are permanently modified according to the instructions. These include, for example, glued parts or cut hoses.

**Summary:**

| Type | Unique Lots | Total Qty |
|------|-------------|-----------|
| **Regular Items:** | | |
| Parts | 181 | 476 |
| Minifigures | 6 | 6 |
| **Extra Items:** | | |
| Parts | 33 | 34 |
| **Counterparts:** | | |
| Parts | 15 | 21 |
| **Alternative Items:** | | |
| Parts | 1 | 1 |

*Table 9 - Counterparts for LEGO Sets on Bricklink*

## 4.4.17.4 Alternative Items

*Alternative* individual bricks and parts differ from regular items and parts across different production cycles. Thus, alternative bricks and parts can have two meanings:

- The shape of the individual brick or part was changed during production, so later versions of the LEGO set may have a different component.
- The original build was modified at some point during production. Some LEGO sets have been modified (bricks or parts added for strength, stability, etc.). Sometimes this is reflected in the different number of individual bricks and parts on the packaging or in the instructions (e.g., additional pages).

**Summary:**

| Type | Unique Lots | Total Qty |
|---|---|---|
| **Regular Items:** | | |
| Parts | 181 | 476 |
| Minifigures | 6 | 6 |
| **Extra Items:** | | |
| Parts | 33 | 34 |
| **Counterparts:** | | |
| Parts | 15 | 21 |
| **Alternative Items:** | | |
| Parts | 1 | 1 |

*Table 10 - Alternative Items for LEGO Sets on Bricklink*

The alternative items play a rather subordinate role for the statistical analysis.

## 4.4.17.5 Minifigures

LEGO minifigures have a long and exceptionally important raison d'être in the LEGO universe. It is well known that they have a significant impact on the performance of LEGO products (especially LEGO sets).

The classic minifigure known to us today has existed since 1978 and consists of a total of nine individual parts. Usually, a minifigure is partially assembled at the factory.[1] Minifigures consist of a head, body or torso with arms and hands, and legs. All three parts have received special attention in recent years from The LEGO Group. Nowadays, some heads have a two-face feature when you turn the head 180 degrees. Also, heads are no longer only in yellow color.

For example, the first LEGO police minifigure had a uniform in the form of stickers that had to be stuck onto the unprinted torso. In contrast to ordinary LEGO bricks and parts, nowadays there are only printed heads, torsos and legs. There are also now different types of hands, for example, with hooks. There are all kinds of legs, such as wooden legs, as known from pirates. Minifigures are equipped with numerous accessories such as musical instruments, tools or technology. But also everyday items such as an umbrella or cutlery can be used by minifigures.

In general, the value of a minifigure is determined by its head, torso, legs and accessories as a whole. As of February 6, 2021, there are over 11,000 different types of minifigures listed on Bricklink. Especially themed areas like Star Wars, Ninjago, City, Monkie Kid, Harry Potter and the Collectable Minifigures Series are known for their wide variety of LEGO minifigures. The statistical survey aims to examine and evaluate the impact of LEGO minifigures on the development of the value of a LEGO set.

---

[1] These individual parts are known as *counterparts*. The name already implies the obvious. These components come pre-assembled from the manufacturer. For example, the pants part of a LEGO minifigure actually consists of three parts
(2 legs + 1 Hip). From the manufacturer The LEGO Group, these parts are already pre-assembled. These factory-assembled parts are a common thread throughout the LEGO universe. A subsequent separation is often laborious and sometimes not possible without damage.

Certain minifigures are carried by a special feature: Exclusiveness or Uniqueness. Exclusive or unique minifigures clearly distinguish themselves from normal minifigures. These include elaborately printed facial features, the lush design of torso, legs and arms, as well as unusual hair parts, headgear and accessories.

Another form of uniqueness and exclusivity is the fact that a particular minifigure only appears in one LEGO set. This can also have an impact on the performance. If an identical minifigure appears in more than one LEGO set, it is strictly speaking no longer a unique and exclusive minifigure. In the LEGO universe, there are very many collectors who focus specifically on collecting unique and exclusive minifigures. More and more often, collectors are willing to pay considerable prices for unique and exclusive minifigures. The value of a minifigure can easily reach four digits value. The prerequisite for this is that the minifigure must meet the higher demands of buyers and collectors, especially due to the individual features and refinements. This niche[1] is correspondingly interesting for LEGO investors. However, even this strategy is not completely free of risks.

Only The LEGO Group knows whether a unique and exclusive minifigure will retain its status. If a minifigure is still exclusive and unique today, it could be easily multiplied significantly as a free gift in a LEGO magazine. This in turn has an impact on the devaluation of the LEGO minifigure in question. In the past, it has already happened several times that identical minifigures are revived in newly released LEGO sets.

Due to their importance in the LEGO universe, a consideration of the number of exclusive and unique minifigures in the statistical study is inevitable

---

[1] Pursuing a niche means being active in a submarket.

## 4.4.18 Last 6 Months Sales in USD on Bricklink

There are very few ways to trace past selling prices of LEGO products over a longer period of time. Well-known platforms like Ebay, Facebook Marketplace, Amazon, etc. do not officially offer any possibilities. Now and then there are third-party programs for one or another platform. These programs calculate the average selling price based on past purchases. Unfortunately, only a few of these programs are still available today (e.g., CamelCamelCamel or Keepa).

For some time now, Ebay has a new feature in which it indicates the price trend based on the sales prices of the last 90 days under searched items. Unfortunately, this feature works worse than good and often not at all. Of course, you can also go to the trouble of finding the average price of a LEGO set yourself. For example, you can arithmetically determine the average price of a LEGO set on Ebay under sold items. Obviously, the more LEGO sets you include in the average price calculation, the more representative the calculated price will be. If you repeat the process at regular intervals, you can even create your own price trend.

Alternatively, you can use Brickeconomy. The platform shows you the current lowest prices, average prices and highest prices from Ebay USA, StockX, Amazon US and Bricklink.[1]

Probably the easiest and fastest way to track the development of sales prices of different LEGO sets is offered by Bricklink. For this purpose, Bricklink has developed a so-called price guide, which provides very different and extremely useful information about a LEGO set.

---

[1] Stand 25.05.2022, Brickeconomy

| Last 6 Months Sales: | | | | Current Items for Sale: | | | |
|---|---|---|---|---|---|---|---|
| New | | Used | | New | | Used | |
| US Dollar | | | | | | | |
| Times Sold: | 7 | Times Sold: | 2 | Total Lots: | 23 | Total Lots: | 8 |
| Total Qty: | 7 | Total Qty: | 2 | Total Qty: | 59 | Total Qty: | 8 |
| Min Price: | US $125.00 | Min Price: | US $135.00 | Min Price: | US $179.97 | Min Price: | US $125.00 |
| Avg Price: | US $171.06 | Avg Price: | US $141.88 | Avg Price: | US $286.51 | Avg Price: | US $211.75 |
| Qty Avg Price: | US $171.06 | Qty Avg Price: | US $141.88 | Qty Avg Price: | US $311.92 | Qty Avg Price: | US $211.75 |
| Max Price: | US $200.00 | Max Price: | US $148.75 | Max Price: | US $400.00 | Max Price: | US $599.99 |

*Table 11 - Price Guide Last 6 Months Sales in USD for LEGO Products on Bricklink*

In Table 11, we can see the example of a price guide on Bricklink. In this chapter, we will first look at the *Last 6 Months Sales*. For this purpose, the relevant part of the Table 6 was highlighted in color, which lists the *Last 6 Months Sales*.

According to Bricklink, the data is live and does not include canceled orders. The prices do not include shipping costs or other possible fees. Incomplete sets are generally not taken into account. The following information are provided:

- **Times Sold**     Number of times an item has been sold.
- **Total Qty**     Quantity of sold LEGO Products[1].
- **Min Price**     Lowest price for which the LEGO product was sold.
- **Avg Price**     Average price for which the LEGO product was sold.
  
  Example     *(USD 150 + USD 125) : 2 pcs. = USD 137.5 per pc.*
- **Qty Avg Price**     Average price by quantity for which the LEGO product was sold
  
  Example     *(USD 150 x 2 pcs. + USD 125 x 4 pcs.) : 8 pcs. =*

---

[1] LEGO items in the sense of sets, bricks, parts, etc.

196

*USD 100 per pc.*

■ **Max Price**        Highest price for which the LEGO product was sold.

Especially the distinction between *Times Sold* and *Total Qty* must be familiar to you. If you find that the *Times Sold* and *Total Qty* numbers are different, it means that there are several LEGO products of the same type in the same order.

Another special aspect is the difference between the *Avg Price* and the *Qty Avg Price*. With the *Avg Price*, each individual sale is included in the calculation, regardless of the quantity of LEGO items within the sale. Therefore, there is no strong influence from bulk discounts. Again, the *Qty Avg Price* includes all sales taking into account the quantities within an order. Experience shows that the *Qty Avg Price* is often slightly below the *Avg Price*.

By considering the Last 6 Month Sales, we represent the period between July 01, 2020 and December 31, 2020. For the statistical analysis, we will therefore take the less favorable *Qty Avg Price* as the reference value.

## 4.4.19 Current Items for Sale in USD on Bricklink

Bricklink is also known as Ebay for LEGO products in the LEGO community. As a result, LEGO products can be bought and sold on the platform all the time. In addition, Bricklink offers the possibility to view *current items for sale*. The name already suggests that these are LEGO sets that are currently for sale on the platform. Description and calculation follow the same way as in the chapter before. The following information is provided:

- **Times Sold**    Number of times an item has been sold.
- **Total Qty**    Quantity of sold LEGO Products[1].
- **Min Price**    Lowest price for which the LEGO product was sold.
- **Avg Price**    Average price for which the LEGO product was sold.
  Example    *(USD 150 + USD 125) : 2 pcs. = USD 137.5 per pc.*
- **Qty Avg Price**    Average price by quantity for which the LEGO product was sold
  Example    *(USD 150 x 2 pcs. + USD 125 x 4 pcs.) : 8 pcs. = USD 100 per pc.*
- **Max Price**    Highest price for which the LEGO product was sold.

This represents only offers and not sales carried out.

---

[1] LEGO items in the sense of sets, bricks, parts, etc.

| Last 6 Months Sales: | | | | Current Items for Sale: | | | |
|---|---|---|---|---|---|---|---|
| New | | Used | | New | | Used | |
| US Dollar | | | | | | | |
| Times Sold: | 7 | Times Sold: | 2 | Total Lots: | 23 | Total Lots: | 8 |
| Total Qty: | 7 | Total Qty: | 2 | Total Qty: | 59 | Total Qty: | 8 |
| Min Price: | US $125.00 | Min Price: | US $135.00 | Min Price: | US $179.97 | Min Price: | US $125.00 |
| Avg Price: | US $171.06 | Avg Price: | US $141.88 | Avg Price: | US $286.51 | Avg Price: | US $211.75 |
| Qty Avg Price: | US $171.06 | Qty Avg Price: | US $141.88 | Qty Avg Price: | US $311.92 | Qty Avg Price: | US $211.75 |
| Max Price: | US $200.00 | Max Price: | US $148.75 | Max Price: | US $400.00 | Max Price: | US $599.99 |

Table 12 - Price Guide Current Items for Sale for LEGO Products on Bricklink

### 4.4.20 Part-Out-Value in USD on Bricklink

Bricklink is the first place to go in the LEGO universe when it comes to sourcing new or used individual bricks, parts or minifigures. The range of current and past LEGO products is unique. The basis is a constantly updating catalog for almost all manufactured products of The LEGO Group. Buying and selling takes place exclusively online, around the clock and thus 365 days a year. When LEGO products are bought or sold, the catalog records the selling prices of the products. Under the heading Price Guide you have the possibility to determine the so-called *Part-Out-Value* of a LEGO set.

The *Part-Out-Value* is the sum of the current average prices of the individual bricks, parts, minifigures and instructions and packaging associated with the LEGO set. Bricklink describes the *Part-Out-Value* as follows:

*The Part-Out-Value displays the total value of all regular items in the inventory of a selected item based on price information when the contents of a set were sold as individual parts.*

Figure 13 - Definition of the Part-Out-Value according to Bricklink

The *Part-Out-Value* can be determined using the following link:

https://www.Bricklink.com/catalogPG.asp

Figure 14 - Determination of the Part-Out-Values in USD on Bricklink

200

The following information is necessary to determine the *Part-Out-Value*:

- **Item Type**  Here you can choose between *set, minifigure* or *gear*.
  *Note*  *For the statistical investigation we choose set.*
- **Item No**  The official LEGO number must be entered here.
  *Note*  *Care must be taken to select the correct additional number in the second field (e.g., -1, -2, -3, etc.).*
- **Include**  It is the price consideration of minifigures, giving you a choice of *Parts and whole Minifigures* or *Parts including Minifigures parts*. With *Parts and whole Minifigures*, the minifigures are considered as a whole in the Part-Out-Value. With *Parts including Minifigures parts*, the components of a minifigure are included as part prices in the Part-Out-Value.
  *Note*  *For the statistical study we choose Parts and whole Minifigures.*
- **Condition**  It is the condition of the LEGO set, giving you a choice of *New* or *Used*.
  *Note*  *For the statistical study we choose New.*
- **Include**  Here you can choose between *Instructions, Box, Extra Parts* or *Break Sets in Set* for selection.
  *Note*  *For the statistical analysis, we select all options.*

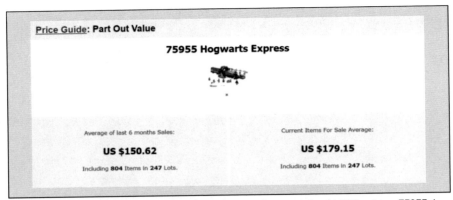

*Figure 15 - Part-Out-Value in USD on Bricklink using the example of LEGO set no. 75955-1 Hogwarts Express.*

As of June 12, 2022, the *LEGO set no. 75955-1 Hogwarts Express* of the Harry Potter theme has a Part-Out-Value of 179.15 USD. We also learn that the Part-Out-Value is calculated from a total of 804 items (individual bricks, parts, minifigures, bonds, packaging, etc.), which are distributed over 247 different lots.

Bricklink has a unique selling point in the LEGO universe with this useful feature. Therefore, LEGO investors should become very familiar with the *Part-Out-Value* function.

## 4.5    Investigation of Hard Factors

Every year, The LEGO Group releases loads of products. There are all sorts of books, clothes, magazines, miscellaneous items like keychains, promotional items and of course sets to build. To date, LEGO sets represent the largest number of LEGO products. The company's product range is limited and unevenly available from continent to continent and sometimes even from country to country.

The LEGO Group does not provide any information about how often a LEGO product is sold globally, not to mention in a single country. We can only speculate about possible reasons. Certainly, The LEGO Group fears that by publishing concrete sales figures (e.g., for LEGO sets or themed areas), speculation about LEGO products as investment vehicles could increase further. Again, a look at product sales would give LEGO investors extraordinary visibility into which LEGO products are selling particularly well and which are not. Concrete sales figures make the frequency of a LEGO product transparent. The official report on the sales volume of a LEGO product would therefore be particularly interesting, because this would make it possible to check the effectiveness of the free market laws respectively supply and demand in LEGO investment.

Certainly, this is a double-edged sword for The LEGO Group. On the one hand, the company is generating ever-higher record sales, driven in significant part by the large number of new LEGO investors or resellers speculating on LEGO products as an investment. On the other hand, The LEGO Group has no real benefit from the high increases in value and selling prices in the secondary market such as Ebay or Amazon.[1] This is another reason why there are no public statements by the company about the new buyers (LEGO investors). It is certainly better for the world's largest toy manufacturer to be perceived as exactly that.

---

[1] In contrast, the company generates additional revenue through arising sales fees from sellers after it acquired the Bricklink platform.

I already wrote that one of the requirements of the statistical survey must be that it is representative. This is achieved primarily by considering an extraordinarily large database. However, there is a special circumstance or limitation in the LEGO universe that can have a central influence on the increase in value of LEGO products. We are talking about LEGO products that are known to be available only under certain circumstances, in certain countries or under other restrictions.

Another restriction is that certain LEGO products can only be purchased in the online store or only stationary stores. In addition, for example, the purchase of the famous *LEGO set no. 10179-1 Millennium Falcon* of the Star Wars theme included a collector's card in a strictly limited edition as an extra. The LEGO Group puts the number of so-called *Black VIP Cards* worldwide at 20,000. The privileged circle of owners has been able to enjoy exclusive rewards and promotions in the past.

For as long as LEGO products have existed, the availability of various LEGO products has been limited. This in turn means that the circle of buyers is also limited in advance. It can be assumed that such LEGO products were very likely produced significantly less and even fewer are available today in new or unopened condition respectively are for sale on the secondary market. There are always plenty of assembled or used LEGO sets. But to find an original, unopened LEGO set in new condition after years is sometimes a true work of art. Surely you already know what I'm trying to point out: Experience has shown that the increase in value of such products is even higher. In general, the limitations can be summarized as follows:

- LEGO products that are not available in all countries due to the political context, costly distribution channels, lack of customer demand or determinations by The LEGO Group. For example, the LEGO themes *Forma* and *LEGO set no. 77942-1 Fiat 500 (Bright Light Blue Edition)* were available exclusively in the United Kingdom. Also, *LEGO sets no. 80101-1 Chinese New Year's Eve Dinner* and *LEGO set No. 80102-1 Dragon Dance* were available exclusively in Asia.

■    LEGO products that were only available locally-limited. For example, both *LEGO set no. 4000016-1 Billund Airport* and *LEGO set no. 40199-1 Billund Airport* (new edition, as of December 31, 2020 still available.), as the name implies, were only available at Billund Airport (Access only for passengers departing from Billund Airport.). This also includes all LEGO sets, which are only available at *LEGOland* (e.g., *LEGO set no. 40346-1 LEGOland Park, LEGO set no. LLCA27-1 LEGOland Pirate with Parrot*, etc.). Another example is the rare example of the Burj Khalifa (*LEGO set no. 21008-1 Burj Khalifa*)[1]. This group also includes LEGO products that could be purchased exclusively for visitors to events (e.g., trade fairs). This also includes raffles after such events (e.g., CCXP Cologne in 2019). A total of 70 LEGO items (LEGO sets, minifigures, etc.) were given out exclusively at the San Diego Comic Convention (Comic-Con International) between 2004 and 2020.[2] Also of interest are the so-called LEGO sets of the Inside Tour, which are even more exclusive. Between 2005 and 2019, there were a total of 15 LEGO sets. This corresponds to one Inside Tour set per year.[3]

■    LEGO products that were only available to purchase for a limited group of people. Of course, the LEGO items from the San Diego Comic Convention could also be included in this category. In addition, between the years 2008 and 2020, there were a total of 14 different LEGO sets that were exclusively gifted to employees. Traditionally, LEGO sets are given to employees around Christmas time. This category also includes LEGO products that could be purchased exclusively by owners of a Black VIP Card (e.g., *LEGO Set No. 5005747 Black VIP Frame* or *Card Display Polybag*).

---

[1] Coincidentally, I am one of the few owners of a new and unopened copy of LEGO set no. 21008-1. I bought this one in 2018 while working abroad in the United Arab Emirates and visiting the Burj Khalifa. Strictly speaking, it is the first LEGO set of my LEGO portfolio.
[2] As of 2022, San Diego Comic Con International (SDCC) is the world's largest comic convention of its kind. The comic event has been held since 1970.
[3] Due to the Corona Pandemic in 2020 and 2021, the LEGO Inside Tour was suspended by The LEGO Group. In 2022, it was held again in the usual manner.

- LEGO products that are included as a complimentary gift with the purchase of LEGO products. We are talking about the so-called GWP's (Gift-With-Purchase). The LEGO Group has various promotions several times a year. In the recent past, in order to receive the giveaway, you had to purchase LEGO products at a certain minimum order value. Each of these giveaways (e.g., LEGO set no. 5006293-1 ROman Chariot or LEGO set no. 5006330-1 VIP Chrome Silver Metal Key Chain, etc.) were strictly limited.

LEGO products in these categories are sometimes very difficult or even impossible for the majority to access. Therefore, they are often considered strictly limited and very rare. As a rule, the very low supply is countered by higher demand, which leads to extraordinary increases in value. The value growth of such LEGO products reached frequently several hundred to thousand percent in the past.

Nevertheless, these are regular LEGO products, which are covered by platforms such as Brickset and Bricklink. However, the inclusion of such LEGO products can have a significant impact on the overall survey. Therefore, it was considered to exclude LEGO products of these groups from the statistical survey. Instead, such products should be considered individually or categorized. Finally and after careful consideration, I decided against excluding these LEGO products from the survey. Accordingly, they have been part of my statistical survey from the beginning. Rather, these LEGO products are also part of the company's product range and demonstrate in an impressive way the dimensions possible in the development of LEGO products. The majority of LEGO products are LEGO sets and can be divided as follows:

- **Ordinary LEGO Sets**
  These are all official LEGO sets. These consist of one or more models or a collection of many different parts.

■ **Accessories products**

These are known as supplements (1950 to 1970) or service packs (1970 to 2001 and 2002 to 2012). These special LEGO sets do not contain models, but a minor number of special parts.

■ **B- and C-Models**

Some LEGO sets include instructions for one or more alternate models. These official alternative models are called B and C models. These LEGO sets do not have their own LEGO number or name. If a LEGO set has an additional B and C model, the LEGO set is still found only once in the statistical survey (e.g., *LEGO set no. 31042-1 Vacation Getaways*). Unofficial alternative models not created by The LEGO Group are referred to as MOC or My Own Creation.

■ **Sub-Products, Partial Products or Groupings (Subs)**

This LEGO category is grouped into one LEGO number. This includes, among other things, the Collectible Minifigure Series. For example, *LEGO set no. 71001 Minifigure Series No. 10* is divided into 17 different minifigures from 71001-1 to 71001-16.

■ **Super Sets or Super Packs**

These are a combination of normal LEGO sets, which are usually also available individually in stores. This type of LEGO sets are rather isolated and rare. They are by far the most common in the Star Wars, Technic, Friends or City themes. An example is the *LEGO set no. 66427-1 City Police Helicopter 4 in 1 Superpack*. This combines *LEGO sets no. 4436-1, LEGO set no. 4437-1, LEGO set no. 4439-1* and *LEGO set no. 4441-1* in one set bundle.

In addition to LEGO sets, there are other LEGO products that are included in the statistical investigation. In contrast to the statistical investigation of LEGO sets, the evaluation of these LEGO products is less detailed. The reasons for any changes in value are more difficult to determine for these LEGO products. Hard and soft factors are often not applicable here. This means that many factors cannot be included in the analysis.

The majority of the presented hard and soft factors are intended for LEGO sets. The additional consideration of other LEGO products is due to the idea of getting a feeling for whether other items of The LEGO Group may also be suitable as an investment.

### Books

This includes official books or books from other publishers that are published under license from The LEGO Group. Books include the history of the LEGO brick or The LEGO Group, ideas for buildings, inventions or games. LEGO books can be found on many shelves and are occasionally collected by people.

### Gears

These include products such as wristwatches, alarm clocks, bracelets, posters, magnets, jewelery, bags, backpacks, clothing, board games, writing utensils, mobile phone cases, key chains and many more. LEGO keychains have become extremely popular and are available in numerous variations. Often it is a minifigure, a single brick or occasionally a miniature set, which is provided by a sturdy metal chain with a key ring at the end. This allows you to attach the keychain to a keyring or backpack. The minifigure should not be removed from the metal chain. As a rule, the size of the LEGO figure is between 7 and 15 cm. Due to their size, LEGO keychains are only suitable for children over 3 years of age, and some variants are even recommended for children over 6 years of age. Movable arms, legs and head allow minifigures to perform poses. There are also special keychains with individual functions such as glowing feet with LED lights (up to 15 minutes, according to The LEGO Group).

These include products such as wristwatches, alarm clocks, bracelets, posters, magnets, jewelery, bags, backpacks, clothing, board games, writing utensils, mobile phone cases, key chains and many more. LEGO keychains have become extremely popular and are available in numerous variations. Often it is a minifigure, a single brick or occasionally a miniature set, which is provided by a sturdy metal chain with a key ring at the end. This allows you to attach the keychain to a keyring or backpack. The minifigure should not be removed from the metal chain. As a rule, the size of the LEGO figure is between 7 and 15 cm. Due to their size, LEGO keychains are only suitable for children over 3 years of age, and some variants are even recommended for children over 6 years of age. Movable arms, legs and head allow minifigures to perform poses. There are also special keychains with individual functions such as glowing feet with LED lights (up to 15 minutes, according to The LEGO Group).

The group of gears also includes the following LEGO products, which, however, are not included in the study:

- **Video-Games**
  This includes computer and console games (e.g., for Sony Playstation, Xbox, Wii, etc.). These types of games are not included in the study. An exception is the LEGO theme LEGO Dimensions. These include occasional minifigures and individual parts, some of which are exclusive to *LEGO Dimensions* sets.

- **Sets from other Manufacturers**
  In 2019, The LEGO Group acquired the Brick and Parts marketplace Bricklink. Even before the merger and even today, there are various LEGO sets that could only be purchased through the Bricklink platform. These include the *Bricklink AFOL Designer Program or Bricklink Designer Program*.

**Game and Trading Cards, Magazines, etc.**

There are also various collectible and playing cards and magazines, for example, of the Ninjago theme.

Finally, all these items represent the entire LEGO product range.

### 4.5.1  Preparation of the Data Records

Due to the extraordinary size of the data record and the manual extraction, it is not possible to determine an exact point in time for the overall actuality of the data record. Rather, the manual extraction of data points on Bricklink and Brickset is the result of many months.[1] It can be assumed that within the period of the data search, occasional changes of already recorded data have taken place (e.g., sales of the last 6 months or the Part-Out-Value). Furthermore, each data point was only extracted once (December 31, 2020). This means that there is no information about the Part-Out-Value of a LEGO set as of December 31, 2019 or price information about sales of the last 6 months of 2013. It is obvious that this information (data points at different times) has an incredible added value for a statistical investigation. Conversely, this means that there is no possibility to examine value developments within different time intervals. A significant advantage would be that you can determine, for example, after how much time the highest sales price would have been achieved. Accordingly, any knowledge gained about a LEGO product always represents exactly the period between release and EOL. Alternatively, it is possible to observe the performance of a LEGO product at different time intervals (e.g., every 6 or 12 months). This seems particularly useful when holding LEGO products as an investment over the long term. By constantly updating the data points, it is possible to identify and evaluate fluctuations. Nevertheless, updating the data is extremely time-consuming.

After the basics were defined, the data points had to be filtered. Depending on the specific questions, an individual determination of the corresponding data set was made. For example, there is a certain number of LEGO sets for certain years, although there is less information about another factor to be evaluated (hard or soft). Consequently, the evaluation is based on the smaller number of available information of the two (hard or soft) factors.

---

[1] As of November 18, 2020, automated retrieval of all data at an arbitrarily determined point in time is not possible.

Thus, it is not necessary to delete incomplete data. On the contrary, incomplete data sets also add value to the overall statistical investigation.

As of December 31, 2020, the compiled data set consists of a total of 339,411 raw data. The Microsoft Excel table created for this purpose comprises a total of 46 columns (data points or hard and soft factors) and 16,891 rows (LEGO products such as sets, books and other items). This corresponds to a maximum of 776,986 possible data points in total. As mentioned earlier, the majority of the hard and soft factors do not apply to LEGO Books and LEGO Other Items. Subtracting these data records results in a maximum total of 710,157 data points. The ratio of existing raw data to maximum possible data points provides information about availability. As a result, a good half or 48 percent of the data points are available between 1961 and 2020. This means that the information on the individual LEGO products varies in its completion degree. The main reason for this is that data points in the past were not recorded in anywhere near the level of detail we are familiar with today.

Furthermore, there is an impact on the statistical collection of those LEGO products that were released in the last quarter of 2020 and associated data points are still incomplete. Bricklink and Brickset also need a certain amount of time after the release of new LEGO products until the data for a LEGO product is completely recorded on their own platforms. The training and maintenance take a lot of time. Accordingly, data records of new LEGO products in particular are only fully available with a time delay. However, the impact on the results of the overall statistics is considered to be extremely minor.

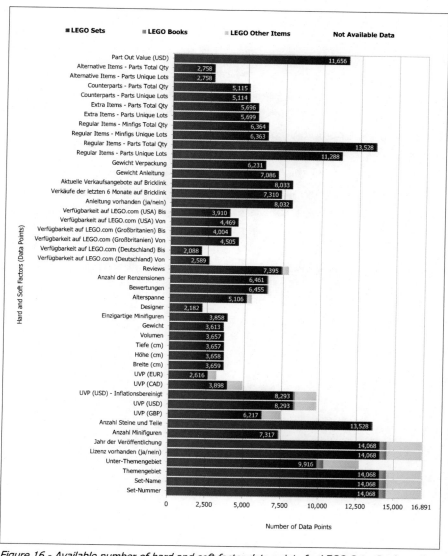

Figure 16 - Available number of hard and soft factor data points for LEGO Sets, Books and Gears

213

It is especially conspicuous that large parts of the data are not available. Especially older LEGO products are hardly or not at all documented. Therefore, the following is an overview of the availability of the data of LEGO sets, LEGO books and LEGO gears. Overall, 63 percent of the data points come from Brickset and 37 percent from Bricklink.

In Figure 16, we see the summary graph of the available and unavailable data records respectively hard and soft factors for LEGO sets, books and gears. The maximum value of the x-axis is 16,891 and represents the sum of LEGO sets (14,068 items), books (475 items) and gears (2,348 items). These are the basis of this statistical survey. LEGO sets represent the bulk of the statistical survey, accounting for 83 percent. The remaining 17 percent are divided between books (3 percent) and gears (14 percent). The survey and analysis is based on a total of 710,157 data points, of which only 339,411 are available. Of these 315,083 data points or 93 percent are attributable to LEGO sets. 3,840 data points or 1 percent are books and 20,848 data points or 6 percent are gears.

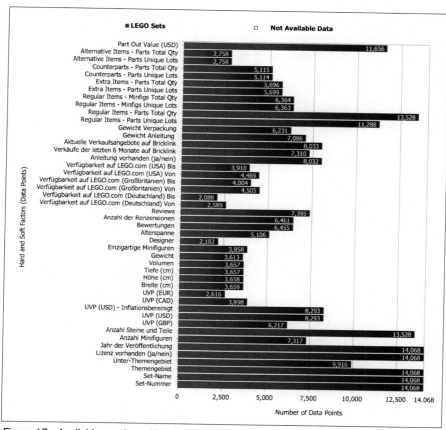

Figure 17 - Available number of hard and soft factor data points for LEGO sets

Due to the important role of LEGO sets in this statistical investigation, the available data points of LEGO sets will be discussed in more detail (Figure 17). A total of 315,083 of 647,128 data points are available for LEGO sets. This corresponds to 49 percent. It should be added here that only 39 percent of the data points are available for LEGO books and gears. This can already be seen impressively in Figure 16. Only hard and soft factors such as the MSRP, set number, set name, theme and year of publication are useful here. This essentially underscores that the product categories LEGO books and

215

LEGO gears play a subordinate role in the LEGO universe. The availability of data points for LEGO sets is much more convincing. After all, the most important information is available for this, so that substantiated statements can be made about every hard and soft factor.

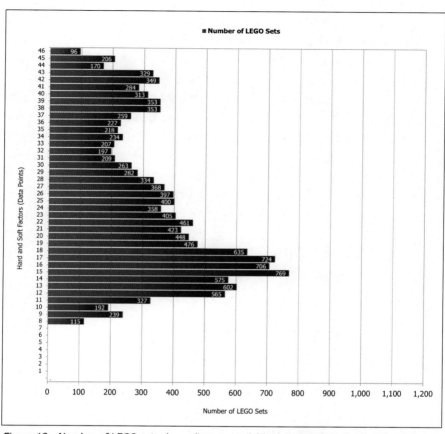

*Figure 18 - Number of LEGO sets depending on available data points for hard and soft factors*

217

Figure 18 gives a very good overview of the number of LEGO sets depending on the available data points. On average, 24 of the total 46 data points are available per LEGO set. A complete data record is available for only 96 of 14,068 LEGO sets. This corresponds to less than 1 percent of all LEGO sets.

Furthermore, a look will be taken at the distribution of data points between the years 1961 and 2020. It has already been pointed out that particularly little information is available from LEGO sets from the early years. This is not least due to the fact that the LEGO platforms we are familiar with, such as Brickset or Bricklink, are only a few years old. Brickset was founded in 1997 and Bricklink in 2000. Until then, there were no independent documentation of data records for LEGO products. Consequently, an extraordinary amount of research was done by Brickset and Bricklink. We can see how the available data points are generally distributed among the individual years between 1961 and 2020 in Figure 19.

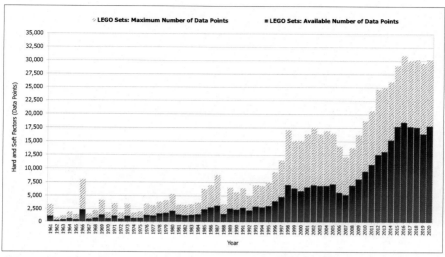

*Figure 19 - Available number of hard and soft factor data points for LEGO sets between 1961 and 2020*

Since 1961, the number of available data points has been steadily increasing. It is also clear that as time goes on, there are more and more data points available per year. This is also logical, because every year numerous new LEGO sets are released. Apparently, the data points available for this behave synchronously. This means that the higher number of LEGO sets successively increases the available data of LEGO sets in a year increases. Conversely, the ratio between available and maximum data points has increased in the past years.

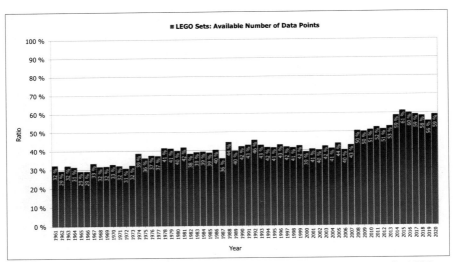

*Figure 20 - Ratio (percentage) of available and maximum number of data points for LEGO sets between 1961 and 2020*

Figure 20 confirms what was already suspected. The jump in recorded data points is especially noticeable in the years 2006 to 2008. From these years on, significantly more data points were documented on Bricklink and Brickset. Since 2006, on average more than 10 percent more data points are available than in the years or decades before.

Again, the question arises as to what data is still missing here, since only 60 to 65 percent of the data has been available on average since 2007. Above all, the MSRP in the USA, Canada, Great Britain and Europe are increasingly not documented. Also, the availability of LEGO sets in the official LEGO online store and retail store for Germany, Great Britain and USA is hardly documented.

It is important to know that The LEGO Group never commits to an exact date in this regard. Rather, LEGO products are removed from the product range without prior notice - from one day to the next. Thus, platforms such as Bricklink or Brickset can only estimate the data points for the appearance and discontinuation, or may have to leave them out completely.

It can be assumed that more and more data points will be available in the future. With more data points, the reasons for the value developments of LEGO products can be determined more easily and even more precisely.

## 4.5.2 Years

Each LEGO product is assigned to a specific date. As a rule, this is the year in which the LEGO product was released. Basically, a year in the LEGO universe begins on January 1 and ends on December 31. LEGO products are released all over the year. In each of these years, completely different information or data points are available. Consequently, these have an impact on the statistical survey and must be taken into account accordingly. Each year, there are a variety of different LEGO products. For example, these may still be available from previous years. Or LEGO products may be new in a given year. Both circumstances add up to the total number of LEGO products available in a calendar year. Of course, the years also differ in terms of their number of individual bricks, parts as well as minifigures. The purpose is to gain as much knowledge as possible from this. At the same time, we want to avoid anticipating topics that will be explored in much greater depth later on.

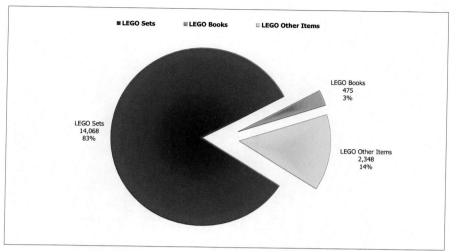

*Figure 21 - Share of LEGO sets, books and gears in the statistical survey*

The first step is to get an overview of how LEGO products are spread in general. The analysis includes a total of 16,891 LEGO products. Of these, 475 are LEGO books. Gears account for 2,348 items. LEGO sets represent the vast majority with 14,068 items. There is no doubt that LEGO sets are much more popular among customers than gears or books. Accordingly, The LEGO Group focuses on this product category. This can be seen particularly impressively in the following Figure 22.

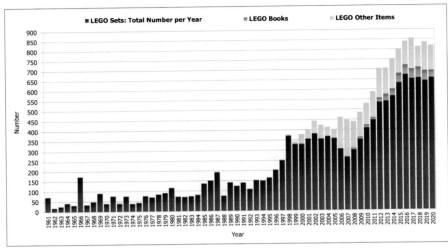

*Figure 22 - Number of LEGO sets, books and gears between 1961 and 2020*

The histogram in Figure 22 provides an overview of the number of LEGO sets, books and gears published annually between 1961 and 2020. Each bar represents the number of LEGO sets, books and gears published in a given year. It must be added that these are exclusively products that were newly released in one year. For example, if a LEGO set was released in the year 2000 and was regularly available until the year 2004, this LEGO set is only considered for the year 2000.

The amount of LEGO sets has been growing rapidly especially in the past 25 years. While the number of published LEGO sets has increased almost every year, there is a noticeable decline between 2004 and 2009. During this period, The LEGO Group had a particularly hard time, with the company on the verge of bankruptcy. The LEGO Group had completely bogged down with computer games, the Legoland theme parks, and children's fashion, with no real expertise in any of these areas. Only a massive restructuring program was able to bring the company back into profit.

Between 1960 and 1969, an average of only 59 LEGO sets were released per year. Between 1970 and 1979, there was already a slight growth with an average of 63 LEGO sets per year. Growth continued unabated between 1980 and 1989, with an average of 111 LEGO sets per year being released during this period. This is nearly twice as much as in the previous decade. In the following decade from 1990 to 2000, the average number of LEGO sets per year nearly doubled to 199 pieces. LEGO sets became especially popular in the 1990s, and The LEGO Group continued to expand its range of LEGO sets.

In the period between 2000 and 2009, the average number of LEGO sets per year grew at a slightly slower pace to 338, not quite doubling. In the current decade between 2010 and 2019, The LEGO Group has again accelerated growth significantly. In this decade, we are averaging 576 LEGO sets per year. This is almost a ninefold increase compared to the first decade between 1961 and 1969.

The LEGO Group is setting a very clear trend here, and we can expect to see more and more LEGO sets in the coming years. This is supported by the fact that we have been offering more than 600 LEGO sets per year since 2015. As long as demand for the LEGO sets on offer does not collapse on the customer side, there will be no reason for The LEGO Group to release fewer new LEGO sets.

Compared to LEGO sets, LEGO books have only played a genuine part in the product portfolio since 2000. In the decades before, there was an average of less than 1 book per year. It wasn't until the years between 2000 and 2009 that The LEGO Group significantly increased the offering to an average of 3.5 books per year. And in the current decade between 2010 and 2019, The LEGO Group has increased growth more than ten times to 37 books per year. An unimaginable development, though LEGO books only appear in the shadow of the success of LEGO sets.

The last category in The LEGO Group's product range is the so-called LEGO gears. Until 1999, there was less than an average of one item per year in the category. Here, too, The LEGO Group has significantly adjusted the offer and released many new items. Between the year 2000 and 2009, the range was noticeably expanded to an average of 89 items per year. To this end, the graph in Figure 22 suggests that in the current decade (2010 to 2019) there has been a slight increase to 130 LEGO Other items per year. Items in this category are nowhere near as long-lived in the market as LEGO sets. Rather, individual gears are replaced by updated versions without really being available in parallel for a long time.

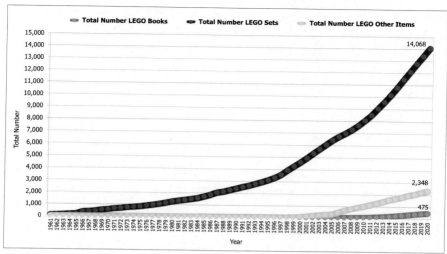

*Figure 23 - Total number of LEGO sets, books and gears between 1961 and 2020*

At this point, it is already obvious that The LEGO Group can, in principle, significantly increase the range of all product categories. However, the display and storage areas in The LEGO Group's stationary stores are limited in terms of space. The stationary stores only carry a fraction of the LEGO products that can alternatively be ordered in the online store. It therefore remains to be seen how The LEGO Group will position its offline and online offers in the future. The bulk of LEGO products will probably continue to be sold primarily through contractors such as Target, Amazon, Costco, Walmart, etc.

Both tendencies and the trend towards more products suggest the following: The LEGO Group is pursuing the goal of increasing overall sales by expanding its product range. This is a typical approach of large companies and corporations. Like most companies, The LEGO Group feels compelled to report certain growth each year. This is most evident when The LEGO Group proudly exceeds its own established growth projections each year. The impact is felt by buyers, collectors and investors. It is true that with the increasing number of new LEGO products, it seems almost impossible to buy all of them. As a result, LEGO investors in particular are increasingly having to decide which LEGO products they ultimately want to invest in.

At this stage of the investigation, it is not yet possible to identify the reasons why LEGO products rise or fall in value. In order to be able to consider this in the further course, it is first necessary to take a fundamental look at the availability of the MSRP's of LEGO products.

A popular phrase nowadays is: The Internet never forgets (and nothing). The meaning behind this is that content can no longer be removed from the Internet. Once posted, they stay there forever. With regard to LEGO products, however, it unfortunately had to be stated that this does not yet apply to the Internet before the year 2000. Prior to the year 2000, the infrastructure of the World-Wide-Web was still in its early stages. And so the MSRP of older LEGO sets is hardly documented or, in some cases, not publicly available at all. *And who remembers the prices on long-ago white or orange sticky labels on the packaging?* It is very unlikely that the MSRP's of older LEGO products will ever be available in the future.

The following Figure 24 confirms why the statistical investigation refers exclusively to USD. For 58 percent or 9,853 of the available 16,891 LEGO products, the MSRP's are available in USD. Nevertheless, the GBP comes on 44 percent or 7,503 data points for UVP's. For CAD only 29 percent or 4,922 data points are available. The least data points are available for the EUR (19 percent or 3,186 data points). This is certainly also due to the fact that the Euro was only introduced in 2002. Since then, 11,776 LEGO products have been published. If one puts these in relation to the existing data points, nevertheless only 27 per cent of the data points for UVP's in EUR are present. Also against the background that Brickset is an American provider, it can be assumed that the focus is rather on USD. Unfortunately, there are no comparable platforms in Europe. This would certainly also be appropriate to check the data points recorded by Brickset against.

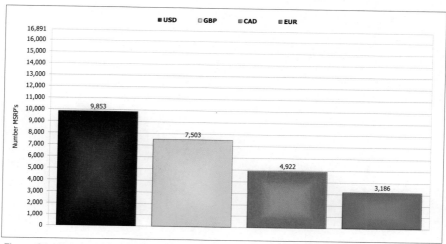

*Figure 24 - Number of available MSRP's in USD, GBP, CAD and EUR on Brickset*

In addition, there is another significant advantage of using the global currency, the U.S. dollar. This currency has existed since the 17th century. In comparison, Germany has already experienced several currency changes since the 17th century. If the EUR were used as the central basis for evaluation, all LEGO products would have to be converted before the introduction of the Euro (2002). Although the Brickset data platform was founded in 1997, Brickset does not document prices for LEGO sets in Deutsche Mark currency (DM). If this were the case and one were to base the study on Deutsche Mark prices, one would not only have to convert all foreign currencies (GBP, USD and CAD) into Euro, but also the Deutsche Mark itself. The constant conversion would undoubtedly lead to inaccuracies.

In total, the MSRP data points of 7,038 LEGO products are missing. Still, for many of these LEGO products, the MSRP in CAD, GBP or EUR is available. Nevertheless, it is not possible to convert this currency to USD that easily. We have already learned in Section 4.2 that The LEGO Group cannot easily determine its selling prices or MSRP in other countries and currencies by considering the currency difference to USD. Of the 9,853 price data points in USD shown in Figure 24, 8,293 data points are for LEGO Sets, 99 data points are for LEGO Books, and the remaining 1,461 data points are for LEGO Other Items. Conversely, this means the following for the represent- ativeness of the evaluation:

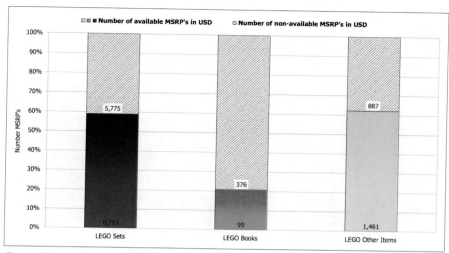

*Figure 25 - Number of available MSRP price data records for LEGO sets, books and gears in USD on Brickset*

For LEGO sets and gears, about 60 percent of the MSRP data records are available in USD on Brickset. For LEGO books, on the other hand, only 21 percent are available. This means that there are basically enough MSRP's data points in USD for a representative evaluation of LEGO sets and LEGO gears. On the other hand, it is difficult to make well-founded statements about LEGO books, since there are too few UVP price data points available.

This would mean that we would have to infer the total range (475 books or 100 percent) from only 21 percent of available price data points. Consequently, the evaluation would be distorted due to the limited data available. Accordingly, a distortion is indicated by the fact that a small number of data points can influence the evaluation in a particular direction (positively or negatively). The significance of the results would be unfavorably influenced. Now that the data on MSRP's are known, we will look at how their availability has developed since 1961.

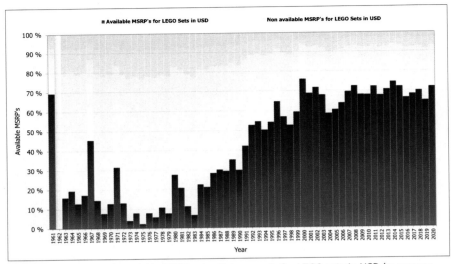

*Figure 26 - Number of available MSRP price data records for LEGO sets in USD by year on Brickset*

The availability of MSRP price data records for LEGO sets in USD has been less consistent in the past. Especially in the years between 1963 and 1990, only between 2 and 45 percent of MSRP price records in USD are documented. No data are available at all for 1962. Overall, there is an average availability of 59 percent between 1961 and 2020 for LEGO sets.

A clear improvement in the data can be seen from 1991 onwards. From 1992 to 2020, an average of 64 percent of the MSRP's in USD for LEGO sets are available. This has a particular impact on the evaluation, which becomes more accurate and thus more meaningful as a result of the improved data situation. This is particularly encouraging since 82 percent of the total 14,068 LEGO sets in the period were released between 1992 and 2020.

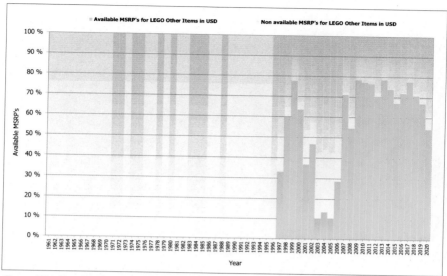

*Figure 27 - Number available MSRP price data records LEGO gears in USD by Year on Brickset*

Basically, the availability for the MSRP data records in USD for LEGO gears looks similarly good. Here, the Brickset platform benefits from the fact that the variety of offers for LEGO gears has only increased significantly since 1997. Almost 99 percent or 2,331 articles of the total of 2,348 LEGO other articles were published from 1997 onwards. Since Brickset only went online in 2000, a large part of the MSRP in USD can be taken into account. This is also clearly shown in Figure 27.

Excluding the early years up to and including 1996, the availability of MSRP price data records in USD for LEGO gears averages 63 percent.

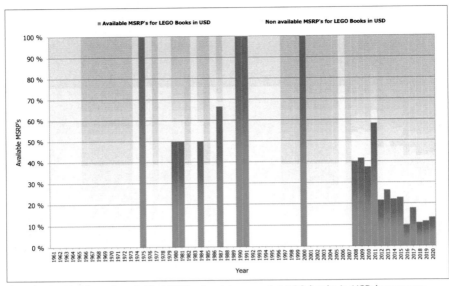

*Figure 28 - Number of available MSRP price data records LEGO books in USD by year on Brickset*

To complete the picture, the availability of the MSRP price data records in USD for LEGO books should also be listed. Figure 28 shows a much worse picture. The years between 2008 and 2020 have the highest number of LEGO books (433 LEGO books or 91 percent of the total 475 LEGO books). Nevertheless, only an average of 20 percent of the price records in USD is available for this period. This, of course, has an impact on the evaluation. Due to the significantly poorer data situation, I have therefore decided to exclude LEGO books and gears from further analysis. To this end, all data records relating to both product categories will no longer be taken into account. On the other hand, the presentation of the MSRP price data records for LEGO sets provides the basis for further analysis. It has already been pointed out that the number of LEGO sets has been steadily increasing for years. This growth should also be reflected in the total annual value of LEGO sets based on the MSRP.

234

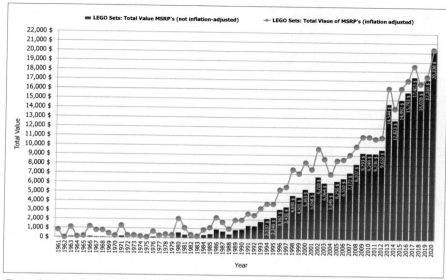

*Figure 29 - Total value of MSRP's for LEGO sets in USD by year*

Collecting LEGO sets has always been an expensive pleasure. Figure 29 makes it clear that this pleasure has become even more expensive in the recent years. In general, we try to capture trends with the help of trend curves. The development of the annual total values for LEGO sets makes this tool obsolete. The rapid growth based on cumulative MSRP's is obvious and fully coincides with the number of new LEGO sets released in a year. Based on MSRP's, over the past 60 years, the total value has increased a total of 35 times over the previous year. Conversely, an even higher total value of LEGO sets has been published almost every second year. In the past 30 years, it has been every 1.5 years. And in the past 10 years, the total value has been increased every year based on the cumulative MSRP's compared to the previous year. As of the current year 2020, the total value is at its peak with a total of USD 20,338. This is the amount you, as a LEGO investor, will have to spend to purchase all of the 2020 released LEGO sets. Since inflation cannot yet be taken into account for this year, this value also

235

corresponds to the total when inflation is taken into account. In 2000, or 20 years ago, the total of all LEGO sets based on MSRP's was only USD 5,363. This represents a 280 percent growth in 20 years. It also seems certain at present that this will continue unstoppably. In this context, it is worth taking a look at the gross sales of The LEGO Group.

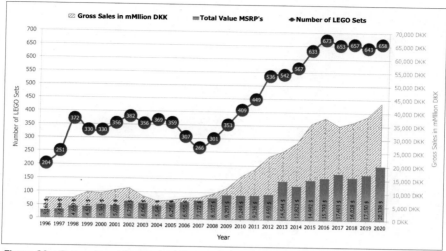

*Figure 30 - Comparison of annual total value (MSRP), total number for LEGO sets in USD and The LEGO Group sales by year.*

Figure 30 illustrates the total number of LEGO sets, their total value based on MSRP's, and the gross sales of The LEGO Group between the years 1996 and 2020. In the 1990s and around the turn of 2000, The LEGO Group had a particularly hard time. Sales losses became widespread. The reason was that many children were switching to videogames and electronic toys. Today, the trend seems to be slowing down and construction toys are a welcome change in the all-too-digital environment.

In addition, The LEGO Group has ramped up an incredibly successful marketing strategy that helps keep the company in people's minds. There is marketing in stores, video games, theme parks and LEGO movies. In addition, The LEGO Group has acquired various licensing agreements that ensure LEGO individual bricks and pieces are becoming more sought after in the world of construction toys. The comparison confirms that there is a correlation between annual sales, number of LEGO sets as their total value. In the long-term view, all three values show a steady growth. Particularly striking is the steep increase from the year 2007, which finds its peak in the current year 2020. The gross sales in million DKK (gray area) move mostly parallel to the total number of LEGO sets (blue line). Undeniably, LEGO sets are the driving force of the company. The average growth between 1996 and 2020 is as follows:

- Gross sales in DKK million compared to previous year:  8 Percent
- Total quantity of LEGO sets to previous year:  6 Percent
- Total value of MSRP's compared to previous year:  9 Percent

Now we know the dependencies among each other. Nevertheless, we want to take a more detailed look at LEGO sets. The following Figure 31 shows the annual development for the total number of LEGO sets compared to the previous year as well as the total value based on the MSRP.

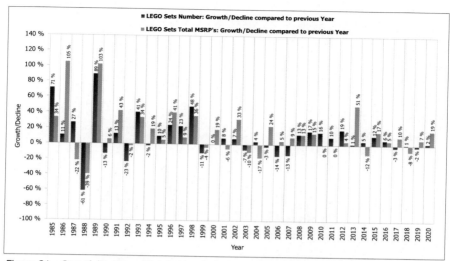

*Figure 31 - Growth/Decline of total value (MSRP) and total number of LEGO sets in USD by year.*

Figure 31 shows how The LEGO Group changes the total range of LEGO sets each year. The total supply refers to all LEGO sets that were released in that year. Between the years 1985 and 2020, there is an average increase in LEGO sets of 17 percent. Conversely, there are 17 percent newer LEGO sets every year compared to the previous year.

The average growth for the underlying total value based on MSRP's is 50 percent. This means that the sum of all MSRP's for LEGO sets is growing faster than the total supply of LEGO sets. This can have very different reasons. For example, we can conclude that the average MSRP per LEGO set is gradually increasing. From 1961 to 2020, the total supply of LEGO sets has increased by a factor of two hundred. If the growth of 17 percent on average continues unhindered, more than 1,000 LEGO sets would be released in a calendar year for the first time in 2023.

We already know that the total value of all annual MSRP's increases faster than the number of new LEGO sets in a year. Consequently, we want to see what relationship can be derived from both quantities.

239

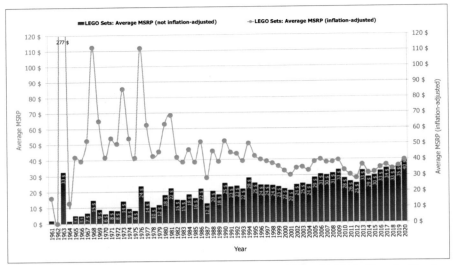

*Figure 32 - Average MSRP of LEGO sets in USD between 1961 and 2020 (with and without inflation adjustment)*

Taking inflation into account, between the years 1965 and 2020, the average MSRP for LEGO sets more than doubled from USD 16 to USD 40. Over the same period, the total annual supply of LEGO sets has increased ninefold. For example, 72 LEGO sets from 1965 are facing a total of 658 LEGO sets in 2020. This is a clear indication that the supply of LEGO sets is increasing at a much faster rate than the average underlying MSRP of LEGO sets. Conversely, there are more and more inexpensive LEGO sets. And yet the average MSRP, taking inflation into account, is increasing over the entire period.

There are various reasons why The LEGO Group increases prices over the years. For example, prices can increase due to more, larger and printed bricks and parts. LEGO minifigures are becoming more complex to design and then print. In addition, there are operating costs, costs for licensing agreements and development costs. Undoubtedly, all this has an impact on why LEGO sets increase in price. The previous explanations about the MSRP form the basis for the following explanations about the determination of the

240

value development of LEGO sets in the overall period between 1961 and 2020. The value development of LEGO sets was determined as of the reporting date of December 31, 2020. In total, there may be up to three different price dates for LEGO sets as of the reporting date of December 31, 2020.

- Last 6 Month 6 Sales in USD on Bricklink
- Current Items for Sale in USD on Bricklink
- Part-Out-Value in USD on Bricklink

For this purpose, we want to evaluate the inflation-adjusted value developments for LEGO sets between 1961 and 2020 below.

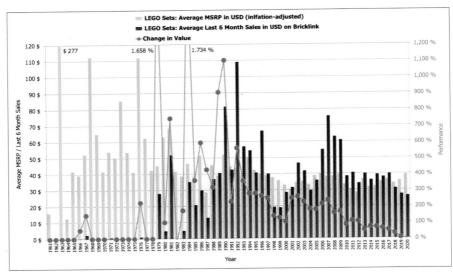

*Figure 33 - Inflation-adjusted performance by sales of the last 6 months in USD on Bricklink for LEGO sets between 1961 and 2020*

In Figure 33, we see value performance based on the last 6 months of sales in USD on Bricklink for LEGO sets between 1961 and 2020. The last 6 months represent the period between July 01, 2020 and December 31, 2020. In addition, the chart shows the inflation-adjusted MSRP as well as the resulting value performance. The majority of the years between 1961 and 1978 (1966, 1967, 1971 and 1976 are excluded) cannot be included due to incomplete data records. However, it can be stated overall that the performance of the sales of the last 6 months in USD on Bricklink for LEGO sets between 1961 and 2020 is extraordinarily different. The total return as of December 31, 2020 varies between -25 and +1,734 percent. Looking at the entire period, it seems that the most successful years of LEGO investment are behind us.

It is also very apparent that with the introduction of the minifigure in 1978, the returns of LEGO sets really exploded in the following years. LEGO

242

sets from 1979 to 1990 have traded on Bricklink with an average appreciation of 675 percent based on sales in USD over the last 6 months. For these years we are talking about ownership periods between 31 and 42 years. LEGO sets from that time are hardly comparable to what we know today. For example, at that time there were only very simply designed minifigures with little to no accessories. LEGO sets were also very simply constructed and had less detail. This was not least due to the fact that only a few different LEGO bricks and parts existed.

Nowadays, there are hardly any LEGO sets from this long-gone era left in unopened condition. And if you do find some on the secondary market, the prices are high. But not everyone knows what to do with these LEGO sets. Nowadays, the main target group is mainly nostalgics, enthusiasts and collectors. LEGO sets from 1979 (1,658 %), 1984 (1,734 %) and 1990 (1,102 %) achieved the greatest increases in value.

You can already guess: It was the beginning of the first minifigures as well as many iconic LEGO sets (e.g., *LEGO set no. 6399-1 Airport Shuttle*). It is also the decades from which much of today's AFOL generation comes. They associate very special memories and emotions with the LEGO sets of that time, which AFOLs are happy to spend a fortune on today (e.g., LEGO set no. 6980-1 Galaxy Commander, market price of 2,500 Euro as of January 18, 2021).

In 1984, sales of the last 6 months in USD on Bricklink for LEGO sets reach their peak. In the following years up to and including 2020, the increases in value are significantly lower. The average increase in value is only 258 percent for LEGO sets sold between 1991 and 2000, and in the later years between 2001 and 2020, the average increase in value is only 127 percent. This is despite the fact that LEGO sets have been subject to significantly lower annual inflation over the past 20 years.

In principle, the high increases in value for LEGO sets between 1979 and 1990 are plausible. In the early years, no one seriously considered buying LEGO sets as an alternative investment or storing them (in large quantities and unopened). If LEGO sets from these years are still available today, they are probably unused or originally packed LEGO sets that have simply been forgotten and reappear years later. These LEGO sets are undoubtedly extremely rare. Accordingly, the demand is high among true collectors, enthusiasts and nostalgics.

The careful reader will have noticed that the performance graph in Figure 33 is extraordinarily similar to the inflation graph in Figure 8 (Section 4.2). This is due to the fact that the MSRP of each calendar year has the same base as a comparison - namely the year 2020. Taking inflation into account, it is calculated how much 1 USD from each calendar year is worth to the comparison year 2020. Accordingly, the entire graph of inflation is reflected imputatively in all graphs of value developments. Imputed in the sense that it is the one that cuts off the gains. In the following, we want to see how the *Current Sales Offers in USD on Bricklink for LEGO* sets are represented between 1961 and 2020 as of December 31, 2020.

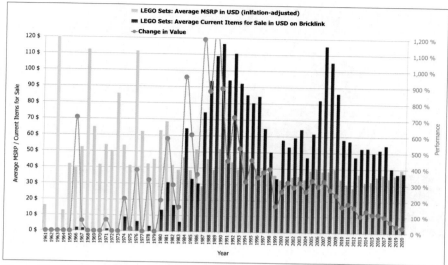

*Figure 34 - Inflation-adjusted performance by Current Sales Offers in USD on Bricklink for LEGO sets between 1961 and 2020.*

In Figure 34, the average *Current Sales Offers in USD on Bricklink* were selected as a price reference. Thus, all sales prices at which available LEGO sets can be purchased on Bricklink as of December 31, 2020 have been taken into account as a measure of value development. This additional information is very helpful because it shows how LEGO sets have developed in value between Sales of the *Last 6 Months in USD on Bricklink* and *Current Sales Offers in USD on Bricklink*.

A direct comparison of the two Figures 33 and 34 does not reveal any major differences at first. The underlying bar chart for LEGO Sets: Average MSRP in USD (adjusted for inflation) is identical in both Figures. Only the price information has changed, which successively leads to different value developments. For a better comparison, the same periods are considered as before.

For LEGO sets between the years 1979 and 1990, the average return is 655 percent. This is slightly less than the *Sales of the Last 6 Months in USD on Bricklink* (675 %). The differences become clearer when looking at the years between 1991 and 2000, where the average increase in value is 400 percent, which in the end is 142 percent more than the *Sales of the Last 6 Months in USD on Bricklink* (258 %). LEGO sets from the years 2001 to 2020 were also able to accelerate their value growth and achieved an average increase in value of 193 percent. That's again an average 66 percent increase over the Last 6 Months of Sales in USD on Bricklink (127 %). In conclusion, LEGO sets have again increased in value on average and this in a period of only 6 months.

In fact, at this point in time, no generally proven cause can be determined as to why LEGO sets have once again risen sharply, especially during this period. Only so much on this, of course, it may be related to the Corona pandemic and the generally increased demand for toys. The LEGO Group also set a new record for sales in the 2020 consolidated financial statements. A correlation to the secondary toy market is certainly very likely.

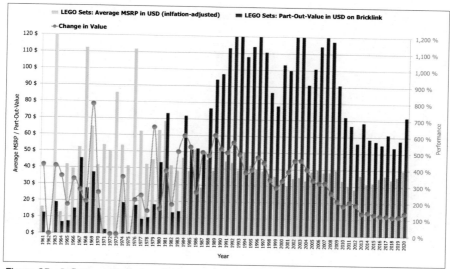

*Figure 35 - Inflation-adjusted performance of Part-Out-Value in USD on Bricklink for LEGO sets between 1961 and 2020*

Finally, we will take a look at the last price information: the part-out value. For LEGO sets from 1979 and 1990, the average value increased by 447 percent, which is slightly lower than the previous price information. This is certainly not surprising. The majority of these are very simple individual bricks and parts, which are still used by The LEGO Group today. This increase in value also remains almost constant between 1991 and 2000 at 419 percent. Similar to the price information before, the average increase of the Part-Out-Value in USD on Bricklink for LEGO sets decreases in the last 20 years. However, the increase in value still averages 237 percent between 2001 and 2020, which is even higher than the previous price information. As a result, current LEGO bricks and pieces in particular are driving value growth even more significantly. It is in the nature of LEGO sets that buying a complete LEGO set is cheaper than buying individual bricks and parts. Therefore, the individual sale of bricks and parts is sometimes the most lucrative.

The recent decline of value of the majority of LEGO sets has made me examine to what extent the value developments are related to the number of LEGO sets sold in a year. For this purpose, I use the already known information from Figure 22 as well as the arithmetic result of the three-price information (*Sales of the Last 6 Months in USD on Bricklink, Current Sales Offers in USD on Bricklink as well as Part-Out-Value in USD on Bricklink*). In the further course of the evaluation, the average performance always refers to the arithmetic mean of the three-price information.

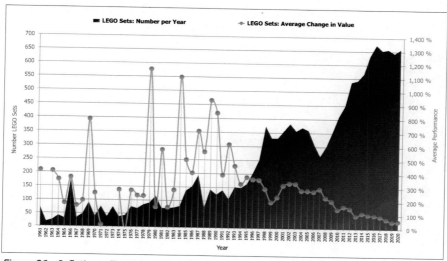

*Figure 36 - Inflation-adjusted average performance for LEGO sets between 1961 and 2020*

By comparing the figures, it becomes clear that the number of LEGO sets is inversely proportional to the average increase in value. Thereby, it can be stated that the increase in value in the recent past has been lower and lower. At the same time, the number of new LEGO sets continues to rise. On closer investigation, this seems quite logical. As the production and availability of a collectible increases, its exclusivity status decreases. Strictly speaking, LEGO products are not (exclusively) collectibles. With the continuous increase in the supply of new LEGO sets, it may be a conscious move by The LEGO Group to reduce the increasing speculation on LEGO products. This at least would explain why the company has been literally flooding the market with new LEGO sets and themes in recent years. It is also clear from Figure 36 that currently the return on LEGO sets is particularly low. LEGO sets from the past 10 years are particularly affected by this, although it is not possible to say whether this will continue in the future. If LEGO products are compared with other capital investments, they still show impressive increases in value that are often unrivaled.

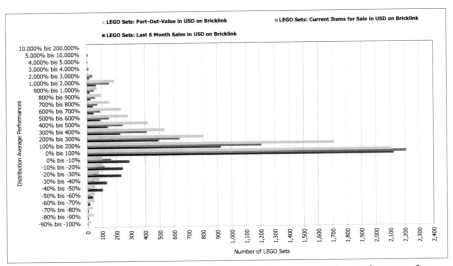

*Figure 37 - Statistical breakdown of the inflation-adjusted average Value performance for LEGO sets between 1961 and 2020*

The previous figures do not show how many LEGO sets have increased or decreased in value. Figure 37 illustrates how this breakdown is presented. For a better overview, the sets have been divided into different groups. Each group defines a range for the amount of value development (positive as well as negative) in percent. It can be seen that LEGO sets are surprisingly likely to increase in value. The chance of acquiring a LEGO set that increases in value reaches an impressive 88 percent. Without a doubt, this is a particularly high hit rate, which is rarely found in other capital investments. If only LEGO sets that have increased in value are taken into account, 56 percent or every second LEGO set achieves an increase in value of between 0 and 200 percent. In turn, 31 percent or every third LEGO set even achieved increases in value beyond 200 percent.

Only 12 percent of the evaluated LEGO sets lost value in the period between 1961 and 2020 and fell below the inflation-adjusted MSRP. Anticipating this, LEGO sets with negative returns have fewer than 1,000 individual bricks or parts and are represented over the entire period from 1961 to

2020. On average, 8 percent of the LEGO sets evaluated lost between 0 and 30 percent. Two other aspects are especially remarkable here. Every second LEGO set that experiences a loss in value has no minifigures. In addition, 85 percent of LEGO sets with negative returns have no licensing agreement.

### 4.5.3 Individual Bricks and Parts

The studded LEGO brick is the characteristic feature of the LEGO brand. It is one of the most famous products in the world and will be given full attention in this chapter. The number of individual bricks and parts of a LEGO set provides information about how much time it can take to assemble or how difficult it is to build. In the following, we will look at the importance of LEGO bricks and parts in the development of the value of LEGO sets.

The so-called *Price-per-Brick* ratio is of central importance. The meaning of the *Price-per-Brick* ratio can be read in chapter 4.4.17. It is important to understand that the *Price-per-Brick* ratio refers exclusively to *Regular Items* in a LEGO set. This means that no further subdivision into *Extra Bricks and Parts, Counterparts* and *Alternative Bricks and Parts* is possible. The reason for this is that only one MSRP is assigned to each LEGO set. In order to determine the *Price-per-Brick* ratio for the categories *Extra Bricks and Parts, Counterparts* and *Alternative Bricks and Parts*, it becomes necessary to know the share of the respective categories in the MSRP.

The same applies to *Sales of the Last 6 Months in USD on Bricklink, Current Sales Offers in USD on Bricklink* and *Part-Out-Value in USD on Bricklink*. Also, for these it cannot be determined what share the individual bricks and parts categories have on the respective price information and consequently what their performance is. Nevertheless, the categories *Extra Bricks and Parts, Counterparts* and *Alternative Bricks and Parts* are included in the evaluation to show possible influences on the performance of the LEGO sets.

This statistical survey is based on a total of 14,068 LEGO sets. It has already been pointed out that not all price information in the form of the *MSRP, Sales of the Last 6 Months in USD on Bricklink, Current Sales Offers in USD on Bricklink* and *Part-Out-Value in USD on Bricklink* as well as the number of *Extra Bricks and Parts, Counterparts* and *Alternative Bricks and Parts* are available for all these LEGO sets. In fact, the data is incomplete in different ways, as for example for a LEGO set only the number of different individual bricks and parts categories is available. Again, for other LEGO sets

252

no MSRP's are available. Moreover, the data set of the three-price information is incomplete. Especially old LEGO sets are no longer available in unopened condition, which is why no current purchase or sales prices are available for them. Therefore, we will first take a look at the available data points.

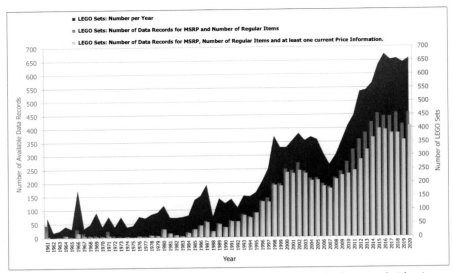

*Figure 38 - Availability of data records for MSRP's, number of Regular Items and at least one price information for LEGO sets between 1961 and 2020.*

The blue graph shows the total number of LEGO sets for one year. The red graph represents the number of LEGO sets for which the MSRP and the number of bricks and parts are available. The yellow graph has a further restriction, where in addition (to the information in the red graph) at least one price information must be available. A special focus is on the yellow graph, which specifies the number of LEGO sets that can be used for the evaluation. It can be seen that in the years 1961 up to and including 1990 there are particularly few data sets available. In this period, only an average of 12 percent data points (yellow graph) is available. Even ignoring the fact that at least one price information must also be available, only 19 percent of the data points are available (red graph). Of course, this has an impact on the subsequent evaluation, where certain gaps cannot be avoided.

The data availability from 1991 onwards looks much brighter. For the period from 1991 to 2020, information is available for 59 percent of LEGO sets, which makes the evaluation much more accurate. For some time now,

The LEGO Group has had to face the accusation that the total number for individual bricks and parts is artificially increased. Customers criticize that in many places fewer but larger or longer bricks or plates would make more sense. Rather, it appears that the number of individual bricks and parts is a powerful selling point. Sometimes this in turn leads to drastic increases in the number of individual bricks and parts in LEGO sets.

There is no doubt that the average number of *Regular Items* in LEGO sets has increased significantly in recent years (Figure 39, red graph). In the period from 1961 to 2002, LEGO sets consist of an average of 113 *Regular Items*. Starting in 2003 up to and including 2020, there are already 242 *Regular Items* in LEGO sets. This corresponds to a growth of over 110 percent. Especially since 2012, a strong increase can be seen, with the average number of *Regular Items* growing by 5 percent per year. An interesting coincidence is that the growth in new LEGO sets during this period is also 5 percent. In contrast, between 1961 and 2001, growth averaged 10 percent annually for new LEGO sets and 26 percent for *Regular Items*.

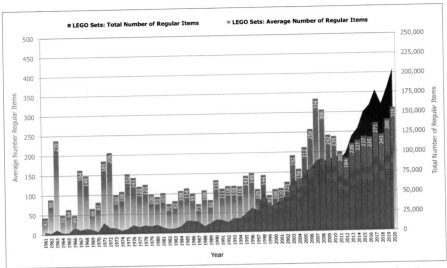

*Figure 39 - Development of the number of Regular Bricks and Parts for LEGO sets between 1961 and 2020*

For the first time since 2020, the total number of all *Regular Items* in LEGO sets is over 200,000. What the graph doesn't tell us is that in 2000, the largest *LEGO set, no. 3450-1 Statue of Liberty*, had a total of 2,882 Regular Items. In 2020, *LEGO set no. 10276-1 Colosseum* has 9,036 Regular Items. A remarkable increase of over 200 percent in 20 years. This impressive increase may be one of the reasons why, unlike in the past, LEGO sets are considered more expensive these days. But LEGO sets have not only become bigger, they have also become more complex. Also, because LEGO sets are becoming more and more detailed. For the first time since 2020, LEGO sets contain an average of more than 300 Regular items. The data confirms the impression of customers that The LEGO Group has noticeably increased the average number of Regular Items in a LEGO set in the recent past. This is not least due to larger *D2C* products. *D2C* or *Direct-to-Consumer* refers to the direct sale of products and services by the manufacturer.

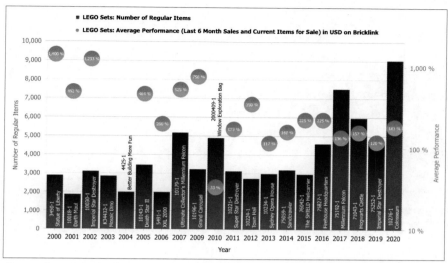

*Figure 40 - Biggest LEGO sets by number of Regular Bricks and Parts between 2000 and 2020*

Figure 40 shows the largest LEGO sets since the year 2000. It is obvious that since 2000, the trend has been towards larger and larger LEGO sets with an increasing number of Regular Items. At the same time, the performance is decreasing more and more. Large LEGO sets have not been exceptional for a long time. Moreover, there are now more and more people who can afford LEGO sets for USD 500 or more.

Because of their essential relevance in the LEGO universe, LEGO bricks and parts are considered by collectors and investors to be a crucial benchmark for the *price-performance ratios* of LEGO sets. We are referring to the average *Price-per-Brick*. Collectors and investors agree and like to consider the *Price-per-Brick ratio* when buying a LEGO set. Basically, the number of Regular Items in a LEGO set can vary significantly. Therefore, it is not possible to simply compare the MSRP of different LEGO sets to find out which LEGO set is the better deal. Nevertheless, for many years, LEGO enthusiasts have been comparing the prices (MSRP) of different LEGO sets to evaluate whether a particular LEGO set is even worth buying. Collectors, on the other hand, are less concerned about the price of a LEGO set being too high.

However, there are people who build LEGO sets and therefore look at how many and which individual bricks and parts they get for their money. Other buyers play with LEGO sets and look at how many features and what entertainment value they get for their money. Thus, it has become apparent in the LEGO universe that the *Price-per-Brick* has grown to be the most significant factor in evaluating the price-performance ratio of a LEGO set. Therefore, the *Price-per-Brick* ratio is given considerable importance these days.

But how exactly is the *Price-per-Brick* determined? Simply divide the cost (MSRP) of a LEGO set by the number of *Regular Items*. The result is an average *Price-per-Brick* of a LEGO set. For example, the *LEGO set no. 21052-1 Dubai* of the *Architecture* theme counts 740 *Regular Price-per-Brick*. The MSRP is USD 59.99. This results in a *Price-per-Brick* of USD 0.1234 per brick. For clear understanding, I would like to point out that the *Price-per-Brick ratio* refers to an average single brick or average part of the LEGO set under consideration. In this context average means that simplistically small bricks (e.g., 1 x 1 Plate), large bricks (e.g., 1 x 6 Brick), small parts (e.g., 4 x 4 Wedge Plate) as well as large parts (e.g., Tires) are identical in their meaning. No sizes of LEGO single bricks or parts are considered. Also, no different colors are considered or whether single bricks or parts are printed. This calculation also ignores the fact that LEGO sets sometimes come with no minifigures at all or with different numbers of minifigures.

This in turn means that with a lower *Price-per-Brick* ratio, customers get more bricks or parts for their money. At least this is the theory and view of the LEGO community from a strictly economic point of view.

*But what role does the Price-per-Brick ratio still play these days?* This question is hotly debated among LEGO enthusiasts. The LEGO Group has explicitly stated that the number of bricks and pieces in a LEGO set is not the only factor in determining the MSRP. The LEGO Group also takes into

account the number of new and different moldings that are required to produce a LEGO set and that have to be produced in advance. In addition,
potential brand licensing costs are factored in.

If, for example, you as a Bricklink seller want to sell the individual bricks
and parts of a LEGO set individually, you should always pay attention to the
*Price-per-Brick*. On the other hand, the question for collectors and investors
of sealed LEGO sets is not easy to answer. So far, there have only been
isolated and occasional studies of LEGO sets that suggest that the *Price-per-
Brick* ratio is not a good indicator of whether a LEGO set is cheap or expensive. In the past, for example, there have been LEGO sets with a comparatively high *Price-per-Brick* ratio that have nevertheless experienced an
above-average increase in value. For example, the *LEGO set no. 21003-1
Seattle Space Needle* from *LEGO Architecture*. This LEGO set dates back to
2009 and cost USD 19.99 at the time.[1] The LEGO set has 57 Regular Items
and no minifigures. This results in a *Price-per-Brick* ratio of USD 0.351.
Based on 48 LEGO sets in the *Architecture* theme series between the years
2008 and 2020, the average *Price-per-Brick* ratio is USD 0.13 per brick.
Within the *Architecture* theme series, the *Seattle Space Needle* is thus considered to be high-priced. Accordingly, the average *Price-per-Brick* of the
LEGO set is almost three times higher than the average Price-per-Brick of
the themed set. As of December 31, 2020, the retail prices of LEGO set no.
21003-1 Seattle Space Needle are as follows: 1.) *Sales in the Last 6 Months
in USD on Bricklink = USD 82*, 2.) *Current Sale Offers in USD on Bricklink =
USD 87* and 3.) *Part-Out-Value in USD on Bricklink = USD 59*. The averaged
selling price is USD 76. Despite the apparent high Price-per-Brick ratio, the
value of the LEGO set increased to 380 percent of the original MSRP. You
should always look critically at the *Price-per-Brick* ratio.

Due to its high significance in the LEGO universe and the fact that so far
only analyses of individual LEGO sets exist, the importance of the Price-per-
Brick ratio and its influence on the value performance of LEGO sets will be

---

[1] Taking inflation into account, this results in an MSRP of USD 23.7 in 2020.

fully examined and evaluated in the following. The focus here is on the extent to which the Price-per-Brick ratio provides information about increases and decreases in the value of LEGO sets. It is of decisive advantage that the relevant data records of thousands of different LEGO sets are available.

We will start with the *Price-per-Brick* ratios based on the MSRP's for LEGO sets in the period from 1961 to 2020. For this purpose, Figure 41 below shows the *Price-per-Brick* ratios based on the original MSRP's (blue graph) as well as the MSRP's after adjusting for inflation (red graph). In addition, the number of underlying data records (gray graph) is taken into account.

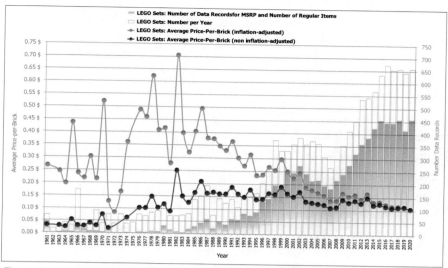

*Figure 41 - Average Price-per-Brick for LEGO sets between 1961 and 2020*

Over the total period between 1961 and 2020, an average *Price-per-Brick* in LEGO sets costs USD 0.27 per brick (adjusted for inflation) or USD 0.12 per brick (not adjusted for inflation). The evaluation is based on 59 percent or 8,250 of 14,068 LEGO sets. No data records are available for the years 1962, 1972, 1973 as well as 1975, therefore these years are not included. The data points for the remaining years are also not completely complete. Figure 41 shows that there are sometimes considerable fluctuations in the *Price-per-Brick ratio*. These are mainly related to the years between 1971 and 1982 and range from USD 0.08 to USD 0.71 per brick (adjusted for inflation) and from USD 0.02 to USD 0.25 per brick (not adjusted for infla-tion). One possible cause can be identified thanks to the underlying data records (gray graph). For this time period, there are particularly few data records, averaging 12 percent, which sometimes give a distorted picture. In addition, the fluctuations in the early years are mainly due to special indi-vidual parts such as motors. Given the comparatively low number of LEGO sets at the time, this had a direct impact on the *Price-per-Brick*.

There was also particularly high inflation in the period between 1961 and 1991. This averaged 5 percent, which explains the large gap between the two graphs (inflation-adjusted and non-inflation-adjusted). The compound interest effect associated with this intensifies (or exposes) the *Price-per-Brick* for this long period due to the depreciation of money. In the period from 1992 to 2020, inflation was comparatively low, averaging 2.2 percent.

In order to assess whether LEGO sets are really becoming more and more expensive, we will look at the blue graph (not adjusted for inflation). This represents the strategic approach of The LEGO Group. Overall, the development of the *Price-per-Brick ratio* looks very consistent over many years. Ignoring the period before 1991, for which less than 50 percent of the data records are available, the average *Price-per-Brick* (not adjusted for inflation) ranges between USD 0.11 and USD 0.31 per brick from 1992 to 2020, with the long-term trend even showing a falling *Price-per-Brick* (1992: USD 0.30 per brick and 2020: USD 0.11 per brick). This shows the efforts of The LEGO Group to keep the Price-per-Brick ratio in an appropriate range. Within this period, the *Price-per-Brick* fluctuates by an average of only 3 percent from year to year. The LEGO Group achieves this by optimizing its production and operating processes. This makes it possible to achieve the very competitive *Price-per-Brick* of an average of USD 0.11 per brick in 2020.

Certainly, for the majority of readers a surprising finding, everywhere you read that LEGO sets are getting more and more expensive. With reference to the *Price-per-Brick*, ignoring inflation, this cannot be confirmed. The average *Price-per-Brick*, which has been falling for years, is not least the result of the introduction of many large LEGO sets with many bricks and parts, which sometimes have a particularly favorable individual brick or part value. For example, LEGO sets of the Art theme have an average of 3,212 bricks and parts. The four LEGO sets available so far each have an MSRP of USD 119.99. As a result, the average *Price-per-Brick* is a very competitive of USD 0.037 per brick. Also, *LEGO set no. 10276-1 Colosseum, LEGO set no. 75979-1 Hedwig* or *LEGO set no. 92176 NASA Apollo Saturn V* have a very low average *Price-per-Brick* of USD 0.06 per brick.

It is primarily about the average MSRP of LEGO sets, which has been increasing for years, which gives customers and LEGO fans the impression that LEGO sets are becoming more and more expensive. This is a false impression.

For adults or AFOL's are especially interesting LEGO sets, which have a large number of individual bricks and parts or have licensing agreements (e.g., Star Wars).

The rising MSRP has another effect. Expensive LEGO sets level the willingness to buy even more expensive LEGO sets in the future. This can be seen in the example of LEGO's *Technic* theme. The following supercars were released between the years 2016 and 2022.

- **2016 - LEGO Set No. 42056-1 Porsche 911 GT3**
  MSRP of USD 299.99; 2,704 Bricks and Parts; 11 Cent per Brick

- **2018 - LEGO Set No. 42083-1 Bugatti Chiron**
  MSRP of USD 349.99; 3,599 Bricks and Parts; 10 Cent per Brick

- **2020 - LEGO Set No. 42115-1 Lamborghini Sián FKP 37**
  MSRP USD 379.99; 3,696 Bricks and Parts; 10 Cent per Brick
  June 2022: MSRP of USD 449.99 or 12 Cent per Brick

- **2022 - LEGO Set No. 42143-1 Ferrari Daytona SP3**
  MSRP USD 449.99; 3,778 Bricks and Parts; 12 Cent per Brick

The *Price-per-Brick* gives LEGO potential buyers a good feeling for the price tendency of the MSRP's. Therefore, the following can be said: In pure terms of *Price-per-Brick*, as well as taking into account currency depreciation or inflation, LEGO sets have become less expensive in the period from 1961 to 2020.

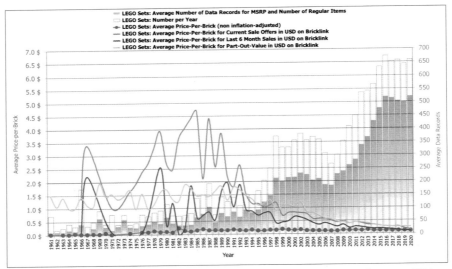

*Figure 42 - Value performance of the average Price-per-Brick for LEGO sets between 1961 and 2020*

After providing an overview of the average *Price-per-Brick* for each year between 1961 and 2020, we will now look at how they have developed. Figure 42 compares the average *Price-per-Brick* (not adjusted for inflation), the value development based on various current price information from Bricklink and the average availability of data records. It should be noted that the calculation of the various discounted price information is based on the inflation-adjusted MSRP. However, in Figure 42, the *Price-per-Brick* is presented based on the MSRP without inflation adjustment. The reason for this is that we first want to reflect the reality that LEGO customers and fans perceive. It must be assumed that LEGO customers and fans do not take into account the inflation of the past years when making their purchase decisions. In addition, we do not know today how inflation will develop in the future. It would therefore be difficult to draw conclusions about future scenarios from Figure 42.

Do not be confused by the multiple graphs in Figure 42. The red graph corresponds to the blue graph in Figure 41 and represents the average *Price-per-Brick* for the period from 1961 to 2020 (not inflation-adjusted). The blue graph shows the current performance of the average *Price-per-Brick* for Last 6 Month Sales in USD on Bricklink. The green graph shows the current performance of the average *Price-per-Brick* for Current Items for Sale in USD on Bricklink. Remaining is the yellow graph, which shows the performance of the average price-per-stone for Part-Out-Value in USD on Bricklink. The difference between the price information and the Price-per-Brick (not adjusted for inflation) reflects the performance.

The availability of data records corresponds to Figure 41. For the total period between 1961 and 2020, the average data records availability is 58 percent. This does not include the years 1961 to 1965, 1968 to 1970, 1972 to 1975, and 1977 and 1978. No data records are available for these 14 years. Based on the MSRP's including inflation, the following average value developments result for the total period of 60 years:

- Last 6 Month Sales on Bricklink:          146 Percent
- Current Items for Sale on Bricklink:      417 Percent
- Part-Out-Value on Bricklink:              323 Percent

The average rise in value based on the three types of price information is 333 percent. Solely the graph for Last 6 Month Sales in USD on Bricklink underperforms the average *Price-per-Brick* in eight different years. For this purpose, it was found that impairments were reached in 1966, 1971, 1976, 1980, 1982, 1983, and 2019 and 2020. This depreciation averages 42 percent. In the current year 2020, the impairment for Last 6 Month Sales in USD on Bricklink amounts to minor 9 percent. This is not unusual. LEGO sets fluctuate in value, especially in years when they are still regularly available online or at retail. In terms of average *Price-per-Brick*, the majority of LEGO sets have increased in value over the past 60 years.

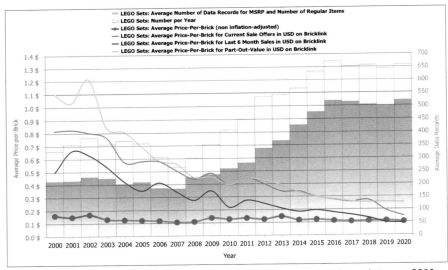

*Figure 43 - Value development of the average Price-per-Brick for LEGO sets between 2000 and 2020*

Since a flattening of the price information can already be seen in Figure 42 from the year 2000 onwards, I would like to enlarge this area in particular. The declining trend from the past to the present is extremely strong at certain times. As the *Price-per-Brick* has been falling since the mid-1980s (Figure 42), so too has the performance of LEGO sets. Currently in 2020, the *Price-per-Brick*, excluding inflation, stands at an average of USD 0.11 per brick. By comparison, in 2020 a single brick still costs an average of USD 0.16 (not adjusted for inflation). Returns significantly declined even more in the period between 2000 and 2020. LEGO sets from the year 2000 increased in value by an average of 221 percent. In contrast, current LEGO sets from the year 2020 have increased in value by only 57 percent. This development is hardly surprising. LEGO sets from the current collection are still available online or at retail.

With this perspective in Figure 43, we get a feeling for the direction in which the *Price-per-Brick* will develop in the future. Certainly, this is to be seen here in a very trivializing way only on the total LEGO set product range. However, to all appearances, LEGO sets in general will generate comparatively much lower returns in the coming years. It just seems to that for each graph, by its gradual horizontal formation, norm ranges are formed. Undoubtedly, there are individual LEGO sets that will resist this development and achieve significantly higher or even lower performance.

In the previous step, we were able to show how the average *Price-per-Brick* has developed from the past to the present. Based on this, the next step is to clarify how the various average Price-per-Bric between USD 0.02 and USD 1.00 per brick for LEGO sets have developed. By taking inflation into account in the value development, the *Price-per-Brick* ratios can be considered independently of the years.

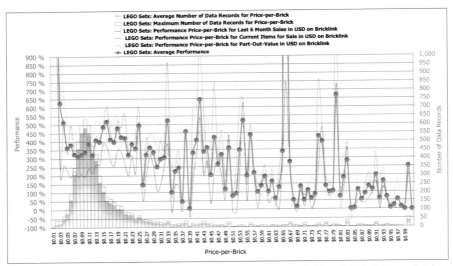

*Figure 44 - Value development of the Price-per-Brick between 0.01 and USD 1.00 per brick for LEGO sets*

Figure 44 shows the percentage performance of various *Prices-per-Brick* in USD. In general, the *Prices-per-Brick* of LEGO sets range from USD 0.02 to USD 224.95 per brick. For simplicity, the range is limited to between USD 0.02 and USD 1.00 per brick. Furthermore, this is the range that applies to most LEGO sets. After accounting for inflation, the analysis does not include any LEGO set that has a *Price-per-Brick* of 0.01 USD per brick. On the other hand, there have been several LEGO sets in history, where based on the MSRP, an average single brick costs only USD 0.01 (i.e., without taking inflation into account).

For example, *LEGO set no. 3443-1 Mosaic, LEGO set no. 4679-2 Bricks and Creations Tub* or *LEGO set no. 4782-1 Box of Bricks*. To understand how representative the performance is for the respective *Price-per-Brick*, the underlying numbers of data records (gray graph) are shown as well. The different price information is done according to the familiar color scheme. Furthermore, I decided to summarize the arithmetic mean of the three-price information in an average graph (red). This includes the arithmetic mean of

Last 6 Month Sales in USD on Bricklink, Current Items for Sale in USD on Bricklink and Part-Out-Value in USD on Bricklink.

For all Price-per-Brick values between USD 0.02 and USD 224.95 per brick, a total of 6,203 data records are available.[1] This corresponds to the number of LEGO sets for which both MSRP (inflation-adjusted), number of Regular Items, and at least one price information is available. With reference to the total number of 14,068 LEGO sets on which the statistical survey is based, this means that 44 percent of LEGO sets are included. Due to the absence of at least one of these crucial data records, the remaining 56 percent or 7,865 LEGO sets cannot be considered further. It cannot be completely ruled out that in these 56 percent occasional surprises are to be found with regard to the value developments. Their influence on this evaluation cannot be assessed. Ultimately, however, only the minimum number of data points available can be taken into account. Nevertheless, the number of available data points is large enough for the evaluation to be representative.

I would like to add that in Figure 44 the *Price-per-Brick* ranges from USD USD 0.02 to USD 1.00 per brick and is based on 5,821 data points respectively LEGO sets. Consequently, the remaining 382 data points are located in the range of USD 1.01 to USD 224.95 per brick. The majority of LEGO sets between 1961 and 2020 have an average *Price-per-Brick* (MSRP, adjusted for inflation) between USD 0.02 and USD 0.50 per brick. Overall, 87 percent of LEGO sets are within this range. Figure 45 illustrates the distribution most clearly. The range between USD 0.01 and USD 0.21 per brick represents 77 percent of the data points available for the statistical survey. The remaining 23 percent thus are in the range greater than USD 0.21 per brick. LEGO sets from this range are significantly less common.

---

[1] The number of data records is the arithmetic mean of the data points for Last 6 Month Sales in USD on Bricklink = 5,201 nos., Current Items for Sale in USD on Bricklink = 5,730 nos. and Part-Out-Value in USD on Bricklink = 7,083 nos.

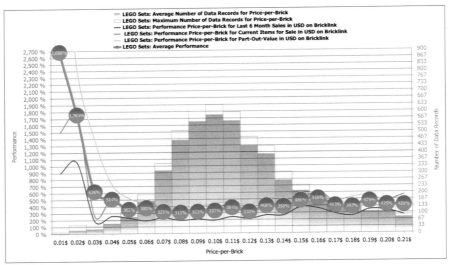

*Figure 45 - Development of the Price-per-Brick between USD 0.01 and USD 0.21 per brick for LEGO sets*

Now that sufficient data records are available for an assessment, the value developments will be analyzed in the following. The first thing that comes to mind is that all *Price-per-Bricks* values have risen. From Figure 41 it is already known that since 1990 the *Price-per-Brick* (MSRP, not adjusted for inflation) has been relatively stable between USD 0.1 and USD 0.2 per brick. In other words, The LEGO Group would like to avoid large fluctuations. The average fluctuation from year to year is less than 6 percent. The range between USD 0.1 and USD 0.2 per brick shows an increasing value growth of 415 percent. The appreciation in the range between USD 0.01 and USD 0.09 per brick looks even better. This includes a total of 27 percent of LEGO sets, with an average increase in value of 810 percent. This is due in partic-ular to the astonishing performance in the range between USD 0.01 and USD 0.04 per brick.

270

| Average Price-per-Brick (not inflation-adjusted) | Average Price-per-Brick (number of data records) | Performance Price-per-Brick for Last 6 Month Sales in USD on Bricklink | Performance Price-per-Brick for Currents Items for Sale in USD on Bricklink | Performance Price-per-Brick for Part-Out-Value es in USD on Bricklink | Average Performance |
|---|---|---|---|---|---|
| 0.01 USD | 3 | 900 % | 1.500 % | 5.663 % | 2.688 % |
| 0.02 USD | 18 | 1.057 % | 1.725 % | 2.506 % | 1.763 % |
| 0.03 USD | 23 | 188 % | 264 % | 1.426 % | 626 % |
| 0.04 USD | 50 | 261 % | 537 % | 743 % | 514 % |
| 0.05 USD | 82 | 233 % | 328 % | 525 % | 362 % |
| 0.06 USD | 161 | 193 % | 497 % | 451 % | 380 % |
| 0.07 USD | 312 | 235 % | 352 % | 388 % | 325 % |
| 0.08 USD | 460 | 194 % | 352 % | 390 % | 312 % |
| 0.09 USD | 552 | 213 % | 354 % | 402 % | 323 % |
| 0.10 USD | 584 | 194 % | 375 % | 441 % | 337 % |
| 0.11 USD | 554 | 245 % | 434 % | 472 % | 384 % |
| 0.12 USD | 431 | 216 % | 326 % | 417 % | 320 % |
| 0.13 USD | 391 | 268 % | 432 % | 525 % | 408 % |
| 0.14 USD | 261 | 265 % | 402 % | 509 % | 392 % |
| 0.15 USD | 208 | 377 % | 495 % | 575 % | 482 % |
| 0.16 USD | 155 | 369 % | 609 % | 577 % | 518 % |
| 0.17 USD | 140 | 292 % | 460 % | 486 % | 413 % |
| 0.18 USD | 130 | 258 % | 401 % | 532 % | 397 % |
| 0.19 USD | 106 | 351 % | 525 % | 561 % | 479 % |
| 0.20 USD | 105 | 338 % | 485 % | 453 % | 425 % |
| 0.21 USD | 78 | 270 % | 566 % | 424 % | 420 % |
| 0.22 USD | 72 | 201 % | 338 % | 424 % | 321 % |
| 0.23 USD | 71 | 319 % | 390 % | 444 % | 385 % |
| 0.24 USD | 46 | 212 % | 429 % | 433 % | 358 % |
| 0.25 USD | 59 | 516 % | 603 % | 365 % | 495 % |
| 0.26 USD | 40 | 63 % | 173 % | 203 % | 146 % |
| 0.27 USD | 35 | 203 % | 423 % | 335 % | 320 % |
| 0.28 USD | 33 | 316 % | 325 % | 449 % | 363 % |
| 0.29 USD | 26 | 251 % | 321 % | 435 % | 335 % |
| 0.30 USD | 26 | 109 % | 271 % | 372 % | 251 % |
| 0.31 USD | 19 | 150 % | 406 % | 332 % | 296 % |
| 0.32 USD | 21 | 251 % | 346 % | 319 % | 305 % |
| 0.33 USD | 29 | 379 % | 862 % | 329 % | 523 % |
| 0.34 USD | 9 | -9 % | 84 % | 231 % | 102 % |
| 0.35 USD | 11 | 145 % | 224 % | 305 % | 225 % |
| 0.36 USD | 11 | 133 % | 345 % | 254 % | 244 % |
| 0.37 USD | 18 | -2 % | 49 % | 94 % | 47 % |
| 0.38 USD | 26 | 452 % | 475 % | 448 % | 458 % |
| 0.39 USD | 5 | -37 % | 1 % | 57 % | 7 % |
| 0.40 USD | 15 | 181 % | 596 % | 218 % | 332 % |
| 0.41 USD | 10 | 324 % | 583 % | 315 % | 407 % |

Table 13 - Statistical distribution of Prices-per-Brick between USD 0.01 and USD 0.41 per brick for LEGO sets

That lower *Prices-per-Brick* achieve high increases in value was to be expected. LEGO sets in this category have significantly more room to move up. The preliminary figures confirm what many AFOL's already take into account. A low *Price-per-Brick* has a more positive effect on the value development. The following characteristics are obvious:

- When Price-per-Brick increases, the number of underlying LEGO sets decreases.
- A rising Price-per-Brick has little impact on the performance of *Last 6 Month Sales in USD on Bricklink.*
- A rising Price-per-Brick partially influences the value trend for *Current Items for Sale in USD on Bricklink.*
- A rising Price-per-Brick partly leads to smaller increases of the *Part-Out-Value in USD on Bricklink.*
- In a direct comparison, sales by the *Part-Out-Value* achieve the highest returns, with an only few exceptions.

It can be concluded that, if past experience is any guide, LEGO investors should target LEGO sets that have a favorable *Price-per-Brick ratio*. The summary in Table 14 should be seen as a guide to the average Price-per-Brick. Deviations cannot be excluded, which is why it is recommended to always consider soft factors as well as hard factors in their entirety when evaluating a LEGO set investment.

| Price-per-Brick (not inflation-adjusted) | Investment Grade | Frequency / Probability |
|---|---|---|
| 0.01 to 0.03 | excellent | > 1 % |
| 0.05 to 0.11 | good | 44 % |
| 0.12 to 0.18 | moderate | 28 % |
| 0.19 to 0.25 | low | 9 % |
| from 0.26 | bad | 18 % |

*Table 14 - Roadmap for LEGO set investment based on Price-per-Brick*

So far, only LEGO sets have been considered with regard to their composition of *Regular Items*. The chapter will conclude with an excursus on the other individual bricks and parts categories. These include *Extra Items,*

*Counterparts* and *Alternative Items.*[1] Also for this it must be clarified first whether sufficient data points are available.

Figure 46 only provides an indication of the availability of data records on the number of *Regular Items, Extra Items, Counterparts* and *Alternative Items. Why is that?* The reference LEGO Sets: Number per year is the comparative approach and represents 100 percent of the data records. Measured against the total period from 1961 to 2020, only 42 percent of the data records for *Regular Items* exist (red graph). Looking at the development from 1990 onwards, the average is 63 percent. And since 2010, the figure has risen to almost 70 percent. This also confirms that LEGO products have been significantly better documented in recent years.

---

[1] Minifigures are discussed in chapter 4.5.7.

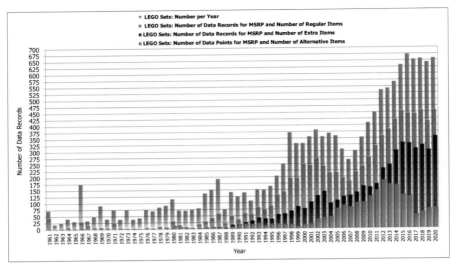

*Figure 46 - Availability of data records on the number of Regular Items, Extra Items, Counterparts and Alternative Items for LEGO sets between 1961 and 2020.*

For *Extra Items* (blue graph), the documented number of available data records per year is significantly lower. However, no statement can be made in this regard as to whether data records are incomplete or whether LEGO sets do not have any *Extra Items* at all. Nevertheless, on the basis of the available data records, an attempt will be made to derive a possible correlation with regard to historical performance. The same applies to the two outstanding data sets *Counterparts* (yellow graph) and *Alternative Items* (green graph).

For the category *Counterparts*, data records are available for only one fifth of all LEGO sets. Again, no conclusion can be drawn as to whether the data set is incomplete or LEGO sets often do without *Counterparts*. Nevertheless, the availability of data records improves significantly from the year 1990 onwards.

Finally, the availability of data records for *Alternative Items* is the worst. It can also be assumed that *Alternative Items* occur less frequently in LEGO sets. The trends for the various individual bricks and parts categories are as follows. Basis are all those LEGO sets for which both MSRP (not adjusted for inflation) and the number of the respective individual bricks and parts category are available.

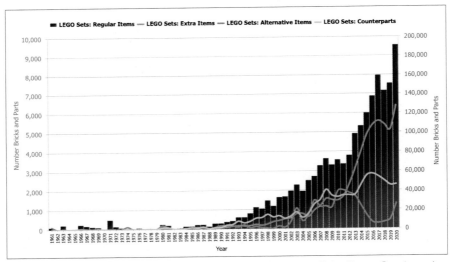

*Figure 47 - Overall development of the number of Regular Items, Extra Items, Counterparts and Alternative Items for LEGO sets between 1961 and 2020*

Understandably, the main category *Regular Items* develops congruently with the number of new LEGO sets per year. Since 1990, the annual growth has been 10 percent, which is significantly higher than the number of new LEGO sets per year (6 percent). As a result, LEGO sets are getting bigger and bigger. The LEGO Group thus gives more weight to the growth in individual bricks and parts than to the number of new LEGO sets.

The development of Extra Items, Counterparts and Alternative Items largely develops in line with each other in the period from 1990 to 2000 without any major fluctuations. From 2001 onwards, the development becomes much more volatile. While Extra Items grow strongly and are therefore included more often in LEGO sets, Counterparts are stagnating. On the other hand, Alternative Items experience particularly large fluctuations and appear in only a few LEGO sets.

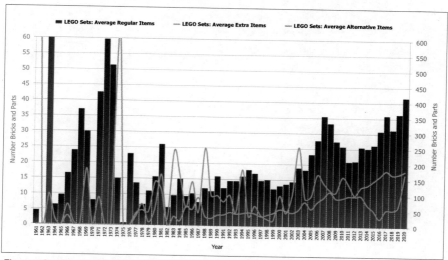

*Figure 48 - Average development of the number of Regular Items, Extra Items, Counterparts and Alternative Items for LEGO sets between 1961 and 2020*

The share of Extra Items, Counterparts and Alternative Items varies strongly from year to year. In the following, the data is transferred into a table to show value changes in connection with the different brick and part categories.

277

| Year | Regular Items | Share of Extra Items to Regular Items | Share of Counter-parts to Regular Items | Share of Alternative Items to Regular Items | Changes in Value Last 6 Month Sales in USD on Bricklink | Changes in Value Current Items for Sales in USD on Bricklink | Changes in Value Part-Out-Value in USD on Bricklink |
|---|---|---|---|---|---|---|---|
| 1961 | 47 | 0 % | 0 % | 6 % | | | 457 % |
| 1962 | 0 | | | | | | 0 % |
| 1963 | 1,444 | 0 % | 0 % | 0 % | - | | 475 % |
| 1964 | 65 | 0 % | 0 % | 0 % | | | 409 % |
| 1965 | 96 | 0 % | 4 % | 0 % | | | 129 % |
| 1966 | 165 | 0 % | 1 % | 0 % | -57 % | 469 % | 493 % |
| 1967 | 239 | 0 % | 1 % | 0 % | 911 % | 1,446 % | 411 % |
| 1968 | 371 | 0 % | 0 % | 0 % | | | 254 % |
| 1969 | 300 | 0 % | 1 % | 1 % | | | 803 % |
| 1970 | 80 | 0 % | 1 % | 0 % | | | 179 % |
| 1971 | 427 | 0 % | 0 % | 0 % | -26 % | 689 % | 1,102 % |
| 1972 | 597 | 0 % | 0 % | 0 % | | | 1,494 % |
| 1973 | 513 | 0 % | 0 % | 0 % | | | 775 % |
| 1974 | 149 | 0 % | 3 % | 28 % | | 358 % | 370 % |
| 1975 | 7 | 0 % | 0 % | 0 % | | 0 % | 0 % |
| 1976 | 229 | 0 % | 1 % | 0 % | -80 % | 386 % | 220 % |
| 1977 | 136 | 1 % | 1 % | 1 % | | 488 % | 114 % |
| 1978 | 68 | 1 % | 3 % | 1 % | | 433 % | 86 % |
| 1979 | 110 | 0 % | 1 % | 1 % | 525 % | 861 % | 293 % |
| 1980 | 156 | 1 % | 2 % | 4 % | -20 % | 548 % | 312 % |
| 1981 | 260 | 1 % | 2 % | 2 % | 328 % | 780 % | 380 % |
| 1982 | 59 | 0 % | 3 % | 1 % | -99 % | 415 % | 79 % |
| 1983 | 97 | 1 % | 0 % | 5 % | -34 % | 915 % | 376 % |
| 1984 | 150 | 0 % | 1 % | 2 % | 477 % | 1,264 % | 445 % |
| 1985 | 95 | 1 % | 3 % | 1 % | 55 % | 1,060 % | 261 % |
| 1986 | 104 | 0 % | 1 % | 2 % | 48 % | 327 % | 205 % |
| 1987 | 77 | 1 % | 2 % | 0 % | 126 % | 1,064 % | 280 % |
| 1988 | 121 | 0 % | 1 % | 1 % | 49 % | 583 % | 338 % |
| 1989 | 112 | 1 % | 1 % | 1 % | 337 % | 911 % | 431 % |
| 1990 | 159 | 1 % | 1 % | 3 % | 495 % | 558 % | 292 % |
| 1991 | 122 | 1 % | 3 % | 2 % | 184 % | 391 % | 390 % |
| 1992 | 145 | 2 % | 3 % | 2 % | 526 % | 774 % | 460 % |
| 1993 | 145 | 1 % | 3 % | 1 % | 246 % | 463 % | 442 % |
| 1994 | 160 | 1 % | 3 % | 2 % | 159 % | 269 % | 327 % |
| 1995 | 181 | 1 % | 2 % | 0 % | 206 % | 397 % | 371 % |
| 1996 | 169 | 1 % | 2 % | 1 % | 240 % | 329 % | 386 % |
| 1997 | 146 | 1 % | 3 % | 0 % | 204 % | 316 % | 385 % |
| 1998 | 149 | 1 % | 3 % | 0 % | 63 % | 366 % | 251 % |
| 1999 | 121 | 2 % | 3 % | 0 % | 51 % | 139 % | 260 % |
| 2000 | 131 | 1 % | 2 % | 0 % | 98 % | 226 % | 339 % |
| 2001 | 136 | 2 % | 2 % | 0 % | 196 % | 268 % | 360 % |
| 2002 | 144 | 1 % | 2 % | 1 % | 156 % | 227 % | 395 % |
| 2003 | 188 | 2 % | 2 % | 2 % | 186 % | 304 % | 345 % |
| 2004 | 182 | 2 % | 1 % | 1 % | 137 % | 222 % | 353 % |
| 2005 | 232 | 1 % | 2 % | 1 % | 110 % | 246 % | 314 % |
| 2006 | 277 | 2 % | 2 % | 3 % | 166 % | 272 % | 271 % |
| 2007 | 356 | 2 % | 2 % | 2 % | 149 % | 268 % | 307 % |
| 2008 | 333 | 2 % | 3 % | 2 % | 101 % | 221 % | 230 % |
| 2009 | 275 | 2 % | 3 % | 2 % | 110 % | 192 % | 172 % |
| 2010 | 258 | 2 % | 2 % | 3 % | 43 % | 155 % | 156 % |
| 2011 | 209 | 3 % | 3 % | 3 % | 71 % | 179 % | 177 % |
| 2012 | 211 | 3 % | 2 % | 2 % | 73 % | 179 % | 195 % |
| 2013 | 256 | 3 % | 2 % | 2 % | 29 % | 110 % | 140 % |
| 2014 | 252 | 4 % | 2 % | 1 % | 40 % | 160 % | 155 % |
| 2015 | 263 | 4 % | 2 % | 1 % | 47 % | 124 % | 123 % |
| 2016 | 309 | 4 % | 2 % | 0 % | 44 % | 124 % | 126 % |
| 2017 | 359 | 4 % | 2 % | 0 % | 38 % | 124 % | 125 % |
| 2018 | 313 | 4 % | 2 % | 0 % | 16 % | 133 % | 119 % |
| 2019 | 364 | 3 % | 2 % | 0 % | -13 % | 66 % | 123 % |
| 2020 | 417 | 3 % | 1 % | 1 % | -9 % | 40 % | 139 % |

*Table 15 - Correlation of the share of the different brick and part categories on the value development for LEGO sets between 1961 and 2020*

Due to inconsistent data availability, the year 1962 must be excluded from consideration. Even otherwise, only few trends can be derived:

- The average number of *Regular Items* is in a continuous upward trend.
- It is particularly noticeable that the proportion of *Extra Items* to *Regular Items* has been increasing since 1962.
- *Counterparts* and Alternative Items make up an average of two percent of the *Regular Items*.

The highest average increases in value were achieved between 1979 and 1998. During this period, there was no consistent development in the shares of *Extra Items*, *Counterparts* and *Alternative Items*.

In summary, the additional brick and part categories do not have any influence on the performance of LEGO sets. Instead, the investigation once again reveals that the value developments of LEGO sets are directly related to the years (and thus the age of a LEGO set). It is no coincidence that LEGO sets increase in value the older they are.

But we don't want to make it that simple. The fact is that the increase in value of LEGO sets does not occur linearly with their age. Consequently, the correlations with other possible influencing parameters must be examined. One of these influencing parameters is possibly the size or number of Regular Items in LEGO sets. To check this, different categories for the number of Regular Items were defined. In the present statistical investigation, the smallest LEGO set considered is *no. 10700-1 32x32 Green Base Plate* and consists of one piece. The biggest LEGO set is *no. 10276-1 Colosseum* with 9,036 Regular Items.

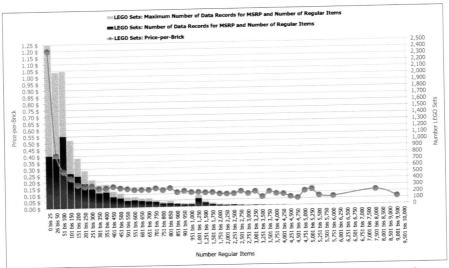

*Figure 49 - Statistical distribution of the Price-per-Brick and the number of LEGO sets from the number of Regular Items*

Of the 14,068 LEGO sets surveyed from 1961 to 2020, 89 percent of LEGO sets have fewer than 500 *Regular Items*. Overall, slightly less than one-third of LEGO sets have between 0 to 25 *Regular Items*. Consequently, The LEGO Group's product range basically consists of a particularly large number of small LEGO Sets.

Furthermore, Figure 49 shows that LEGO sets with up to 200 *Regular Items* also have the highest average *Price-per-Brick*. This is an average of 0.46 USD per brick. LEGO sets with up to 200 *Regular Items* represent 74 percent of the LEGO set product line. As we recall, the average *Price-per-Brick* is USD 0.14 between 1990 and 2020. The higher-than-average *Price-per-Brick* for LEGO sets with up to 200 *Regular Items* might have various root causes. For example, the increased cost of producing small LEGO sets is passed on directly to the customer. The above-average *Price-per-Brick* also suggests that value increases in this area should be more modest.

The average *Price-per-Brick* decreases as the number of *Regular Items* increases. Consequently, the average MSRP is inversely proportional and increases as the number of *Regular Items* increases. LEGO sets with 200 to 1,000 *Regular Items* have an average *Price-per-Brick* of USD 0.14 per brick. LEGO sets of this size represent 23 percent of the LEGO set product line. LEGO sets larger than 1,000 *Regular Items* have an average *Price-per-Brick* of USD 0.09 per brick. LEGO sets of this size represent 3 percent of the LEGO Set product line. It can be proven beyond doubt that as the number of *Regular Items* increases, the average *Price-per-Brick* decreases.

The next step is to examine whether there is a direct relationship between LEGO set performance and the size of the LEGO sets (number of *Regular Items*). In this context, it is often assumed that smaller LEGO sets or sets with a low number of *Regular Items* experience higher increases in value than larger LEGO sets. In this regard, it is speculated that potential buyers (e.g., builders, collectors, investors, etc.) will be much more willing to pay double or triple the MSRP for inexpensive LEGO sets. For example, a LEGO set with a MSRP of USD 19.99 that is worth twice as much after two years (USD 39.98) is still considered relatively cheap in the LEGO universe today.

The following Figure 50 shows the correlation between average performance and the number of *Regular Items*. The availability of the data appears as follows:

- **Last 6 Month Sales in USD on Bricklink**
  38 percent or 5,298 of 14,068 LEGO Sets

- **Current Items for Sales in USD on Bricklink**
  42 percent or 5,837 of 14,068 LEGO Sets

- **Part-Out-Value in USD on Bricklink**
  52 percent or 7,265 of 14,068 LEGO Sets

- **Average Performance / Change in Value**
  44 percent or 6,133 of 14,068 LEGO Sets

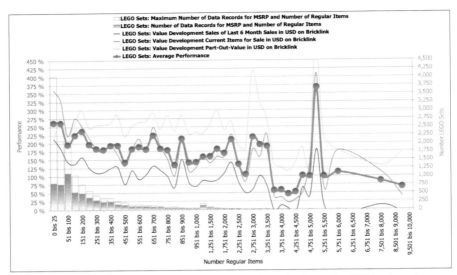

*Figure 50 - Performance in relation to the number of Regular Items for LEGO sets up to 10,000 bricks and parts*

Only LEGO sets were considered for which the MSRP and the number of *Regular Items* were available. In general, it can be observed that the performance decreases as the number of *Regular Items* increases. For example, LEGO sets with up to 500 *Regular Items* achieve an average return of 207 percent. LEGO sets with more than 500 and less than 1,000 *Regular Items* grow in value by an average of 178 percent. And LEGO sets with more than 1,000 *Regular Items* still increase in value by 138 percent. The trend is obvious. So, there is an elevated risk that with increasing size of the LEGO set, lower appreciation in value will be achieved. Looking only at the sales of the Last 6 Months Sales in USD on Bricklink (blue graph), even losses in value were observed for larger LEGO sets.

The largest gain in value, 516 percent, is in the range between 5,001 and 5,250 *Regular Items*. From a rational point of view, this is LEGO set no. 10179-1 Ultimate Collectors Millennium Falcon. Therefore, a generalization for this range does not seem appropriate. Especially not because it is the most famous example in the LEGO universe when talking about LEGO Investment.

In addition, the value developments for the total range between 1 and 10,000 *individual bricks and parts* follow. This should give LEGO investors an overview of which is the most profitable sales option.

▪ **Last 6 Month Sales in USD on Bricklink**
88 Percent

▪ **Current Items for Sale in USD on Bricklink**
166 Percent

▪ **Part-Out-Value in USD on Bricklink**
242 Percent

In summary, the sale of individual LEGO bricks and parts (*Part-Out-Value in USD on Bricklink*) again generates the majority of the highest increases in value. Excluded are LEGO sets with a size up to 100 *Regular Items*. The results confirm that the sale of complete LEGO sets is much more promising for this segment. These are very often LEGO sets for children (themed areas such as Clikits, Unikitty, Belville, 4 Juniors, etc.). It can be assumed that LEGO sets of these themes are sold in large quantities. In addition, these are often uninteresting for AFOL's and especially MOC'ers due to the associated individual bricks and parts as well as colors (purple, pink, turquoise, etc.). These reasons ensure that LEGO sets with up to 100 Regular Items have lower part-out values.

We have previously based our evaluation of the performance exclusively on the total number of *Regular Items*. The total number of *Regular Items* is the result of the multiplication of the number of unique lots and the corresponding quantity of single bricks and parts. For simplification, I would like to give an example. *LEGO set no. 4431-1 Ambulance* consists of 187 *Regular Items*. These are distributed over 92 different types of bricks and parts (unique lots). Dividing the total number of *Regular Items* (187 pieces) by the number of unique lots (92 pieces) gives the average number or quantity of different types of bricks and parts. For the example *LEGO set no. 4431-1 Ambulance*, each single brick and part type exists on average about twice. With this ratio, two additional hard factors can be examined to see if they have a direct influence on the performance of LEGO sets.

For this purpose, the number of unique lots in LEGO sets must first be determined. Assuming that for the evaluation of the MSRP, the number of unique lots and at least one current price information is available, the resulting availability of the data points is as shown in Figure 51 below.

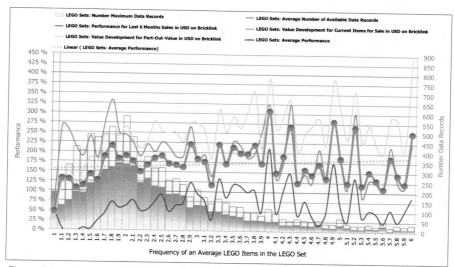

*Figure 51 - Value performance depending on the average frequency of a single LEGO brick and part in the LEGO set*

A maximum of 11,288 LEGO sets are applicable for the evaluation. The ratio between the number of *Regular Items* and the number of unique lots for LEGO sets ranges from 1.0 to 643.1. However, as shown in Figure 51, the vast majority of LEGO sets have a ratio between 1.0 and 6.0. 10,507 of the total 11,288 LEGO sets fall into this range. Of these, data points are available for 6,056 LEGO sets, or 57 percent.

The additionally selected indicator for the frequency of an average LEGO brick or part in a LEGO set does not seem to be very appropriate to provide a correlation to the performance. The fluctuations in value development are too strong depending on the LEGO individual bricks or parts. Thus, no clear tendency can be derived.

But repeatedly you can read and hear (e.g., LEGO set reviews) that some LEGO sets are significantly better because these contain unique individual bricks and parts. Conversely, these unique bricks and parts only appear in a few other LEGO sets, or at best none at all. This can be a decisive indica-tion why LEGO sets develop differently in value. It also explains why LEGO sets of the same size achieve such different *Part-Out-Values* in USD on Bricklink. The composition of the LEGO set in terms of individual bricks and parts undoubtedly has an impact on its future value performance. Due to the complexity of the composition of the LEGO set in terms of individual bricks and parts, a statistical survey exclusively on the topic of individual bricks and parts is definitely needed.

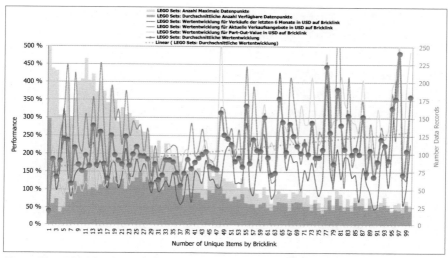

*Figure 52 - Value development depending on the frequency of unique bricks and parts in LEGO sets*

In the final step, the available data points from Brickset and Bricklink will be used to analyze to what extent the total number of unique lots influences the performance of LEGO Sets. A maximum of 11,289 LEGO sets are considered for the following exploration. Of these, data points are available for 5,897 LEGO sets. These refer to a value range of unique lots in LEGO sets from 1 to 1,013 pieces. Ultimately, Figure 52 only represents the value range between 1 and 100 unique lots. This range represents 70 percent of the available data points. However, it is difficult to interpret a clear trend. No range in Figure 52 stands out in such a way that a correlation between value performance and the number of unique lots becomes apparent. The clue to a trend is given by the red linear trend line. Basically, the higher the number of unique lots in a LEGO set, the higher the linear trend. Nevertheless, this trend is on shaky ground at best, because the fluctuations are extraordinarily high. Despite this, the data points are sufficient to infer that a higher number of unique lots increases the probabilities of upward trends in the value of LEGO sets.

In conclusion, it could be demonstrated that the *Price-per-Brick* still plays an important role in the evaluation of LEGO sets as an investment. Especially in the context that the *Price-per-Brick* tells nothing about the quality of a LEGO set, as this is not only limited to the number of individual bricks and parts. Therefore, the *Price-per-Brick* should never be used in isolation when LEGO investors are analyzing potential LEGO sets for investment. This would ignore many other factors (e.g., total weight or Weight-per-Brick, amount of minifigures, licensing agreement, etc.). Particularly the weight metric can provide crucial information about which LEGO sets are rising or falling in value. The number of individual bricks and parts influences the level of detail and complexity of a LEGO set. In turn, weight gives us a sense of physical size. The following additional considerations are not taken into account by the *Price-per-Brick*:

- LEGO bricks and parts are different in size, shape and color. This is especially noticeable when comparing two LEGO sets of different themes. By using different individual bricks and parts, the *Price-per-Brick* ratio can differ substantially. For example, *LEGO set no. 31202-1 Mickey Mouse* from the Art theme has an average *Price-per-Brick* of USD 0.045 per brick (MSRP = USD 119.99; number of bricks and parts = 2,658 pieces). In contrast, *LEGO set no. 42126-1 Ford F-150 Raptor* from the Technic theme has a significantly higher calculated *Price-per-Brick* of USD 0.073 per brick (MSRP = USD 99.99; quantity of bricks and parts = 1,379 pieces).

- If a LEGO set is under a license agreement, this can also have an impact on the Price-per-Brick. For example, *LEGO set no. 75903-1 Haunted Lighthouse* from the Scooby-Doo theme has a *Price-per-Brick* of USD 0.128 per brick (inflation-adjusted MSRP = USD 53.98; number of bricks and pieces = 420). This compares to *LEGO set no. 41904-1 Picture Holders* from the Dots theme without a license agreement. The LEGO set has an inflation-adjusted MSRP of USD 14.99 and 423 single bricks and parts. This results in an average *Price-per-Brick* of only USD

0.035 per brick. The difference in the two *Price-per-Brick* ratios is obvious. The influence of the underlying license Scooby-Doo with the rights holder Warner Bros. Entertainment Inc. on the *Price-per-Brick* cannot be ignored.

- *Does the LEGO set contain large individual bricks or parts such as plates, boat hulls, struts, tires or animals? If so, what size are these parts? How many of the large bricks and parts are included in the LEGO set? Are the large bricks and parts easy to make (like a 2- or 3-part mold)? Or are they difficult to make (like a 5- or 6-piece mold)?* All of these factors affect the price of each brick and simply cannot be generalized using an average *Price-per-Brick.*

- *Are LEGO bricks and parts printed? How many individual bricks and parts are printed and how large are they?* For example, in the *LEGO sets Harry Potter Hogwarts Moments no. 76382 to 76385,* the book cover is a full print on a special 10 x 16 tile.

- *Does the LEGO set have pre-assembled or assembled parts? Are these simple or complex assemblies?* Again, the number and size are important.

LEGO sets have a large number of different individual bricks and parts. In the case of large bricks and parts, The LEGO Group requires a larger quantity of ABS (acrylonitrile-butadiene-styrene copolymer) material for production.[1] Again, LEGO bricks and parts are sometimes made from other types of plastic materials, such as HIPS or High Impact Polystyrene, PA or Polyamide, MABS or Methyl Methacrylate Acrylonitrile Butadiene Styrene Polymer, MTPO or Metallocene Thermoplastic Polyolefins, PC or poly-carbonate, PE or polyethylene, POM or polyoxymethylene, PP or polypropylene, TPU or thermoplastic polyurethane, SEBS or styrene-ethylene-butylene-styrene and TP or thermoplastic polyester.[2]

---

[1] ABS is the material that The LEGO Group has been using to make classic DUPLO and LEGO bricks. ABS is a hard and scratch-resistant plastic.
[2] https://www.lego.com/de-de/sustainability/product-safety/materials/

Different parts tend to lead to difficulties in manufacturing or assembly. The complexity of LEGO bricks and parts must be factored into the *Price-per-Brick* consideration. The isolated consideration of the *Price-per-Brick* bears unimagined risks.

Small LEGO sets achieve higher growth in value. However, large LEGO sets are very popular and are in high demand among children and adults alike. This is due in part to the building fun that larger LEGO sets provide. Many children cannot afford large LEGO sets. Consequently, they are the potential buyers of such LEGO sets in the future. For years, it can be observed that people are more and more often willing to fulfill the (expensive) dream of the LEGO set from their own childhood.

The main argument against large LEGO sets is the more difficult storage. Larger outer packaging is required for shipping, which also takes up more space. It is tedious to bring them to the post office. Usually, you have to transport them by car. Also, large LEGO sets are discounted less often and heavily. In addition, large LEGO sets correlate particularly with the AFOL market, which limits the circle of interested parties at least temporarily.

Many LEGO investors have their eye on the large LEGO sets in particular. It only takes a single incentive to sell, for example, 300 Euro in sales. This is significantly less effort than, for example, achieving the same sales with 10 Euro LEGO sets. It is easier to convince one person than six, four or three. Also, the (buying and selling) administration and logistics must be in place for just one LEGO set. These are all costly capacities.

Here are a few final words from my own experience: Never buy a LEGO set if the focus is on the fact that it is the largest LEGO set (e.g., of the theme). The LEGO Group is aware of the coveted selling point that it is the largest Technic or Star Wars set. The frequent release of ever larger LEGO sets happens much more often than you might think.

## 4.5.4 Themes

Designated theme series or themed areas are product lines produced by The LEGO Group according to a core concept. After the introduction of minifigures in 1978, owner Kjeld Kirk Kristiansen pursued a new strategy. A series of LEGO sets was designed and marketed, which he called a *System within a System*. The three original themed worlds were born: Town, Castle and Space. These were to be based on the present, past, and future. The next step was for The LEGO Group to create areas within these themed worlds in 1987. The company also produced product lines using parts outside the standardized LEGO system, such as Technic, Fabuland, and later Duplo.

Over the years, numerous themes have been introduced, including licensed themes such as Star Wars in 1999. Adults become junior architects with LEGO sets from the Architecture theme. Car fans become engineers with LEGO sets from the Technic theme area and city planners with Creator. Themes differ from each other to a great extent. The main differences are type, number of related LEGO sets, price, license agreement, age range, availability, composition and number of individual bricks or parts, amount of minifigures and much more. The themes cover a number of different genres, ranging from fantasy and western to science fiction and horror. All of these features and attributes characterize a theme and play an important role in pricing. For example, themes with large moldings (e.g., dinosaurs, large figures or so-called big figures, etc.) are inherently more expensive because special large moldings have to be produced for them. Such additional costs are of course included in the price of the LEGO set and thus passed on to the customer.

It has already been demonstrated that some of these factors have an impact on the future performance of LEGO sets. It can be assumed that if many factors are combined, different value developments are inevitable. Also, it is impossible to show all factors in dependence of the respective theme, clearly in a diagram. Instead, we will examine step by step possible influences from subject areas that can lead to changes in the value of LEGO sets.

Again, the central benchmark is the value development of average MSRP's to the already known current price information like *Last 6 Month Sales in USD on Bricklink, Current Items for Sale in USD on Bricklink* as well as *Part-Out-Value in USD on Bricklink*. First, an overview of the general development of themed areas in the LEGO universe will be given.

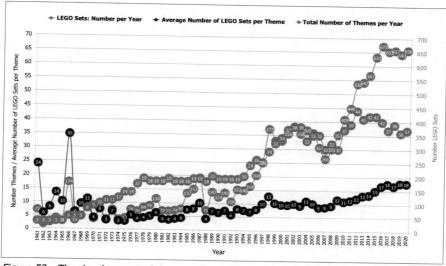

*Figure 53 - The development of the number of LEGO themes, sets and the average number of LEGO sets per theme between 1961 and 2020*

It is well known that the annual number of LEGO sets (green graph) has been steadily increasing since 1961. However, what is new is the fact that the number of LEGO themes (red graph) has also been rising continuously since 1961. In the period between 1961 and 2020, the number of themes increased by an average of 7 percent annually. Conversely, this corresponds to an average of 4 new theme areas per year. Between 2000 and 2019, it is already an average of 5 subject areas per year and in the current year 2020, it is already another 7 new subject areas. Interestingly, there were a total of 19 years without new themes in the period between 1961 and 2000.

The growing number of themes is certainly also somewhat necessary in order to meet the demand from customers for current topics and ultimately to be able to offer them. Themes reflect the development of new television and cinema films, series, computer and console games, and many more. Target groups are addressed directly through thematic areas and targeted marketing.

Since 1961, the number of new LEGO sets has grown by an average of 18 percent per year. As a consequence, the average number of LEGO sets in a themes (blue graph) also increased. Taking into account all LEGO sets as well as themes, a theme consisted of an average of 10 LEGO sets in the period between 1961 and 2020. There are 820 sub-themes assigned to the total of 145 themes. Thus, a theme is subject to an average of 5 to 6 sub-themes. The consideration seems to be meaningful for many reasons. On the one hand, it can be used to investigate whether the success of a themes is caused by all or only individual associated sub-themes. It is also possible that there are themes which are particularly successful precisely because there are no sub-theme areas.

We start by investigating whether there is a correlation between the number of LEGO sets within a theme and its performance. Since 145 themes can only be represented very poorly in a chart or table, additional minimum requirements had to be established.

Basically, we have to sort out 4 themes for which no MSRP's are available.[1] In addition, 19 themes are excluded, for which less than 40 percent of the MSRP data records are available.[2] Furthermore, 2 additional themes have to be excluded from the investigation, as for none of them at least one current price information is available.[3] In total, 120 LEGO theme areas remain for the investigation.

For the remaining themes, the inflation-adjusted MSRP varies from an average of USD 5 to USD 221. Based on 81 of 90 related LEGO sets, the *Mixels* theme has an average inflation-adjusted MSRP of USD 5. This makes it the lowest priced theme in the LEGO Universe. Again, based on 2 out of 2 related LEGO sets, the *Ghostbusters* theme has an average inflation-adjusted MSRP of USD 221. Thus, Ghostbusters is the most expensive theme in this statistical survey.

---

[1] Among the themes are Dino 2010, Forma, Minitalia as well as PreSchool.
[2] These include Assorted, Basic, Building Set with People, Dacta, Education, Fabuland, Hobby Set, Homemaker, Legoland, Make and Create, Master Builder Academy, Miscellaneous, Promo-tional, Stranger Things, Serious Play, System, Trains, Universal Building Set and Znap.
[3] These concern the themes Originals as well as Collectable Minifigures.

Based on 120 themes and 7,230 (out of a total of 10,833) related LEGO sets, the average inflation-adjusted MSRP is USD 29.23 for the period from 1961 to 2020. The number of related LEGO sets to a theme varies from 1 to 1,228 LEGO sets. On average, there are 90 LEGO sets assigned to each theme. *LEGO set no. 17101-1 Boost Creative Toolbox* is the only LEGO set in the Boost theme. The theme with the most LEGO sets is Duplo (1,228 pieces).

The following Figure 54 shows these 120 themes, including the number of associated LEGO sets, as well as the average performances.

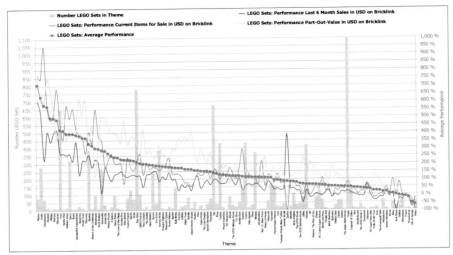

*Figure 54 - Average performance of 120 LEGO themes*

As expected, the average performance of the different LEGO themes varies significantly. The weakest performance was achieved by the LEGO theme Primo with -66 percent. However, the LEGO theme *Avatar - The Last Airbender* achieved the highest performance with an average of 904 percent. Both themes represent extremities and could not be more different. The LEGO theme *Primo* was available in stores between 1995 and 2005. The individual bricks and parts are extremely similar to those of *Duplo* and are therefore primarily aimed at babies and pre-school children. This theme has a total of 56 sets. The LEGO theme *Avatar - The Last Airbender* counts only 2 sets, which were available in 2006 and 2007. This themes are the illustration of a television show. This was licensed and broadcast by Nickelodeon. Both LEGO sets were only sold in the USA and Canada. With only two associated LEGO sets, *Avatar - The Last Airbender* is the second smallest LEGO themed area after the Boost themed area, in terms of number of LEGO sets. It can be assumed that these peculiarities of both LEGO themes are partly responsible for their respective success or failure.

296

In the following, we will look at the 10 LEGO themes that have the highest or lowest performance. Some LEGO themes have performed remarkably well or poorly. Nevertheless, the limited data points in Table 16 provide few clues as to the reasons that led to the corresponding performance changes. However, it is striking that both themes with increases and decreases in value turn out to be quite different in size (in terms of the associated number of LEGO sets). It is important to know that within the LEGO community it is often said that the essence or the character of a theme unfolds with its size. These include themes that are a main pillar of The LEGO Group, such as Star Wars, City, Creator, Friends, Marvel Super Heroes, Harry Potter, and so on. The listed themes can still be found in the LEGO Set product range today.

| No. | LEGO Themes | Number of underlying LEGO Sets in Theme | Average Performance |
|---|---|---|---|
| 01 | Avatar The Last Airbender | 2 | 904 % |
| 02 | Pirates | 84 | 709 % |
| 03 | Castle | 281 | 632 % |
| 04 | Adventurers | 72 | 581 % |
| 05 | Western | 20 | 570 % |
| 06 | Vikings | 7 | 499 % |
| 07 | Batman | 15 | 497 % |
| 08 | Dinosaurs | 12 | 486 % |
| 09 | Town | 647 | 422 % |
| 10 | Spider-Man | 11 | 417 % |
| 01 | Primo | 9 | -66 % |
| 02 | Life of George | 1 | -58 % |
| 03 | Powered Up | 44 | -22 % |
| 04 | Fusion | 25 | -12 % |
| 05 | Dimensions | 20 | -10 % |
| 06 | Galidor | 68 | -8 % |
| 07 | Jack Stone | 4 | -1 % |
| 08 | Baby | 10 | 5 % |
| 09 | Boost | 2 | 5 % |
| 10 | Action Wheelers | 56 | 18 % |

Table 16 - The 10 LEGO themes with the highest and lowest performance

The LEGO Group's annual published financial results show that everyday themes such as City and Creator continue to be sales drivers. They do not become boring for customers, originate from the imagination and can be integrated into different worlds. Nevertheless, the increase in value of both themes is rather below average. According to the evaluation, the City theme has an average increase in value of 144 percent. The Creator theme area achieves a somewhat lower average increase in value of 116 percent.

Themes with particularly few LEGO sets are therefore difficult to classify (especially in terms of popularity). This generalization cannot be confirmed by the analysis of Table 16. According to this, themes with particularly few associated LEGO sets achieved both very high increases and decreases in value. For example, themes such as Prince of Persia, The Angry Birds, Boost, Life of George or Jack Stone are considered failures in LEGO circles. This is also reflected in the average performance. For example, Prince of Persia only achieved an increase in value of 111 percent and The Angry Birds only 50 percent. Compared to other investments, these are undoubtedly still high returns. However, in the LEGO investment, these are comparatively weak increases in value. Neither theme was well accepted by LEGO customers. Consequently, The LEGO Group decided not to continue with either theme.

So far, no correlation between the number of LEGO sets belonging to a theme and its average performance could be determined. Nevertheless, I would like to exclude a possible causality between these two variables in the following.

It is difficult to identify a clear trend from the performance changes shown in Table 17. None of the factors (e.g., Number of underlying Themes or LEGO Sets) provides sufficient indication that it is driving the corresponding performance. The performance as a function of the number of underlying LEGO sets appears inconsistent. The weak performance of particularly small LEGO themes with less than 5 underlying LEGO sets can only be explained to me by the fact that these are poorly perceived by customers due to their small size.

| Number of underlying LEGO Sets in Themes | Number Themes | Number LEGO Sets | Average Performance |
|---|---|---|---|
| ≥ 1,000 | 1 | 1,228 | 49 % |
| ≥ 500 and < 1,000 | 3 | 2,102 | 260 % |
| ≥ 400 and < 500 | 3 | 1,280 | 104 % |
| ≥ 300 and < 400 | 4 | 1,467 | 257 % |
| ≥ 200 and < 300 | 3 | 798 | 371 % |
| ≥ 100 and < 200 | 10 | 1,311 | 142 % |
| ≥ 50 and < 100 | 19 | 1,377 | 161 % |
| ≥ 25 and < 50 | 17 | 609 | 125 % |
| ≥ 20 and < 25 | 10 | 219 | 169 % |
| ≥ 15 and < 20 | 8 | 129 | 287 % |
| ≥ 10 and < 15 | 13 | 159 | 194 % |
| ≥ 5 and < 10 | 17 | 123 | 177 % |
| ≥ 1 and < 5 | 12 | 31 | 115 % |

Table 17 - Relationship between the number of related LEGO sets in a theme and the average performance

The evaluation is even more astonishing as this range includes themes like *The Simpsons* (127 %), *Ghostbusters* (113 %) as well as *Minion - The Rise of Gru* (66 %). These are strong brands that many people still know today, and yet they experience significantly worse performance than many other LEGO themes. In each of these three LEGO themes, there are (so far) only two LEGO sets. In contrast, the LEGO theme with by far the highest average increase in value of 904 percent. *The Avatar - The Last Airbender* theme also includes only two LEGO sets. We will take this strikingly good or bad performance as an opportunity to examine how much these increases or decreases in value vary within the LEGO themes. The following Figure 55 shows particularly impressively how strongly the changes in value vary within a theme. In contrast, the average value development shows only a section of the range. In each theme, there are LEGO sets that have risen in value, in some cases significantly higher than the average value development of the theme. But there are also individual LEGO sets in each LEGO theme, which show higher losses in value. Consequently, it is not sufficient to simply buy all LEGO sets from a successful theme area.

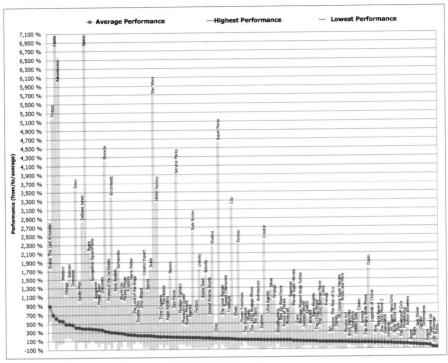

*Figure 55 - Average performance of 120 LEGO themes*

For example, the Castle theme has the third-best value increase with an average of 632 percent. *LEGO set no. 0011-3 Castle 2 for 1 Bonus Offer* is the most successful LEGO set in the Castle theme area, with an inflation-adjusted increase in value of 11,951 percent. In contrast, *LEGO set no. 88091-1 King Mathias (Series 1) Limited Edition with Map and Cape* from the same Castle theme achieved a 38 percent loss in value as of December 31, 2020. Thus, the theme on its own is no guarantee for the success of any belonging LEGO set. It is clearly visible in Figure 55 that, with a few exceptions (e.g., *The Simpsons, Dino, Ghostbusters, The Angry Birds* or *Universe*), LEGO sets are subject to strong fluctuations within a theme area. The difference between the best and worst LEGO set in a theme averages

300

an astonishing 1,242 percent. This makes it all the more important for LEGO investors to choose the right LEGO set even within a theme.

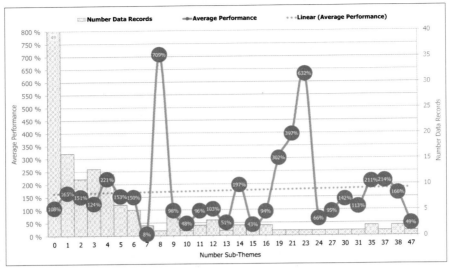

*Figure 56 - Average performance of LEGO sub-themes*

The following themes have the most sub-themes (performance): Bionicle 38 units (331 %), BrickHeadz 19 units (302 %), Castle 25 units (632 %), City 30 units (144 %), Collectible Minifigures 35 units (not available), Duplo 47 units (49 %), Friends 24 units (66 %), Marvel Super Heroes 27 units (95 %), Ninjago 31 units (113 %), Star Wars 37 units (214 %) and Town 35 units (422 %).

Ultimately, no correlation can be identified between the performance and the number of sub-themes. The fact that themes with an average of 8, 21 and 23 sub-theme areas experience significantly higher increases in value seems to be more of a coincidence. As a result, no further investigation is carried out into the most profitable and least profitable sub-topic areas.

Instead, I would like to go even further and check whether the availability of a theme over time (from, to) is potentially related to its performance. For this purpose, the difference between the release date and the discontinuation date (EOL) of each associated LEGO set for a theme is considered. Finally, the difference represents the duration of availability of a theme. For

LEGO themes that have not yet been discontinued at the time of the statistical investigation, the date of December 31, 2020 is assumed. Due to the good data record situation, all 120 themes can be taken into account for the following graphical evaluation in Figure 57. The duration of the themes is given in months. These range from 1 month to 52 months respectively 4.33 years. As you can see from the X-axis of Figure 57, there are gaps in the time axis, whereby there is not a theme for every duration. For example, as of December 31, 2020, there is no theme available in the market for either 24 or 25 months. Consequently, this duration was omitted from the X-axis. For other durations, there were several topics, whereby I use the arithmetic medium.

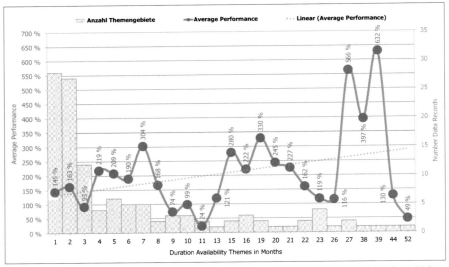

*Figure 57 - Correlation between average performance and duration of availability for LEGO themes*

Also here, an inconsistent development can be observed, whereby, to my astonishment, especially the longer durations generate the highest value developments:

- The *Castle* theme stayed for 39 years from 1978 to 2016. The average increase in value is 632 percent as of December 31, 2020.
- The *Space* theme stayed for 38 years from 1978 to 2015, with an average appreciation of 397 percent as of December 31, 2020.
- The *Town* theme stayed for 28 years from 1987 to 2004. The average appreciation is 566 percent as of December 31, 2020.

On the contrary, I suspected that the value of themes with short availabilities in particular would increase. Looking at Figure 57, a more differentiated picture appears. LEGO themes that only remain in the LEGO universe

304

for a short time do not manage to establish themselves and settle eventually. For example, LEGO themes with an availability of 6 months or less only achieve an average increase in value of 154 percent. LEGO themes that have been available for 7 to 12 months have increased in value by 161 percent. If a LEGO theme manages to stay between 12 and 24 months, chances are good that it will achieve an average increase in value of 205 percent. And LEGO themes available for more than 2 years achieved an average increase in value of 351 percent.

It seems reasonable to presume that, in addition to the availability of the theme in terms of time, the related content or the popularity of the theme also plays an important role for its performance. For example, the above-mentioned themes Castle, Space and Town all have one thing in common: These themes were already extremely popular during their lifetime and they obviously still are today. It can be assumed that LEGO themes are only on sale for a long time if The LEGO Group perceives a high demand for them or sells an above-average number of LEGO sets for a theme. Looking at the three themed areas Castle (281 sets), Space (323 sets) and Town (647 sets), it can be stated that in total, 1,251 LEGO sets are sold. This much can be said, based on all 148 LEGO themed areas, an average of 113 LEGO sets are contained in one themes.

LEGO investors should therefore focus their attention on LEGO themes that are particularly in demand. Obviously, it is not absolutely necessary that the theme area is subject to a licensing agreement. The three themed areas Castle, Space and Town also achieved high increases in value without any underlying licensing agreement.

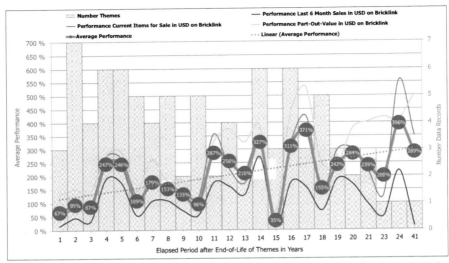

*Figure 58 - Relationship between average performance and expired time after End-Of-Life for LEGO themes*

In order to further examine which influential factors have led to the success of some themes, we will also look at how the value of themes has developed in the period after the End-Of-Life. The basis is all LEGO sets of a theme, for which the End-Of-Life date as well as at least one current price information is known. According to these criteria, a total of 89 of the 120 themes are still available for analysis. This results in a deficit of 31 themes. These are the 31 subject areas that have only been published in the current year 2020. Even if themes are already End-Of-Life, strictly speaking not even a single year has passed for a change in value to be observed.

*So, what do I expect from this analysis?* First and foremost, I hope to gain insights to the effect that a tendency can be drawn as to when LEGO themes reach their performance peak in retirement. Figure 58 indicates a correlation that the growing gap between EOL and the cutoff date of 12/31/2020 has an impact on the appreciation of themes. To determine how long a theme has been retired, the following procedure was undertaken. First, the arithmetic mean of the EOL date of all associated LEGO sets for a theme was determined. The expired time after the EOL is then the difference to the status of the present evaluation as of December 31, 2020.

As expected, the performance of themes immediately after retirement is very low. Accordingly, the value increases one year after the EOL averaged 67 percent. Just two years after the official EOL, the average increase in value was still 95 percent. However, extraordinary variations in value can be seen in the years that follow, with LEGO themes increasing significantly in value over the longer term. This is supported by the graph *Last 6 Month Sales in USD on Bricklink* as well as Part-Out-Value in USD on Bricklink, which also forecast clear upward trends. Only the underlying graph Current *Items for Sale in USD on Bricklink* is much more uncertain in its forecast and shows only a moderate value growth.

The literal collapse in performance 15 years after EOL can be explained as a result of two of the underlying three LEGO themes. The two LEGO themes *Baby* and *Primo* were already less popular during their lifetime. This is now evident many years later after the LEGO themes have been retired.

In general, LEGO investors should keep in mind that as time passes after the EOL of a LEGO set or theme, there is always a risk that LEGO collectors and fans who are enthusiastic about building can lose their interest in old LEGO sets or themes. Over the years, it is not unusual that people's areas of interest change. The evaluation of Figure 58 does not confirm this. Holding on to LEGO themes for too long does not have a negative effect on the return. Rather, it confirms once again that themes are in an upward trend overall, but that the individual popularity of a theme should not be underestimated. The popularity of a theme is very often associated how large LEGO sets are. For clarification, I have reviewed LEGO themes in terms of the average number of Regular Items. In this respect, LEGO themes experience a wide range. For example, *LEGO set no. 4521221-1 C-3PO - Chrome Gold (SW 30th Anniversary Edition)* from the Star Wars theme consists strictly of only one part (minifigure). However, *LEGO set no. 75192-1 Millennium Falcon - UCS (2nd Edition)* from the same Star Wars theme consists of a total of 7,513 Regular Items. On average, Star Wars LEGO sets have

469 Regular Items. This illustrates how much LEGO sets vary within a theme in terms of their Regular Items.

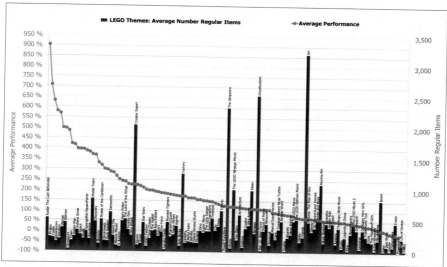

Figure 59 - Correlation between the average performance and number of Regular Items for LEGO themes

In fact, the historical performance is not related to the average number of Regular Items. The performance as a function of the number of Regular Items can be generalized as follows:

| Average Number of Regular Items | Average Performance |
|---|---|
| ≥ 3,000 and < 2,000 | 66 % |
| ≥ 2,000 and < 3,000 | 156 % |
| ≥ 1,000 and < 2,000 | 118 % |
| ≥ 900 and < 1.000 | not available |
| ≥ 800 and < 900 | 188 % |
| ≥ 700 and < 800 | not available |
| ≥ 600 and < 700 | 180 % |
| ≥ 500 and < 600 | 239 % |
| ≥ 400 and < 500 | 153 % |
| ≥ 300 and < 400 | 168 % |
| ≥ 200 and < 300 | 216 % |
| ≥ 100 and < 200 | 211 % |
| ≥ 75 and < 100 | 144 % |

| ≥ 50 and < 100 | 121 % |
|---|---|
| ≥ 1 and < 50 | 88 % |

Table 18 - Ranking according to the number of Regular Items as well as average performance of LEGO themes.

Table 18 shows particularly well the trends of the smaller LEGO themes. For example, LEGO themes with 100 to 300 Regular Items have more than doubled on average. These include well-known and successful themes such as *BrickHeadz, Castle, Bionicle, Town, Space* and *Spider-Man*. Themes with better performances only occur in the range of 500 to 600 Regular Items. These mainly include themes with licensing agreements, such as *Harry Potter, Jurassic World, The Lord of the Rings* or *The LEGO Batman Movie*. It can also be concluded that themes with an average of more than 1,000 regular bricks and pieces increase less in value.

With release of a new theme, the number of related LEGO Sets is usually not known. Oftentimes, The LEGO Group does not share this information. Sometimes they just don't know either. Primarily, the company wants to be flexible in case the LEGO theme is successful. In this case, the company can tie on the success of the LEGO themes by releasing more LEGO sets at a later time.

Investing in entire theme series can be time-consuming and costly. A very good example is the LEGO theme *BrickHeadz*. This series was launched with *LEGO set no. 41585-1 Batman* in 2017. Since then, 96 different BrickHeadz have been released as of December 31, 2020. Meanwhile, the theme has a large fan community and so there are always collectors who place great emphasis on a complete collection. As a result, LEGO BrickHeadz are bought more often, which are less popular, but ultimately may not be missing in the collection (e.g., *LEGO set no. 40350-1 Chick*). At least this is the argument of some LEGO investors. A preprogrammed dilemma, because it is not known how many more BrickHeadz sets will appear eventually. Most recently, there have been constant rumors about the discontinuation of the

BrickHeadz, which have ultimately not proven true to this day. As of November 31, 2022, there are 138 different BrickHeadz models, according to Brickset.

The speculation about the last official LEGO set of a theme series seems all the more interesting. Basically, you can never be sure that The LEGO Group will not announce more LEGO sets after all. However, it can be assessed how the return of the first LEGO set of each theme is. The first LEGO set of a theme always has a special rank. This LEGO set is sometimes given both an ideal and emotional value. It is not uncommon for the first LEGO set in a theme to be symbolic of the theme itself.

In Figure 60 we see a comparison of the performance of the first LEGO set of a theme (red graph) and the average performance of the related themes (blue graph). If the red graph exceeds the blue graph, the performance of the first LEGO set of the theme was higher than the average performance of the theme itself. For the evaluation, the data records of 61 percent or 91 of the 148 LEGO themes. This also means that for 57 first LEGO sets a crucial data records (e.g., MSRP or at least one current price information) is missing. Therefore, these 57 first LEGO sets cannot be considered further.

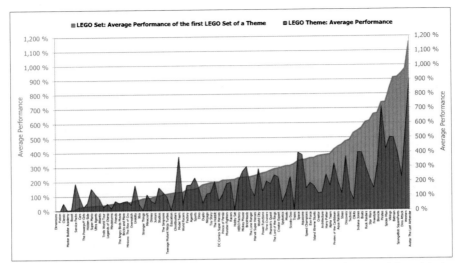

*Figure 60 - Comparison of the performance of the first LEGO set in a theme and the related theme*

Overall, 71 percent or 64 first LEGO sets of a theme show a higher performance than the associated LEGO theme. This means that the chances of a LEGO investor acquiring the first LEGO set of a theme area are 71 percent. Particularly pleasing is the finding that the 64 first LEGO sets outperformed the corresponding theme by an average of 111 percent.

A total of 29 percent or 26 of the 91 first LEGO sets performed worse in value than the corresponding LEGO theme. The average performance of the first LEGO set was only 14 percent lower than that of the theme.

Price spikes after a LEGO set is retired are often caused by LEGO themes being completed by collectors. This can simply happen when people (e.g., collectors) have missed out on the first LEGO set of a theme for individual reasons. For example, because the concerned person had no interest in LEGO products at that time. A good example of this are Modular Buildings. This is a sub-theme of Creator Expert. Together with *LEGO set no. 10182-1 Cafe Corner, LEGO set no. 10190-1 Market Street* and *LEGO set no. 10185-1 Green Grocer* were released at a time when LEGO products were not as popular as we know today. These LEGO sets have tremendous collector value today and are hard to find in new and unopened condition. Many fans of Modular Buildings today would love to complete their collection with these three LEGO sets, but have to pay a lot for them.

I would like to close this chapter with a comparison. On Bricklink there is an overview of the most popular LEGO themes. The purpose is to clarify whether the popularity of a theme or sub-theme can be used as an indicator for its performance. The so called *All Time Favorite Themes* are chosen by the Bricklink community. Every member has the possibility to choose his favorite theme when registering on Bricklink. The overview is independent of the member's country of residence. For this purpose, the election takes place continuously.

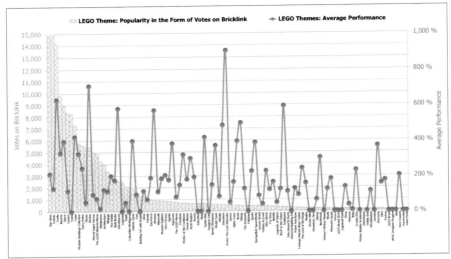

*Figure 61 - Comparison of popularity on Bricklink and related average performance for LEGO themes*

With the introduction of new themes by The LEGO Group, there is a constant change of the most popular theme on Bricklink. Over the past 50 years, Bricklink has identified that City, Space, Castle and Pirate themes are constantly topping the popularity scale. These genres are extremely popular and sought after by fans.

There are already more than 250,000 members who have voted on Bricklink. This makes this public poll certainly one of the most representative of its kind. Star Wars is currently at the top. With only half as many votes, the Technic theme is in second rank, followed by Castle in third rank. Finally, there seems to be no direct correlation here either. Just because a LEGO theme is extraordinarily popular on Bricklink does not seem to predetermine an above-average increase in value. For example, the LEGO theme Mindstorms is still in 15th place on the popularity scale, yet according to this statistical survey, the theme only achieves an average return of 20 percent. Even apparently less popular themes such as Toys Story (62nd place) achieve higher increases in value (122 %).

Taking into account the previous hard factors, it appears very difficult in principle to understand why the values of LEGO themes develop so differently. Among many LEGO collectors, a great preference for certain themes has emerged over the past decades. Classic themes such as knights, pirates or westerns from the 80s and 90s have enjoyed great popularity among collectors for years. LEGO collectors focus primarily on themes that they like. Therefore, as a LEGO investor, you increase your chances if you focus on LEGO themes that are trending well. In turn, other themes are rarely collected. For example, LEGO sets from the City theme sell very well, but the City theme is rather unpopular among collectors. In particular, themes such as City, another major factor comes into play. Collectors try to continuously complete the themes they collect. Thus, the theme is a demarcation of the collecting passion. In the case of themes with knights or pirates, this is fairly easy to do, since LEGO sets for these themes are only released at irregular intervals. LEGO topics around the topic City are supplied yearly with new LEGO sets. A demarcation is hardly possible for collectors here. For anti-cyclical investors certainly a very interesting circumstance. If a LEGO themes is unpopular during its lifetime, there will be correspondingly little supply in the future. Interesting opportunities can arise here, which is why I personally even have a particularly strong focus on LEGO sets and themes that are apparently unpopular at first (e.g., *LEGO set no. 75222-1 Betrayal in Cloud City*).

Fundamental insights are certainly possible in later chapters (e.g., weight and licensing). Nevertheless, it is important to be interested in the themes in which you want to invest. Questions for this can be: *How popular is the theme?* Here you need to do some research. Licensed LEGO sets e.g., Star Wars, Harry Potter or Lord of the Rings are often much more popular than more general LEGO sets (e.g., City or Friends). This is not least due to the fact that products for popular series, movies, etc. sell particularly well.

### 4.5.5  Weight

Earlier chapters have already suggested that the isolated view of the average *Price-per-Brick* is an outdated approach. This single factor does not seem to be sufficient to evaluate whether the price structure of a LEGO set is appropriate and the individual value performance is the result of it. Therefore, this approach will be followed in the form that in a first step a possible relationship between the average *Price-per-Brick* as well as the average *Weight-per-Brick* will be identified. A relationship between the *Weight-per-Brick* and the *Price-per-Brick* is conceivable due to the number of Regular Items, which are included in both factors. The second step is to investigate to what extent a relationship between both factors (*Weight-per-Brick* and *Price-per-Brick*) has had an impact on the performance of LEGO sets in the past. Themes can be left out of this framework, as they are merely a categorical summary of LEGO sets.

The smaller LEGO bricks and pieces are, the higher is their weight for a certain volume (e.g., the assembled LEGO set). For example, a 1 x 1 brick weighs exactly 0.44 grams. Thus, six 1 x 1 bricks weigh a total of 2.64 grams. However, in comparison, a 1 x 6 brick weighs only 2.42 grams. Although six individual 1 x 1 bricks cover the same space as a single 6 x 1 brick, they weigh about 10 percent more. A single 1 x 1 plate weighs 0.2 grams. In contrast, a single 2 x 4 plate weighs exactly 1.2 grams. Even in this example, individual bricks with the same volume have a higher weight of about 33 percent. Accordingly, in principle, an identical LEGO set (in terms of volume) can be constructed with different individual bricks and parts so that it has different weights.

In the past, the weight of LEGO sets was of little or no importance. Since LEGO sets have become larger and thus more expensive, weight has become increasingly important in assessing the price composition of a LEGO set. This is not least due to the fact that The LEGO Group has recently been releasing more and more LEGO sets in such a form, which have already existed comparatively similar. An appropriate example is *LEGO set no.*

*10225-1 R2-D2* at an MSRP of USD 179.99 from 2012, which was reissued in a very similar form in 2021. *LEGO set no. 75308-1 R2-D2* has an MSRP of USD 199.99.[1] If we ignore the hard factors such as weight, number of individual bricks and parts, minifigures, etc., the customer undoubtedly perceives the new identical LEGO set as more expensive (+ USD 20). Of course, we already know that material and production costs increase in 10 years. Already between 2012 and 2020 (9 years), the inflation rate was 14.14 percent. Therefore, if the number of bricks and parts, weight, etc. remained the same, an MSRP for *LEGO set no. 75308-1 R2-D2* of about USD 205 would have been reasonable.

For LEGO investors, there is no question that weight must be considered as an additional factor in evaluating a LEGO set. The weight factor, in addition to the number of Regular Items, allows LEGO sets to be evaluated in terms of their physical condition. Unlike the number of Regular Items, which is a measure of complexity and detail, weight gives a sense of the size of a LEGO set.

For LEGO designers, weight is the primary determinant in figuring out whether a LEGO set is within a given budget. In sum, the weight and number of Regular Items give an idea of how much LEGO you will get.

By additionally considering weight, LEGO sets can be evaluated in terms of the following factors:

- Average gross to net weight ratio
- Average share of packaging, instructions, individual bricks and parts, minifigures in total weight
- MSRP per gross or net weight
- Relationship between Price-per-Brick and Weight-per-Brick

---

[1] For LEGO investors, the example of *LEGO sets no. 10225-1 and 75308-1* is an extremely interesting case, since ideally comparative values (e.g., change in value) are available for an almost identical LEGO set. The extent to which such new editions can be used at all to evaluate the price and value structure of LEGO sets will be discussed in more detail later..

- Price information for Last 6 Month Sales in USD on Bricklink per Regular Items
- Price information for Current Items for Sale in USD on Bricklink per Regular Items
- Price information for Part-Out-Value in USD on Bricklink per Regular Items
- Average performance or change in value for Regular Items

The following is a comprehensive overview of the annual development of the weight of LEGO sets. Since LEGO sets have been changing in shape and color for years, and numerous new bricks and parts are continuously being introduced, it can be assumed that these changes have an impact on the weight of LEGO sets. In order to be able to show changes in the past, the terms gross weight and net weight of LEGO sets need to be distinguished in advance.

The gross weight is the sum of the net weight of the individual bricks, parts, instruction/s, package/s and other content/s (e.g., sticker/s). Bricklink records the gross weight of many LEGO sets as well as the net weight of associated instructions and packaging. There are already many studies that have determined the average net weight of a minifigure. From experience, this varies between 10 and 12 grams per minifigure. In this evaluation, we calculate 11.5 grams per minifigure for the full period. Subtracting the weights of package/s and instruction/s from the gross weight of the LEGO set gives the net weight for the individual bricks, parts, sticker sheet/s and minifigure/s. The data availability for gross weights and net weights is as follows:

- **Number of Records for Gross Weight of LEGO Sets:**
  25.7 Percent or 3,613 of 14,068

- **Number of Records for Net Weight of Instructions:**
  50.4 Percent or 7,086 of 14,068

- **Number of Records for Net Weight of Package:**
  44.5 Percent or 6,263 of 14,068

- **Number of Records for Net Weight of LEGO Sets:**
  17.5 Percent or 2,460 of 14,068

- **Number of Records for Minifigures in LEGO Sets:**
  1,780 of unknown

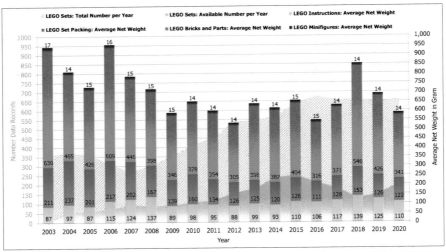

*Figure 62 - Average gross and net weights in grams for LEGO sets between 2003 and 2020*

In principle, data availability is poor. Up to 2003, there is practically no data on the various weights, which is why these years are excluded. The data situation only improves with the year 2003, with only an average of 26 percent of data records available for the period between 2003 and 2020. Nevertheless, a representativeness for the further statistical survey of the weight is given.

Figure 62 summarizes all annual net weights. The sums of the annual net weights give the corresponding gross weights. Annually, the gross weight fluctuates between -22 and +24 percent. Overall, the average gross weight of LEGO sets decreases by 4 percent annually between 2003 and 2020. Some LEGO sets will be significantly lighter in 2020 than they were in 2003.

The main driver is falling net weights for individual bricks and parts, min-ifigure/s, instruction/s, and package/s. The drop in the net weight of pack-age/s and individual bricks and parts is particularly evident. Whereas in 2003 an average of 630 grams of individual bricks and parts were included in a LEGO set, by 2020 this figure is down to just 341 grams. This represents a reduction of around 46 percent. A very similar situation emerges when we look at the weight of the package/s. In 2003, the average packaging material weighed 211 grams. In 2020, the average weight was only 122 grams. This corresponds to a reduction in packaging weight of 58 percent. The decreasing net weight can be explained as follows: We already know that The LEGO Group is increasingly releasing larger LEGO sets, so the average net weight of individual bricks and parts can only decrease because significantly smaller individual bricks and parts are more often being used by The LEGO Group. As a result, the average weight of a LEGO individual brick or part decreases. Consumers appreciate this very much because it generally results in more beautiful models with more depth of detail.

The net weights for minifigure/s and package/s are also decreasing from 2003 to 2020. The latter is mainly due to the fact that The LEGO Group is increasingly releasing smaller LEGO sets. During the period under review, only the average weight of the instruction/s increased. This, in turn, will not surprise one or the other reader. It is no secret that The LEGO Group has been making its instructions progressively simpler in the recent past. Nowadays, the instructions include much more building steps, with each step involving far fewer individual bricks and parts. The simpler building steps, with fewer bricks and parts per step, make it possible for children to build larger LEGO sets.

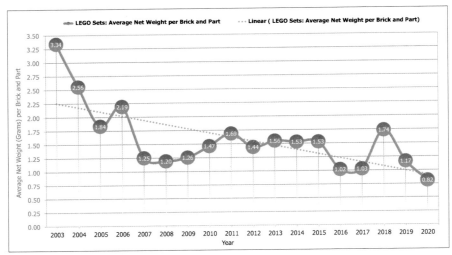

*Figure 63 - Average net weight per LEGO brick or part in grams*

The average net weight for a LEGO brick or part recorded in Figure 63 shows a clear downward trend of -13 percent annually on average from 2003 to 2020. In 2020, a single brick or part in a LEGO set weighs an average of 0.82 grams. In 2003, a LEGO brick or part weighed an average of 3.34 grams. This represents a reduction in weight of around 75 percent. At the same time, this confirms the trend that LEGO sets are increasingly containing smaller bricks and parts. This must undoubtedly also be reflected in the average MSRP per gram.

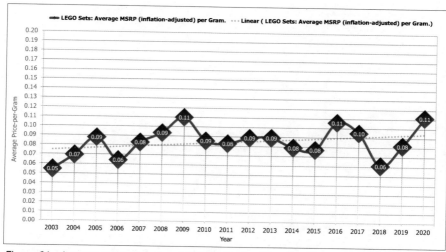

*Figure 64 - Average price per net weight (MSRP per gram)*

Over the same period, a slight increase in the MSRP per gram can be identified. It must be added here that in the case of Figure 64, the weight refers exclusively to minifigures and individual bricks and parts. From this it can be concluded that an average gram of LEGO costs about USD 0.08. Thus, you can quickly compare the price structure of different LEGO sets and themes.

After the correlation between MSRP, weight, number of individual bricks and parts has been itemized, the two hard factors Price-per-Brick and Weight-per-Brick are to be combined in the following. Ideally, this will provide an explanation of the extent to which both factors influence the performance of LEGO sets. The data records of 2,460 LEGO sets are available for this evaluation.

The red graph shows the average Price-per-Brick as a function of the average Weight-per-Brick. For example, in the past a LEGO set with an average Price-per-Brick k of USD 0.2 per brick weighed an average of 1.8 grams. The blue graph represents the past performance as a function of the Price-per-Brick (right Y-axis or red graph) and the Weight-per-Brick (X-axis).

323

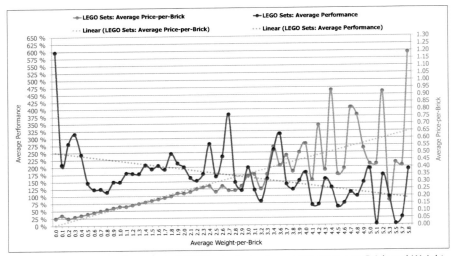

*Figure 65 - Average performance of LEGO sets depending on the Price-per-Brick and Weight-per-Brick*

In the previous example, LEGO sets with an average Price-per-Brick of USD 0.2 per brick and an average Weight-per-Brick of 1.8 grams per brick, have achieved a 246 percent increase in value. Both graphs are highly volatile in places, with an overall trend emerging. As a result, the range with a Price-per-Brick k of USD 0.25 per brick, for example, has seen a variety of past value trends. For LEGO sets since 2003, the associated average Weight-per-Brick has been between 2.2 and 3.2 grams per brick. This range achieved an average increase in value between 82 and 153 percent. The opposite trends of both graphs give a clear picture that in the past, as the average Price-per-Brick increased, the average Weight-per-Brick also increased, while lower value increases were achieved (blue graph). Again, a lower average Price-per-Brick automatically led to a lower Weight-per-Brick. Both factors ensured that higher increases in value were achieved.

Finally, the Price-per-Brick (red graph) relative to the x-axis (Weight-per-Brick) shows us the average structure or composition of LEGO sets. In addition, the following Figure 66 shows the underlying number of data points for the Price-per-Brick and Weight-per-Brick ratios. For this purpose, the graph Price-per-Brick was replaced by the number of data records.

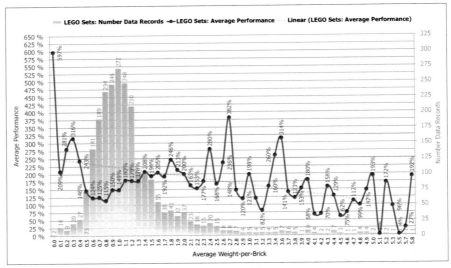

*Figure 66 - Data records complementary to Figure 65*

Figure 65 presents a diagram that can be used as a forecasting tool for the future development of LEGO sets. It is important to keep in mind that the average time horizon is 18 years. This in turn means that the value developments shown may have been achieved earlier but never later than after 18 years. Furthermore, these are average performance data. Of course, these may deviate in individual cases, with both higher and lower performance possible. In the present case, three different indicators of price information were used. This manifests in particular the arithmetic determination of the increase in value.

At the end of the chapter, various examples will be simulated to show investors how to use Figure 65. The randomly chosen example is *LEGO set no. 7137-1 Piraka* from the Bionicle theme. The LEGO set has 15 Regular Items, a total net weight of 66 grams and an MSRP of USD 7.99, or USD 9.52 after adjusting for inflation.

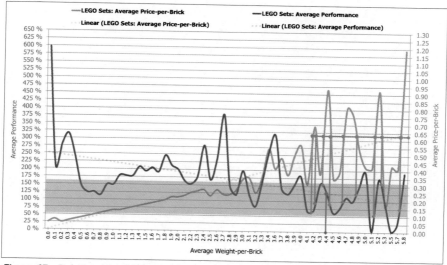

*Figure 67 - Relationship of Price-per-Brick and Weight-per-Brick using the example of LEGO set no. 7137-1 Piraka*

*LEGO set no. 7137-1 Piraka* is from 2010 and has a Price-per-Brick of USD 0.63 per brick and a Weight-per-Brick of 4.4 grams per brick. According to Figure 65, a Weight-per-Brick of 4.4 grams per brick results in average value increases of 129 percent (dark green). Again, according to Figure 67, a Price-per-Brick of USD 0.63 per brick results in several average increases in value. In the past, these have been in the range of 52 to 158 percent (light green lines), which corresponds to an average increase in value of 105 percent. Thus, we have two increases in value based on empirical values over the past 18 years. The arithmetic average of the two increases in value is 117 percent[1].

Looking at our three-price information reveals that *LEGO set no. 7137-1 Piraka* has achieved the following value developments as of December 31, 2020: For *Last 6 Month Sales in USD on Bricklink*, there is no comparative value because the LEGO set has not sold once in the past 6 months. For

---

[1] x = (129 %+105 %) / 2 = 117 %

327

*Current Items for Sale in USD on Bricklink*, the LEGO set is for sale for an average of 29 USD. Taking into account the MSRP after adjusting for inflation, this represents a 206 percent increase in value. As described earlier, we always look at average performance in this analysis, which is why we also want to look at value by *Part-Out-Value in USD on Bricklink*. As of December 31, 2020, the LEGO set no. 7137-1 Piraka has a *Part-Out-Value in USD on Bricklink* of USD 17. Taking into account the MSRP after adjusting for inflation, this represents a 78 percent increase in value. Consequently, we get a documented average appreciation of 142 percent[1]. This current value increase is 18 percent higher than the forecast (117%) according to Figure 67.

I would like to present a second example. The *LEGO set no. 42056-1 Porsche 911 GT3 RS* has a total of 2,704 Regular Items, a net weight of 2,458 grams and an MSRP of USD 299.99.

---

[1] x = (206 %+78 %) / 2 = 142 %

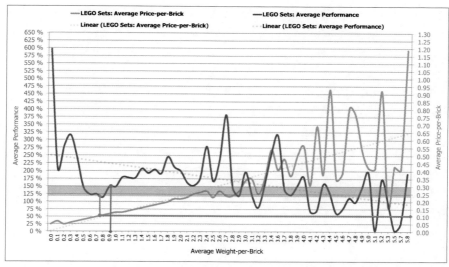

Legend:
- —— LEGO Sets: Average Price-per-Brick
- —— LEGO Sets: Average Performance
- ····· Linear (LEGO Sets: Average Price-per-Brick)
- ····· Linear (LEGO Sets: Average Performance)

*Figure 68 - Relationship of Price-per-Brick and Weight-per-Brick using the example of LEGO set no. 42056-1 Porsche 911 GT3 RS*

This results in a Price-per-Brick of USD 0.11 per brick and a Weight-per-Brick ratio of 0.91 grams per brick. At this point, you can already see the significant difference between the two LEGO sets, with the Porsche having a much lower average Weight-per-Brick. According to the statistical survey or Figure 68, a Weight-per-Brick of 0.91 grams per brick resulted in a 150 percent increase in value in the past. For a Price-per-Brick ratio of USD 0.11 per brick, the increase in value was 120 percent. We again assume an arithmetic mean of 135 percent. With an MSRP of USD 299.99, or USD 323.56 after adjusting for inflation, the current value after calculation is USD 760.37.

Looking at the three-price information reveals that *LEGO set no. 42056-1 Porsche 911 GT3 RS* has achieved the following performance as of December 31, 2020: For *Last 6 Month Sale in USD on Bricklink*, the average price sold is USD 582. This represents an average inflation-adjusted appreciation of 80 percent. For *Current Items for Sale in USD on Bricklink*, the

LEGO set is for sale for an average of 788 USD. This represents an average inflation-adjusted appreciation of 144 percent. As of December 31, 2020, the LEGO Porsche has a *Part-Out-Value in USD on Bricklink* of USD 838. Taking into account the MSRP after adjusting for inflation, this corresponds to a value increase of 159 percent. Consequently, we get a current average appreciation of 128 percent. This current value increase is only 7 percent below the forecast according to Figure 68.

Admittedly, the isolated consideration of the weight of LEGO sets is also not an adequate means of determining the value. Only with the help of the two ratios Price-per-Brick and Weight-per-Brick a meaningful and helpful indicator seems to be found, so that LEGO investors can judge the future value development of LEGO sets.

### 4.5.6 Time

The previous findings have shown that the timing factor plays a significant role in the performance of a LEGO set. However, the factor time must
be distinguished between the release date (from), the expiration date (to),
the age of a LEGO set and the lifetime of a LEGO set. Strictly speaking, the
release date and the expiration date are specific dates in the form of days.
In contrast, age and lifetime are specific periods of time. The period between the release date and the expiration date is the lifetime of a LEGO set.
Whereas the difference between the day of consideration (e.g., today) and
the expiration date defines the age of a LEGO set. Thus, the age tells how
long a LEGO set has been retired.

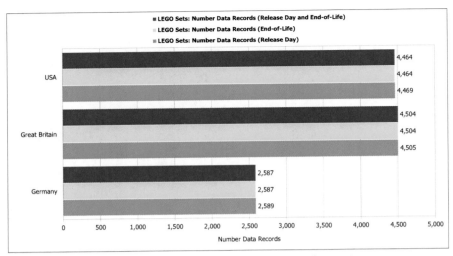

*Figure 69 - Number of data records for availability of LEGO Sets by country on https://www.lego.com*

Both release date and expiration date are best recorded on the Brickset platform. Here the platform distinguishes in principle even in the countries Germany, Great Britain and USA. The data records of Brickset document the availability on The LEGO Group Online Shop at *https://www.lego.com*

Especially for the USA and Great Britain, there are significantly more data records available compared to Germany. This may certainly also be due to the fact that Brickset as a platform has its origin in England. In addition, it is very pleasing that almost the same number of data points are documented for the release date and the expiration date. LEGO sets with only one of the two data records cannot be considered for the present evaluation. Both data records are needed for consideration in order to calculate the lifetime of a LEGO set. Also, the expiration date is needed to determine the age of a LEGO set. In this regard, another graph has been included in Figure 69, which shows the set of data records for LEGO sets for which both the release date and expiration date are available.

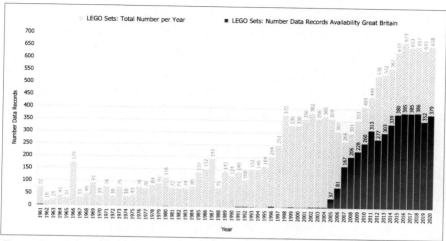

*Figure 70 - Number of data records for availability of LEGO sets by year in United Kingdom at https://www.lego.com*

The data set for Great Britain marginally exceeds available data records of the USA (+40 LEGO sets). This is why the data set from Great Britain is used for further analysis. Thus, we have 32 percent or 4,504 data records of the available 14,068 LEGO sets. The distribution of the available data between 1961 and 2020 is shown in Figure 70.

For the years between 1961 and 2004, almost no data records are documented. The same applies to data points from Germany and the USA. From 2004 onwards, the data situation slowly brightens up. For the years 2007 to 2020, data points are available for 60 percent of LEGO sets. Accordingly, the focus is on these years. Unfortunately, these are the years that experienced significantly lower value growth. It is therefore essential to check the validity of the following evaluation. The first part of the chapter is dedicated to the lifetime and availability of LEGO sets between the years 2007 and 2020.

| | | |
|---|---|---|
| Germany: | 530 Calendar Days or 1.45 Years |
| Great Britain: | 536 Calendar Days or 1.47 Years |

- USA: 526 Calendar Days or 1.44 Years

The listed values are average durations of LEGO sets according to *https://www.lego.com*. Surprisingly, all three countries are very close to each other. Nevertheless, I was personally expecting the average availability to be significantly higher. The reason for this is that in forums and other social medias it is always said that the average lifetime is two years. The lifetime or availability of LEGO sets varies considerably in certain cases. Of course, this depends on many different factors, such as number of sales of the LEGO set. Other important influencing factors for the lifetime or availability are the assigned theme or whether a license agreement exists. In addition, it can be assumed that the increasing number of new LEGO sets per year decreases the lifetime or availability. The following chart shows the lifetime and availability of LEGO sets in the UK by year.

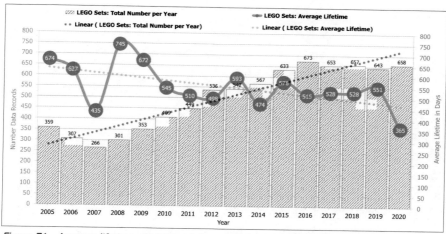

*Figure 71 - Average lifetime of LEGO sets by year in the United Kingdom*

The gray graph is the same as from Figure 70 and represents the course of new LEGO sets per year. The red graph shows the average lifetime for LEGO sets from the respective year. For both graphs, the corresponding linear trend graph has been colored accordingly. A look at these two confirms the initial assumption. There is a tendency for the average availability or lifetime of LEGO sets to decrease as the number of new LEGO sets has been increasing for years. One argument for this is that The LEGO Group is limited in space in its official retail stores. Many LEGO stores have existed for several years. These were originally planned and designed for much smaller capacities or numbers of LEGO sets. On the other hand, each year the largest possible number of LEGO sets must be displayed in the company's own stores. With the space limitation and at the same time strong increase of new LEGO sets, LEGO sets have to be taken out of the store shelves need to be exchanged more quickly.

With regard to Figure 71, it must be added that many LEGO sets from 2020 are not yet retired. Consequently, the year 2020 must be disregarded in the evaluation, as significantly higher lifetimes are still possible here. Of

335

course, this will only become apparent with the next few years, how high the lifetimes really were.

LEGO investors should assume that this trend will continue over the next few years. You should constantly monitor the development in this regard. With the average lifetime or availability of LEGO sets, purchases can be planned better. We already know that purchases should be made as close as possible to the End-of-Life date in order to tie up as little space and capital as possible. Up until now, we have only looked at the average lifetime or availability of LEGO sets. The lifetime or availability have a significant impact on the supply and demand of LEGO sets. In theory, this means that if LEGO sets are only available for a short time, it can be assumed that fewer LEGO sets will be sold. At the same time, fewer LEGO sets will find their way to the secondary market. Accordingly, LEGO sets with short lifetimes should experience higher increases in value than LEGO sets with longer lifetimes. Figure 72 shows that the lifetime and availability of LEGO sets have a significant impact on their performance. If lifetime or availability of a LEGO set in stores rises, the performance in turn falls. Conversely, the shorter a LEGO set's lifetime or availability, the higher its performance. LEGO sets with short lifetimes or availabilities have less chance to spread widely or to completely saturate the market. Rather, when the LEGO set is discontinued or becomes unavailable, demand for it will remain or increase. This demand is matched by little supply, which impacts the change in value. GWP's from The LEGO Group are an appropriate example. These complimentary items are only ever officially available for a fairly short period of time. The fact that the demand is significantly higher than the supply is especially shown by the later sales in the secondary market such as Ebay or Facebook Marketplace. After a GWP is no longer officially sold through The LEGO Group, the traded quantities of the products in the secondary market increase. In general, GWP's are known to generate comparatively high returns.

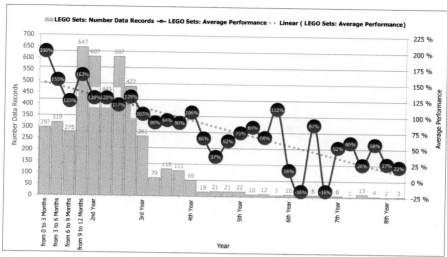

*Figure 72 - Correlation between lifetime and performance of LEGO sets*

Referring to Figure 72, LEGO sets that have only been officially on sale for up to 3 months achieve an increase in value of up to 200 percent. In turn, LEGO sets that have been officially available for more than 8 years only achieve an average increase in value of between 22 and 27 percent. According to the evaluation, a LEGO set loses an average of 2 percent return with each additional month it is officially on sale. According to Figure 72, 62 percent of LEGO sets are officially available between 9 and 30 months. As many as 20 percent of LEGO sets have a maximum runtime of nine months. Experience shows that the lifetimes or availabilities differ between LEGO themes. For example, as of the end of 2021, there are a total of nine LEGO sets in the *Chinese New Year* series. Neglecting the two LEGO sets that are currently (as of July 2022) still available, the remaining seven LEGO sets were always officially available for around one year.

Figure 73 illustrates the available data records of all theme areas for which the average lifetimes are available. The data records of 3,954 LEGO cover a total of 86 out of 148 themes. The dependency between themes and performances is less evident in Figure 73. However, the same tendency

337

can be seen overall, meaning that the higher the lifetime of a LEGO theme, the more likely it is that a lower return will be generated than for themes with shorter lifetimes. The lifetime of a theme ultimately depends on the success of the theme. Higher increases in value are particularly likely with short lifetimes or availabilities.

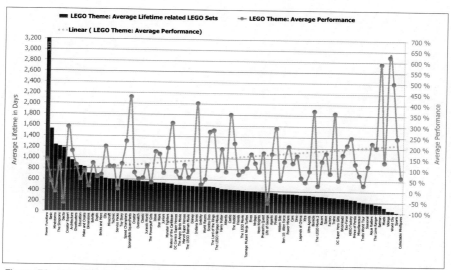

*Figure 73 - Correlation between lifetime and average annual performance of LEGO themes*

We will conclude the section with a look at the data records that show the relationship between average performance and age of a LEGO set. For this purpose, we use the EOL date of each LEGO set. The time period is defined from End-Of-Life to the reporting date of this study (December 31, 2020). Based on my experience, the majority of LEGO sets increase slightly during the official life or availability. Very often, there is a spike in demand as the EOL or retirement begins, which drives up the price of the affected LEGO sets. The central question is whether there are signs from which point in time LEGO sets increase or decrease in value. It may be possible to better determine when to buy and sell.

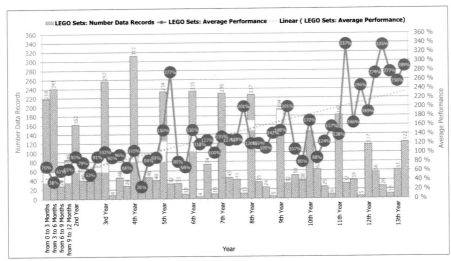

*Figure 74 - Average performance by age of LEGO sets as of December 31, 2020*

In Figure 74, we see the performance of LEGO sets with increasing age after End-Of-Life. The evaluation is based on 4,102 LEGO sets. This means that an average of 25 LE-GO sets are used for each month. There is no doubt that LEGO sets increase with the beginning of retirement. Overall, the overall trend is stable, but certain intervals have clearly volatile dips. It can be seen that all the over- and undershoots (e.g., from year 4 only 26 percent) happen in months for which few data records are available. For example, year 4 had a particularly high average of 26 percent for LEGO sets from the *Dimensions* theme. The *Dimensions* theme is one of the worst performing LEGO themes with an average performance of -10 percent. In addition, if the gap between EOL and the reporting date as of December 31, 2020 is short, the LEGO set was probably only recently removed from official sale. It is then still too early for an increase in value.

Just because a LEGO product is old does not automatically mean it is worth more. Older LEGO products, especially before the millennium, are sometimes clearly different from today's products. LEGO products are continuously improved. There are many new colors and shapes. For many years

340

LEGO sets have been getting bigger, more detailed and the construction more complex. The quality of workmanship and materials continue to improve. Nowadays LEGO sets are produced in large quantities. In contrast to the last century, the toys are distributed and marketed worldwide.

On the other hand, old LEGO sets have two decisive advantages. They have a certain charm or are considered nostalgic and have long since been retired. So there is a very high probability that we will not see them again in identical form and composition. These crucial facts make old LEGO sets desirable - especially among collectors.

As we have already seen from the evaluation, this is no guarantee for an increase in value. Exclusive sets such as The Simpsons or Ideas are on the market for between 1.5 and 2 years. If these LEGO sets sell very well, the The LEGO Group can extend the lifetime of these sets. LEGO sets that are real blockbusters (e.g., *LEGO set no. 10220-1 Volkswagen T1 Camping Bus* or *LEGO set no. 10252-1 VW Beetle*) usually do not have a fixed End-Of-Life date. This is where The LEGO Group weighs in on post-production. LEGO sets from the UCS (Ultimate Collectors Series) are officially available for an average of three years. Basic building sets such as baseplates and boxes of LEGO bricks currently labeled Classic, as well as railroad tracks, generally have a life span of just over two years.

Of course, there are always exceptions. *LEGO set no. 8038-1 The Battle of Endor* from the Star Wars theme was officially available for almost two years. *LEGO set no. 10221-1 Super Star Destroyer* was on the market for 6 years. It is not uncommon to see significantly different lifetimes for individual LEGO sets within themes. Themes such as Star Wars or Super Hero persevere for a long time, with their marketability also stuttering. In contrast, LEGO sets from The Longe Ranger, Prince of Persia and Pirates of Caribbean IV were available for an exceptionally short time.

### 4.5.7 Minifigures

In 1978, The LEGO Group patented the modern yellow minifigure with movable legs and arms, heads with the iconic face. Minifigures quickly became the secret stars and have driven the development of LEGO themes that have taken them through the city, sent them into space or had them fight medieval battles. The classic minifigures in *City* to *Star Wars*, *Ninjago* and *Friends* bring life to the LEGO universe.

Meanwhile, the standard smiley face is on a variety of printed faces, which first appeared in 1989 with the theme of *Pirates*. Minifigures now come with different colored arms, legs or hands. They were also followed by alternative body parts such as hooked hands and wooden legs. The LEGO minifigure we know today consists of nine main parts, seven of which are movable. With the introduction of hands, minifigures were equipped with other accessories and accessories. In addition, The LEGO Group has noticeably improved its printing techniques over the past decades.

For the first time in 1999, licensed movie characters of the Star Wars universe were produced. As a result, we now get incredibly-detailed LEGO minifigures. Bodies or torsos sometimes have printed front and back, double-sided faces, printed arms, accessories, front and side printed legs. There are numerous different variations for each of these parts. In the implementation of new LEGO minifigures, the Danes regularly outdo themselves and presumably there will be more fantastic innovations in the future.

Together with LEGO sets, LEGO minifigures have become a profitable collector's hobby over the past 10 to 15 years and occupy a kind of special position in LEGO investment. Even The LEGO Group has promoted minifigures as a collector's item and dedicated a separate theme to them in 2010 with *Collectable Minifigures*.

Missing parts and elements affect the value of a LEGO set, but not as much as a missing minifigure. In certain cases, a missing minifigure can cost as much as the entire LEGO set itself. Because each individual minifigure has its own personality and history.

The isolated trade of LEGO minifigures has developed into a dedicated market. LEGO enthusiasts quickly realized that minifigures from sets or polybags could be sold on platforms like Bricklink or Ebay for sometimes more than the belonging LEGO sets. While LEGO minifigures and sets are tangibly linked, minifigures can dramatically affect the value of sets. The popular minifigures are also known as the currency of the LEGO world. Individual minifigures can sell for dozens, if not hundreds and even thousands of US dollars

Basically, there are no official MSRPs for minifigures (except *Collectable Minifigures Series*). Rather, minifigures are included in the MSRP of the belonging LEGO set. The prices or values of individual minifigures are based on supply and demand. Accordingly, the isolated consideration of the value development of minifigures without a basic reference is not feasible. The value development can only be assessed together with the belonging LEGO set.

A serious aspect in the past was that LEGO minifigures were not easy to categorize and track prices. This originated from the nature of a LEGO minifigure. A standard LEGO minifigure consists of a head, torso (including arms) and legs. For each of these components there is an individual part number. However, The LEGO Group does not have a part number for a complete (assembled) minifigure. Due to the increased commitment of the LEGO community, own nomenclatures and numbering systems have been developed for the multitude of minifigures without official numbers. Here we differ the numbering of Bricklink or Brickset, which make it much easier for both fans and collectors to identify LEGO minifigures. If you are more interested in the history of the minifigures, I recommend one of the numerous LEGO minifigure books, which deal exclusively with this topic.

Experience shows that especially sought-after and thus later expensive minifigures are in LEGO sets and rarely occur alone (e.g., *Collectible Minifigure Series*). It is extremely important that these are original LEGO sets and therefore minifigures. Especially with the valuable LEGO figures, there are fakes, figures from other manufacturers or unbranded figures, which may look particularly similar to the original. The type and completeness of a figure or minifigure is important for its evaluation.

Since the launch of minifigures in 1975, it is impossible to imagine the LEGO universe without them and they have become extremely popular. Although the focus here is on minifigures, it is important to know that The LEGO Group has designed numerous other figures in many different scales and origins, some of which have been around since 1975. These figures include System (minifigures), Friends (minidolls), Technic, Belville, Friends, Scala, Duplo, Bionicle, and Fabuland. These figures appear in LEGO sets in different ways. We distinguish each of these figures in a LEGO set by uniqueness, varied (Unique Lots) and totality (Total Qty = Quantity).

Unique figures occur in their composition (shape and color) only once in the LEGO universe. This restriction is necessary because it often happens that the identical (unique) minifigure appears in different LEGO sets. Moreover, it is common knowledge that the more often an identical (unique) LEGO figure appears in different LEGO sets, the higher the probability that this figure will be traded in higher quantities on the secondary market later. We remember: A high supply leads to a lower demand.

So, it happens repeatedly that an identical LEGO figure is included several times in a set (e.g., *LEGO set no. 75165-1 Imperial Trooper Battle Pack*). In the present evaluation the following data records are available for LEGO figures.

| | | |
|---|---|---|
| ▣ | LEGO Sets with Figures: | 6.363 von 14.068 LEGO Sets |
| ▣ | Unique Figures: | 8.358 in 6.363 LEGO Sets |
| ▣ | Varied Figures: | 16.246 in 6.363 LEGO Sets |
| ▣ | Totality Figure: | 17.196 in 6.363 LEGO Sets |

A total of 17,196 LEGO figures appear in 6,363 of 14,068 LEGO sets. This means that there is an average of 2.7 LEGO figures in a LEGO set. Of these 17,196 LEGO figures, almost 49 percent or 8,358 LEGO figures are unique. They appear only once in the LEGO universe in identical form. The 17,196

LEGO figures are distributed over a total of 16,246 different slots in LEGO sets. This means that identical LEGO figures appear on average only once in a LEGO set. Examples in which the same LEGO figures appear more often in a LEGO set would be the so-called Battle Packs from the Star Wars theme area.

Between 1975 and 2020, a total of 17,196 figures found their place in 6,363 LEGO sets. This means that LEGO figures appear in 37 percent of LEGO sets. The number of figures in LEGO sets ranges from 0 to 80 figures (*LEGO set no. 3695-1 Fabuland Minifigure Retailer Box*). The graphical breakdown can be seen in Figure 75 below. According to this, there has also been a strong focus on LEGO figures in recent years, with growth strongly resembling that of LEGO sets. It can be assumed that this trend will continue in the coming years.

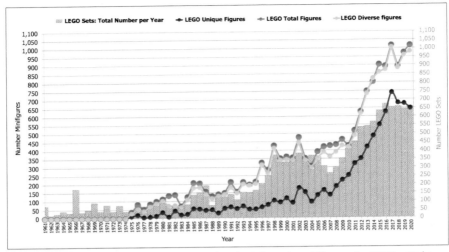

*Figure 75 - Annual number of unique, varied and total number of figures for LEGO sets between 1961 and 2020*

Now that we know how the number of LEGO figures in general has developed, we will focus further on the famous LEGO minifigure. After all, it is the LEGO minifigure that has a huge fan base and is collected by large numbers of people around the world. The individual value of certain LEGO minifigures has long-term effects on the associated LEGO sets. Thus, the LEGO minifigure takes a special position in the LEGO universe. Last but not least, it is characteristics such as the loving design, strong licensing agreements and the depiction of real or fictional characters that make LEGO minifigures so successful. Since their introduction in 1987, the dimensions of the minifigures have been largely set in stone. Of course, this rigidity comes with certain limitations, especially in terms of scale. This has been overcome by redesigning some parts, such as shorter legs to represent children and smaller figures. Longer torso parts and headdresses also work well to represent figures that are slightly taller than the average person. For example, original printed torsos give a minifigure a big belly (e.g., Minifigure Bro Thor SH753). It was only due to themes involving fantasy and science fiction that

The LEGO Group had to realize that characters with much larger proportions could not be represented by minifigures.

In order to determine the influence that exclusively LEGO minifigures have on the performance of LEGO sets, various criteria must be defined. First of all, all LEGO themes or sets are excluded from the analysis if they contain other types of figures (different from LEGO minifigures). This includes a total of 60 out of 148 themed areas: 4 Juniors, Action Wheelers, Baby, Belville, Ben 10, Bionicle, Boats, Books, Boost, Brick Sketches, Brick-Headz, Bricks and More, Building Set with People, Bulk Bricks, Cars, Classic, Clikits, Collectable Minifigures, Dacta, Dots, Duplo, Elves, Explore, Fabu-land, Forma, Freestyle, Friends, Fusion, Galidor, Games, Gear, Hero Factory, Hobby Set, Homemaker, Jacket Stone, Life of George, Mickey Mouse, Mindstorms, Minitalia, Miscellaneous, Mixels, Model Team, Originals, Pre-School, Primo, Quatro, Samsonite, Scala, Serious Play, Service Packs, Spybotics, Super Mario, System, Technic, The Powerpuff Girls, Trolls World Tour, Unikitty, Universal Building Set. All listed themes either have no mini-figures or the included figures are not minifigures in the classic sense.

In addition, LEGO sets that do not include minifigures or for which no price information is available were excluded. This includes LEGO sets from the following seven themes: Architecture, Art, Dino 2010, Dinosaurs, Power Functions, Powered Up and Znap.

This results in LEGO sets from 53 of the original 148 themes that feature at least one minifigure. These 53 themes are based on a total of 3,326 LEGO sets. These 3,326 LEGO sets include a total of 7,012 unique minifigures. This equates to an average of 2.1 unique minifigures per LEGO set. In addition, these 3,326 LEGO sets contain a total of 13,431 minifigures. Thus, on average, 4 minifigures appear in one LEGO set.

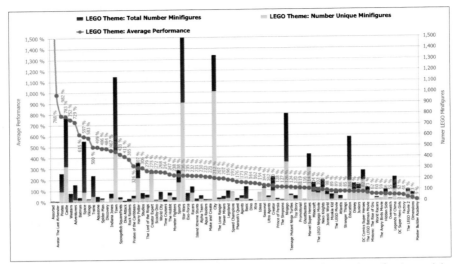

*Figure 76 - Average performance of LEGO themes depending on the number of unique mini-figures and the total number of minifigures*

Despite the continuously growing popularity of LEGO minifigures among buyers and especially collectors for years, an isolated analysis of the value development of LEGO themes does not seem to clearly confirm this trend. Especially LEGO themes with many unique minifigures and a high total number of minifigures sometimes achieve only modest increases in value. Thus, many unique minifigures or a high total number of minifigures are not a self-evident guarantee for above-average returns of a LEGO set or theme. An extraordinary phenomenon are LEGO sets, where the included LEGO minifigures exceed the total value (especially the RRP) of the LEGO set significantly.

For example, LEGO set no. 75212-1 Kessel Run Millennium Falcon of the Star Wars theme was released in 2018 at an MSRP of USD 169.99.[1] As of December 31, 2020, LEGO set no. 75212-1 has an average appreciation,

---

[1] In my personal LEGO portfolio, I was able to purchase *LEGO set no. 75212-1 Kessel Run Millennium Falcon* for about 96 Euro. This corresponds to a discount of about 44 percent.

after accounting for inflation, of 62 percent and costs an average of approximately USD 276. At the same time, the seven included minifigures have an average value (Current Items for Sale in USD on Bricklink) of approximately USD 220. Taking into account the 1,383 Regular Items conservatively with USD 0.075 per item and the value is USD 323.73, if you decide to sell all individual parts. This corresponds to an increase in value of 90 percent and is, compared to the average value of the new or unopened LEGO set, USD 47 or 28 percent higher.

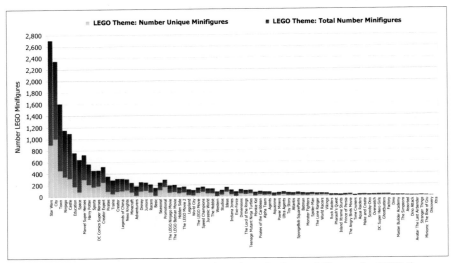

*Figure 77 - Total number of minifigures and number of unique minifigures for LEGO themes*

The Star Wars theme is the third largest LEGO theme in terms of the number of published LEGO sets and has the highest total number of LEGO minifigures. *Star Wars* sets represent over 10 percent of all LEGO minifigures. Conversely, this indicates the immense role that the *Star Wars* or Disney license plays for The LEGO Group. However, when it comes to the share of unique LEGO minifigures, *Star Wars* (11 percent) is beaten by the *City* theme (12 percent). This is certainly a conclusion that most of you would have suspected, but the *City* theme literally sparkles with the largest share of unique minifigures. Nevertheless, for many buyers (especially collectors), the *City* theme and the contained LEGO minifigures are uninteresting, due to the lack of a licensing agreement. The level of detail of the LEGO minifigures of both themes is also very different. Therefore, it can be strongly assumed that LEGO minifigures have little or no impact on the performance of *City* sets.

It is extremely difficult to make statements about associated minifigures based on the performance of LEGO themes. In Figure 77, an attempt was made to show a correlation. Unsurprisingly, the themes with the most min-ifigures are *Star Wars*, *City*, *Town*, *Ninjago* and *Castle*. At least on the basis of these data records, no comprehensible correlation can be established be-tween the changes in value and the number of unique minifigures or the total number of minifigures.

Rather, there is a clear need to include the values of all individual mini-figures in this comparison. In this context, the *Part-Out-Value* would cer-tainly be able to provide information about the share of *Regular Items* as well as minifigures in the development of values.

Without a doubt, the demand for a LEGO set also depends on its price. When a LEGO set is priced lower, for example, in the range of 10 to 40 USD, the demand is certainly higher. Corresponding LEGO minifigures in these sets are therefore more frequently available than LEGO minifigures in more expensive sets. While high-priced LEGO sets attract a lot of attention, they are less in demand because only experienced builders and dedicated LEGO fans are willing to pay 200 USD or more.

LEGO themes are not sufficiently suitable to illustrate the relationship be-tween unique minifigures or the total number of minifigures and the average performance. Rather, in each theme area there are different LEGO sets with a different number of unique minifigures. The total number of minifigures for individual LEGO sets within a theme also varies significantly. Instead, it is necessary to look at LEGO sets in detail neglecting the themes. Figure 78 below illustrates the relationship between the total number of LEGO mini-figures and the average growth in the value of LEGO sets.

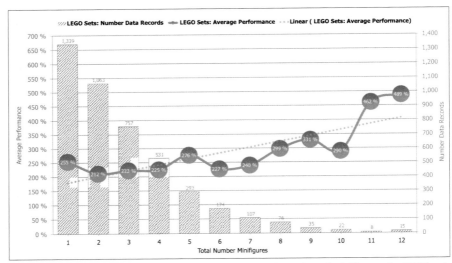

*Figure 78 - Correlation of average performance and total number of minifigures for LEGO sets*

Based on 4,463 LEGO sets, the average performance can be shown as a percentage of the total number of LEGO minifigures. The majority of LEGO sets have between 1 and 12 minifigures. The average increase in value of LEGO sets with a total number of minifigures between 1 and 12 pieces is 238 percent. It is well evident that there are particularly many LEGO sets with up to 5 minifigures. Not surprisingly, the total number of LEGO sets decreases as the total number of minifigures increases. For example, in the statistical survey, there are only 15 LEGO sets that contain 12 minifigures. However, the most exciting fact is certainly that as the total number of LEGO minifigures rises, the average value of the sets increases. Accordingly, LEGO sets with 11 or 12 minifigures increased in value particularly strongly. It is interesting to note that the uniqueness of the minifigures does not reflect the same increase in value.

352

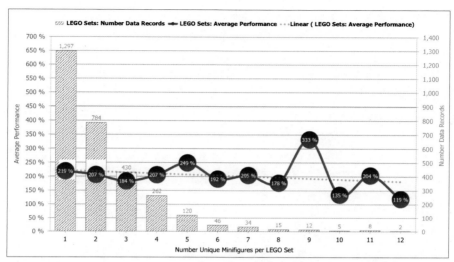

*Figure 79 - Correlation average performance and unique minifigures for LEGO sets*

In Figure 79, we see the average performance of LEGO sets as a percentage of the number of unique minifigures. Again, the focus is on the range between 1 and 12 (unique) minifigures, which represents 99.4 percent of LEGO sets. In contrast to Figure 78, the average performance falls slightly as the number of unique LEGO minifigures increases. If, on the other hand, the performance graph would rise as the number of unique minifigures increases, this would indicate that buyers and collectors care about the uniqueness of the minifigures themselves. Instead, what is practically present is a volatile environment that indicates that the type of minifigure is of particular importance. For example, what character the minifigure represents and what role it is assigned (e.g., in the associated film). The average increase in value of LEGO sets with 1 to 12 unique LEGO minifigures is 210 percent.

Despite this, LEGO sets with unique minifigures achieve a comparatively stable increase in value. For example, considering that a LEGO set contains exactly one unique minifigure, there are only 58 LEGO sets that have fallen

353

in value. These 58 LEGO sets are limited to the themes *City* (18), *DC Super Hero Girls* (1), *Dimension* (16), *Education* (1), *Explore* (8), *Factory* (1), *Juniors* (1), *Legends of Chima* (4), *Sports* (1), *Teenage Mutant Ninja Turtles* (1), *The LEGO Batman Movie* (1) and *The LEGO Movie 2* (5). This makes it clear that LEGO sets with minifigures are generally much more likely to increase in value.

Many factors determine the price or value of a LEGO minifigure. As already mentioned, the uniqueness and exclusivity or rarity of the minifigure explicitly contributes to this. If a LEGO minifigure appears exclusively in a LEGO set, this increases its value. A famous example is certainly the minifigure Boba Fett (Bricklink ID sw0107) from the LEGO set no. *10123-1 Cloud City* in 2003. As of the end of January 2022, the minifigure Boba Fett is offered on Bricklink for prices between 1,700 and 3,500 USD. Last 6 Month Sales average USD 1,200 on Bricklink. At the same time, the related LEGO set is only available once on Bricklink (new and unopened) and is offered for USD 3,852.43. The selling price in the last 6 months averaged USD 2,139.48 on Bricklink (5 pieces). This is in part because the Boba Fett minifigure is highly desirable among collectors. By the way, the MSRP of the LEGO set was only USD 100 or USD 142 (adjusted for inflation).

Speculations and bets on the next Boba Fett minifigure are already underway. Basically, this is not an isolated case. Such enormous increases in the value of LEGO minifigures are certainly rare, but it cannot be ruled out that such a scenario will repeat itself. Especially considering the background when a LEGO set including the associated minifigures gain fame and desirability after the EOL (as in the example of Boba Fett). Therefore, there are always speculators who purchase large quantities of various LEGO minifigures (especially Star Wars), in the hope that the Boba Fett's story will be repeated.

Generally speaking, the total value of the minifigures in low-priced LEGO sets is not very high. It gets more exciting when a unique minifigure appears in a very high-priced LEGO set. Again, this has happened many times in the past and seems to be taking on a routine. The LEGO Group understands the popularity of unique minifigures among collectors and rewards them when they purchase high-priced LEGO sets. For example, only *LEGO set no. 75222-1 Betrayal in Cloud City* features a version of the Lando Calrissian minifigure. As of the end of January 2022, the Lando Calrissian minifigure is priced between USD 130 and USD 160 on Bricklink. *LEGO set no. 75222-1 Betrayal in Cloud City*, which has since been retired, was retailing at an MSRP of USD 350.

A look at my personal holdings reveals that the LEGO set could certainly be purchased at a 25 to 30 percent discount. Without going into too much detail, you can already see the point I'm trying to make. The LEGO minifigure of Lando Calrissian already weighs in at a good 50 percent of the investment cost at the time (MSRP including discount) according to its value today. There is a total of 21 minifigures in the LEGO set, seven of which are unique and therefore exclusive to this LEGO set. Their current total value (Current Items for Sale in USD on Bricklink, as of the end of January 2022) is an impressive USD 454.58. Perhaps this is an excellent example of the magic and extraordinary increase in value of LEGO minifigures.

In fact, both Boba Fett and Lando Calrissian have already appeared several times in different versions in the LEGO universe. Sometimes there were already similar minifigures before, sometimes modified and revised LEGO minifigures appeared later. Especially with LEGO minifigures, although a minifigure has already been released several times, a certain minifigure can always provide surprises in terms of its value development. As a rule, this goes hand in hand with a particularly elaborate design. If there are also relatively few models on the secondary market, a strong return is predetermined. It has already been observed several times in the past that new LEGO minifigure models in particular have achieved significant increases in value compared to their predecessors.[1]

---

[1] We will go into more detail about the same later in relation to LEGO sets.

Of special interest is the character of a LEGO minifigure. People very often (consciously or unconsciously) build a connection with main and side characters of stories. Personality and character attributes determine the behavior of these. These are well-known personalities from books, movies, series, TV, music or sports. We quickly empathize and sympathize with the character. They can also be role models or idols that we simply like. The LEGO Group is aware of these connections, which is why experience shows that such figures are among the most elaborately designed. This is often a reason for their later price increases. The popularity of the character also determines their price. On the other hand, unpopular characters are less in demand and therefore usually cheaper.

Ultimately, it depends on how strong the limitation of the LEGO minifigure is. For example, in 2012 at the New York Toy Fair, an Iron Man minifigure was released only 125 pieces. This exclusive version was the only time Iron Man's helmet was printed on his head. Of course, many other Iron Man minifigures were made, but these all come with a separate helmet, which is attached to the headpiece. But the rest of the printing is also different on this limited-edition version. These subtleties and details make the LEGO minifigures so interesting for collectors that as of the end of January 2022, this extraordinary Iron Man's minifigure has traded for an average of USD 1,380 on Bricklink over the past 6 months.

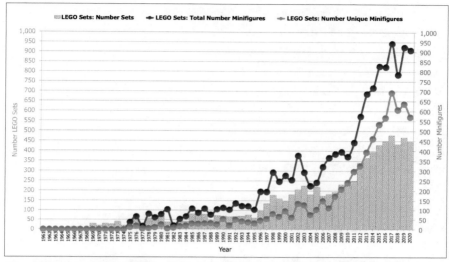

*Figure 80 - Annual development of the number of unique minifigures as well as the total number of minifigures for LEGO sets between 1961 and 2020*

Such examples are steadily repeated in the LEGO universe. The LEGO Group has been providing us with more and more of these unique LEGO minifigures for years. Both the number of unique minifigures and the total number of minifigures in LEGO sets is on a continuous upward trend. The LEGO Group has been increasing the number of unique minifigures by an average of 21 percent per year since 1976. The total number of LEGO minifigures is also growing at an annual rate of 21 percent over the same period. At the same time, between 1976 and 2020, the annual share of unique minifigures in the total number of minifigures grows from 28 to 63 percent. This trend seems to be unbroken, whereby we are already witnessing an average share of 69 percent over the past five years. This discovery makes it all the more exciting to observe the development of LEGO sets over the past few years for the near future. It seems reasonable to assume that as the number of unique minifigures increases, the effect on the development of the value of LEGO sets will grow.

357

With a few exceptions, LEGO minifigures are available exclusively by purchasing LEGO sets. Under normal circumstances, Star Wars minifigures are not sold separately. When buying a LEGO set, you should therefore keep a critical eye on the associated minifigures. As an example, I would like to mention the *LEGO set no. 70917-1 Ultimate Batmobile*. As of December 31, 2020, the different price information are as follows:

- Last 6 Month Sales in USD on Bricklink:     USD 259.04
- Current Items for Sale in USD on Bricklink:     USD 185.96
- Part-Out-Value in USD on Bricklink:     USD 381.78

The share of minifigures includes the following ratio. The data points were obtained from Bricklink on January 28, 2022:

| Number | Description | Current Items for Sale in USD on Bricklink |
|---|---|---|
| 1 | Alfred Pennyworth - Batsuit | USD 23.74 |
| 1 | Batgirl, Yellow Cape, Dual Sided Head with Smile | USD 6.88 |
| 1 | Batman - Utility Belt, Head Type 4 | USD 5.79 |
| 1 | Flying Monkey - Evil Smile | USD 61.66 |
| 1 | Flying Monkey - Teeth Bared | USD 61.96 |
| 1 | Polka-Dot Man | USD 66.55 |
| 1 | Robin - Green Glasses, Smile / Scared Pattern | USD 11.49 |
| 1 | Wicked Witch | USD 24.77 |
| **8** | | **USD 262.84** |

*Table 19 - Value of minifigures in LEGO set no. 70917-1 Ultimate Batmobile (as of January 27, 2022)*

This is a simple way to determine the impact of minifigures on the value of the respective LEGO set. The breakdown in Table 19 shows that already the 8 included minifigures are traded at a total value of USD 262.84 on Bricklink. This means that the trade value of the minifigures is higher than both the *Last 6 Month Sales in USD on Bricklink* and *Current Items for Sale in USD on Bricklink.* Taking into account the *Part-Out-Value in USD on Bricklink,* the difference between Part-Out-Value and Minifigures is 118.94 USD. This difference of 118.94 USD effectively represents the value of the remaining individual bricks and parts. Thus, the price per brick is USD 0.08 per brick and part.

As a LEGO investor, you need to keep an eye out for such LEGO sets. It is especially helpful to monitor the value of LEGO minifigures over a defined period of time. For example, a simple tracking spreadsheet will be sufficient. Once a LEGO set is released, it usually takes a few months for the value of the associated LEGO minifigures to stabilize. Of course, it occasionally happens that identical LEGO minifigures appear in other LEGO products (e.g., sets or magazines). This has a strong influence on the value of a minifigure. For example, if an identical LEGO minifigure from a relatively expensive LEGO set (e.g., USD 200) is included in an inexpensive LEGO set (e.g., USD 25), experience shows that the value of the LEGO minifigure will drop. Interested buyers can grab this minifigure for a lower amount. To ease your fears a little bit: *It is rather rare that The LEGO Group puts minifigures from particularly expensive LEGO sets into extremely inexpensive sets.* Because in the meantime, these LEGO minifigures are a major factor of many potential buyers.

LEGO sets without minifigures have an average increase in value of 211 percent. In contrast, LEGO sets with minifigures have increased in value by an average of 266 percent. Minifigures from the *Star Wars, Harry Potter, Ninjago, Marvel Super Heroes* and *DC Comics Super Heroes* themes are particularly sought-after and, in some cases, achieve high increases in value. It can also be assumed that this will remain the case in the medium term. The majority of collectors and completionists are focused on these themes. As long as The LEGO Group continues to publish minifigures in the usual way, this trend will most likely continue.

Many investors focus on popular LEGO sets and underestimate the value of LEGO minifigures. Yet many of the small figures are a real boost to your portfolio. Also, the sale of LEGO minifigures is less space and capital inten-sive. Nevertheless, these rarely come alone. Therefore, you should have a plan B for the individual bricks and parts included in the LEGO set. Which is why you usually can't avoid a Bricklink store. Of course, LEGO minifigures can also devalue a set quite decisively if the associated minifigures are of no interest. In principle, investors should include minifigures in their decision when choosing their LEGO investments. Bricklink is an excellent source for this. There are also numerous books on minifigures that go far beyond this chapter.

## 4.5.8 Age Groups

The age categorization is a recommendation for each age level, according to the respective developmental level. By doing so, The LEGO Group offers children the opportunity to become more skillful through their play and to develop new problem-solving abilities. Age classifications on LEGO sets should therefore be used as a rough guide for purchase. Regardless of age recommendations, many LEGO sets become collector's items. Both owners and retailers of these LEGO sets are well outside the age range.

The LEGO Group is the world's largest toy manufacturer and already offers play sets for children from 1.5 years (*LEGO Duplo theme*). *Duplo* bricks are larger LEGO bricks with rounded corners in a scale of 2:1 and offer a great introduction to the world of building. The age recommendations of LEGO *Duplo* range up to 7 years (e.g., *LEGO set no. 7880-1 Big Pirate Ship*). With this range, mainly toddlers can play, learn and much more.

*Juniors* follows Duplo with the target group of children between 4 and 8 years. Visually, the LEGO sets contain a mixture of relatively large bricks and individual bricks as we know them. The LEGO *Junior* sets become more complex in content as the number of smaller pieces increases. These LEGO sets let children create their own worlds, as well as improve their own dexterity and imagination.

This is followed by the age group from 5 to 12 years. The complexity increases as well as the number of smaller and more detailed individual bricks and parts. These LEGO sets include themed areas such as *City*, *Marvel Super Heroes*, *Star Wars*, *Friends*, etc. With sets in this age category, children can learn the ability to solve problems and playfully try out new roles. However, already complex robots can be designed, which help to develop the visual imagination.

This is followed by the second last category for LEGO sets between 12 and 16 years. This includes *Creators*, *Batman Movie*, *Ninjago*, *Nexo Knights* or *Technic* and is aimed at teenagers and young adults with a deeper understanding of structure and construction. The *Technic* theme particularly stands out, with associated LEGO sets being partly controlled electronically, by app or computer.

Finally, we have the 18+ category. This does not mean that buyers have to be at least 18 years old to understand and build these LEGO sets. Rather, this is clever marketing by The LEGO Group to reach adult builders. As a result, LEGO sets in this age category are sometimes only marginally harder to build. Rather, it is the content reference, which should appeal to adults. Of course, certainly few children also partly several hundred USD for a LEGO set of this age category. Not infrequently, this type of LEGO sets is also too large to play with. Therefore, they are often rather so-called display models.

LEGO collectors are known to focus on one or more LEGO themes. There are also collectors who buy thematically, for example, to expand their city (buildings, cars, roads, minifigures, etc.). Of course, the passion for collecting can also be diverse and cross-themed. In my LEGO investment journey so far, I have met few if any collectors who therefore buy LEGO sets that are not very challenging structurally. Many collectors complain that these sets rarely have interesting individual bricks or parts, minifigures are very simply designed and the LEGO sets are thus rather uninteresting for their purposes. In this respect, the question came up in the context of the statistical investigation as to whether the official age recommendation on LEGO sets by The LEGO Group has any influence on their value development.

Of the known 14,068 LEGO sets, age recommendation information according to The LEGO Group is available for 5,420 LEGO sets, or 39 percent. In total, there are 57 different age recommendation categories by age: 18+, 16, 16+, 14+, 12 to 16, 12, 12+, 11 to 16, 11+, 10 to 16, 10 to 15, 10 to 14, 10+, 9 to 16, 9 to 14, 9 to 12, 9+, 8 to 16, 8 to 14, 8 to 13, 8 to 12, 8+, 7 to 16, 7 to 14, 7 to 12, 7 to 9, 7+, 6 to 16, 6 to 14, 6 to 12, 6 to 10, 6 to 9, 6+, 5 to 12, 5 to 10, 5 to 9, 5 to 8, 5+, 4 to 99, 4 to 12, 4 to 10, 4 to 9, 4 to 8, 4 to 7, 4+, 3 to 15, 3 to 12, 3 to 8, 3 to 6, 3+, 2 to 6, 2 to 5, 2+, 1 to 5, 1 to 4, 1 to 3 and 1+

These age recommendations can be summarized as follows:

- Ø 15 years:       4 percent or 195 of 5,420 LEGO Sets
- Ø 12 years:       8 percent or 429 of 5,420 LEGO Sets
- Ø 10 years:       27 percent or 1,487 of 5,420 LEGO Sets
- Ø 8 to 9 years:   54 percent or 2,915 of 5,420 LEGO Sets
- Ø 4 years:        7 percent or 394 of 5,420 LEGO Sets

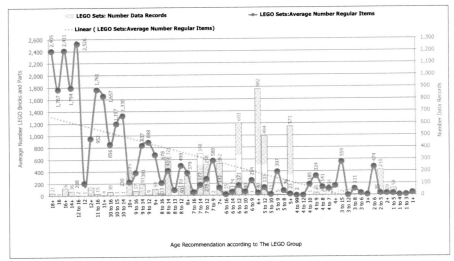

*Figure 81 - Correlation between average number of Regular Items and age recommendation according to The LEGO Group*

Figure 81 shows the correlation between the age recommendation according to The LEGO Group and the average number of Regular Items. To simplify matters, the age recommendation according to The LEGO Group was given on the x-axis and age ranges were combined. The graphical representation confirms that the average number of Regular Items increases with the age recommendation. This increases the building fun and demand, especially for adults and experienced builders.

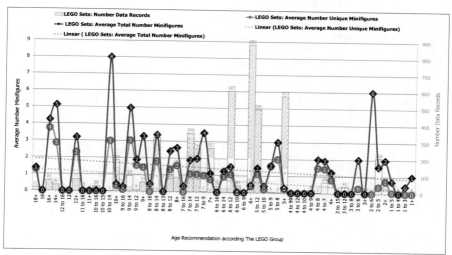

*Figure 82 - Correlation of average total number of minifigures, number of unique minifigures and age recommendation according to The LEGO Group*

For the number of unique minifigures and the total number of minifigures, the result is a similar situation as before. As the age recommendation increases (slightly) according to The LEGO Group, the number of unique minifigures and the total number of minifigures in LEGO sets increases. This is certainly a surprising finding, as LEGO minifigures are ideally designed to be played with. However, it can be assumed that LEGO sets including minifigures with high age recommendations according to The LEGO Group are rarely or never played with. Nevertheless, in such LEGO sets the average total number as well as the number of unique minifigures is higher. Of course, this is no coincidence. The LEGO Group has long understood that LEGO minifigures have a completely different raison d'être for adult collectors and builders. Today, they are considered small collectible trophies and decorative accessories that give life to LEGO models. For collectors, many LEGO minifigures have more and more often a high value.

365

It is certainly not very surprising that LEGO sets also increase in MSRP with increasing age recommendation according to The LEGO Group. Consequently, the MSRP is not very meaningful for the age recommendation. Rather, the average *Price-per-Brick* should be used to assess whether different pricing of LEGO sets goes hand in hand with the age recommendation according to The LEGO Group.

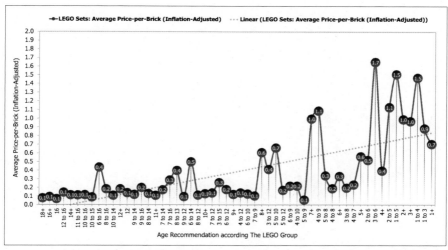

*Figure 83 - Correlation of average total number of minifigures, number of unique minifigures and age recommendation according to The LEGO Group*

According to Figure 83, the development of the average Price-per-Brick (adjusted for inflation) is contrary to the development of the average number of regular bricks and parts in Figure 81. LEGO sets for younger target groups (between 1 and 10 years) are sometimes significantly more expensive than LEGO sets for teenagers and adults (12 years and older). So buyers of LEGO sets with a low Price-per-Brick get more individual bricks and parts for their money. Of course, parents are less concerned about such things when they buy LEGO sets for their loved ones. Especially if you only consider the retail price, LEGO sets for younger target groups still seem cheaper than a LEGO Star Wars set for USD 199.99 at first glance, thanks to their relatively lower retail price.

However, LEGO investors should use all available information to evaluate future LEGO investments. For this reason, we will look at how LEGO sets of the various age recommendations according to The LEGO Group have developed in value in the past.

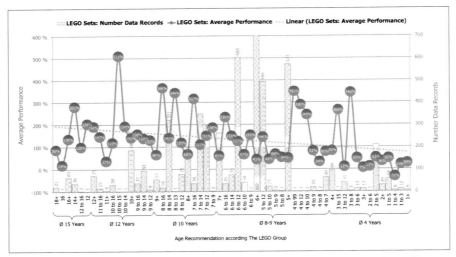

*Figure 84 - Average performance of LEGO sets by age recommendation from The LEGO Group*

Due to the relatively unclear trend, I decided to adjust the age recommendations according to The LEGO Group. For this purpose, the lowest (1 year) and highest age (18 years) were first determined according to The LEGO Group. Thus, the performance of a range such as 6 to 12 years represents LEGO sets for 6, 7, 8, 9, 10, 11 and 12 year olds. The same applies to all the other ranges. On the one hand, this gives us significantly more data (250 instead of 57) per one year age range. In addition, we get a smoothed progression for the performance of LEGO sets with age recommendations between 1 and 18 years.

368

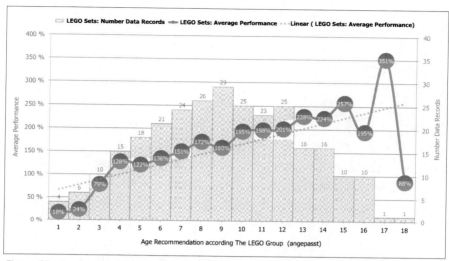

*Figure 85 - Average performance of LEGO sets according to adjusted age categorization by The LEGO Group*

Figure 84 shows more clearly that in the past, the age categorization had a lasting influence on value development. Therefore, it can be said that LEGO sets have increased more in value with increasing age recommendations. In addition, the development reflects the common feeling about the value development, for example that LEGO sets for children under 3 years (e.g., *Duplo* theme) could not hold their own as an investment in the past. At least these were able to increase in value overall, but were clearly beaten by higher age categories. This should not come as a surprise, as themes in this age category (up to 3 years) often do not meet the high demands of (adult) collectors. In particular, the range between 4 and 15 years is ideal. With each additional year, higher value appreciation is achieved. Also, this range represents by far the most published LEGO sets. However, in the range for LEGO sets with age recommendations between 16 and 18 years, value increases have been much more volatile. In this range in particular, LEGO sets are generally more sophisticated, which is why the vast majority of collectors and adults are already buying them.

### 4.5.9  Licensed

The LEGO Group credits much of its global success and awareness to the conclusion of various licensing deals over the past decades. Licensing deals are among the most successful marketing activities, as they can significantly increase attention for a product. In this regard, licensing provides an opportunity for companies to enter the international market and raise awareness of their own products. For every USD a manufacturer invests in a concession, it saves part of the marketing costs in return. This is because licenses with cinema, television, computer game producers or car brands bring a high degree of brand recognition. These costs incurred by the licensee (The LEGO Group) are passed on directly to the consumer, making the products more expensive. The fast-moving business of licensing involves various risks for the toy industry, and yet hardly any manufacturer can avoid it today, because the licensing business is extraordinarily attractive for sales and margins. It is remarkable that The LEGO Group itself has managed to turn the tables. For years, other companies have been acquiring licenses from The LEGO Group in order to make their products better known with the brand (e.g., Adidas).

The LEGO Group can look back on a large number of licensing collaborations:[1] Shell, BMW, McDonalds, Ferrari, Arla, Maersk, Exxon, Dano-ne, Nesquik, Deutsche Bahn, Weetabix, Esso, Star Wars, Harry Potter, Avatar, NHL, NBA, Discovery Channel, Little Robots, Ben10, Marvel and DC Comics, Lone Ranger, Sponge Bob, Bob the Builder, Thomas and Friends, Pirates of the Caribbean, Lord of the Rings, The Hobbit, Bugatti, Spielbergs Studios, Galidor, Ford, Coca Cola, Ferrari, Indiana Jones, Prince of Persia, McLaren, Speed Racer, Vestas, Disney Cars, Mickey Mouse, Mercedes Benz, Toy Story, Lamborghini, Nvidia, Julus & Friends, Porsche, Tine, Little Forest Friends, Winnie the Pooh, ran Fußball, Telekom, Minec-raft, Back to the Future, Turtles, Netflix, Volkswagen, various airlines, various ferry lines and Disney Fairy Tale. The world's largest licensor is the Walt Disney Company, which

---

[1] Whether it is a LEGO set with license agreement, you can see at Brickset.

also owns Marvel Studios and Pixar. In 2012, the U.S. entertainment giant secured the rights to *Star Wars* through its multibillion-dollar takeover of Lucasfilm. There is hardly a well-known toy manufacturer that can ignore products such as *Star Wars*, *Frozen* or *Cars*.

It is known that The LEGO Group entered into the first licensing agreement with *LucasArts* and *Star Wars* in 1999. This licensing agreement has now been in place for over 20 years and is one of the most important licensing agreements in The LEGO Group's history. Whenever a new movie, series or book is released, The LEGO Group designs numerous new LEGO *Star Wars* sets. In turn, this generates a strong increase in sales for The LEGO Group.

Licenses attract attention, tell stories and transport emotions. Every now and then, The LEGO Group tries to invent and tell such stories itself. For example, LEGO *Ninjago* is one of these own creations. Today, *Ninjago* comprises more than 400 sets, there are movies and a lot of merchandise. *Ninjago* is certainly the most successful own license of The LEGO Group. In Figure 86 below, we see the ratio of LEGO sets with and without licensing agreements between the years 1999 and 2020.

As the release of new LEGO sets has increased in recent years, the number of LEGO sets with licensing agreements has also increased. In the first year 1999, only 29 LEGO sets had a license cooperation. However, in 2020, there were already 260 LEGO sets. In the current year 2020, the share is 39.5 percent. In the period shown, there were always slight downturns, but the overall picture shows a clear trend that the share of LEGO sets with a licensing agreement is steadily increasing. Overall, the share has averaged 38 percent since 2010.

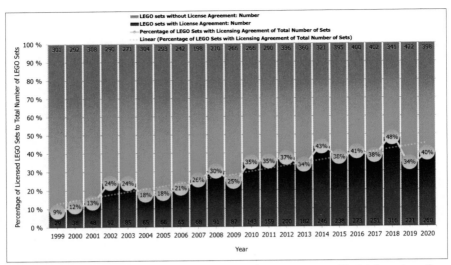

*Figure 86 - Percentage of LEGO sets with license agreement compared to total number of LEGO sets from The LEGO Group between 1999 and 2000*

A company like The LEGO Group is happy to be paid for the right to use [their intellectual property]. The right of use is acquired either for a fixed period or for an indefinite period. Usually, the cost of license agreements is passed on to the customer, making the product more expensive accordingly. Therefore, it is often said that LEGO sets with license agreements are comparably expensive. The main reason for this is, of course, the additional costs due to the license itself. These arise from the transfer of the rights of use by the licensor (e.g., BMW) to the licensee (The LEGO Group). There is no information about the license rates. It is unknown whether lump-sum fees, minimum license fees or cost-sharing are agreed upon.

To assess the proportion of licensing fees in the total cost of a LEGO set, it is ideal to compare two identical LEGO sets, one with a licensing agreement and one without. For an optimal benchmarking, both LEGO sets should have the same bricks, parts, minifigures, etc. The only difference should be that one LEGO set has a licensing agreement, while the other LEGO set does not. Although The LEGO Group has hundreds of LEGO sets with and without a license agreement, there are no such identical LEGO sets. All LEGO sets that could be considered for such a comparison ultimately differ too much in certain factors to make the comparison representative. Instead, let's look again at the *Price-per-Brick* for LEGO sets with and without a licensing agreement.

For optimal comparison, certain themes have been omitted. The reason for this is that these themes have particularly high *Price-per-Brick* ratios due to their nature (e.g., less individual bricks and parts, high proportion of technical parts, different types of figures, etc.). These include Duplo, Galidor, Dimensions, Sports, Collectible Minifigures, Baby, Scala, Boost, Mindstorms, Serious Play, Dacta, Fabuland, Service Packs, Forma, Powered Up, PreSchool, Power Functions, Ben10, Primo and Education.

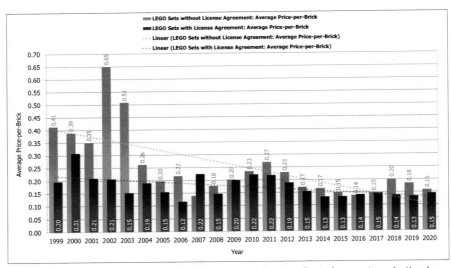

*Figure 87 - Average performance of LEGO sets according to adjusted age categorization by The LEGO Group*

For the period from 1999 to 2020, data records are available for a total of 5,382 LEGO sets. Thereof, 1,678 LEGO sets or 31 percent have a licensing agreement. This results in 3,704 LEGO sets, or 69 percent, which are not subject to a licensing agreement. For LEGO sets without a licensing agreement, we see a sharp decline in the average *Price-per-Brick* since 1999. The average *Price-per-Brick* was USD 0.41 in 1999. In 2020, it is 59 percent less, or USD 0.16 per brick. This is not a surprise, as it has already been explained that The LEGO Group has ensured that the average *Price-per-Brick* becomes more favorable by improving production, materials, structures as well as organization in the past. On average, the *Price-per-Brick* for LEGO sets without a license was USD 0.25 per brick.

However, more surprising is the fact that since 1999, the average *Price-per-Brick* for LEGO sets with a licensing agreement has remained almost unchanged or has fallen slightly. On average, this is USD 0.18 per brick and at times fluctuates between USD 0.12 and USD 0.31 per brick. With regard to the *Price-per-Brick*, LEGO sets with a license agreement were comparatively cheaper in the past than LEGO sets without a license agreement. Today, however, there is a persistent belief that LEGO sets with licenses are (significantly) more expensive than LEGO sets without licenses. This is not least due to the fact that LEGO sets with license agreement consist of significantly more regular bricks and parts and consequently have higher MSRPs.

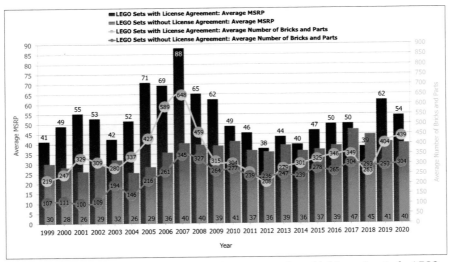

*Figure 88 - Comparison of average MSRP and average number of bricks and parts for LEGO sets with and without license agreement between 1999 and 2020*

Figure 88 provides an enlightening explanation of why the majority of customers believe that LEGO sets with licensing agreements are comparatively more expensive than LEGO sets without licensing agreements. If we focus only on the MSRP, this is probably correct. From 1999 to 2020, the average MSRP of LEGO sets with licensing agreements was higher than the average MSRP of LEGO sets without licensing agreements. Nevertheless, it must be taken into account here that in the same period from 1999 to 2020, the average number of individual bricks and parts of LEGO sets with a licensing agreement predominated. Only in 2012 and 2018, LEGO sets without a licensing agreement had an average slightly higher number of individual bricks and parts. Over the entire period, LEGO sets with licensing agreements had an average of 347 individual bricks and parts. In contrast, LEGO sets without a licensing agreement averaged only 234 individual bricks and parts. Licensed models were therefore 48 percent larger on average.

We have already learned that the *Price-per-Brick* is only relevant if we include information about the weight per individual brick and part. Even when it comes to weight, we have to keep the previously defined restrictions regarding the themes. This is even more important when evaluating the average *Weight-per-Brick*, because themes such as Scala, Duplo or Fabuland sometimes have very large and therefore heavy individual bricks and parts.

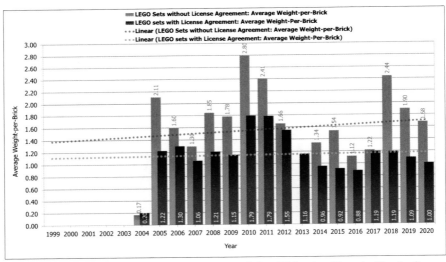

*Figure 89 - Comparison of average Weight-per-Brick for LEGO sets with and without a licensing agreement between 1999 and 2020*

The result shows a well-balanced picture. The *Weight-per-Brick* between LEGO sets with and without a license agreement differs only slightly in the period from 1999 to 2000. The average *Weight-per-Brick* for LEGO sets with a license agreement was 1.16 grams per brick. In contrast, individual bricks and parts of LEGO sets without a license agreement had an average weight of 1.68 grams per individual brick. Substantially larger individual bricks and parts are thus in LEGO sets without license agreement. If this is put into perspective, individual bricks in LEGO sets without a licensing agreement are on average 40 percent larger. Taking into account the fact that LEGO sets with a license agreement have 48 percent more bricks and parts, it can be said that the volume of LEGO sets with and without a license agreement was approximately the same between 2004 and 2020.

Therefore, it cannot be conclusively determined why LEGO sets with licensing agreements were cheaper on average. However, it seems reasonable to assume that The LEGO Group calculates with higher sales figures and can therefore offer these products at a lower price. It is therefore all the more exciting that the performance of LEGO sets with and without licensing agreements is examined in the following.

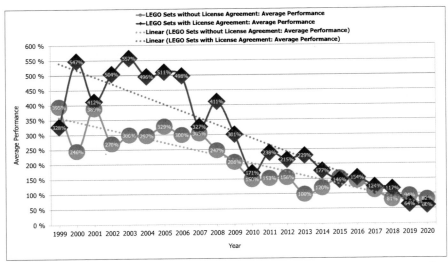

*Figure 90 - Comparison of the average value development of LEGO sets with and without licensing agreements between 1999 and 2020*

Finally, the result of the comparison should come somewhat as less of a surprise that the values of LEGO sets with licensing agreements have risen higher in the majority. Accordingly, LEGO sets with licensing agreements have achieved the higher value increases in 18 of 22 years. Based on 1,657 data points between 1999 and 2020, LEGO sets with licensing agreements increased in value by an average of 299 percent. LEGO sets without a licensing agreement (3,582 data points) increased in value by an average of 210 percent.

In total, there were only 14 of 1,657 LEGO sets with a license agreement that decreased in value. The loss in value is moderate with an average of 14 percent below to the MSRP. These LEGO sets include, for example, various *Star Wars Buildable Figures*. Of the 3,582 LEGO sets without a license agreement, 169 LEGO sets or 5 percent have fallen in value. Their loss in value is also noticeably higher at an average of 25 percent. As many as 24 themes are affected by this, whereby the highest number of LEGO sets without a licensing agreement with a loss can be attributed to the *Legends of*

*Chima*, *City*, *Explore* or *Friends* themes. It is also noticeable that a reverse picture prevails in 2019 and 2020, with LEGO sets with a licensing agreement increasing less in value. The majority of LEGO sets of these years are still available at retail. This seems reason enough that LEGO sets without licensing agreements are more stable in value in the short term.

Long-term oriented LEGO investors should prefer LEGO sets with license agreements. According to the results so far, there is a higher chance that these sets will increase in value significantly more. It should be taken into account that the average lifetime and availability of LEGO sets with and without license agreements differ. Based on 1,530 data points, LEGO sets with a license agreement are officially available in retail stores for an average of 475 calendar days or 1.3 years. Based on 2,974 data points, LEGO sets without a license agreement were available for an average of 571 calendar days, or 1.6 years. The shorter availability or lifetime will also ultimately have been a contributing factor to the greater increase in value of LEGO sets with licensing agreements. Figure 91 shows that the value development is independent of the age categorization according to The LEGO Group.

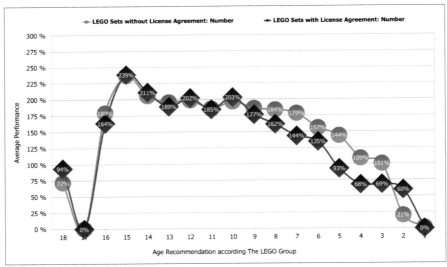

*Figure 91 - Comparison of average performance taking into account age categorization according to The LEGO Group for LEGO sets with and without license agreement between 1999 and 2020*

In addition, Figure 92 illustrates the average distribution of LEGO minifigures (total number of minifigures and unique minifigures) for LEGO sets with and without license agreements. The total number of minifigures ranges on average between 2.9 and 3.7 minifigures per set. Thus, LEGO sets with licensing agreements have about one more minifigure on average. However, the difference in the number of unique minifigures is remarkable. LEGO sets with licensing agreements have an average of 3.3, while LEGO sets without licensing agreements have an average of only 2.8. This confirms what we have already observed. When buying LEGO sets with licensing agreements, you often get more for your money - and ultimately even a better return.

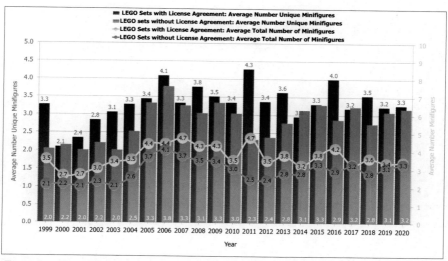

*Figure 92 - Comparison of total number of minifigures and number of unique minifigures for LEGO sets with and without licensing agreement between 1999 and 2020*

## 4.5.10 Avoiding New Editions or Re-Releases?

The LEGO Group offers a very diversified range of LEGO sets. The selection includes LEGO building sets of a wide variety of themes, with each theme having its own character as well as a distinctive look. The themes range from everyday city life (e.g., *World City*), to ninja adventures (e.g., *Ninjago*), to well-known realistic licensed sets from *Harry Potter* or *Star Wars*. Over the past 10 years, an average of six new themes and 584 new LEGO sets have been released each year. Both the range of LEGO themes and LEGO sets have always been limited in time. Based on 148 themes, the average availability or lifetime of a theme is 7.5 years. Based on 4,504 LEGO sets remain in official stores for an average of 536 calendar days or 1.47 years.

Over the course of time, The LEGO Group has recognized the trend toward the re-release of LEGO sets. Re-releases or new editions are primarily targeted at new buyers in order to win them over as customers. For collectors and owners of older models (especially the original model), new editions or re-releases are often a bitter pill to swallow. *Who is not happy to have models that are no longer available?* Clearly, self-interest takes precedence over that of the community. Precisely because many LEGO sets have relatively short lifetimes or availabilities and many themes or models are still popular after years (e.g., *Star Wars*), it happens that The LEGO Group re-launches LEGO sets that have long been discontinued.

Re-releases are the repeated production of a product that has already been manufactured, e.g., due to increased demand. This is to be distinguished from so-called new editions. In the case of new editions, the old design is usually reinterpreted, the LEGO set is redesigned and finally published. New editions are characterized by, among other things, revisions, additions or changed equipment. Often this happens with a certain time gap between the old and new edition. It also happens that the new edition directly follows the previous version or goes directly over.

This applies not only to LEGO sets, but also to LEGO minifigures. The LEGO Group has become aware over the years that due to its own (but absolutely necessary) artificial shortage of LEGO sets, the demand is sometimes not yet satisfied. *Who has not experienced the feeling of still wanting to own a LEGO set from your childhood?* In addition, LEGO investors and resellers sometimes demand high prices for particularly rare pieces. While this does not harm The LEGO Group, it does miss out on additional sales and profits. The publication of legal alternatives by competitors and illegal plagiarism by other companies, such as Lepin, has a negative impact on The LEGO Group's market share. As a consequence, it is understandable why The LEGO Group repeatedly opts for new editions or re-releases. The *Star Wars* theme is an excellent example of this. The universe of the same theme is limited in terms of the total number of figures, vehicles, aircraft and buildings. If The LEGO Group were to construct each of these components only once as a LEGO set, the Star Wars theme would already be saturated for The LEGO Group.

Consequently, there is no certainty that desired rarities such as LEGO set no. 71006-1 The Simpsons House or *LEGO set no. 75827-1 Ghostbusters Firehouse Headquarters* will not be re-issued in the past, since this has already been the case several times. For example, the iconic Star Wars model of the Millennium Falcon. It is important for LEGO investors to be aware that certain iconic LEGO sets, such as the Star Wars Millennium Falcon, will be reissued again and again.

Since new editions and re-releases cannot generally be predicted and ultimately avoided, LEGO investors must deal with the subject. It is important to understand the influence of new editions or re-releases on the performance of the predecessors. For many years, the point of view has persistently been that new editions or re-releases contribute to a significant reduction in the value of the predecessors.

| LEGO Set | 01 | 02 | 03 | 04 | 05 | 06 | 07 | 08 | 09 | 10 | 11 |
|---|---|---|---|---|---|---|---|---|---|---|---|
| | | | | | Numbers of the New Edition or Re-Release | | | | | | |
| Fire Stations | 866% | 219% | 243% | 21% | 79% | 10% | | | | | |
| Police Stations | 397% | 344% | 73% | 74% | 69% | 69% | 60% | 8% | | | |
| Train Station | 331% | 415% | 436% | 206% | 215% | 123% | 123% | | | | |
| Gas Station | 985% | 337% | -9% | 26% | | | | | | | |
| Rocket Launch Station | 368% | 466% | 168% | 75% | -31% | 22% | | | | | |
| Cargo Train | 462% | 354% | 354% | 278% | 359% | 264% | 173% | 131% | 71% | 75% | 21% |
| Passenger Train | 525% | 341% | 83% | 39% | 19% | | | | | | |
| Mobile Operations Center | 411% | 132% | 55% | 62% | 15% | | | | | | |
| Mobile Crane | 135% | 164% | 372% | 256% | 130% | 49% | 115% | 55% | | | |
| Camper | 499% | 179% | 0% | | | | | | | | |
| Rescue Aircraft | 500% | -17% | 59% | | | | | | | | |
| Cargo Ship | 360% | 199% | 42% | | | | | | | | |
| Taj Mahal | 317% | 70% | | | | | | | | | |
| Carrousel | 673% | 106% | | | | | | | | | |
| Ferris Wheel | 401% | 108% | | | | | | | | | |
| Ecto-1 | 191% | 98% | 60% | | | | | | | | |
| Saturn V | 70% | 71% | | | | | | | | | |
| Ship in the Bottle | 63% | 56% | | | | | | | | | |
| Pirate Ship | 837% | 548% | 686% | 326% | 43% | | | | | | |
| Castles | 1.965% | 1.039% | 1.156% | 1.103% | 1.707% | 1.484% | 321% | 943% | 333% | 235% | 238% |
| Dragons | 411% | 271% | 282% | 211% | 176% | 143% | 108% | 108% | 64% | 66% | 56% |
| The White House | 122% | 54% | | | | | | | | | |
| Burj Khalifa | 201% | 93% | | | | | | | | | |
| Las Vegas | 70% | 40% | | | | | | | | | |
| Solomon Guggenheim | 145% | 55% | | | | | | | | | |
| Batmobil (small) | 609% | 73% | 103% | 36% | 45% | 24% | 27% | | | | |
| Batmobil (large) | 460% | 74% | 66% | | | | | | | | |
| Batman's Cave | 435% | 96% | 29% | 64% | 42% | | | | | | |
| Knight Bus | 213% | 30% | | | | | | | | | |
| Attack on the Burrow | 354% | 64% | | | | | | | | | |
| Hogwarts Express | 375% | 485% | 548% | 218% | 43% | | | | | | |
| Hogwarts Castle | 284% | 385% | 614% | 188% | 62% | | | | | | |

| | | | | | | | | | | | |
|---|---|---|---|---|---|---|---|---|---|---|---|
| Hagrids Hut | 412% | 447% | 213% | 28% | | | | | | | |
| X-Wing (small) | 357% | 450% | 159% | 179% | 90% | 81% | 111% | 43% | | | |
| X-Wing (large) | 440% | 121% | | | | | | | | | |
| Y-Wing (small) | 175% | 274% | 159% | 102% | 13% | | | | | | |
| Y-Wing (large) | 609% | 148% | | | | | | | | | |
| Millennium Falcon (small) | 270% | 471% | 114% | 51% | 58% | 40% | | | | | |
| Millennium Falcon (large) | 369% | 86% | | | | | | | | | |
| AT-TE | 547% | 388% | 307% | 79% | | | | | | | |
| AT-AT | 414% | 307% | 128% | 118% | 33% | | | | | | |
| Death Star | 362% | 82% | 71% | | | | | | | | |
| Yoda | 260% | 52% | | | | | | | | | |
| Snowspeeder (small) | 322% | 101% | 140% | 132% | | | | | | | |
| Snowspeeder (large) | 676% | 108% | | | | | | | | | |
| Tie Fighter & Y-Wing | 198% | 393% | 234% | | | | | | | | |
| Tie Fighter | 378% | 108% | 55% | 149% | 52% | 25% | 67% | | | | |
| Tantive V | 170% | 74% | | | | | | | | | |
| Slave 1 | 701% | 833% | 445% | 445% | 184% | 168% | 97% | | | | |
| Imperial Star Destroyer | 592% | 265% | 114% | 161% | 46% | | | | | | |
| Imperial Shuttle | 270% | 232% | 147% | 132% | | | | | | | |

Table 20 - Evaluation of the value development of 51 LEGO sets as well as their new editions or re-releases

For the present evaluation in Table 20, LEGO sets from a wide variety of LEGO themes were compared. A total of 51 LEGO sets from 22 themes are available. Nevertheless, LEGO set new editions and re-releases can be found in all themes and price ranges. For each of these LEGO sets first editions exist today different numbers of new editions or re-releases, which are modified in form and appearance. Exceptions are the new editions of *LEGO set no. 21313-1 Ship in a Bottle* and *LEGO set no. 21309-1 NASA Apollo Saturn V.* The re-releases with the same name (*LEGO set no. 92177-1* and *LEGO set no. 92176-1*) are identical to the previous versions.

Overall, the number of new editions or re-releases (not including the LEGO set first editions) adds up to 235 pieces. On average, this corresponds to about 4 to 5 new editions per LEGO set. Excluded from the analysis are

62 LEGO sets for which no sufficient data records (MSRP or at least one current price information) are available. Thus, 51 LEGO set first editions could be compared to their 173 LEGO set re-releases or new editions. As a result, Table 20 gives us an overview of how permanent re-releases or new editions of LEGO sets have developed in value.

LEGO sets that have been re-released or reissued most often are freight trains, castles and dragons. Of the latter two, there are 19 new editions or re-releases. In Table 20, only those LEGO sets are considered that are comparable with each other.

With the help of the diverging color scale per LEGO set, it is possible to visually distinguish which new edition or re-release has performed well or badly. It is particularly noticeable that first edition LEGO sets still generate the highest value growth in the majority of cases. This is true for a total of 41 out of 51 LEGO sets. In the remaining 10 cases, the LEGO set with the highest increase in value is the 2nd or 3rd new edition or re-release.

In addition, Table 20 shows quite impressively that also in 40 out of 51 cases, the new editions or re-releases also have the lowest increase in value. This is all the more astonishing because new editions or re-releases are usually more challenging and significantly more detailed in their design. However, it is important to keep in mind that in these 40 cases, the LEGO sets were released on average in 2018. In the clear majority, these LEGO sets are still available in retail and online stores. Consequently, it can be assumed that an increase in value has not yet occurred.

For the LEGO sets on which Figure 93 is based, the average performance can be summarized as follows, depending on the number of new editions or re-releases.

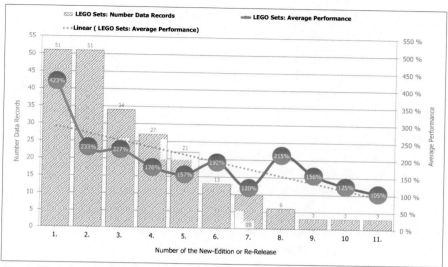

*Figure 93 - Average performance as a function of the number of new-editions or re-releases for LEGO sets*

The first editions of the 51 LEGO sets achieved an average increase in value of 423 percent. Even the first re-release or new edition increased on average only 233 percent in the past. Certainly, this is still a remarkable increase in value. But it is also only about half of what the first edition returned. With each new edition or reissue, the increase in value decreases. For example, three LEGO sets were identified that had an astonishing eleven new editions or re-releases. These only increased by an average of 105 percent in the past.

The new edition or re-release of a LEGO Set achieves on average 8 percent less appreciation compared with the previous version. Nevertheless, the average increases in value are still impressive. This proves beyond doubt that new editions or re-releases are always less lucrative than the first edition.

Unfortunately, Figure 93 does not give any indication as to how much the first edition of a LEGO set loses value at the exact moment when the new editions or re-releases are published. In order to evaluate this, price information is needed at different points in time (before and after the release of the new editions or re-releases). However, since no one except The LEGO Group knows if or when a new edition or re-release will be published, price information would need to be continuously monitored and documented. Looking back on my experience, this is a very time-consuming undertaking for 14,068 LEGO sets. Automation for retrieving the data points would be essential.

The matter is also being hotly discussed on the Internet. Especially LEGO collectors and a few LEGO investors have already noticed such effects in the past. Usually, the first edition of a LEGO set has a certain iconic status in the LEGO universe and especially among collectors. Also, LEGO sets first editions have already had many years to age and consequently gain in value. New editions or re-releases still have their full lifetime ahead of them at the time of their release. It is also unclear at this point, for example, how many years they will remain on the market or whether more will appear. These constant uncertainties mean that LEGO investors have to be patient until new editions or re-releases hopefully develop positively in value.

The factor of timing also plays a significant role. Therefore, the following section will look at how long the time intervals are between the first edition and the subsequent new editions or re-releases. In Figure 94, the annual average between the individual editions was determined on the basis of the 51 LEGO sets (first edition) and their 173 new editions or re-releases. This should give LEGO investors a feeling for the intervals at which new editions or re-releases have been published by The LEGO Group to date.

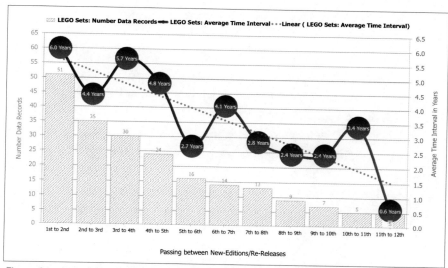

*Figure 94 - Average period of time in years between the different editions or re-releases of LEGO sets*

The graph in Figure 94 is very similar to the graph in Figure 93, although the latter has a completely different message. Nevertheless, a correlation is recognizable. The first new edition or re-release of a LEGO set appears on average after 6 years. Further new editions or new issues appear at increasingly shorter intervals. Due to the significantly shorter intervals between new editions or re-releases, LEGO buyers and collectors can expect a new edition or re-release of a certain LEGO set to appear in the foreseeable future. Of course, this has a lasting effect on the value development of such LEGO sets. If it is foreseeable that a LEGO set of the same type will appear every one or two years, there are little reasons for the predecessor model to increase exceptionally in value.

In principle, The LEGO Group is able to release a new edition or re-release for any LEGO set. With the release of more detailed and beautiful new editions or re-releases, there is little incentive for buyers to buy an old predecessor model. Simply because it is easier to get a new model at a lower price.

There was a time many years ago when you could easily buy any LEGO set to benefit from its appreciation in value. This was especially true for LEGO sets of the Star Wars theme. That time seems to be over for now. The LEGO Group regularly releases new editions or re-releases of particularly popular LEGO sets. It could be proven that it is irrelevant that new editions or re-releases are sometimes significantly more detailed or show more attention to detail. In general, new editions try to reflect the colors of the original even better. And with each new edition, a LEGO set becomes more modern (e.g., smoother edges). To make matters worse, The LEGO Group also wants to outdo the predecessor models in terms of size and number of individual bricks and parts. This makes many buyers and collectors lose their desire to hunt for the first edition. Nevertheless, there will always be only one original or first edition.

New editions of LEGO sets are generally not a good LEGO investment. This includes especially those LEGO sets for which it is expected that they will be re-released again and again in different time frames. This includes in particular all accessories such as rails and railway switches, but also sets such as police stations, fire stations or freight trains. These LEGO sets are essential in the LEGO universe and they always find their regular place in the LEGO catalog every year. Although each LEGO set is a little more unique.

LEGO investors should consider such LEGO sets as an investment strategy each year. For example, if The LEGO Group designs a very intricately-detailed police station, its outstanding features might make it worthwhile as an investment after all. It also helps your return on investment if you purchase the LEGO sets at the highest possible discount.

## 4.6 Investigation of Soft Factors

The reasons for the increase and decrease in the value of LEGO sets cannot always be derived by years, themes, weights, number of individual bricks or parts or minifigures. As in many other areas (e.g., real estate), there are not only hard factors but also soft factors that influence value development.

In contrast to hard factors, soft factors are various key figures that cannot be measured at all or only with auxiliary indicators. Their significance and importance often depend on subjective assessments. Nevertheless, they can be decisive for the performance of a LEGO product. The importance of soft factors in today's world is steadily increasing and should not be ignored when making investment decisions. In the LEGO universe, these include, for example, the fun of building and playing, rarity, customer ratings, exclusivity, scale or controversy of LEGO sets.

Officially, there is no measurable weighting of hard and soft factors. For example, a LEGO product may have an excellent MSRP (hard factor). Nevertheless, it is simply not interesting for customers due to a poor visual appearance (soft factor). As a result, the LEGO set is inappropriate as an investment. The consideration must be done individually. The search for LEGO products that meet all requirements (hard and soft factors) is extremely difficult. The appreciation of a LEGO set is often emotional. A particularly drastic example of this is that someone cannot live without a certain LEGO set. In a way, looking for LEGO sets as a proper investment is like looking for right company shares on the stock market. In the stock market, everyone is trying to find the next Apple, Facebook or Tesla stock. In the LEGO world, investors are trying to find the next *LEGO set no. 10179-1 UCS Millennium Falcon* or the next *LEGO set no. 10182-1 Cafe Corner*.

## 4.6.1 Exclusivity, Rarity and Limitation

Exclusive, rare or limited LEGO sets make the hearts of LEGO investors beat faster. Basically, the three terms have one common denominator: limited availability. Products tend to become valuable when they are produced only in small quantities and for short periods of time, and new editions or re-releases can be ruled out if possible. Nevertheless, the terms have completely different meanings in the LEGO universe.

- The term *rare* expresses that a raw material, product or other (e.g., a service) occurs comparatively less often. In the LEGO universe, this proportionality is measured by comparison to similar LEGO products or LEGO sets. Unfortunately, this theoretical definition does not provide any numerical orientation, which is why the following illustrative example is intended to help with understanding and orientation. It is assumed that LEGO set no. XYZ was produced and sold 50,000 times in a period of 3 years until its official End-of-Life. After LEGO set no. XYZ is retired, some sympathy gradually arises followed by increased demand for LEGO set no. XYZ. In our example, of the former 50,000 units sold, only 20 new or unopened LEGO sets no. XYZ are still available for purchase on the secondary market (e.g., Ebay, Amazon, etc.). If these 20 LEGO sets are now faced against 500 collectors, there will be a real bidding battle, with the price or value increasing significantly. There are few offered LEGO sets no. XYZ a very high number of demands. This example makes it clear that the rarity of a LEGO set (e.g., due to a low production quantity) can undoubtedly be a catalyst for LEGO sets to increase in price or value. Ultimately, the interplay of supply and demand determines whether a value can be placed on the rarity of a LEGO set. The rarest LEGO set is of little use to an investor if there is no buyer even after years. It is well known that supply and demand regulate the price in this case as well. It is also possible for The LEGO Group to create an unintended rarity. This happens, for example, through misprints or special details, but also unique and limited editions, rare misfabrication, unusual color of the base material, deformation or incorrect painting.

We also distinguish LEGO sets in terms of their *exclusivity*. A LEGO set is exclusive if it is only available to a certain group of interested parties or buyers. For example, only The LEGO Group sells LEGO Set No. 75980-1 Harry Potter Attack on the Foxhole in its online store or its own retail stores. Of course, The LEGO Group labels its exclusive products in its own online store or brick-and-mortar retail stores. In addition, The LEGO Group is increasingly selling LEGO products that were previously only available on an exclusive basis on a semi-exclusive basis. For this purpose, the products are made available to other exclusive partners for regular retail after a certain period of time and usually until the End-of-Life. It should be noted that all exclusive LEGO sets are still officially available from The LEGO Group. Again, there are some LEGO sets that are not sold in retail stores. These include LEGO sets from San Diego Comic Con and employee Christmas gifts. There are also LEGO sets that are only available at LEGOland parks worldwide. Due to the Covid 19 pandemic, many LEGOland exclusive sets were sold at other retailers in 2020 and 2021, such as Target (USA) or in LEGOland's own onlinestore. The reason for this may have been that there was an oversupply of these exclusive LEGO sets at LEGOland parks around the world when they were closed due to the Covid 19 pandemic. In order to sell these LEGO sets, The LEGO Group passed on some of the inventory to other retailers. Regardless, it is unclear how long LEGOland sets will be generally available. Brickset does not document any records on this. With an average increase in value of 150 percent, it is recommended to take a look at the local store when visiting the LEGOland theme park. Another category of exclusive LEGO sets are so-called LEGO employee gifts. These LEGO sets are given exclusively to employees and are not available in official stores. Often, employee gifts are an giveaway from The LEGO Group to celebrate certain milestones. For example, LEGO set no. 4002019-1 Star Wars Holiday X-Wing Starfighter was given to employees to celebrate the 20th anniversary of the licensing agreement with Star Wars in 2019. Currently, the Star Wars Holiday X-Wing Starfighter is trading well above USD 1,000. There may also be some unintended exclusivity by The LEGO Group. This happens in case of production errors (e.g., wrong printing) or modification (artist's signature on packaging) of the existing item.

- The term limited means that a certain product is restricted to a certain number. The reason for the limitation can be manifold. For example, it may be a special addition or a test product. Strictly speaking, every LEGO set released so far has been limited. Ultimately, the reason is that there has not been a LEGO set that has not been discontinued at some point. When we talk about limited LEGO sets in the LEGO universe, we are referring to LEGO sets with significantly limited quantities. Even at the production stage, LEGO sets are deliberately artificially scarce. It is no secret that limited items usually increase in value more. Limited LEGO sets (e.g., special editions or special releases) are thus the main focus when looking for potential LEGO investments. Such LEGO sets tend to fetch higher selling prices. The LEGO Group is aware of the popularity of so-called limited LEGO sets. Especially often these attract the interest of collectors and sometimes lead to utopian prices. This in turn leads to harsh criticism and accusations within the LEGO community. Accordingly, The LEGO Group is now very keen to avoid limitations as far as possible. Nevertheless, they occur occasionally (e.g., LEGO Bricklink Designer Program) and should enjoy the full attention of the LEGO investor.

Unfortunately, there are few reliable sources that clearly and unequivocally document whether a LEGO set was distributed exclusively or produced in limited quantities. Therefore, we will consider exclusive, rare and limited

LEGO sets together for further evaluation. With the help of Brickset, we were able to identify a total of 223 LEGO sets (as of February 15, 2022) that are documented as exclusive, rare or limited. In principle, the data availability of such LEGO sets is significantly worse than for normal LEGO sets. Nevertheless, complete records is available for 44 LEGO sets. Figure 95 impressively shows that exclusive/limited/rare LEGO sets achieve considerable increases in value. The average MSRP of the 44 LEGO sets considered is USD 51 after adjusting for inflation. Here, the most expensive LEGO set is no. 2000451-1 The Panama Canal with an MSRP of USD 249.99. This LEGO set was exclusive to Panama, with production quantities said to be only 40,000 pieces. The average appreciation for all 44 LEGO sets is 425 percent. This varies from -4 to +1,268 percent. Few of these LEGO sets are only minifigures. Among the 44 LEGO sets, *LEGO set no. 2000451-1 The Panama Canal* is the largest LEGO set with 1,180 Regular individual bricks and pieces. On average, the 44 exclusive/limited/rare LEGO sets come to 201 Regular Individual bricks and pieces. Particularly impressive is the fact that there is a total of only 17 minifigures in the entire 44 LEGO sets. The average increase in value of exclusive/limited/rare LEGO sets with minifigures is 359 percent. In contrast, exclusive/limited/rare LEGO sets without minifigures achieved an average increase in value of 449 percent.

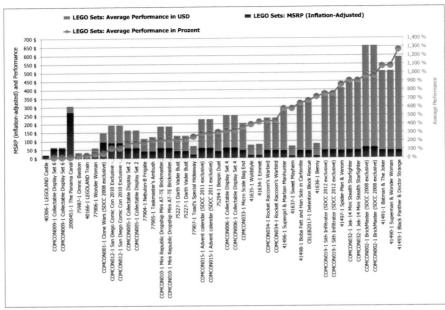

*Figure 95 - Average performance for exclusive, rare or limited LEGO sets*

We can therefore conclude that for these types of LEGO sets, the included LEGO minifigures are barely responsible for the increases in value. Looking only at the two-price information *Last 6 Month Sales in USD on Bricklink* and *Current Items for Sale in USD on Bricklink*, these 44 LEGO sets have increased by an average of 129 percent in the last 6 months. Furthermore, one thing in particular stands out in the evaluation: The average Part-Out-Value in USD on Bricklink is only 39 percent of the value for Current *Items for Sale in USD on Bricklink*.

It is thus also clear that, similar to the minifigures, the Regular Items are hardly responsible for the extraordinary increases in value. Therefore, it is assumed that exclusive/rare/limited LEGO sets barely have special individual bricks or parts. In addition, these exclusive/limited/rare LEGO sets already have a relatively high Price-per-Brick of USD 0.46 per brick (based on MSRP). As of December 31, 2020, the average Part-out-Value is only USD

398

70, whereas some LEGO sets trade for over USD 1,000 on Bricklink. The high price and value increases are rather the result of exclusivity, limitation and rarity of these LEGO sets.

Of course, the few LEGO minifigures included are just as limited and thus arouse the interest and desire of collectors. It is less common for exclusive/rare/limited LEGO sets to be parted out to sell LEGO individual bricks and parts as well as minifigures on their own. This in turn leads to minifigure collectors having to buy entire LEGO sets. The already too low amount of supply is thus confronted with an even higher supply.

In the future, the search for exclusive/rare/limited LEGO sets is likely to become more difficult. The LEGO Group has changed its own policy as of May 1, 2019, to the effect that LEGO sets will no longer be launched only in certain regions. In the past, the outcry among interested parties and collectors was too great. Up to this point, The LEGO Group had repeatedly released various LEGO sets in isolated countries. Nevertheless, The LEGO Group continues to leave itself open to various options:

- Pilot projects like *Forma* to test markets and opportunities without making them available to the general public.
- Gifts-With-Purchase campaigns through LEGO Store at Home and LEGO Brand Retail.
- Products that are sold only after specific experiences (e.g., LEGOland, LEGO House and LEGO Brand Retail Stores).
- Special event sets (e.g., Comic-Con, LEGO Inside Tour).

Exclusive/rare/limited LEGO of the LEGO Inside Tour stand out particularly strongly. As of 2022, this tour takes place in groups four times a year and lasts 2.5 days each time. The tour is exclusive to Billund and participation currently costs just about 2,000 Euro per person. Participants receive a LEGO set as a gift at the end of the tour. These individualized LEGO sets are considered the most limited LEGO sets, as they are exclusively for participants. Each LEGO set will be handed out with a group photo of the participants on the back of the box. This special gift will be given to four groups with an average of 20 people. Thus, there are only 80 copies of this LEGO set in circulation worldwide. With that comes incredible value gains of between USD 1,000 and USD 7,000 on Bricklink. The biggest hurdle is not selling his LEGO set. It is much more difficult to get a place on the LEGO Inside Tour, which can only be obtained by drawing lots.

There is hardly a company that understands how to create hype around new products so well. VIP pre-purchase privileges are announced and advertised weeks in advance. Many smaller gift sets or so-called Gift-With-Purchases are meanwhile added to purchases directly from LEGO online and retail stores. The LEGO Group is focusing specifically on LEGO sets with blockbuster characters, which will initially only be offered exclusively through its own online and retail stores. Quite a few of these GWP's are traded directly in the first days after addition over USD 80. Considering that it is a free gift, the reduction in price of the actual purchase is very lucrative. Since the return on investment is determined at the point of purchase, it's a good idea to time your LEGO online and retail purchases accordingly. The LEGO Group has also recognized this trend and has recently shown itself to be extraordinarily willing to constantly announce new GWP's. To illustrate how The LEGO Group's Gift-With-Purchases have developed in the past, a total of 46 different GWP's from the period 2011 to 2020 were evaluated in terms of their performance in the following Figure 98.

Instead, only the average price or value in USD is shown in Figure 96. The total value of all 46 GWP's amounts to USD 2,108. The average prices or values vary between USD 4 and USD 157. For example, *LEGO set no. 5004938-1 NINJAGO Minifigure Collection* has a value of USD 156.70. That's not bad for a gratis LEGO set.

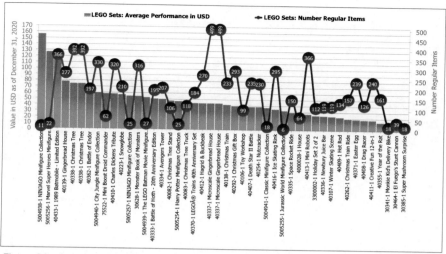

*Figure 96 - Average performance for Gift-With-Purchases (GWP)*

This specific LEGO set is one of the so-called Bricktober sets, which was exclusively available at Toys'R'Us in 2017. To get this one, you had to buy LEGO sets for a certain amount in one of the numerous Toys'R'Us stores. If you think now that these sets are hard to get, I can reassure you. I myself was able to grab five Bricktober sets in 2018 through specific purchases at Toys'R'Us (1 x *LEGO set no. 5005254-1 Harry Potter Minifigure Set*, 2 x *LEGO set no. 5005256-1 Marvel Super Heroes Minifigure Set*, as well as 1 x *LEGO set no. 5005257-1 Ninjago Minifigure Set*). Currently, the value of these four LEGO sets is around USD 400. In return, I have purchased LEGO sets for 225 USD (MSRP).

## 4.6.2 Stickers and Printings

It's impossible to talk about LEGO investment without addressing the weak point in the LEGO universe. There is no topic LEGO enthusiasts agree on as much as when it comes to printed bricks or stickers on bricks. For example, the majority of LEGO sets in the Friends theme have printed bricks and pieces. LEGO sets of the 4 Juniors theme series also come exclusively with printed individual bricks and parts. It is certainly understandable that The LEGO Group does not want to impose stickers on this young target group. Again, the expensive top seller *LEGO set no. 75192-1 Millennium Falcon*, which has an MSRP of USD 799.99, only comes with stickers. Many LEGO fans and collectors take issue with this. The main arguments for or against stickers and printed individual bricks or parts can be summarized as follows:

- On the one hand, printed items are seen as price drivers. On the other hand, most buyers are willing to pay more for printed bricks and parts.
- A sticker rarely comes alone. If a sticker is needed, other stickers often follow. The background to this is the effort and printing costs involved in producing sticker sheets.
- The adhesion of stickers is often doubted. This is not least due to the fact that many adults of today find heavily worn parts with stickers in their old LEGO collections. If you believe The LEGO Group, the adhesion of stickers has developed considerably in recent decades.
- Stickers are less able to withstand direct sunlight.
- Stickers are difficult to position. Customers complain about crooked application, unsightly bubbles as well as sticking in the wrong orientation or on non-planar elements.
- For value and longevity, printed individual bricks and parts are simply better.
- Printed bricks and parts are usually difficult to reuse (e.g., for own designs or MOCs).

- For a premium product, which LEGO wants to be, printed bricks and parts should be standard.
- Color deviations between an individual brick and sticker are unavoidable. Only rarely does The LEGO Group succeed in matching the colors of the stickers to the underlying individual brick or part.

Stickers are above all one thing: A matter of taste. It is particularly advantageous that there is no obligation to use stickers. You can simply omit them, which is certainly to the detriment of the overall look of the LEGO set. Likewise, stickers can be removed even after years and the individual bricks or parts can be used elsewhere. Of course, after the removal of the stickers are rarely further to use.

One thing that is indisputable is that both stickers and printed elements visibly increase the richness of detail in a LEGO set. There are also more and more competitors that rely exclusively on printed parts. Therefore, the topic will remain particularly exciting in the coming years, to what extent The LEGO Group will be impressed by this behavior of the competition or will take action itself.

A statistical evaluation of LEGO sets with stickers and/or printed individual bricks and parts is not the scope of this analysis. The individual recording of these seems to be too time-consuming and so far, there is no documentation about which LEGO sets use printed single bricks and parts as well as stickers. Furthermore, it is highly doubtful that stickers or printed bricks and parts have a noticeable impact on the performance of LEGO sets. Nor is it possible to say whether people decide not to buy a LEGO set because it comes with (the less desirable) stickers. You can read again and again in posts or forums that people boycott a LEGO set because of the stickers, but the number should be vanishingly small.

### 4.6.3   Other Tips

### 4.6.3.1   Display-Set or Play-Set

Toys should be safe and fun. Children judge the value of a toy by its play functions or the fun they have with it. Whether a LEGO set has a high play value is subjectively in the eye of the beholder (e.g., fantasy and imagination). However, it is obvious that a train with different wagons offers more diverse play possibilities than a train with identical wagons. Also, the play value depends on various factors such as design, shape, color, size, weight, construction and mechanics. In addition, the evaluation of the toy can only take place taking into account the age and developmental stage of the child. A possible approach would be, for example, to divide the hours of play by the purchase price.

In contrast, adults rather evaluate the display capability. The term describes the ability or capacity of a LEGO set to convince as a showcase model (e.g., a "wow effect" in the form of an extraordinary display or charisma). Both display capability and play value cannot be measured. These soft factors are so subjective that one would rather have to do a study with a large number of test persons to substantiate or refute these capabilities with numbers.

The display capability can also be reduced to various factors. For example, whether the design of the construction matches the original (e.g., *LEGO set no. 75827-1 Ghostbusters Fire Department Headquarters* or *LEGO set no. 42043-1 Mercedes-Benz Arocs 3245*). This is certainly also a major reason why the Nexo Knights theme area rose significantly worse in value (83 percent). The theme is characterized by a future world with colorful robots, vehicles and knights without any reference to the Middle Ages. The following additional characteristics can have a lasting impact on the price or value of a LEGO set:

## Building Ideas

When you build a car or a train from LEGO bricks, each building step is usually repeated - once left, once right. Then again, there are LEGO sets such as *LEGO set no. 70840-1 Welcome to Apocalypse City!* Customers report that the building and playing experience is much more varied and adventurous. Certainly, this can also lead to discovering details during construction that inspire building projects of their own. Surely it is no coincidence that the increase in value of the LEGO set is 150 percent. *LEGO set no. 70840-1* is subordinate to *The LEGO Movie 2* theme, which itself has only achieved an average increase in value of 19 percent.

## Alternative Buildings

B-models are a term that generally applies to toys for assembly, but is especially important for LEGO sets in the Technic theme. In addition to the A-model, which is usually the name giver for a sold LEGO set or is shown on the packaging, there is occasionally also a B-model. The B-model is a model that can be built with the same bricks and parts as the A-model. It is usually a similar model and is advertised on the back of the product box. It can be built instead of the A model. Often, the B-model requires slightly fewer individual bricks and parts than the A-model. Instructions for the B model are either included as well or are available online at The LEGO Group. In *LEGO set no. 42044-1 Jet Plane*, the A model is a jet plane and the B model is a propeller plane.

### 4.6.3.2 Scaled Sets

Buyers of LEGO sets rarely expect them to be constructed to scale. It is well known that this already fails with the LEGO minifigures, which, with a few exceptions, are always the same size. Nevertheless, an approximate scale accuracy is advantageous for a LEGO set - especially if minifigures are included. As positive examples, the Modular Buildings or Speed Champions themed series are particularly noteworthy. This is contrasted, for example, by *LEGO set no. 71006-1 The Simpsons House*. Although the house is in principle playable and displayable with minifigures, the proportions of rooms, furnishings and minifigures do not correlate. For example, the kitchen is just as wide as the couch. When a LEGO model is so small that no minifigure can fit inside, it is what is known as macro scale (for example, *LEGO set no. 71043-1 Hogwarts Castle*). In the near future, these models will have to be monitored particularly closely to see what influence macro figures have here.

### 4.6.3.3 Possible Combinations of Different Themes

The LEGO universe offers a variety of themes. The combination of LEGO sets within a theme will not be discussed further here. Instead, various LEGO sets are ideal for combining with each other - i.e., with other themes. For example, the vehicles of the Speed Champions theme series can ideally move in a city (e.g., *City*, *Modular Buildings*, etc.). Another example is the combination of the *Ninjago* and *Monkie Kid* themed series. Both action-animation TV series are set in a fictional world, a place inspired by Chinese and Japanese myths and culture, and are ideal for complementing and expanding each other. Various strategies can be derived from this. Having the right LEGO sets can definitely attract significant interest from collectors later on. For example, look at *LEGO set no. 21310-1 Old Fishing Store* from the Ideas themes. There is probably no better LEGO set in the LEGO world than *LEGO set no. 70419-1 Wrecked Shrimp Boat* from *Hidden Side*, which can be parked right in front of the *Fishing Store*.

### 4.6.3.4   Popular Sets due to constant Demand and Reviews

It is in the nature of LEGO investment that again and again LEGO sets are less attractive during their lifetime or availability. The more surprising is then when these in retirement (clearly or conspicuously) increase in value (i.e. *LEGO set no. 75222-1 Betrayal in Cloud City*). Usually, the reason is obvious that too few LEGO sets have made it to the secondary market. Again, it can be said that particularly desired LEGO sets during their lifetime, this also remain for the time being, once the LEGO sets are retired. There are enough indications for this. For example, when a LEGO set is constantly sold out in the official LEGO online or retail stores. There are plenty of examples of this from the past. For example, the *LEGO set no. 10277-1 Crocodile Locomotive* sold out exceptionally often in the LEGO online store between its release on July 01, 2020 and the official EOL on December 31, 2021. This is an extremely well-known indicator of a future supply shortage. Of course, it also symbolizes the popularity of the locomotive.

In addition, it is never a bad idea to read the customer ratings or reviews of a LEGO set (e.g., Amazon, Brickset, Brickpicker, LEGO Onlineshop, etc.). This allows you to quickly get a differentiated assessment picture of the LEGO set. You should pay special attention to the overall rating as well as the ratio of positive to negative ratings. Two negative evaluations, which oppose 100 positive ones, can be Classifieds as little meaningful. Buyers' rating scores for the same LEGO set can vary widely. Therefore, you should read the content carefully. Try to fade out emotional ratings and focus entirely on the facts. Especially in view of the fact that you as a LEGO investor rarely or never build a LEGO set, this source seems particularly helpful and educational.

In the process of the data collection carried out in this investigation, all existing reviews or so-called ratings at Brickset were also evaluated. In total, the complete data is available for 4,547 or 32 percent of 14,068 LEGO sets.

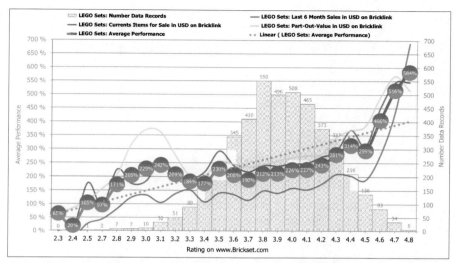

*Figure 97 - Correlation between ratings on Brickset and the average performance of LEGO sets*

Surprisingly, the rating on Brickset turns out to be an extremely useful indicator of the performance of LEGO sets. It is obvious that there is a connection between the increase in value of a LEGO set and the rating on Brickset. According to this, there is an average increase in value of between 20 and 584 percent between the ratings of 2.3 and 4.8. Basically, it can be ruled out that the ratings took place after a LEGO set increased in value. Rather, Brickset users rate LEGO sets anytime they are posted on Brickset. Obviously, this is an extremely helpful indicator to find potential LEGO investments.

### 4.6.3.5  Controversial LEGO Sets

A rare flop is known from 1979. The *Scala* theme, designed for young girls aged five to seven, focused mainly on jewelry. These LEGO sets consisted of decorative elements from which necklaces, bracelets and rings could be assembled. In 1979, the jewelry elements came on the market, but were not a great success. The LEGO sets disappeared from the shelves two years later in 1981.

However, there are other types of controversial LEGO sets, which were significantly more profitable in terms of their performance in the past. *LEGO set no. 42113-1 Bell Boeing V-22 Osprey* from the LEGO *Technic* series takes a special spot in this regard. The detailed replica for rescue missions was released by The LEGO Group in 2020. However, in the real world, the aircraft's primary use is military. It's important to note that The LEGO Group has had a policy of not creating military-themed LEGO sets for quite some time. Following calls from peace activists not to release the LEGO set, The LEGO Group decided to conduct an intensive review for and against the introduction of *LEGO set no. 42113-1 Bell Boeing V-22 Osprey*. Although the LEGO set does not glorify violence, there is no military reference on the packaging and it does not contain any weapons, The LEGO Group finally bowed to the pressure and decided not to release the LEGO set. However, at this time it was already possible for various buyers to purchase the LEGO set in retail stores. The LEGO Group announced that a small number of the *V-22 Osprey* had already been distributed to retailers, so even a few had been sold. The LEGO sets that were sold were not recalled by The LEGO Group, which certainly makes them collector's items with strictly limited quantities. A fortunate outcome for buyers as it turns out in hindsight. Within a few days, the *V-22 Osprey* shot up to 1,000 Euro on Ebay and other sales platforms, well off an original MSRP of 139.99 Euro. It is still unclear what will happen to the stock of LEGO sets still owned by The LEGO Group. A statement from the company suggests that it is highly likely that the parts will be reused for other LEGO sets.

Another example is the Indiana Jones themes. The theme includes numerous representations of military features from the World War II and Cold War era, including both a Pilatus P-2 with markings for the German Air Force and a fictitious Nazi Airborne Bomber. Such LEGO sets appeal to a very special group of buyers who are generally left out of LEGO products. Increasingly, this clientele is looking to the competition, which additionally thematize and offer military sets in particular. LEGO sets from the Indiana Jones theme have an average appreciation of 397 percent as of December 31, 2020.

# 5.   My LEGO Portfolio (as of June 30, 2022)

## 5.1   Overview

In this chapter, I would like to extend the previous findings from the statistical investigation with experiences from my personal LEGO portfolio. I started the statistical survey at the beginning of 2019. Whereas my own LEGO portfolio goes back to the beginning of 2018. From the beginning, I have been documenting a particularly wide variety of data points about my own LEGO portfolio. The goal is to optimize my personal purchases or sales (e.g., type of LEGO sets, timing for buying or selling, etc.) through continuous monitoring and documentation.

Due to my constant purchases and the relevant documentation in my personal LEGO portfolio, this chapter also provides more in-depth insights into the performance of LEGO sets. This is accompanied by further criteria, which a promising LEGO investment should bring with it. With this knowledge, we move directly into the processes of acquiring and later selling LEGO sets. These processes go beyond theory. Rather, practical experience is required for this. Therefore, it made sense to include experiences from my personal LEGO portfolio of the past five years. *After all, practical experience is what you get when you don't get what you want.* Due to the significant size that my personal LEGO portfolio has meanwhile taken on, it is only possible to go into detail about individual selected LEGO sets to a limited extent.

I have started seriously with the LEGO portfolio with my first purchase of the *LEGO set no. 75192-1 Millennium Falcon* on January 15, 2018. At that time, I had only one other LEGO set (*LEGO set no. 21008-1 Burj Khalifa*), which is strictly speaking a souvenir. However, with respect to the purchase date, the LEGO set of the *Burj Khalifa* represents my oldest LEGO set in the LEGO portfolio. Still today I own both LEGO sets. As of June 02, 2022, there are 533 LEGO sets from 47 different themes in my portfolio. These are genuine realized purchases. With a few exceptions, I own the vast majority of my LEGO sets only once. A handful of LEGO sets I even own three to six times. All LEGO sets in my portfolio are new respectively unopened respectively sealed. The total quantity is distributed as follows:

- Single:            423 LEGO Sets or 79 Percent
- Twice:             44 LEGO Sets or 17 Percent
- Three-Times:    1 LEGO Set or 1 Percent
- Four-Times:     2 LEGO Sets or 2 Percent
- Five-Times:     1 LEGO Set or 1 Percent
- Six-Times:      1 LEGO Set or 1 Percent

All 533 LEGO sets were purchased between January 15, 2018 and June 02, 2022. Taking into account the release or discontinuation date, there are significantly older LEGO sets in my LEGO portfolio. The current oldest *LEGO set no. 8836-1 Sky Ranger* was released in 1992. How I acquire such older LEGO sets, I will explain later. The last purchase in my LEGO portfolio was the *LEGO set no. 76906-1 1970 Ferrari 512 M* on June 02, 2022.

I have consciously chosen to consider the complete period of my personal portfolio, even though the previous statistical investigation considers the performance of LEGO sets only until December 31, 2020. Rather, the additional 18 months until June 30, 2022 are intended to reveal further deeper insights (especially the course of the value performance among different time periods). Conversely, this means that the LEGO sets in my portfolio had another 18 months to develop further in price or value. The previous statistical survey only looked at the MSRP as well as the various price information as of December 31, 2020. In my own LEGO portfolio, much more information regarding price or value is documented. So, in addition to the MSRP and my purchase price, the discount (in percent) is recorded. Furthermore, various price information is always determined at the middle and end of each calendar year. Since the journey of my own LEGO portfolio started a few months before this book and the statistical investigation, the types of price information differ to some extent. For my own LEGO portfolio, I consider Current Items for Sale in Euro on Bricklink, Part-Out-Value in Euro on Bricklink, and Current Items for Sale in Euro on Ebay Classifieds. By regularly documenting the price or value development, for example, the right time to sell can be defined. In practice, it is then seen when the price or value of a LEGO set is at its highest, before it starts to fall again in subsequent periods.

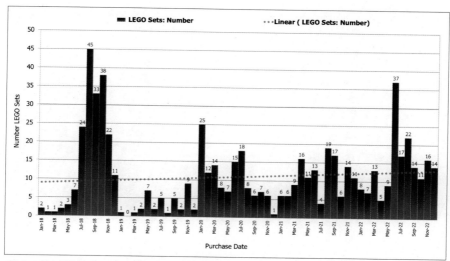

Figure 98 - Overview of my LEGO portfolio by number of LEGO set purchases per month between January 2018 and June 2022

First, I would like to give an overview of how my LEGO purchases have been distributed on a monthly basis. Figure 98 illustrates my monthly purchases of LEGO sets between January 2018 and June 2022. In the period of about 4.5 years, I bought an average of 10 LEGO sets per month. Here you can already see that I did not set myself any guidelines on how many LEGO sets I buy per month at most, because the purchases vary between 0 and 45 units per month. This approach is only possible if they keep their capital flexible and have access to sufficient storage space.

Throughout the period, there are clear fluctuations between the individual months. For example, I bought the most LEGO sets (13 to 18 units) in the months from July to November. However, I bought the fewest LEGO sets in the months from December to June. I will go into more detail about the reasons later.

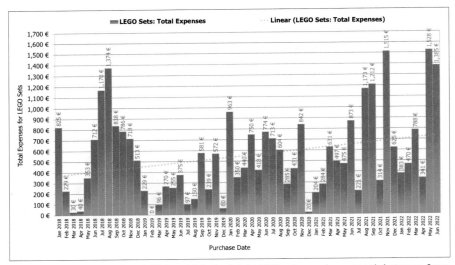

*Figure 99 - Overview of my LEGO portfolio by total LEGO set spend per month between January 2018 and June 2022*

A slightly different picture can be seen when looking at the total monthly purchases in Euro. Figure 98 shows that since 2018, purchases of LEGO sets per month have fallen slightly. In contrast, total monthly spending on new LEGO sets has been increasing over the same period (Figure 99). Over the 54-month period, an average of 533 Euro per month was invested in LEGO sets. This corresponds to approximately 17.40 Euro per day over a period of 1,644 days.

Figure 99 also shows that my LEGO purchases are unsteady and inconsistent. For example, there are months in which I have a high total expenditure but only buy a few LEGO sets (e.g., November 2021). On the other hand, there are months in which I spend relatively little money on many LEGO sets (e.g., March 2020). This is partly because I keep my monthly budget for LEGO purchases flexible. For example, I try to buy more LEGO sets in months with particularly good deals or high discounts. Overall, I see slightly increasing spending per month in my LEGO portfolio. As of June

2022, the total invested capital is 28,777 Euro. Over the entire period, this corresponds to an average purchase price of 53.91 Euro per LEGO set.

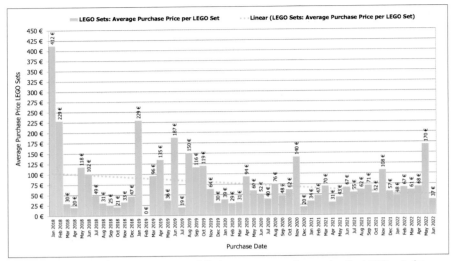

*Figure 100 - Overview of my LEGO portfolio by average purchase price for LEGO sets between January 2018 and June 2022*

As unexperienced as I was, my LEGO investment journey began with, among other things, the purchase of *LEGO set no. 75192 Millennium Falcon* from the *Ultimate Collector Series*. I bought this on January 15, 2018 at the original MSRP of 799.99 Euro. Initially, I had no feeling for the subject of LEGO investment and bought mainly according to personal taste and preference. True to the motto what would I like to build later, if the LEGO sets do not increase in value. I also still lacked any sense of possible discounts, which is why I had purchased the *Millennium Falcon* at MSRP. As of June 2022, the *Millennium Falcon* is still available. Thus, the purchase was clearly too early. The highest discount I know of on the *Millennium Falcon* to date has been about 30 percent off MSRP. If I sold the *Millennium Falcon* at the present time, I would be making a loss. *Who would buy a LEGO set at MSRP when you can get it for 10 or 20 percent off?* Therefore, I will continue to keep the Millennium Falcon in my portfolio, at least until it eventually goes into well-deserved retirement. So far, it's impossible to estimate when that will be. But when that time comes, all buyers who have already bought at a discount and much later will be in a much better position.

Large LEGO sets with high purchase costs are especially demanding on budget and storage capacity, which is why usually no or only a few more LEGO sets are purchased in the same months.

My total of 533 LEGO sets are distributed over 47 different themes. This corresponds to about one third of all themes published so far. The themes include between 1 and 82 LEGO sets. On average, I have 11 LEGO sets from one theme. The themes with the fewest LEGO sets include *Stranger Things*, *Ghostbusters*, *Knights Kingdom*, *Legends of Chima*, *Racers*, *Sports*, *The Simpsons* etc. Of all of these, I own only one LEGO set. With 82 LEGO sets, *City* is my largest theme in terms of number of LEGO sets. This might come as a surprise to experienced investors in particular. Because among investors, collectors and fans, the *City* theme is considered rather unpopular and an even worse investment. From my personal point of view, the average increases in value are the *City* theme among my top 10.

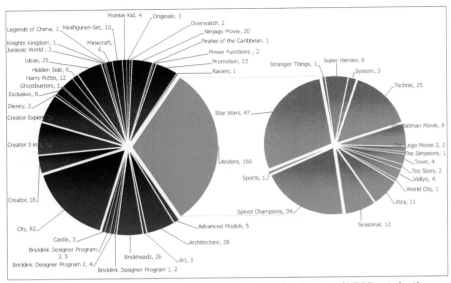

*Figure 101 - Overview of my LEGO portfolio according to distribution of LEGO sets by themes*

My second largest theme in the portfolio is *Star Wars* with 47 sets. It is followed by *Speed Champions* (34 sets), *Creator 3in1* (33 sets), *Creator Expert* (29 sets) and *BrickHeadz* (26 sets). The size of LEGO sets vary from 1 to 7,513 Regular Items. The smallest LEGO sets include *no. 88000-1 AAA battery box* or *no. 8883-1 M-Motor*. The largest LEGO set in my portfolio is the aforementioned *UCS Millennium Falcon*. All 533 LEGO sets together comprise 406,779 Regular Items. This is approximately the sum of all Regular Items of the LEGO themes *Technic* and *City* between 1961 and 2020.

The average size of my LEGO sets in the portfolio is 769 Regular Items. At first glance, this seems very high. From the statistical survey, we can see that between 2018 and 2020 LEGO sets have an average of 278 Regular Items. So my LEGO portfolio is focused on much larger LEGO sets. This is certainly also due to the fact that LEGO sets have been designed larger and larger for a few years now. Nevertheless, my personal LEGO portfolio covers the full range of LEGO set sizes.

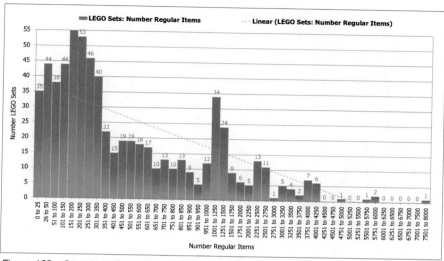

Figure 102 - Overview of my LEGO portfolio by distribution Number of Regular Items for LEGO sets between January 2018 and June 2022

It has always been very important to me personally to diversify as much as possible in this regard. For example, if you only buy LEGO sets with more than 2,500 Regular Items, you run several risks. First of all, the circle of buyers for such large LEGO sets is considerably limited. This is not least due to the fact that such LEGO sets generally have a higher RRP. In this respect, it is particularly important to keep in mind when choosing LEGO sets that in the future you will still have to find someone who is willing to pay (much) more than your purchase price.

A large number of LEGO sets and an even larger number of Regular Items suggest that there are also a lot of LEGO minifigures in my portfolio. Regarding the number of minifigures and unique minifigures, the structure is very mixed. In my LEGO portfolio there are 30 percent or 163 LEGO sets without minifigures. This applies especially to the *Architecture, BrickHeadz* and *Technic* themes, which account for about 50 percent of the total. Consequently, 1,497 minifigures are distributed among the remaining 370 LEGO sets.

421

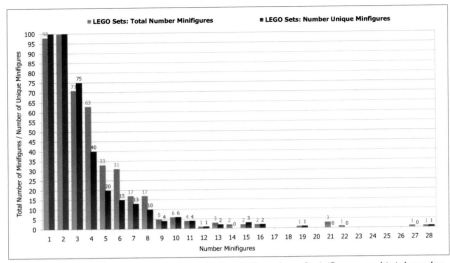

*Figure 103 - Overview of my LEGO portfolio by total number of minifigures and total number of unique minifigures*

This corresponds to an average of 4 minifigures per LEGO set. The LEGO set with the most minifigures is *no. 75159-1 Death Star*. In total, this LEGO set has 27 minifigures, whereas as of June 2022, 9 minifigures are unique or are only included in this LEGO set. In total, 1,154 minifigures or 77 percent of the minifigures are unique. That's slightly more than an average of 3 unique minifigures per LEGO set. It's no surprise that the most minifigures come from those LEGO themes to which the most LEGO sets belong. This already shows the strength of *Star Wars* sets. Despite almost twice as many LEGO *City* sets in my depot, *Star Wars* sets come to more minifigures. The number of unique minifigures is also greatest in LEGO sets of the Star Wars theme.

Finally, I would like to briefly discuss the masses of so many LEGO sets. Because it is certainly difficult to estimate the total weight of 533 LEGO sets. The total gross weight of the LEGO sets in my portfolio is 553.783 kilograms. Thus, a LEGO set weighs on average 1.063 kilograms.

422

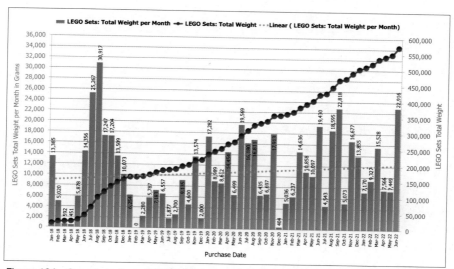

Figure 104 - Overview of my LEGO portfolio by total weight in kilograms for LEGO sets between January 2018 and June 2022

## 5.2    Buying LEGO Sets before Retirement

A crucial success factor and guarantor for consistently positive returns in LEGO investment is the purchase price. *The profit lies in purchasing is an old merchant's rule.* It is still valid and even more so in LEGO Investment. It has already been explained that the non-binding selling price is not mandatory for retailers. Both online retailers and retail stores have the flexibility to set their own sellling prices. LEGO sets are more popular than ever, which is why more and more retailers are placing the products in their assortment. As a result, competition among retailers is increasing. To be competitive, LEGO sets are increasingly offered at a discount. So it is very likely that LEGO sets are available at different prices at different retailers. Therefore, you should always compare prices before buying. Every retailer has a different strategy, so it happens that prices change sometimes every hour to make retailers competitive again.

However, you should not try to wait to buy LEGO sets until you think that the current offer price is the lowest price so far. This doesn't work very well on the stock market or with LEGO sets. It is unlikely that you will correctly estimate this point in time. Rather, this has often resulted in LEGO investors missing out on a LEGO product. If a LEGO set catches your attention because the discount is above average, it's a good move to buy it. Above average is of course vaguely worded. How can you recognize such a scenario? Personally, since the beginning of my journey in LEGO investment, I have been watching the prices of LEGO sets almost every day and sometimes several times a day on comparison portals. If you do this for a very long time, you can soon estimate whether the current price is lucrative or even better offers can be expected.

This sounds very time-consuming, especially at the beginning. But the benefits will quickly become apparent. I have also noticed that a particularly worthwhile offer is rarely a one-time event. If you have found a particularly great discount on a LEGO set, there is a very high probability that the offer will come back again at a later date. I would say that the probability is 100 percent. Of course, I can't prove these numbers, but just about every LEGO set is discounted sooner or later. I also don't know of any LEGO set that was only discounted once. There is far too much competition from online stores and retailers who have to undercut each other. If you watch the prices of LEGO sets daily, you can approach the lowest price. If you find the LEGO set of your choice at, say, 40 percent off, you shouldn't be upset when it's offered at more than 40 percent off later. If you are still convinced of this LEGO as an investment, you should rather consider buying a further set.

You would not be the first LEGO investor who is not able to call a LEGO set his own because he meticulously keeps hoping for an even lower purchase price. I have had this experience as well and so I am currently not (yet) a happy owner of the *LEGO set no. 75827 Ghostbusters Firehouse Headquarters*. This LEGO set, with an MSRP of USD 349.99, has never been available at a particularly deep discount. Even more surprisingly, it was retired from one day to the next. Before this was noticed, the LEGO set was already abruptly sold out in online and retail stores. As of February 2022, the LEGO set is trading between USD 800 and USD 900 on the secondary market. Currently, the increase in value continues without hindrance. The two- to threefold price as compensation for pain is certainly also one thing: apprenticeship money. I never really got over the fact that I don't own the *Ghostbusters Firehouse Headquarters*. But I have learned that you should never speculate on the lowest price.

By constantly monitoring the prices, you automatically acquire a hunting instinct that focuses your learned knowledge and intuition for interesting LEGO products (e.g., when a LEGO set is sold out again and again). Price comparisons such as Brickmerge, Idealo, Brickwatch and many more show the current lowest selling price for LEGO sets. Get into the habit of regularly checking the major platforms for deals and prices. You can also set a price alarm on many platforms. The price alert automatically informs you by email when the set price or the desired discount in percent is reached.

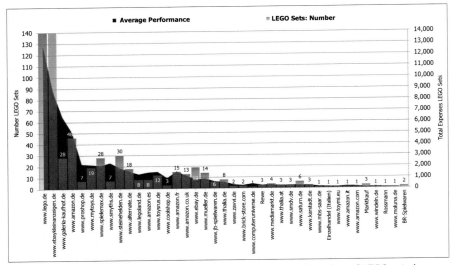

*Figure 105 - Overview of my LEGO portfolio by total spend and number of LEGO sets by dealer*

In the previous chapters of the statistical survey, the discount could not be taken into account in the value performance, as no data is available on this. It is also a fact that the discounts on LEGO sets vary greatly and are only a snapshot. There is no platform that documents discounts on LEGO sets. Therefore, it seemed helpful to me that I describe my own experiences in this regard and support them with meaningful data from my extensive purchases.

In total, I bought all 533 LEGO sets from 39 different online and retail stores. Of these, 491 LEGO sets, or 92 percent, were purchased from German-speaking retailers. These 491 LEGO sets were distributed among 32 different online and retail retailers. The remaining 42 LEGO sets were mostly purchased from online retailers abroad. Insofar as you buy LEGO products abroad, pay attention to the currency differences. Only seven LEGO sets were purchased from physical retailers. The purchases are distributed unevenly among the different retailers, which has different reasons.

My purchases from The LEGO Group stand out most dramatically. This applies to both online and retail purchases, which have been summarized in Figure 105. Over the past 4.5 years, I have purchased 129 LEGO sets directly from The LEGO Group for a total of 7,833.80 Euro. This represents 27 percent in terms of total LEGO portfolio spending. Basically, direct purchases from The LEGO Group are not well known for the fact that they come with particularly high discounts. The LEGO Group rarely offers discounts on its own products, and if it does, they can rarely keep up with those of the competition. Instead, it is the (partially) exclusive LEGO sets that attract customers. And this is guaranteed to be successful, as you can see in my case.

If you always buy directly from The LEGO Group, a LEGO set will potentially go End-Of-Life later. Ongoing sales of LEGO sets signal to The LEGO Group that there is still higher demand. Consequently, in the past, individual LEGO sets have continued to be produced, availability has been extended, and End-Of-Life has been delayed. To mitigate this, it is recommended to buy directly from private individuals, for example (e.g., Ebay or Ebay Classifieds).

A surprise is certainly the fact that I bought 110 LEGO sets on Ebay Classifieds. However, I only spent a total of 3,580.14 Euro on them. This indicates that I essentially buy smaller LEGO sets on Ebay Classifieds. However, purchases on Ebay Classifieds account for 12 percent of my LEGO portfolio. If you relate the share to the total number of my LEGO sets, it is 21 percent. For me, Ebay Classifieds is a great platform to buy LEGO sets that have long since been discontinued. I have had extremely positive experiences with the platform. But more about that later.

Galeria-Kaufhof and Amazon Germany follow on second and third place, where I have spent 2,823.63 Euro and 2,202.59 Euro so far. Both online retailers are always convincing with particularly good offers and high discounts. Taken together, these four retailers already account for 57 percent of the total spending in my LEGO portfolio.

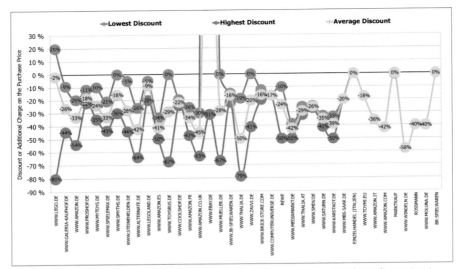

*Figure 106 - Overview of my LEGO portfolio by lowest, average, and highest discounts at online and retail stores*

In principle, I can say that I am not passionate about online shops or retailers. In this respect, I do not prefer any dealer. Rather, the purchase rate is essentially dependent on the LEGO offers or the number of discounts. Also, occasionally there is no way around online or retail dealers, because they are in partnership with The LEGO Group, so that they are allowed to distribute, for example, (partially) exclusive LEGO sets. As described above, this is one of the main reasons to buy directly from The LEGO Group.

Figure 106 gives an overview of how different my discounts are at the various online and retail retailers. The lowest, average and highest discount is shown for each retailer. If the value is above the wide black line or 0 percent, this corresponds to a surcharge. This means that I also bought LEGO sets for which I paid more than the RRP.

For this, I omitted all purchases on Ebay Classifieds. The clear majority of my LEGO sets, which I have purchased on Ebay Classifieds, was already retired at the time of purchase. As a consequence, the purchase price was usually already above the MSRP. Nevertheless, I make sure to buy only

LEGO sets that already achieve a (significantly) higher value or selling price. For the present evaluation, this is not relevant and not representative. Rather, this corresponds to a kind of bargain hunting on the digital flea market. Of course, Ebay Classifieds can also be worthwhile if you want to buy current LEGO sets. For example, it is possible to activate search requests. This way, offers come in regularly. In addition, you have the opportunity to negotiate the price. Even if this is sometimes excluded by sellers, asking costs nothing.

Ignoring my purchases on Ebay Classifieds, 423 LEGO sets were purchased in the past, with discounts to MSRP ranging from -18 to -37 percent. Cashback programs like Shoop, Payback as well as VIP points were not considered here. Of these 423 LEGO sets, I purchased 29 percent or 122 LEGO sets without a discount. The majority or 110 LEGO sets are direct purchases (online and retail) at The LEGO Group. Outside of The LEGO Group, this still results in 12 LEGO sets without discount.

Certainly, one or the other reader wonders why to buy an expensive product like LEGO sets without discounts? Just a moment ago I had explained in detail that discounts are always possible. Now for this, it is worth taking a closer look at the LEGO sets that were purchased without discounts. Among the 12 LEGO sets are no. 21310-1 Old Fishing Store, *no. 10259-1 Winter Village Station* or *no. 77942-1 Fiat 500 (Bright Light Blue Edition)*. The first two LEGO sets are already retired and increased by an average of 163 percent. The third LEGO set was sold exclusively through a dealer in the UK and could be ordered only temporarily to Germany. In this respect, you should always assess whether the purchase of the LEGO set without discount does not seem reasonable. However, in the example of the *LEGO set no. 21310-1 Old Fishing Store*, this was also a lucky coincidence. I had the Old Fishing Store already once in my LEGO portfolio. Coincidentally, this was available at short notice before retirement at a dealer, so I confidently struck - despite the MSRP. In retrospect, it turned out that this was an absolute stroke of luck.

In the official The LEGO Group online or retail stores are hardly (good) discounts to obtain. Accordingly, I only get an average discount of -2 percent in my LEGO portfolio. This is not least due to my recent purchases (*LEGO set no. 10291-1 Queer Eye - The Loft of the Fab 5* as well as *LEGO set no. 21328-1 Seinfeld*). Surprisingly, there was a 30 percent discount on both LEGO sets. A truly rare occurrence, especially considering that both LEGO sets were released just a few months prior at the time of the discount.

In general, my purchases from the official LEGO Store are limited to exclusive offerings such as *BrickHeadz* or *Monkie Kid*. Here, the limited availability seems lucrative, as fewer investors have access to them and the themed areas are noticed by fewer buyers. In general, people are quite reluctant to buy directly from the manufacturer. Especially because the discount is comparatively low here.

The best deals on the latest LEGO sets are undoubtedly available at official LEGO wholesalers such as Costco, Amazon, Walmart, and so on. Also, at these larger retailers, you generally have a very good chance of not coming away empty-handed when LEGO sets are on sale. These retailers have a much larger inventory than a small retailer in their town.

Certainly, a direct comparison between retailers is not easy. Without question, the discount depends on many factors. For example, individual LEGO sets are rarely offered with more than 25 or even 30 percent (e.g., Star Wars Ultimate Collectors Series). Other LEGO sets or themes are sometimes offered with discounts of over 50 percent (e.g., *Vidiyo* or *City*).

Just because there is a 50 percent discount on a LEGO product doesn't mean you have to buy it and that it will actually increase in price or value. LEGO products with particularly high discounts over a very long period of time should make you wonder and be particularly questioned. In this context, I would like to briefly discuss when LEGO sets are offered permanently cheap. For example, *LEGO set no. 10274-1 Ghostbusters ECTO-1* has been on sale since November 16, 2020. It only took a few weeks and the *ECTO-1* was offered at a 30 discount by various retailers. Since then, the LEGO set has been consistently available at 30 percent off. In the meantime, the

*ECTO-1* was even available at 40 percent below MSRP. So far, there are hardly any empirical values for such cases. Therefore, it is advisable to monitor the *LEGO set no. 10274-1 Ghostbusters ECTO-1* beyond its End-Of-Life. Because to what extent the *ECTO-1* later represents a sensible investment, must then be seen. However, I personally assume that demand will be covered in the medium term. Buyers had many months and even years to buy this cheap. Also, there are guaranteed enough LEGO investors who speculate on a success of the *ECTO-1*. How the *ECTO-1* will develop in the long run remains exciting.

Another example is the *LEGO set no. 70828-1 Pop-Up Party Bus* from The *LEGO Movie 2* themes, which was released in Germany on December 27, 2021. *The Pop-Up Party Bus* could be purchased effortlessly for many months at a discount of between 50 and 75 percent. Experience has shown that such LEGO sets have a particularly hard time when they are retired. The probabilities of profitable returns are extremely low. A LEGO set which is offered in the market for months with comparatively high discounts is not particularly popular. Rather, retailers want to sell off the LEGO set to make room for new inventory. Stored and unsold goods cost dealers' money and are also dead capital. Customers and collectors who are really interested in the LEGO set have usually long since stocked up on enough LEGO sets. It is not recommended to invest in such LEGO sets. It is extremely easy to buy any LEGO set that is discounted. Experience has shown that this is not the most successful way to achieve good long-term returns. Readers who are already active in LEGO investment will surely agree with me that LEGO offers and discounts fluctuate seasonally. In my experience, especially the time before Christmas is an ideal time, in which there are particularly many cheap offers for LEGO sets. Therefore, I would like to compare below whether there is a correlation between my monthly purchases and the discounts. In Figure 107, the monthly purchases are shown as a blue bar chart. The associated average rebates between 2018 and 2022 are captured as a red line graph. This can be of use to evaluate your own purchasing behavior. Also, for this evaluation, all purchases on Ebay Classifieds are disregarded.

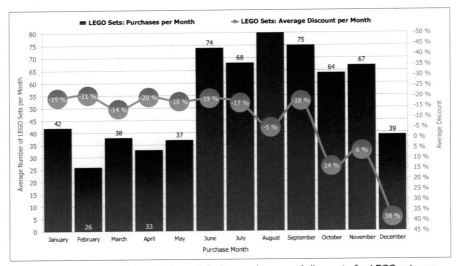

*Figure 107 - Overview of my LEGO portfolio by purchases and discounts for LEGO sets per month*

I have a flexible budget for my LEGO purchases. Therefore, my spending on LEGO sets varies between months. However, I usually make my selection of which LEGO sets to include in my portfolio early after new LEGO sets are announced or released. Consequently, I make very few impulse purchases as far as the type of LEGO set is concerned. On the contrary, my purchases are very spontaneous when the LEGO set in question reaches an attractive discount. Because the fact is that attractive or high discounts are extremely rarely offered permanently. Rather, they fluctuate on a short-term time scale (usually a few days to weeks). As a result, the purchases shown in Figure 107 can be Classifieds as unconscious. This hint is particularly important for me, because it gives the evaluation of figure 107 more significance.

It is hardly surprising that I bought an above-average number of LEGO sets in the months from June to September. Especially during this time, higher discounts and good deals are more likely. Because especially in the quiet summer months, companies like The LEGO Group have a harder time

432

selling. There is a lot of traveling, out-of-town activities. Customers are usually less interested in shopping than in the colder seasons. Domestic activities such as building LEGO sets also take a back seat during this time. Companies like The LEGO Group try to compensate for such weaker months and phases by offering particularly high discounts and making their products more palatable to customers. This is also reflected in my buying behavior.

And although I buy a comparatively normal amount of LEGO sets in the other months from October to March, the discounts are significantly lower, especially in these months. An exception to this is the month of December. In the LEGO universe, this is considered the best month to buy LEGO sets. Companies want to clear their warehouses at the end of the year or in the (pre-) Christmas period to make room for new products. My buying behavior shows that I bought the least LEGO sets in December. The number of LEGO purchases in December make up only 5 percent of my LEGO portfolio. At the same time, it can be confirmed that I also got the highest average discount in the month of December. It also shows that already from November companies like The LEGO Group try again to lure customers for Christmas purchases with higher discounts. This has averaged -41 percent in December over the past 4 years. In the months of February to May, my average discount is only -18 percent. Especially in these months there is an increased demand for LEGO sets. This in turn leads to lower discounts.

One reason for my deviant buying behavior could be that I try to buy anticyclically. Anticyclical behavior refers to processes that move against the general expectation or against the usual patterns of behavior. Anticyclical shopping allows you to purchase products at low prices. Winter shoes are a lot cheaper in the summer than in the high season. Of course, in boutiques they are no longer offered and the buyer has to find other ways to acquire winter footwear. *This behavior does not correspond to that of the masses. What does this mean in LEGO investment?* Experience has shown that LEGO products with a Christmas connection are relatively expensive, especially around Christmas time. This can be observed very well, with LEGO sets of the Winter Village Collection theme available at a significantly higher discount, especially in the summer. Collectors and investors do not have LEGO sets on their radar during the warm summer months, if at all. *Honestly, who care about Christmas when it's over 30 degrees Celsius in the summer?*

Of special interest is the fact that LEGO sets with a license agreement offer higher discounts on average compared to LEGO sets without a license agreement. Ignoring my purchases on Ebay Classifieds, the following average discounts as well as average value changes for LEGO sets with and without a license agreement result.

- **186 LEGO Sets with License Agreement**
  Average Discount of 25 Percent

- **223 LEGO Sets without License Agreement**
  Average Discount of 19 Percent

In fact, The LEGO Group generally gives higher discounts on LEGO sets with licensing agreements. The impact of the discounts is easier to imagine if you compare the purchase prices with the MSRP. So, my 533 LEGO sets come to a cumulative MSRP of 36,579.96 Euro. I actually paid a total of 28,768.61 Euro. This corresponds to a savings of 7,811.35 Euro, or 21 percent.

An old stock market wisdom by Carl Mayer von Rothschild says: *Buy to the sound of cannons, sell to the sound of trumpets*. This wisdom is applicable to LEGO investment. The basic idea behind it is that the opinion of the majority leads to an exaggeration. This exaggeration can affect both the price or value of a stock and the opinion about a particular LEGO set. For example, if the majority of buyers for a LEGO set are negative and have a consistently bad impression of it, it is quite likely that many potential buyers, collectors as well as investors will oppose a purchase. Youtube channels, blogs and other social media in particular reach a very large audience these days. If a LEGO set receives consistently negative reviews, it quickly becomes unpopular. This is where the term cheerleader comes in. In the LEGO universe, the term is associated with a person (e.g., a product tester) whose opinion and thoughts about a LEGO set dictate the general mood of the community about that very LEGO set. An ideal example of this is *LEGO set no. 75286 General Grievous Starfighter* from the *Star Wars* themes. The heavily criticized LEGO set was literally taken apart by various Youtubers. On Brickset, it only achieved a 3.6-star rating. On The LEGO Group homepage, there is even only a 2.4-star rating. For the majority, the price-performance ratio is inadequate. The LEGO set's recommended retail price was USD 79.99, although the LEGO set could easily be purchased at a discount of over 40 percent during its lifetime. The Starfighter has been discontinued since December 31, 2021. Unsurprisingly, there are comparatively few offers for the LEGO set on the secondary market right now. It should be worth a look to see to what extent the Starfighter will develop in value in the future. A very similar fate befell *LEGO set no. 75222-1 Betrayal in Cloud City*, which has already been presented. This LEGO set is also part of the *Star Wars* theme and had consistently bad reviews during its lifetime. The community had absorbed the bad vibes about the LEGO set, which is why this set ended up in very few households. Personally, I can't recall any product review of the LEGO set that was halfway positive. A look at Bricklink shows a worldwide stock of less than 65 pieces as of December 31, 2020. As of December 10, 2022, there are only 46 left. Beyond that, of course, there are people who own the LEGO set and don't list it on Bricklink. For example, in my personal inventory there are two unopened copies that are not for sale on Bricklink.

My average purchase price of *LEGO set no. 75222-1 Betrayal in Cloud City* is 273.22 Euro. This represents a 22 percent discount to the original MSRP of 349.99 Euro. As of December 10, 2022, the offered selling price is 756.08 Euro. In my case, this corresponds to an impressive 177 percent increase in value.

The example shows that before you find yourself in the comments of reviews about LEGO sets, you should take a deep breath, think about it and ask yourself if you are not just jumping on the bandwagon of the masses. This is especially heretical to see if you have never had the LEGO set in your hands to form your own opinion. So don't just run with it and form your own objective opinion instead.

Many LEGO investors are put off by negative reviews. This is partly understandable. As a LEGO investor, you rarely get to see the LEGO set being built. Rather, you have to settle for pictures and videos to get an impression of what you are investing in. Also, in view of the fact that you can only experience the inner structure of a LEGO set in this way.

So, it is quite possible that significantly fewer of these LEGO sets will be sold and make their way into the secondary market. A LEGO investment is certainly interesting if only comparatively few LEGO sets are later available for sale on the secondary market. Of course, the reverse is also possible. This refers to exaggerations that lead to numerous purchases and even hoarding of LEGO sets.

A good example of this is the *LEGO set no. 21319-1 Central Perk* from the Ideas themes. The set was released in 2019 with an MSRP of 69.99 Euro. The EOL has already been delayed various times. As of July 10, 2022, the LEGO set can still easily be purchased at a 30 percent discount. For an Ideas set with 1,070 parts, 7 minifigures and a Part-Out-Value on Bricklink of 178.57 Euro (equivalent to 236 percent off the MSRP), this is a very worthwhile investment. The opinions of the LEGO community are correspondingly positive. As of July 10, 2022, 1,583 pieces are listed for sale on Bricklink. As of December 10, 2022, there are even 2,218 units worldwide. Of course, these are all new and unopened LEGO sets. In addition, the LEGO set has already been parted out numerous times and the individual bricks and parts have been put up for sale on Bricklink. Certainly, there will be readers who feel that the 2,218 pieces are quite few, considering the size of the worldwide LEGO community. This does not take into account those LEGO sets that are stored in the basement and have not yet received an listing on Bricklink. Keeping in mind the quantities offered by other LEGO sets, LEGO set no. 21319-1 Central Perk is certainly one of the most offered LEGO sets on Bricklink. For example, *LEGO set no. 75954-1 Hogwarts Great Hall* makes it to only 1,119 listed LEGO sets on Bricklink. At first glance, the secondary market for *LEGO set no. 21319-1 Central Perk* seems saturated. Based on experience, it will take many months or even years before there is any perceptible performance at all.

In Germany, the best purchase price of a LEGO set can usually be found online. On the other hand, some of you may have seen photos of so-called clearance sales at the American retailers WalMart or Target. Such phenomena are quite unlikely in Germany and are not known to me until today. From time to time, LEGO sets in the USA are literally being sold off. In Germany, we have a high density of different retailers. These range from Amazon to Ebay to Ebay Classifieds, Smyth Toys, Facebook Marketplace, MyToys or the LEGO Store itself. As of July 2022, the comparison portal Brickmerge lists 57 different LEGO retailers. There is never a shortage of offers. Whether these are good or bad is a question to be evaluated elsewhere. If we have found a lucrative LEGO offer, we can try to increase the amount of our discount with so-called cashback programs. In Germany, the best-known providers are Shoop, Andasa or Questler. Registration is free of charge and quickly done. Customers who make a purchase on the merchant's site via these portals sometimes benefit from special discounts and are credited with a certain amount of cashback on the amount spent. They can then exchange this for money or other goods (e.g., gift cards). However, this also means that only those who spend money earn cashback.

The providers can vary greatly in terms of the number, selection and discounts of the partner stores as well as the duration of the repayment. It is worth comparing them in advance, and registering with several providers if necessary. Which retailers cooperate with the respective cashback providers varies constantly. The amount of cashback can also vary. Cashback rates usually range between 2 and 8 percent. This usually refers to the pure net merchandise value of the non-returned items. Coupons, VAT, any service fees and shipping costs are not taken into account here.

As you can see, this can significantly increase your return on investment. With LEGO Investment, you can't avoid buying LEGO products on the Internet. Therefore, I can only advise everyone who wants to approach the subject of LEGO investment, to sign up for cashback programs. For example, over the past 4.5 years, I have had an average cashback rate of 2 percent across all my LEGO products (533 pieces). Directly affected by this are 198 LEGO sets for which I received cashback. The realized purchase price is 11,536 Euro, whereby I generated a cashback of 574 Euro. This again corresponds to an average cashback rate of 5 percent. It should be noted that I did not incur any additional costs. I merely purchased the LEGO products, which I wanted to buy on the Internet anyway, via a small detour.

As an alternative to cashback programs, there is also Payback. Payback is probably the best-known free bonus program with over 2,000 partner companies (as of August 2022). You can collect Payback points when shopping in partner stores or when making purchases on the Internet. One point corresponds to a value of 1 Euro cent. The points can later be redeemed for rewards and the like (e.g., vouchers). In addition, once you have collected a certain number of points, you can have them transferred to your bank account in cash.

Thus, we distinguish these two types of cashback only in their implementation via so-called affiliate links or as a bonus program. Of course, there are many more providers on the market. The best way to find out about them is on the Internet, because there is also a constant fluctuation on the market of cashback programs. It is also advisable to distribute your purchases among different retailers. Of course, you are free to decide what you want to do with the cashback. I, on the other hand, have always let this flow into new LEGO sets to further increase my return on investment.

## 5.3    Performance

In this chapter, the performance of my LEGO portfolio will be presented in detail. The performance shows whether I have had a good hand in the choice of my LEGO sets. As of June 30, 2022, my personal LEGO portfolio has an average total value of 59,710 Euro. This is the result of the arithmetic average of real offer prices on Bricklink (*Current Items for Sale in Euro on Bricklink* and *Part-Out-Value in Euro on Bricklink in Euro*) and *Current Sale Offers on Ebay Classifieds in Euro*. Accordingly, the Current Sale Offers of all LEGO sets on Ebay Classifieds would reach a total of 39,567.21 Euro. Taking into account the Current Items for Sale on Bricklink, the value of all 533 LEGO sets totals 56,648.09 Euro. Not surprisingly, my personal LEGO Depot also reaches the highest value due to the Part-Out-Value on Bricklink. This amounts to 82,915.16 Euro.

With an invested capital of 28,776.60 Euro, this corresponds to a value increase of 107 percent in 4.4 years or a calculated return of 25 percent per year.

| | Current Sale Offers on Ebay Classifieds | Current Items for Sale on Bricklink | Part-Out-Value on Bricklink |
|---|---|---|---|
| Purchasing Cost | 28,776.60 € | | |
| Value | 39,567.21 € | 56,648.09 € | 82,915.16 € |
| Performance | + 10,790.61 € | + 27,871.49 € | + 54,138.56 € |
| Return of Investment | + 37 % | + 97 % | + 188 % |
| Average Return | + 107 % | | |
| Return per Year | + 9 % | + 22 % | + 43 % |
| Average Return per Year | + 25 % | | |

Table 21 - Performance of my LEGO portfolio (as of June 30, 2022)

The calculated return per year is the result of dividing the total return by the time period. However, the calculation does not take into account that my personal LEGO portfolio has grown unsteadily. Every year, different numbers of LEGO sets were bought, which had different prices. This in turn has an impact on the individual value changes, which most likely developed differently from year to year. Therefore, in the following we will see how my LEGO portfolio has developed every 6 months.

| | | Current Sale Offers on Ebay Classifieds | Current Items for Sale on Bricklink | Part-Out-Value on Bricklink |
|---|---|---|---|---|
| 15.01.2018 | Purchasing Price | | 10,051.18 € | |
| from | Total Value | 13,063.50 € | - | - |
| 17.11.2019 | Performance | + 3,012.32 € | - | - |
| 2 Years | Total-Return | + 30 % | - | - |
| | Return per Year | + 15 % | - | - |
| 01.05.2020 | Purchasing Price | | 15,942.96 € | |
| 2,5 Years | Total Value | 21,829.62 € | 26,271.01 € | 42,702.66 € |
| | Performance | + 5,886.66 € | + 10,328.05 € | + 26,759.70 € |
| | Total-Return | + 37 % | + 65 % | + 168 % |
| | Return per Year | + 15 % | + 33 % | + 67 % |
| 31.12.2020 | Purchasing Price | | 17,915.38 € | |
| 3 Years | Total Value | 24,576.77 € | 31,815.50 € | 49,075.52 € |
| | Performance | + 6,661.39 € | + 12,900.12 € | + 31,160.14 € |
| | Total-Return | + 37 % | + 78 % | + 174 % |
| | Return per Year | + 12 % | + 26 % | + 58 % |
| 30.06.2021 | Purchasing Price | | 22,197.03 € | |
| 3,5 Years | Total Value | 30,089.50 € | 40,146.35 € | 60,606.79 € |
| | Performance | + 7,892.47 € | + 17,949.32 € | + 38,409.76 € |
| | Total-Return | + 36 % | + 81 % | + 173 % |
| | Return per Year | + 10 % | + 23 % | + 49 % |
| 31.12.2021 | Purchasing Price | | 25,942.88 € | |
| 4 Years | Total Value | 34,504.00 € | 51,145.69 € | 70,964.44 € |
| | Performance | + 8,561.12 € | + 25,201.81 € | + 45,019.56 € |
| | Total-Return | + 33 % | + 97 % | + 174 % |
| | Return per Year | + 8 % | + 24 % | + 44 % |
| 30.06.2022 | Purchasing Price | | 28,776.60 € | |
| 4,5 Years | Total Value | 39,567.21 € | 56,648.09 € | 82,915.16 € |
| | Performance | + 10,790.61 € | + 27,871.49 € | + 54,138.56 € |
| | Total-Return | + 37 % | + 97 % | + 188 % |
| | Return per Year | + 8 % | + 22 % | + 42 % |

Table 22 - Detailed performance of my LEGO portfolio (as of June 30, 2022)

Having started my LEGO investment journey in January 2018, it wasn't until a little over two years later in November 2019 that I documented my first performance. In these two years, there is no documentation of the performance of my LEGO portfolio. For the first time in November 2019, I only followed the Current Sale Offers on Ebay Classifieds. Only from May 2020, I have monitored and documented every six months in addition to Ebay Classifieds the price or value developments on Bricklink (Current Items for Sale in Euro on Bricklink and Part-Out-Value in Euro on Bricklink).

Overall, the performance of my LEGO portfolio can be summarized as following. Since 2020, I have recorded a stagnant price and value development on Ebay Classifieds. One possible reason for this is that many LEGO sets are not yet retired. On the other hand, LEGO sets that are already no longer available have only been retired for a few months. My increases in value based on sale listings from Ebay Classifieds total 37 percent, or an average of 11 percent per year. Compared to Ebay Classifieds, Bricklink has seen steady increases in value. Since my first record in 2019, higher prices or values have been achieved every 6 months. As of June 2022, my increase in value for Current Items for Sale listings on Bricklink is 97 percent, or an average of 22 percent per year. This means Bricklink claims its place as a best-selling platform over Ebay Classifieds. Not surprisingly, also in my own LEGO portfolio the Part-Out-Value according to Bricklink rose by far the most significantly in price or value. As of June 2022, the total increase in value is 188 percent, or an average of 42 percent per year.

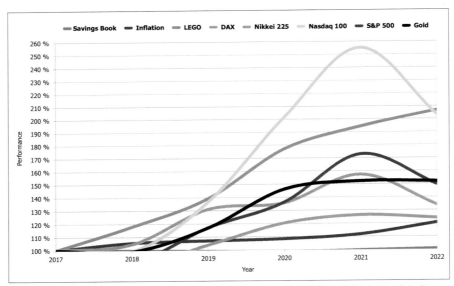

*Figure 108 - Comparison of the performance of my personal LEGO portfolio to stock indices, gold as well as savings account between 2018 and 2022*

In addition, I would like to show a comparison of the performance between my personal LEGO portfolio, the most important international stock indices, an ordinary savings account and gold in the period from January 2018 to June 2022. In a direct comparison, I was able to generate a higher return with my personal LEGO portfolio than the other asset classes. Only the tech-heavy Nasdaq 100 was able to stand up to the fast pace of LEGO as an alternative investment. Between 2018 and 2022, the Nasdaq 100 increased in value by 103 percent. Over the same 4.5-year period, my average appreciation is 107 percent (see Table 21). In short, both my personal LEGO portfolio and the Nasdaq 100 more than doubled in value over the period under consideration.

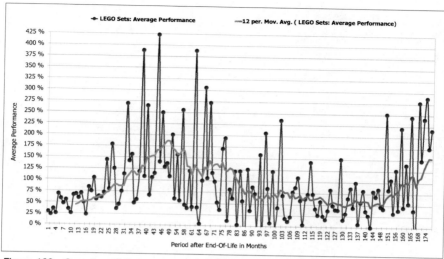

Figure 109 - Overview of the average performance of my LEGO portfolio by month with the start of retirement

The data points used so far provide another interesting insight. By looking at value and price trends every six months, it is possible to see how LEGO sets in my portfolio have performed after retirement. Only LEGO sets that are already retired are considered for this. Also, this time all purchases on Ebay Classifieds are taken into account. Especially these purchases offer a considerable added value for the evaluation. The fact that I bought LEGO sets on Ebay Classifieds that were already retired allows to identify especially long-term effects in the LEGO investment. In order to determine price or value developments depending on the past period after retirement, the difference between expiration date or EOL and the observation days known from Table 22 (November 17, 2019, May 1, 2020, December 31, 2020, June 30, 2021, December 31, 2021, and June 30, 2022) were determined for all LEGO sets.

In the result different time indications in months arise. To these different time indications, the corresponding value developments of a LEGO set can

443

be assigned to the observation days mentioned above. Now only the average value from equal periods (e.g., 1 month after retirement) had to be calculated. As a matter of course, these are again average values. The result is shown in Figure 109. The LEGO sets in my portfolio allow the observation of the performance up to 180 months or 15 years after retirement.

The graph for the value developments in Figure 109 suggests that LEGO sets achieve the highest increase in value directly in the first 48 months of retirement. Between the 49th and 150th month, many LEGO sets give up these gains. The predominant picture is one of stagnation and declines in value. An exciting development can be seen for the period between 150 months (or 12.5 years) and 180 months (or 15 years) after LEGO sets have been removed from the market. From this time on, LEGO sets seem to experience a real revival. The average value increases visibly and almost reach the previous highs (48 months and 4 years). It is very likely that very few investors or speculators have deliberately held on to LEGO sets for so long. Therefore, it can be assumed that the supply is very low, which is why such LEGO sets are rarer. In addition, nowadays rare LEGO sets are particularly attractive and arouse covetousness. The fact that new editions of the LEGO set are already available in the same period can be damaging to the value development. This must be checked in each individual case.

Time is an essential factor when it comes to investing money. In general, the longer the investment period, the stronger the interest effect. However, even in LEGO Investment, a long investment period does not automatically guarantee a profitable investment. Again, a short-term investment horizon does not seem to be particularly promising in LEGO Investment. In fact, most of my appreciation so far has also been due to the long-term holding period. Currently, a LEGO set is in my possession for an average of 2.4 years (difference between purchase date and June 30, 2022).

In addition, the complex and detailed recording of my LEGO portfolio makes it possible to scrutinize my own buying behavior in terms of timing and point of entry. With every purchase of a LEGO set, the date of purchase (day/month/year) is documented. With the semi-annual update of the value changes, I can also see when a LEGO set will be retired. The difference between the purchase date and the official End-Of-Life indicates how close I buy LEGO sets to their official End-Of-Life. Neglecting my purchases on Ebay Classifieds, my buying behavior varies between - 1,673 days and + 609 days to End-Of-Life. Minus days represent the number of days I purchased LEGO sets before they were retired. Again, plus days show how many days after official retirement I purchased a LEGO set.

Based on 423 LEGO sets (not including purchases on Ebay Classifieds), I have purchased a total of 41 LEGO sets after the official EOL. These are usually single purchases from stationary retailers. It happens again and again that retailers such as WalMart sell discontinued LEGO sets with a significant delay. Here you always have to be very fast. I bought the remaining 382 LEGO sets before the official retirement began. Of these 382 LEGO sets, 272 LEGO sets are already retired. I bought these 272 LEGO sets on average 305 days or 10 months before the official End-Of-Life. On average, these LEGO sets were officially available for 651 days or 1.8 years. The availability ranges from a few months to several years. This in turn means that on average I buy LEGO sets at the halfway point of their available lifetime.

In my experience, buying a targeted LEGO investment between the 12th and 18th month of official availability can be judged as reasonable. As a sidenote, I would like to point out that 16 percent of my LEGO sets had an official availability of less than 12 months. At first, this may sound quite contradictory. But now it is also the case that there are currently very many retailers. If a LEGO set goes into retirement and is consequently no longer available in the official LEGO online as well as retail stores, other retailers generally still have remaining stocks. Thus, for a short time, there is still the possibility to get your hands on the desired LEGO set.

Personally, I have also bought LEGO products earlier when I was convinced of the discount. Many investors dislike this approach. Basically, this is true, because with each purchased LEGO set you block storage capacity and the return counts from day 1. And yet I have already given enough reasons why such a procedure is occasionally not harmful. Of course, it is inevitable that you miss a LEGO set, for example, because it is retired after six months. If the LEGO set is still identified by them as a strong investment, it is worth taking a quick look at the secondary market. LEGO products in retirement take very different lengths of time to develop in value.

Experience shows that even in the days and weeks following the EOL, when official retailers no longer have any LEGO sets in stock, it is still possible to purchase the coveted LEGO set on the secondary market at a reasonable price. According to Figure 109, the average change in value of LEGO sets a few weeks to months after the official EOL can still be described as reasonable.

I have already been told in detail that my purchases on Ebay Classifieds have a special status. In the majority, these are LEGO sets, which are already retired at the time of purchase. But more about this in chapter 5.4. The LEGO purchases on Ebay Classifieds do not happen in the classical sense, such as LEGO sets with discounts to buy. Many of my purchase prices on Ebay Classifieds were already above the MSRP. That is why all purchases on Ebay Classifieds are not considered for the further evaluation. From my total of 533 LEGO sets, 423 LEGO sets are considered in the further analysis. These were purchased in the period between January 15, 2018 and June 1, 2022. This corresponds to 1,599 calendar days or 52.6 months or 4.3 years. Of the 423 LEGO sets, 302 LEGO sets have already been retired. Consequently, 122 LEGO sets are still regularly on sale and can still be purchased as of June 01, 2022. The average holding period of the remaining 302 retired LEGO sets is 889 calendar days or 2.4 years. The total purchase price for these 423 LEGO sets is 25,196.46 Euro. Again, the MSRP of these LEGO sets is 32,197.64 Euro. Thus the average discount amounts to scarcely - 22 per cent. In this regard, it should first be illustrated whether a higher discount also leads to higher increases in value.

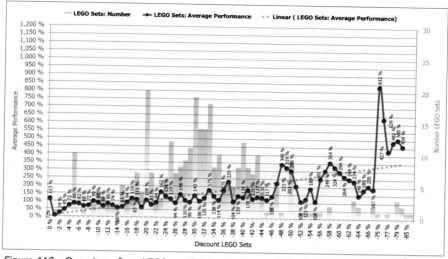

*Figure 110 - Overview of my LEGO portfolio by average performance by month with the start of retirement*

Figure 110 shows the relationship between the level of the discount and the change in value. A linear relationship can be seen between the two. As the discount increases, so does the change in value. An average discount of - 22 percent results in an average increase in value of 159 percent. If purchases from The LEGO Group are additionally neglected, this even results in an average discount to MSRP of - 29.7 percent. Nevertheless, this significantly higher average discount only leads to an average value increase of 147 percent (Ebay Classifieds in Euro = 61 percent, Current Items for Sale in Euro on Bricklink = 133 percent and Part-Out-Value in Euro on Bricklink = 247 percent). This in turn shows the significant impact of my purchases directly from The LEGO Group.

Of the 423 LEGO sets, I have purchased 123 LEGO sets at the MSRP. As of June 30, 2022, these have increased in value by an average of 171 percent (Ebay Classifieds in Euro = 83 percent, Current Items for Sale in Euro on Bricklink = 157 percent and Part-Out-Value in Euro on Bricklink = 296 percent). In direct comparison, my purchases at MSRP (or without discount) have increased in value more than all purchases with discounts. *What could be the reason for this?*

In total, 90 percent or 100 LEGO sets were purchased directly from The LEGO Group's online store and retail stores. This includes a particularly large number of exclusive LEGO sets (e.g., BrickHeadz or Chinese New Year) as well as Gift-With-Purchases, which have risen very sharply in price or value and ensure that purchases of LEGO sets at MSRP have developed particularly well. The connection between the extraordinary increases in value and purchases at MSRP is clearly to be found in the exclusivity of LEGO sets. In no way does this mean that you should simply buy any LEGO sets at the MSRP, because they easily increase in value.

## 5.4    Buying retired LEGO Sets

So far, we have assumed that the targeted LEGO sets for our investment portfolio are purchased only in official online and retail stores. However, the crucial disadvantage here is that patience and time in particular are required from the date of purchase until the LEGO investments increase in value. This can sometimes take months. However, experience shows that it will even take years. It takes time that the supply decreases and at the same time the demand for the LEGO set increases. Of course, it also happens that LEGO sets are found for sale, although they are already no longer produced by The LEGO Group and are de facto retired. This can be, for example, the sale of stored leftover products. Corresponding dealers sell the LEGO products as long as they can keep them in stock and there is demand.

In recent years in LEGO investment, I noticed a way to speed up the process between retirement and appreciation. By coincidence, I have increasingly discovered unopened or new LEGO sets on the Internet and finally bought those that were already older and retired. This turned into a real pursuit, as my personal LEGO portfolio reflects.

I simply looked for LEGO sets that are undervalued and thus represent bargains. How long such a LEGO set is already retired, does not matter. The main thing is that this is no longer available in official retail and online stores. Although the purchase can be tempting, as the prices on the secondary market are significantly lower, this brings certain risks. Many counterfeits are offered on the secondary market. Selling counterfeits can make you a criminal offender. In the worst case, you are therefore not only stuck with the LEGO set, but have also lost the purchase price, since you can not resell the item.

The LEGO Group, retail department stores, and even smaller toy stores should no longer sell the LEGO set. It should literally no longer be available to the broad mass of the population. *You are surely wondering where else you can buy such bargains?* In my case, I can recommend you Ebay Classifieds, Ebay or Facebook Marketplace. Complementing my regular LEGO purchases from official retailers and online retailers, I have also bought LEGO sets from Ebay Classifieds several times since 2018. Nowadays, 20 percent or one-fifth of my personal LEGO portfolio consists of purchases on Ebay Classifieds. Ignoring inflation adjustments, I was still able to purchase 69 of the 110 LEGO sets on Ebay Classifieds for less than the official MSRP. The average discount was - 38.75 percent.

Again, the remaining 41 LEGO sets were purchased at a higher price compared to the MSRP. The premium is on average + 62.61 percent. Strictly speaking, I have thus helped the sellers to a return of + 62.61 percent. All 110 LEGO sets were worth more at the time of purchase. These are therefore so-called bargain purchases, where a LEGO set can be purchased (significantly) below the regular market price.

The supply of new and unopened LEGO sets on the aforementioned platforms, which are already retired, is literally unlimited. Every day numerous new offers are added, again others disappear. For example, just recently I bought *LEGO set no. 4957-1 Ferris Wheel* from 2007 in new and unopened condition for 179 Euro including shipping. A look at Bricklink tells us that the LEGO set is only available five times on Bricklink at the same time in new and unopened condition. Here it must be taken into account that Bricklink is a global platform. *LEGO set no. 4957-1 Ferris Wheel* is currently available for sale at prices between 296 Euro and 750 Euro. The average offer price is 482 Euro. The requested selling prices on Ebay Germany are almost identical. For Ebay Classifieds Germany, I could only find a selling price of 340 Euro. Thus, the real value is 65 to 319 percent higher, based on the called offer prices on Bricklink.

This is especially surprising since there are usually several of the same LEGO product listed. And yet it happens again and again that a listed LEGO product is significantly cheaper than its competitors. *But how can this be?* Of course, there is no clear answer to this question. The following scenarios are conceivable and probable.

- Sellers are not aware of the real value of the LEGO set. This is often the case with so-called basement or attic finds.
- Sellers who need to sell a LEGO product as soon as possible, for example, to free up space (e.g., collectors).
- Sellers need the money otherwise.
- These are LEGO sets, which are owned more than once. This happens very often in families with children (for example, double gift). Usually the LEGO sets then remain sealed somewhere.
- The LEGO set has not been played with so far and should not be played with in the future. This also applies especially to families where the children are already grown up.

One person's gain is another's loss, because one knows more than the other. That was, is and will always be the case. Often, in the run-up to the sale, insufficient or even no research is done on what the own LEGO sets are worth. Many sellers simply do not know what they sometimes have for small treasures. The various online marketplaces are like the Wild West in this respect. For buyers, this can be a good thing. For example, a LEGO set that usually trades for 150 Euro is offered well below its resale value. For you, as a bargain hunter, this means above all that you have to be vigilant and quick. As a rule, you are not the only one looking for such LEGO sets. At the same time, you have to make sure that you know what you are getting for your money by asking questions (e.g., requesting additional pictures). For buyers, such queries often involve unpleasant extra work. In the popularity scale, your queries naturally put you behind prospective buyers who buy the LEGO set without any conditions. But believe me, if you buy products from strangers on the Internet, you should insist on a minimum of security. Too often buyers have complained that they received an opened LEGO set, although it was described as unopened. In my experience, the following risks must be assessed.

- Basically, you should look at and evaluate offers with sense and understanding. Do not be naive and trust your knowledge of human nature and your gut feeling. Especially generous offers and obvious bargains should always be questioned. No one has anything to give away. *Are the pictures expressive enough?* If, for example, the offer comes with five different pictures of the LEGO set, each with a different background (e.g., different rooms in the background), you should specifically question this and draw the seller's attention to it.

- *How sure are they that it is a serious seller or sale?* For example, it often happens that supposed collectors sell a high-priced LEGO set, whereby the seller has only been registered on the platform since the day of the sale (or a few days before). This is a popular scam. Such accounts are sooner or later discovered by the selling platforms and excluded from the sale. Consequently, new accounts always have to be created for the next scam. Have an eye on how long the seller has been registered on the platform and what their reviews are like. For example, buyers and sellers of Ebay classifieds can voluntarily rate each other after each transaction. Basically, there is a mutual interest to be rated positively if you want to buy or sell other products here later.

- If the seller offers many different LEGO sets, this can be a good sign. Ideally, sellers have other non-LEGO products to offer. And in the best case, the sale offers have been active for several days or weeks. In my experience, they scammers do not make this effort. But you should be vigilant here as well.

- Pay attention to how sellers respond to your requests. A friendly tone and a quick response are generally positive. Of course, it also happens that someone is time-bound or absent for a longer period of time (e.g., work and vacation) and therefore reacts late. This does not have to be interpreted negatively.

- Be careful what payment and shipping methods are offered. Scammers like to avoid any form of secure payment such as PayPal Buyer Protection or Ebay Classifieds Buyer Protection. Instead, the ominous sellers specifically demand bank transfer or PayPal by friends (without buyer protection). This in turn should make you suspicious, because the cost of such buyer protection is usually borne by you as the buyer (or you calculate it into your offer negotiation). Usually, this is a percentage surcharge of the provider to the actual purchase price. Familiarize yourself with the different types of buyer protection. There are no reasons for a seller to be against payment with buyer protection, unless he or she has something to hide. The same applies vice versa for shipping by insurance.

- In the recent past, it has been common for scammers to hack into the existing accounts of long-time users in order to post or sell high-priced LEGO sets. The scammers mainly target accounts that have very good ratings and have existed on the platforms for a long time. The bad news for you is that such accounts are difficult or impossible to detect. Some platform providers notice this, for example, because the fraudsters register from another country and block the accounts. However, you cannot rely on this, because this can sometimes take a few days and in that time various buyers have fallen for the scam. If you are unsure, you should first observe the desired product. If it is still available after several days, you can usually breathe a sigh of relief. In the same way, you can write to the support if there have been any problems with the account in the past few days. If you decide to buy, you should insist on buyer protection, insured shipping or pick up the goods directly.

- Basically, it is always recommended to pick and pay cash. So you can inspect the desired product in peace, negotiate the price if necessary and easily still withdraw from the purchase. Fortunately, there are still many private individuals who offer this form of sale. Unfortunately, there are also black sheep here. Recently, scammers have used this method to offer high-priced LEGO sets. In the sales ads, the buyer is lured by means of pickup and cash payment. Well, knowing that this leaves a first positive impression and puts many buyers in security. In practice, it then often looks like that buyers in times of high fuel prices and to avoid the additional time but prefer to insist on shipping. Fraudsters deliberately abuse this convenience. For example, if the money is transferred by bank transfer or other means of payment without buyer protection, the seller usually discontinues contact. And what happens if they accept the offer involving pickup? Of course, the fraudulent sellers find the most outlandish reasons why a pickup is not possible after all. Often the scammers are based abroad and of course they do not have the LEGO product in question. The sales ads are fictitious and there are plenty of pictures on the Internet. Even if they insist on payment via buyer protection, the seller will usually break off contact or find an excuse.

As in all areas of life, such scam machines will never completely disappear. Therefore, it can't hurt to occasionally read up on the subject on the Internet and keep an overview of common scam schemes.

The sellers are multifaceted. There are mothers who sell the LEGO of their adult children or enthusiasts partially or completely dissolve their collection. With some you can negotiate very well, others are not willing to negotiate. Asking basically costs you nothing but time. If a LEGO set has been for sale for a long time, many sellers often become more willing to a discount.

Be aware that you are by no means the only interested party. So don't be upset if you don't get the LEGO set you've been eyeing. Some LEGO sets are so coveted that buyers like to go directly for the offered selling price. I have also done this several times when the price of the LEGO set was already very attractive. Regardless of whether you win the bid or not, it is always a good idea to ask the seller if they have other LEGO sets. Not every seller advertises all his products at once. You have a much better chance if LEGO sets are not yet advertised for the general public on Ebay or Ebay Classifieds.

The main advantage of this approach is that LEGO sets are already retired. You no longer have to wait until the LEGO set reaches its retirement and (hopefully) increases in value. Waiting for the future retirement is therefore obsolete, which already gives you a huge head start in terms of time. Undoubtedly, this approach is considerably more time-consuming than if they buy LEGO sets as usual from Amazon or WalMart. This is mainly because you have to keep a constant eye on the secondary market. The most time is spent browsing the various sales platforms several times a day. In addition, you have to make price inquiries for interesting LEGO sets, as well as occasionally communicate with the seller. This is necessary because there are now many competing bidders and LEGO sets can be sold within minutes of posting the sale ad. Also, there is no guarantee of spotting such bargains. So you can expect to spend a lot of time without locating even one LEGO set. On the one hand, there may simply be a lack of offers or a LEGO set may have already been sold to someone else. You should not be afraid to try your hand at this. If, after a start-up phase, you find that you do not enjoy this approach, you should simply concentrate on your strategy.

Moreover, The LEGO Group releases new and very good LEGO sets every year. Therefore, you should ask yourself whether such a hunt for bargains is financially an option for you. For me, such purchases are to be seen as a bonus to my LEGO portfolio. I personally do not want to rely exclusively on this strategy or approach. I'm especially interested in LEGO sets from a long time ago, when LEGO investment didn't play a role.

As of June 30, 2022, there are 110 LEGO sets in my personal LEGO investment portfolio, all of which I purchased through Ebay Classifieds between 2018 and 2022. These are various LEGO sets from 1992 to 2020, and the EOL date of each set can be found on Brickset. According to this, the LEGO sets have already been retired for an average of 4,828 days or 13.2 years. Even if it only plays a minor role, I would like to mention that my average discount to the MSRP is only - 1 percent. Compared to the MSRP, I paid significantly more in some cases. For example, I bought *LEGO set no. 6463-1 Port Moon Racer* for 15 Euro, where the former MSRP is only 3.99 Euro. This corresponds to a premium of almost 276 percent. I was also able to buy *LEGO set no. 5005255-1 Jurassic World - Toys'R'Us Bricktober Mini-figure Series 2018* for 5 Euro. Taking into account the former MSRP of 29.99 Euro, this corresponds to a discount of more than 83 percent. However, with this strategy, it only plays a minor role whether they buy the LEGO set above or below the MSRP. Of course, despite all this, the cheaper you get the LEGO set, the better for your return. Why the MSRP is less significant, I would like to show below. For this, I have directly documented the current value on Bricklink and Ebay Classifieds for each purchase. Already at the time of purchase, the average increase in value on Bricklink and Ebay Classifieds was 97 percent higher. Also in the subsequent period, these LEGO sets have steadily increased in value on average.

As a result, my purchases on Ebay Classifieds increased by an average of 64 percent annually within the first three years. After three years, the average total increase is a whopping 193 percent. An extraordinary return within three years, thanks to the fact that the LEGO sets were retired at the time of purchase.

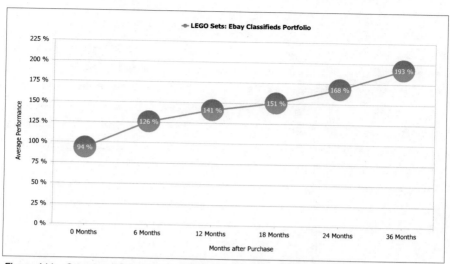

*Figure 111 - Overview of my LEGO portfolio by average performance in months with start of purchase for Ebay Classifieds.*

## 5.5    Arrival of the LEGO sets

A large number of LEGO purchases are now made over the Internet. This reveals a very significant disadvantage compared to stationary retail, which buyers tend to neglect or deliberately ignore. Products that we order on the Internet cannot be checked for their function, quality, packaging, and much more. Retailers on the Internet also usually use standardized product images. A decorative add-on here is the reference that the images shown are for reference only and that the actual product may differ. This refers in particular to the condition of the packaging. Private sellers on Ebay or Ebay Classifieds, who do not offer pickup, make more use than ever of their smartphones and provide their own snapshots for this purpose. As a rule, these are less professional than the official pictures of large department store chains. But in the meantime, custom pictures are required by many sales platforms. An ad without its own photos can quickly be deleted by the operator.

In principle, there is little to criticize about this, as long as the pictures are really of the product. As always, there are also black sheeps here. Again and again, you see crafty sellers who use the original product images of the manufacturer. Of course, this does not help us as a buyer. Rather, we would like to see real photos of the product in order to be able to assess to what extent the asking price is justified or whether we still have room to negotiate. It is also advisable to ask the seller for more photos in advance. Occasionally, the seller shies away from this effort and does not act in a customer-oriented manner. Everyone must assess this for yourself, whether he or she wants to continue to do business with the seller.

And this is where we need to dive a little deeper. We've already talked about how important the appearance and condition of the packaging of a LEGO set can be to potential buyers. So unless you are buying your products from a physical store, when you buy online you need to make sure you know what the condition of the product or packaging is before and after shipping. If it is a retail store, the risk is definitely lower than if you buy from a private individual. Nevertheless, there is still a residual risk. After 4.5 years in LEGO investment and purchases from 40 different online and retail retailers, I have had personal experiences that could not be more different.

Of these 40 dealers, there is only one platform on which I have purchased LEGO sets exclusively from private individuals. Of course, this is Ebay Classifieds. As already described, these 110 purchases on Ebay Classifieds account for 21 percent of my LEGO investment portfolio. In contrast, I have purchased the vast majority of LEGO sets (79 percent) from commercial sellers. At this point, I don't even want to evaluate which form is better or worse. Both have their advantages and disadvantages. Rather, I would like to give helpful tips and advice on what to look for when buying.

First of all, I would like to point out another fact, which many LEGO investors, but also collectors and hobby shoppers forget. It is true that the actual purchase of the LEGO set is made through a retailer or a private person. However, it must be taken into account that the following shipment, as long as you do not pick up the product on site, is carried out by an external transport service provider. Consequently, an additional instance is interposed before we hold the LEGO set in our hands.

In my experience, the majority of damages to LEGO sets are due to the transport route. I do not want to go into any causes, backgrounds, etc., as these are as varied as the range of The LEGO Group itself. Consequently, it is extremely important to check the LEGO set for completeness and conditions immediately after arrival. It is not enough to just check the outer packaging or the shipping box. The product may also have suffered damage, even if it is apparently protected by outer packaging. Simply because, for example, the shipping company has omitted filling material such as bubble wrap or packaging chips. This happens primarily when buying from private individuals. After having had such experiences on Ebay Classifieds, I always advise the seller to send the LEGO set in an outer packaging with filling material after the order has been successfully placed. So far, all sellers have shown understanding and have responded to my request without charging additional costs.

Of course, I would like to receive the LEGO set as it is shown in the photos. After all, I paid for this condition and the seller received his money. Many sellers do not understand when the outer packaging arrived damaged and you complain about the LEGO set to the seller just because the box of the LEGO set has an ugly dent. Sellers are then happy to point out that the actual product is still suitable for its original purpose (building and playing). In principle, this is probably correct, since the outer packaging serves, among other things, to protect the LEGO set. Many sellers do not take into account that one is a LEGO investor and/or reseller and is more or less dependent on the impeccable condition. Unfortunately, there are no comparative and empirical values in this regard, to what extent a LEGO set loses value due to damaged outer packaging.

You should always make the seller aware to use outer packaging including filler material. Insured shipping also minimizes your risk and is strongly recommended. For this, it is advisable to consult the shipping conditions of the respective transport service provider. You are also welcome to inform the seller which transport company you prefer. The surcharge will usually have to be paid by them. Whether the seller agrees to this, sometimes requires your persuasion. Basically, I always use insured shipping for LEGO products from 20 Euro purchase price. Of course, a pickup is recommended in any case, but here you should carefully weigh the time and costs (e.g., gasoline, etc.).

Nowadays, LEGO investors are highly sensitive when it comes to their LEGO investments. More and more often, we read reports of LEGO sets from reputable retailers arriving at the customers with damage (usually to the outer packaging). Complaints are handled much more routinely by the majority of large retailers and usually without much discussion or problems. There are usually entire departments dedicated to this. Depending on the company, damaged products from a customer are handled differently.

Personally, I remember a case where I bought *LEGO set no. 71043-1 Hogwarts Castle* online. The MSRP of the LEGO set at that time was still 399.99 Euro, whereas the *Hogwarts Castle* was listed in the retailer's online store for 339.99 Euro. A discount of 15 percent was unique at that time. Full of anticipation, I received the LEGO set a few days later. The anticipation was quickly dampened, because the outer packaging of the LEGO set had significant damages. Among other things, a tear of about 5 cm in length decorates the front of the packaging. After I contacted the online store to report the incident, they were extremely willing to make a compromise. Unfortunately, an exchange of the product was out of the question, because the item was sold out indefinitely and a subsequent delivery was uncertain at that time. In return, I was granted a further discount of 10 percent. This reduced my purchase price to around 306 Euro or by 24 percent compared to the MSRP. For me, this is a calculable loss, which will certainly affect the value of this unique LEGO set. In what amount this discount can turn out, remains to be seen. Last but not least, it also depends on how high the supply and demand is after the LEGO set is retired.

I'm sure you're wondering why I didn't just return the Hogwarts Castle and wait for another opportunity to buy the LEGO set at a later date. First of all, it wasn't clear if such an offer would come again. At that time, the LEGO set was sold out everywhere. Rumors were already circulating that the End-Of-Life was near. Also, I still had in mind that I had already once painfully missed out on LEGO set no. 75827-1 Ghostbusters Fire Headquarters because I waited too long to buy it and speculated on the highest possible discount. I wanted to avoid a repeat of that at all costs. In addition, at this time, buyers reported in various forums that their accounts in various online stores were banned because the affected users had complained too often when returning LEGO sets. Even the smallest minor damage was returned by them. It is unclear why the buyers were banned from the affected online stores. The users are not informed about any reasons and ultimately the provider has a completely free hand with whom it wants to do business. However, in the end, the users or buyers were very sure that it must have been due to their own return behavior, because they all shared this in common. At the time, both the online store of The LEGO Group and Amazon were affected.

Incidentally, with the blocking also the collected VIP points at The LEGO Group or collection points of the Amazon credit card was lost. It should be said that simply logging in again does not circumvent this block. Even the big companies are learning and can no longer be fooled so easily. Now, in any case, I personally want to avoid such things and reduce my returns to a minimum and really only complain about those LEGO sets that leave me no other choice.

Nevertheless, I would like to give a tip along the way, if you do receive a damaged LEGO set. It can be helpful to argue that the LEGO set is intended as a gift. And it does not look so good to the receiver if the packaging has clearly visible damages. If you do receive a LEGO set with damaged packaging and you don't want to claim it, I recommend selling it on Ebay or Ebay Classifieds. The return rate on Ebay is far lower than what you would see on Amazon, and the buyer's expectations are often lower. When a person buys on Amazon, they often don't realize they are buying from a third-party seller. They often think they are buying directly from Amazon and expect a brand new and pristine product. People who buy on Ebay know that they are buying from smaller private individual sellers or small businesses and are more lenient about condition based on experience. Of course, this does not relieve them of the obligation to clearly state the condition of their LEGO set by providing sufficient description and photos.

## 5.6    Running Costs

The following topic is trivial in itself, but not to be neglected in the long run. An investment usually generates ongoing costs. The costs associated with an investment are of fundamental importance for an investment decision. You need to know what price you have to pay for an investment. Ongoing costs are generally all types of costs incurred to hold and operate an investment. In other words, they are incurred throughout the life of the investment. Ongoing costs can vary greatly depending on the investment. As an investor, it is especially important to pay attention to ongoing costs because they reduce the return. For a relatively small LEGO investor, additional costs can have a significant impact on their profit margin. Traditional ongoing costs include the management fee, management compensation or custodian fees. These relate in percentage terms to the cost of acquisition or even the performance of the investment (e.g., in the case of equity funds). However, these types of ongoing costs do not exist in LEGO Investment. In the case of LEGO Investment, we have running costs that go beyond the purchase price and VAT. We distinguish the following types of running costs:

**Storage**

If you operate the subject of LEGO investment in small form, where I count a stock of less than 50 medium-sized sets, usually your own apartment is enough for storage. Perhaps you also see yourself as a so-called flipper, so the short-term and prompt sale of acquired LEGO sets. In both exemplary cases, you can assign a subordinate role to the topic of storage. If you are far beyond this quantity and are already considering renting external space, storage takes on a completely different dimension and greater importance. I suspect that you are not yet confronted with such a need. However, as long as the inventory for LEGO Investment grows, you either have to think about renting storage space or limit your revenue and inventory to the space that is currently available. This, of course, comes with other ongoing costs of leasing such warehouse space. However, for most investors, the costs will be limited to shelving. The storage costs are by far the largest part of the running costs. It is self-explanatory that these must be reduced to a minimum. If you store the LEGO assortment at home, it is up to you to decide how much of the storage space (e.g., rent, electricity, heating, etc.) you want to include in your return calculation.

## Insurance

LEGO sets, individual bricks or minifigures can sometimes increase significantly in price and in some cases take on extreme values. It is impressively easy to reach several thousand Euro of LEGO inventory in a relatively short time. I can confirm this personally, but I also see it with some other investors. And should something unexpected happen to the collection, you need to make sure they are adequately insured. With the right insurance for your investment, you can sleep peacefully at night. *Or are you willing to risk losing thousands of dollars to avoid an insurance fee?* Before asking an insurance company about this, you should check if your growing LEGO investment portfolio can be covered by homeowners' insurance. Some insurance agencies are willing to add your LEGO Investment to the home coverage. Alternatively, there are special insurance policies for collectors, which are more expensive. Such insurances cover their LEGO collection in case of mail loss, theft, fire, floods, natural disasters or breakage. In addition, the fees for such insurance are very affordable. Don't be surprised if the insurance agencies don't believe you at first that your LEGO portfolio is worth thousands of dollars. Although you may find a better understanding from a specialized agency, most insurance companies are not aware of the climate of the LEGO collector market. If you have a small LEGO collection or live in an area that is largely unaffected by the above risks, you may consider foregoing insurance until it becomes necessary. I don't need to remind you that you do so at your own risk.

### Shipping Costs

In principle, you should always try to pass on the shipping costs to the buyer. This seems to be a very fair solution in view of the fact that the sender bears the effort for the shipping. This includes not only the careful packing, but also effort, travel and time to drop off at the parcel store. So, if you are a seller, you should always try to let the buyer take care of the shipping. For this, you can use small helpful tricks. For example, you can charge the product from the beginning of the shipping and offer a free shipping. If you want to achieve a certain fixed price in any case, you should increase the purchase price by 5 to 10 percent from the outset. This can make both the buyer and you as a seller happy. The buyer gets some discount and the good feeling to have haggled, while you get your purchase price, which you had already envisaged.

### Fees e.g., by Payment Service Providers or Sales Platforms

Other costs to consider when investing in LEGO are the fees for selling LEGO sets on various platforms such as Ebay, Amazon or Bricklink. The service used here, as well as the storage costs can have a serious impact on the return on LEGO investment. The relevant fees of the providers vary at different intervals again and again and should be compared occasionally. Ebay, Bricklink and Ebay Classifieds are the most widespread. However, the later only operates in Germany. On top of that, fees can be added for the respective type of payment. Bank transfers are popular because there are no fees, but there is no protection for the buyer. Increasingly widespread is PayPal. Here we distinguish with buyer protection or without (PayPal to friends and family). With the former, the company protects you if your purchase is damaged or does not arrive at all. The more detailed modalities you should read in advance. Of course, PayPal charges a certain fee for this service. Personally, all transactions are handled by me exclusively through PayPal. For particularly cheap LEGO sets purchases, I like to waive the PayPal fees and take the manageable risk. This, of course, everyone must decide for themselves personally.

## Additional Material Costs e.g., for Shipping

This includes everything the seller uses in both the packaging and shipping process. There are costs associated with the boxes, packing tape, paper and ink for label printing, bubble wrap, and other protective items. Each individual material will cut into your profit if you don't include the extra cost in the selling price. There are cost-cutting measures here as well, which we will address. Savings can happen primarily on shipping boxes and filler material. If you buy most LEGO products online, as I do, you will soon have a collection of shipping boxes to call your own. There is really no need to buy separate new shipping boxes or cartons later. Even the stuffing from your own purchases is great for shipping later after the sale. On the pressure of dispatch labels, you should completely refrain. This can now be done wonderfully with a smartphone and QR codes. This saves you money on the purchase and maintenance of a printer.

## Various Costs e.g., Fuel Consumption during Pick-Up

I am sure that the majority of people neglect or insufficiently consider this type of cost when calculating their return. Unless you get all your LEGO investments from the Internet, there are various costs to consider that come up in connection with trips to retailers where you look for interesting LEGO offerings. The most obvious cost here is the fuel of your means of transportation. Driving to the various retailers costs you money at the gas station, which ultimately leads to a reduction in profit. Whether you want to take this into account or not is basically up to you. The actual costs vary depending on the type of vehicle, fuel efficiency, distance and current oil prices. Wear and tear costs of the means of transportation are often overlooked in my opinion, but can also greatly reduce their profit margin. These include loss or reduction in resale value, wear and tear on materials such as tires, brakes and engine, and pretty much anything that powers your vehicle. Of course, it's again up to you how much you want to prorate insurance, taxes, and the cost of financing or leasing. Both the cost of fuel consumption and the various costs of wear and tear can be calculated using driving cost calculators on the Internet. These are constantly updated and tell you how much each kilometer costs. In order to get a feeling for this, you should calmly set up different calculations. As an advice you should try to do as many purchases as possible online. Sellers like Amazon, eBay, etc. often have very good discounts on LEGO products and also often offer free shipping. In this regard, there is no need to get in the car and drive down all the retailers, which will be much more expensive in the long run. If, on the other hand, you still hesitate and prefer to hunt for LEGO bargains in your area, I give you the following advice: As soon as you find an attractive offer, you should buy as many LEGO sets as possible. The more you buy of the product, the more you spread your cost per LEGO set.

All of the above costs must be considered individually. It is therefore difficult to compare different LEGO investment portfolios. A person who buys all LEGO sets in retail stores will probably earn worse returns due to the cost of their own vehicle than someone who buys exclusively online. To what extent your labor hour is an ongoing cost item is something you must decide for yourself. This includes all expenses associated with buying, holding and selling. Costs associated with the purchase can be many and varied. These include travel time to pick up a particular LEGO product from a vendor or local post office, but also the meticulous search for future purchases, for example, on the Internet. There are also working hours, where you have to take care of administrative issues while holding the LEGO products. These include, for example, the frequent updating and revision of inventory documentation. Also, if you have insurance for your investment, you must keep it constantly up to date. Only if the status is currently documented, a full property value protection can be guaranteed.

The greatest effort is certainly to sell the LEGO sets. Among other things, you have to prepare the sales advertisements (e.g., take photos, create descriptions, etc.) and put them online. You are constantly confronted with questions, which you of course have to answer as quickly as possible. A large part of your working time is also spent on packaging and shipping. If you add up all of these expenses and multiply them by a unit cost per labor hour, the bottom line in LEGO investment is probably not much. In all likelihood, many LEGO sets will generate a negative return on investment by taking into account all of the time expenditures. The number of sets that experience a positive return will be much smaller. Even if you consider the whole subject of LEGO investment more as a hobby, your lifetime is very precious. If you find yourself going to various retailers in your area on a weekly or even daily basis, there is no longer any question of it being a hobby. In this case, you must honestly consider to what extent you are taking into account expenses in the form of your working time. After all, a quick look at what the store around the corner has can quickly become a time-consuming endeavor (travel time, entering the store, checking market values on your phone through Bricklink, etc.). All these expenses increase many times over if you are thinking of selling LEGO bricks. There are similar reports of experience from various LEGO dealers on Bricklink.

## 5.7    Sales Process

To make money in LEGO investment, you have to sell off the LEGO sets in time. Here, too, you are on your own, and there are a few things to keep in mind. Although the Internet is full of wisdom and advice, years of experience are hard to replace. Especially when it comes to selling, experiences couldn't be more different. Experiences vary between different selling platforms, time periods, frequency of sales, and many others. For example, if a LEGO investor sells 30 LEGO sets per month, he will gain more knowledge about selling in a month than a small investor with, say, 5 sales per month.

Inevitably, this chapter is far from breaking down all the advice and suggestions. Nevertheless, people will try to get the most out of their LEGO sales. Experience has shown that it is particularly difficult to sell high-priced or low-popularity LEGO sets. You should have a certain amount of patience and not rely on hasty sales due to lack of money. If the LEGO set for sale is still available in retail and online stores, it is decidedly too early to sell a LEGO set. This is especially true if the LEGO set is still distributed by The LEGO Group or other major retailers are selling it (e.g., Amazon). *Why would anyone pay more for a product that is easily still available at a discount?*

We have already addressed exceptions in the form of flipping sales. In this particular form, it can certainly be worthwhile to sell off LEGO sets directly after acquisition and before they are available to the masses. However, the time window for this is limited. There is always a remaining risk that one's own sale will overlap with availability in the overall market. As a result, you may not get the markup you were hoping for. You may have to be patient until the LEGO set is retired. This should be well thought out beforehand. We will therefore mainly deal with the classic sale, in which a LEGO set is to be sold after a certain holding period.

Selling is not difficult, but it takes time. Time to establish yourself as a trustworthy seller. Time to wait for prices to rise to a level you feel comfortable with. You can monitor the current prices of LEGO sets on Bricklink, Ebay or Ebay Classifieds. Both Bricklink and Ebay have the advantage that they record real finished sales. These are ideal guideline prices. Of course, as a seller, you are free to set your own prices. In principle, you can use random prices or your own ideas for pricing. This even happens quite often, for example when LEGO investors are in first possession of a new GWP.

An even more extreme case was not so long ago, when The LEGO Group announced the discontinuation of *LEGO set no. 42113-1 Bell Boeing V-22 Osprey* after a short-lived production. This happened at a time when some pieces of this LEGO set had already been sold. The buyers, who were unaware until then, could consider themselves lucky. They were now owners of an official and highly limited LEGO set, which henceforth aroused the covetousness of collectors. For such events, there are often no comparative prices of past sales. As a consequence, prices have to be assumed. This is done, for example, via the Part-Out-Value or by arbitrarily thinking up a fictitious price or value.

It can be observed that this price corrects downward as the supply of the LEGO set increases. As is so often the case, this is regulated by the market mechanisms of supply and demand. In the case of the LEGO Osprey, prices ranged from initially over 1,000 Euro to later just under 500 Euro per piece. Bricklink offers a good way to get an overview of the value of certain LEGO sets over the span of the last 6 months. At the same time, the site provides information about the current average selling price offered.

On Ebay, there is a partially comparable function called *Price Tendency*. This is a statistical list that calculates the average price achieved in auctions of an identical product in the past. Unfortunately, this price is not always displayed for current offers and is therefore very unreliable. Originally, this feature was introduced to show bidders whether it is still worth bidding on the item under consideration. A quick glance at the price trend shows whether they may still be making a bargain here. Alternative sites such as Ebay Classifieds, Amazon, etc. do not offer statistics for this and you have to calculate the average bid prices (not sales prices!) yourself using current offers. Both platforms usually do not offer the possibility to look up past prices.

For price monitoring on Amazon there is a helpful tool called *Keepa*. The function is available for all common Internet browsers and allows price development graphs for millions of products. The price monitoring (alarm) can be activated directly from the Amazon product page and informs you as soon as the product price falls to or below your desired price. The graphical representation gives you a helpful indication of a possible average selling price.

Ebay and Bricklink are the largest online brokerage platforms. The models of the two providers differ only slightly. A big difference is that on Ebay (but also Ebay Classifieds) sometimes entire collections are offered in an auction. In contrast, you will find only individual LEGO products on Bricklink. This also reflects the strength of Bricklink, where prices of individual LEGO products are documented very accurately and can be checked individually.

The most important factor influencing consumer choice is price. Consumers want value for money and will not spend more than they think a LEGO product is worth. Should you ever fail to find a suitable comparison price on Ebay, Amazon or Bricklink, you can also try the following: Decide what price they really want and then add 10 percent to that figure. If a customer wants to haggle, you can give them a 10 percent discount. This will make both parties think you got a good deal.

*Not getting any bids?* Maybe the price is too high or there is not much demand for what you are selling. Just hang in there and eventually you will always find a buyer. Of course, only if the price is realistic. If you need to sell, you should keep the selling price below the competition. Bricklink helps you again with this. Here, not only the average selling prices are displayed, but also the lowest and highest price. You should always have an overview of how many identical LEGO sets are concurrently available on the general market. Here it may be worthwhile to hold out until there are no or very few identical LEGO sets left on the market. You remember: supply and demand. If there is no competition for your LEGO set, you set the market price.

In any case, the appearance of your sales ad is crucial, which is why you should consider the following tips and hints.

471

- Describe exactly the condition of your LEGO product. This will help them avoid disputes and bad reviews.

- Provide the right details when selling. Although photos can sometimes reveal the most important information to a buyer, you need to make sure you include the descriptive information in full. This includes the correct LEGO set number, especially if there have been multiple versions of the same named set. *Do you note the condition, the age both in terms of the year it was released and the year you bought it?* Also tell them something about how you took care of the LEGO (with care). It may sound a little crazy, but this will make prospective buyers more willing to buy the LEGO product.

- As a seller, you need to make sure that the listing title contains as much relevant information as possible. As you can imagine, the keywords in the title are crucial for quick and clear visibility. This happens when buyers start searching for phrases with a particular website search engine. Obviously, the most important keywords are included in the title. These include the LEGO brand, set name and number, and a brief description of condition. Errors, for example, in the product or brand name should be strictly avoided. Otherwise, you should clearly and unambiguously distinguish between new and used products. This nevertheless actual unmistakable distinction is used again and again gladly, in order to deceive buyers partly. To the grammatical games belong among others like new, as good as new, new(value), brand new, almost new, new wo. figures and many more. But I have also seen countless sale ads where the LEGO set was clearly described as new. The pictures then showed, for example, an opened package, with the individual plastic bags inside still sealed. The following condition descriptions are common and unofficially recognized in the (international) LEGO world:
  - MIB or Mint in Box: All parts of the LEGO set are in the box. However, the (plastic) inner bags may have already been opened. The

building instructions should be included and the box may show signs of use or damage.

- MIMB or Mint in Mint Box: All parts are in the box and the inner bags are still closed. The building instructions must be included.
- MISB or Mint in Sealed Box: For collectors this is the highest quality condition. All parts are in the box, inner bags are closed, plus the package is still sealed, thus unopened. So, these LEGO sets should look brand new. Especially with older LEGO models, however, it may be that storage marks on the cover are unavoidable. Traces are usually mentioned in the item description, however.

If you are unsure about the condition description in the title or if you already have negative experiences, you can of course continue the condition in more detail in the description. You can also briefly refer to damaged packaging in the title. However, you should always go into more detail about the damage in the description and support the whole thing with pictures.

Use the blank space for the description to make sure you give as much details as possible. Also make sure to repeat the information from the title again. It is imperative that you prevent any misinterpretation by buyers. Dealing with returns or other buyer issues takes valuable time and should already be described in the best possible way here. Of course, you should also show the payment options. Here you should always keep in mind that you should also cover the payment method. Describe the shipping details. Let customers know how you will ship the items. Shipping in an outer box is preferred by buyers. Also, you should make it clear that in the event of an exchange, the original item condition will be guaranteed. It can cause you a significant loss of value if the LEGO product comes back to you opened. Finally, you should also take the time to create your own template. While this is not a deal breaker, it does make your listings more professional than most. You should ideally keep all the info short and sweet with bullet points, answering any questions about the product.

- Photos are the first impression. A high-contrast background can make a big difference. Also, you can tell a story with pictures. Add many of your own and only high-quality color photos from different angles to your ad. This should help prospective buyers understand unmistakably what you are selling. You should pay special attention to the seals, possible damage such as cracks, erasures, bulges, etc. Photos increase their chance of making a sale. I always take my photos in daylight and choose a light and neutral background. Some photos I edit afterwards with simple editing tools for color and contrast.

- As a good seller, you should always act in a friendly manner. Of course, it's not about being friends with every buyer. Nevertheless, you should always be helpful and adopt a friendly tone. Try to answer questions as quickly and competently as possible. Sellers live by their reputation. The reputation is reflected in their ratings. The internet is full of dubious people and fraudulent scams. Set yourself apart from such people and their competitors.

- Follow the hints and advice to make your LEGO selling experience as enjoyable and easy as possible, as well as get the most money.

- Even in November and December before Christmas, LEGO investors can take advantage of increased demand by raising prices. Parents buying gifts for their child would perhaps bid more than usual as they are anxious to get the right gift in time for Christmas.

## 5.8    Sales Platforms

There are many ways to sell your LEGO products or even entire LEGO collections. After we have already broken down how and when they achieve the best possible price, we will now turn our attention to the various sales platforms. The aim is to show the advantages and disadvantages of these. Basically, the platform providers differ in many respects. For example, not every platform is suitable for selling LEGO sets and the sales fees could not be more different. One could devote a separate book to this topic without hesitation. The following remarks are therefore intended as a summary. In any case, you should take a look at the services, fees and experience reports before you go to the trouble of posting your complete collection.

### Facebook Marketplace

Facebook Marketplace is an online shopping channel where Facebook users can buy, sell or even give away items. This makes Facebook's Marketplace the equivalent of Ebay Classifieds. Those who want to sell something upload a picture of the LEGO product, along with a brief description and the purchase price they have in mind. Those who want to buy something can contact the seller directly via Facebook Messenger. Both buyer and seller rarely know each other. Only how long the user has been registered and a link to his or her public profile are visible. In the worst case, it could even be a fake account. There is no proof of identity like on Ebay. Selling on Facebook's Marketplace has been possible in Germany since mid-2017. A sales ad can contain up to 10 photos including a product description. The Facebook company does not charge any direct fees, neither for buyers nor for sellers. This point is particularly interesting and makes Facebook's Marketplace a serious competitor. In return, you pay with the currency of the network: your personal data. Facebook's Marketplace is one of the few places on the Internet where you can also grab serious bargains. The company subjects new listings on the Marketplace to extensive checks.

However, at the end of the day, the platform merely establishes contact between sellers and interested parties. These then regulate the modalities among themselves. Both payment and shipping can be individually agreed between buyer and seller. If the buyer bails out or the seller fails to deliver, Facebook only offers the option of reporting the offending user. Payments via PayPal (among other payment options with buyer protection) and insured shipping represent a minimum of security. Send the item only after it has been paid in full. Alternatively, the traditional pickup and cash payment, which is sometimes still the safest option. As a buyer, you should always be suspicious if a seller offers a LEGO product at a particularly low price. More useful tips on how to sell safely on Facebook's Marketplace can be found at *https://de.wikihow.com/Betrug-auf-Facebook-Marketplace-verhindern*.

## Ebay Classifieds

Ebay-Kleinanzeigen is the largest online classifieds portal in Germany and a kind of digital flea market. Here you can place ads or buy all sorts of things in your area or near you in Germany. Products can be offered at a fixed price, on a negotiated basis or given away. Negotiation basis shows of course that people are willing to negotiate. This tends to encourage potential buyers to contact sellers and negotiate. For example, if you have the only product of a particular LEGO set, you should take that into account when setting the price. Unlike Ebay, its little brother Ebay Classifieds is completely free for sellers. Only if you place more than 50 ads within 30 days, you will have to pay a fee. Due to the anonymous registration without age and name verification, there is no protection mechanism on the part of Ebay Classifieds. When you should be skeptical about Ebay Classifieds, you can read in countless reviews on the Internet. Another disadvantage is that Ebay Classifieds is not open to international buyers and therefore not as present as Ebay. Classically, they pay at Ebay Classifieds cash, provided that the buyer collects the goods from the seller. As a rule, this is only worth-while for local purchases or sales. Nevertheless, you can specify on the platform a radius for purchases and sales of up to 500 km (manual input in the address bar of your Internet browser). As an alternative payment, buyers and sellers often agree on PayPal with each other. Recently, you can also pay directly through Ebay Classifieds. This secures their purchase, so they get their money back if the purchased product does not arrive or does not correspond to the agreed condition. For the seller, the service is completely free. The buyer pays a small fee, which depends on the amount of the purchase price. In return he gets security. I have only had very good experience with this service. Nevertheless, you should always be vigilant, because there are always fraudulent activities by buyers and sellers. The best way to protect yourself from fraud is to meet the buyer and seller and hand over the goods and money on the spot. If you should nevertheless switch to shipping, always insist on insured shipping. Thus, they can save a lot of trouble in case of emergency. The prices on Ebay Classifieds can compete with those of Bricklink or Ebay.

## Ebay

Ebay is by far the best-known auction platform on the Internet, which has played a major role in the growth of the LEGO market for many years. On any given day, there are more than 300,000 LEGO listings on Ebay Germany (as of March 19, 2022). LEGO products are one of the five most active categories. Since there are now countless pages and discussion forums about Ebay, I will limit myself to basic tips. Every day thousands of transactions are listed dealing with LEGO sets, bricks and minifigures. Selling on Ebay is preferred by most investors, because this is where most buyers hang out, always on the hunt for rare LEGO and bargains. Registration is free of charge. Advantage of Ebay is that you get sold with a very high probability of an item of max. 10 days offer length. This is especially useful if you urgently need money or space. This usually requires that you design the offer as an auction with a reasonable starting price. Thus, as a seller, you leave the price development to the bidding behavior of interested parties. However, this carries the great risk that the item sold will be significantly under-priced. Another disadvantage is that if the product is sold for less than you imagined or planned, you will still have to pay the Ebay sales fee. So, you should prefer to buy now, but at the same time avoid fantasy prices. If you are a new seller with few or no reviews, customers are often hesitant to buy. Not only Ebay has a bad reputation in this re-spect, when freshly registered users sell or buy without reviews. The Internet is also overflowing with reports of experiences. It is advisable to read various reports to get a feel for possible scams. So, before you start listing your products, you should first collect positive reviews. For this, it is recommended to make some (small) purchases on Ebay, also to get used to the Ebay process. Buyers feel comfortable with a seller with positive reviews between 90 and 100 percent. Another useful tip comes from the company itself. Accordingly, Ebay recommends that good times - to let an auction expire - are Friday and Sunday evenings from 17 to 21 o'clock. According to Ebay, the website is busiest on Sunday evenings. So, you should try to finish auction then to get the best price. When you sell products on Ebay, you pay a sales commis-sion of the final selling price (excluding shipping and handling charges). These fees are increased from time to time, so you should check the current fee level on Ebay. Especially interesting can be so-called Ebay sales days, where the sales commission is capped particularly low. From the past, such promotional days are known, where the selling price - regardless of the amount of the item sold - is a few Euro. You can create up to 320 offers free of charge every month (as of June 2022). Offer fees they pay only if you want to post more than 320 offers in a month.

## Second-Hand Stors

Second-hand stores exist both online and offline. The original idea behind these stores is, as the name suggests, the purchase of used LEGO sets and individual parts. Since the recent past, it can be observed that these stores also buy new, sealed or unopened LEGO sets. Of course, only if the price is right and/or the goods are of increased interest to the buyer. The buy and sell stores are located in almost all major cities. With the store owners you can very often make acquaintances, which makes future sales much easier. This can prove to be an advantage. The actual seller will sometimes call them first when this comes to merchandise of interest to them.

## Flea Market

It can certainly be worthwhile to dare to look beyond your own horizons. Corona gave flea markets in particular a huge boost. People longed to bustle and haggle among their peers. Anyone who has ever visited a flea market knows that LEGO is also traded here. Often, however, these are second-hand goods, and the offer can differ greatly between flea markets. Now the question arises, to what extent the sale of unopened LEGO sets is suitable here? Basically, it depends primarily on the conditions on site. It is crucial that there are potential LEGO buyers at the flea market, so that all the work is not in vain. A flea market for clothing is certainly the wrong place to want to bring his valuable LEGO to the customer. It's essential for you to have LEGO customers who recognize the value of your products and are willing to pay. You will have a hard time selling a LEGO set to an unknowing family with (young) children for three to four figures. In addition, you should find out to what extent the premises look like. If the flea market is typically not covered, this poses dangers to your expensive possessions. Other sources of danger at flea markets should not be neglected either. The goods live from being examined. Accordingly, your product is taken into the hands before the right customer strikes. Of course, the packaging may suffer. It can be an advantage to talk to interested parties and fellow collectors. From this, long-term contacts can be formed, which may appear important later on. Also need to prepare for the fact that buyers at flea markets bring a great willingness to bargain and haggle. This can be partly for you as a seller very demoralizing. For this LEGO fan meetings are clearly more suitable. Here are usually dedicated LEGO collectors around, who certainly have great interest in their LEGO products.

## Bricklink

Bricklink is considered Ebay for LEGO products. The whole thing started as a fan project and parts database. Over the years, the platform grew through increasing supply and greater reach. In 2019, The LEGO Group fully acquired the trading platform. Contrary to users' fears, the platform itself has changed rather little, so you can currently still buy and sell LEGO individual bricks and parts, as well as entire LEGO sets in new or used condition. You can join Bricklink for free and the signup process is very simple. To open a Bricklink store as a seller, you need at least one valid feedback as a buyer. If you are considering opening a Bricklink store, you can refer to numerous posts on blogs or forums, as well as lots of video material on Youtube. For example, Bricklink wants to make the classification as logical as possible and has created numerous categories to which the individual bricks and parts are manually assigned. Due to the many different individual bricks and parts, the immense number of categories seems overwhelming and clear for non-professionals. On the other hand, the sale of complete LEGO sets is much easier. Bricklink is only available in English and sees itself as an international hub for private and commercial LEGO trade. Since there are both international buyers and sellers, the platform has a very high visitor frequency. A major advantage is that the international audience is used to paying for shipping. Thus, eternal discussions about shipping costs are a matter of the past and there is no longer a need to calculate or include shipping costs in the selling price. At the same time, there is a high level of competition on both the buyer and seller side due to the international nature of the market. Thus, it can sometimes take months or even years to successfully sell a LEGO product. Unlike Ebay and Ebay Classifieds, Bricklink listings run indefinitely. Offered LEGO products are offered at fixed prices. In addition, Bricklink has a dual function where you can document your LEGO products exclusively as a collection. The whole collection can be documented here simply or you place the individual products for sale. At the present time (January 13, 2022), the fee model consists of three levels and is very clearly and simply designed. If you sell LEGO products between USD 0 and USD 500, you will be charged 3 percent. If you sell LEGO products between USD 500 and USD 1,000, you will be charged the previously calculated 3 percent plus 2 percent for the value of goods above USD 500 to USD 1,000. If you sell LEGO products above USD 1,000, you will be charged the previously calculated 3 percent (from USD 0 to USD 500) plus 2 percent (for USD 500 to USD 1,000) plus 1 percent for the value of goods above USD 1,000.[1] Consequently, Bricklink is much cheaper than Ebay or Amazon in terms of its fees. Both buyers and sellers can view the number of sales and the selling prices of each LEGO product. The price guide shows historical sale prices based on six months of data from the platform. There are four columns, the two on the right show the current selling prices. The two columns on the left show the prices an item sold for, both new and used. The price guide is available for every item in the catalog that has been sold at least once in the last six months.

---

[1] https://www.Bricklink.com/help.asp?helpID=38

## Amazon

The world's largest e-commerce platform always has very good LEGO deals and, unlike most of the competitors, the offers are usually still available after a few days. According to the company, every second German regularly buys something on Amazon. This means that the online giant dominates German online retail. On no other platform you will reach so many customers. In this respect, the effort required to sell on Amazon is extraordinarily high. However, the effort is rewarded, because on the one hand you address a very large group of buyers, as well as experience shows that the highest prices are retrieved and paid (especially for retired LEGO sets). The latter appearance is sometimes deceptive, because the prices must be artificially inflated, so that after paying the commission to Amazon enough remains as profit for you. Therefore, one reads again and again that the Amazon prices for older sets are far exaggerated and hardly reflect the market value. The phenomenon leads so far that sellers orient their pricing on it. So it happens that sellers on Ebay Classifieds justify the high selling price by the Amazon offers. According to experience these sellers are hardly to be instructed and accordingly you should not invest energy in unnecessary price negotiations. As a rule, an adjustment of the price follows promptly if no buyer is found. After a seller account is not easily created, the desired items can be posted. The offer creation with Amazon is in principle free. Fees are incurred only when selling. Accordingly, you can be experimental with the selling price. Personally, I lack any sales experience with Amazon, which is why I can only refer to experience reports on the Internet at this point. However, there are more and more voices that selling LEGO via Amazon is becoming more difficult. Amazon feels here noticeably the pressure from private sellers. However, since Amazon itself also sells LEGO, it will certainly have less interest in bringing competition onto its platform in the future. The whole thing should continue to be observed critically.

## Own LEGO Shop

You may even want to set up your own website where you sell LEGO products. This can be especially effective if you specialize in a particular niche. You could even experiment with search ads to drive traffic to their website. This type is especially recommended if you are not forced to sell the products as soon as possible. Thanks to different providers like Shopify, your own LEGO store can be implemented very quickly these days.

# 6.    Epilog

There are many alternative tangible asset investments, but few are as exceptional as LEGO sets. Today, The LEGO Group's assortment is huge and growing steadily from year to year. With the continuous fluctuation, LEGO sets are available for purchase on the market for very different lengths of time. It is quite possible that in a few years there are over 1,000 different LEGO sets available. Unless you have limited budget and storage capacity, your choice must be carefully considered. It is not necessary to collect everything. And the fear of missing out on a LEGO investment is something we should probably get out of the habit of. Those who approach the matter with a certain idea of completeness and several areas of collection will be faced with ever greater expenses and challenges here in recent years. If you buy like the crowd, you will only have the return like the crowd. So, you should start to see the wide range of LEGO products as an opportunity and not as a problem.

If you want to achieve the highest possible return, you cannot buy randomly. After all, not every LEGO product automatically achieves high returns. The challenge for investors lies in identifying which sets will be in demand in the future. In a way, a demand forecast is part of every investment. To win more often than you lose in this game, you have to have an advance in knowledge. That is what the superior investor has. He or she knows more than others about future trends. If you now manage to buy the identified LEGO sets at a decent discount, nothing will stand in the way of the increase in value. Therefore, there is a very high probability that LEGO sets will continue to increase in value in the future.

# 7.    Glossary

| | |
|---|---|
| TLG | The LEGO Group |
| USD | United States Dollar |
| GBP | Great Britian Pound |
| DAX | German Index of Stocks |
| S&P 500 | Standard & Poors 500 |
| Nikkei 225 | Nikkei Heikin Kabuka |
| NASDAQ 100 | National Association of Securities Dealers Automated Quotations System |
| DM | Deutsche Mark |
| EOL | End Of Lego / End Of Line / End Of Life |
| AFOL | Adult Fans Of LEGO |
| ETF | Exchange Traded Fund |
| GWP | Gift With Purchase |
| MOC | My Own Creation |
| UCS | Ultimate Collector Series |
| MSRP | Manufacturer's Suggested Retail Price |
| QTY | Quantity |
| pcs. | Pieces |
| D2C | Direct-to-Consumer |
| g | Gramm |
| PPP | Price-Per-Piece bzw. Preis-pro-Stein |
| ROI | Return of Investment |

## 8.     Useful LEGO Pages

- https://www.lego.de
- https://www.bricklink.com
- https://www.brickpicker.com
- https://www.brickset.com
- https://www.brickwatch.net
- https://www.brickpicker.com
- https://www.brickeconomy.com
- https://www.peeron.com
- https://www.valuebrick.at
- https://www.1000steine.de
- https://www.brickmerge.de
- https://www.stonewars.de
- https://www.promobricks.de
- https://www.klemmbausteinlyrik.de
- https://www.jangbricks.com
- https://www.zusammengebaut.com
- https://monevator.com/investing-in-lego
- https://berndbiege.de/kleines-klemmbaustein-abc
- https://blog.feedspot.com/lego_blogs
- https://thebrickblogger.com
- https://rebrickable.com
- https://brickinsights.com

## 9.     Risk Disclosure

LEGO Investment is a form of investment that involves risks. All explanations, reports, presentations, etc. (*publications*) are for information purposes only and do not constitute a trading recommendation regarding the purchase or sale of LEGO products. The publications are not to be equated with a professional financial analysis, but merely reflect the opinion of the author (*publisher*).

Every investment (*financial instrument*) is associated with opportunities, but also with risks, up to and including total loss. The general principle is that the risks increase with the opportunities, i.e., the greater the potential returns on an investment, the greater the risks of incurring losses with the investment.

Buy and sell orders should always be limited for your own protection. Each investor trades at his own risk.

The publisher and the authors working for him do not assume any guarantee for the topicality, correctness, completeness or other quality of the publications.

For the correctness and/or completeness and/or timeliness of the individual information the author or third party does not take over guarantee.

## 10.    Conflict of Interest Notice

The publisher and the authors are not remunerated for the publications or for other services provided by third parties. The publisher and the authors declare that there is no conflict of interest with the present contents.

The client of a publication, the publisher and the author may hold products of the company discussed in the publication at the time of publication and may have the intention to acquire or sell such products. This gives rise to the possibility of a conflict of interest.

Individual statements on products in the publication are generally not trading recommendations and cannot be equated with a financial analysis.

The prices quoted in the respective publications for products discussed are more current prices prior to the respective publication, unless further explained.

## 11.  General Disclaimer

The publications are for information purposes only. Information and data in the publications originate from sources that the publisher/author considers to be reliable and trustworthy at the time of preparation. The publisher/author has taken the greatest possible care to ensure that the data and facts used and on which they are based are complete and accurate and that the estimates and forecasts made are realistic.

However, the publisher does not guarantee the accuracy, completeness, and timeliness of the information contained in the publications.

The publisher is not obliged to update the information. He points out that subsequent changes of the information contained in the publications and the opinions of the publisher or the author contained therein may arise. In the event of such subsequent changes, the publisher is not obligated to communicate them or to publish them at the same time. The statements and opinions of the publisher or author do not constitute a recommendation to buy or sell a financial instrument.

The publications do not contain any offer to conclude an investment advisory, investment recommendation or investment brokerage contract between the publisher or the author on the one hand and the person who perceives the publication on the other hand. The publisher and author also do not accept offers to conclude investment advisory, investment recommendation or investment brokerage contracts.

The acquisition of financial instruments with low trading liquidity and low capitalization is highly speculative and represents a very high risk. Due to the speculative nature of companies presented in the publications, it must be expected that capital reductions or even total losses may occur in the case of investments. Every investment in financial instruments is associated with risks. An investment decision must not be made on the basis of publications. Publications or the information contained therein are not suitable to serve as a basis for a binding contract of any kind whatsoever or to be relied upon in such a context.

The publisher is not responsible for consequences, especially for losses, which follow or could follow from the use of the information and opinions contained in publications. In particular, the publisher and author do not guarantee that profits can be achieved or that specific price targets can be reached as a result of the acquisition of financial instruments that are the subject of publications.

The publisher and its employees may hold positions in financial instruments that are the subject of publications. The publisher and the authors reserve the right to liquidate such positions from time to time, even if they have expressed positive views on the respective financial instrument in publications.

Publisher and authors are not professional investment advisors.

The publisher and the author are active for third parties in connection with publications. They receive remuneration from third parties for publications, which may lead to a conflict of interest, to which reference is hereby expressly made.
The information and opinions of third parties reproduced on the publisher's Internet pages, in particular in the chats, do not reflect the opinion of the publisher, so that the publisher accordingly accepts no responsibility for the topicality, correctness, completeness or quality of the information.

## 12.    Copyright

# 13.   List of Figures

493

495

# 14.    List of Tables

Made in the USA
Columbia, SC
16 August 2024

92b18f07-81bf-4e05-976f-7a05a5e6c95dR03